The Antipatriarchal Jesus

The Antipatriarchal Jesus

Psychoanalysis, Christianities, Love, Ethics, and Democracy

DAVID A. J. RICHARDS

CASCADE *Books* • Eugene, Oregon

THE ANTIPATRIARCHAL JESUS
Psychoanalysis, Christianities, Love, Ethics, and Democracy

Cascade Books
An Imprint of Wipf and Stock Publishers
199 W. 8th Ave., Suite 3
Eugene, OR 97401

www.wipfandstock.com

PAPERBACK ISBN: 979-8-3852-4258-0
HARDCOVER ISBN: 979-8-3852-4259-7
EBOOK ISBN: 979-8-3852-4260-3

Cataloguing-in-Publication data:

Names: Richards, David A. J., author.

Title: The antipatriarchal Jesus : psychoanalysis, Christianities, love, ethics, and democracy / David A. J. Richards.

Description: Eugene, OR : Cascade Books, 2026 | Includes bibliographical references and index(es).

Identifiers: ISBN 979-8-3852-4258-0 (paperback) | ISBN 979-8-3852-4259-7 (hardcover) | ISBN 979-8-3852-4260-3 (ebook)

Subjects: LCSH: Jesus Christ—Psychology. | Patriarchy.

Classification: BT590.P9 .R53 2026 (paperback) | BT590.P9 (ebook)

01/06/26

For Philip Blumberg and James Gilligan

Who made it possible

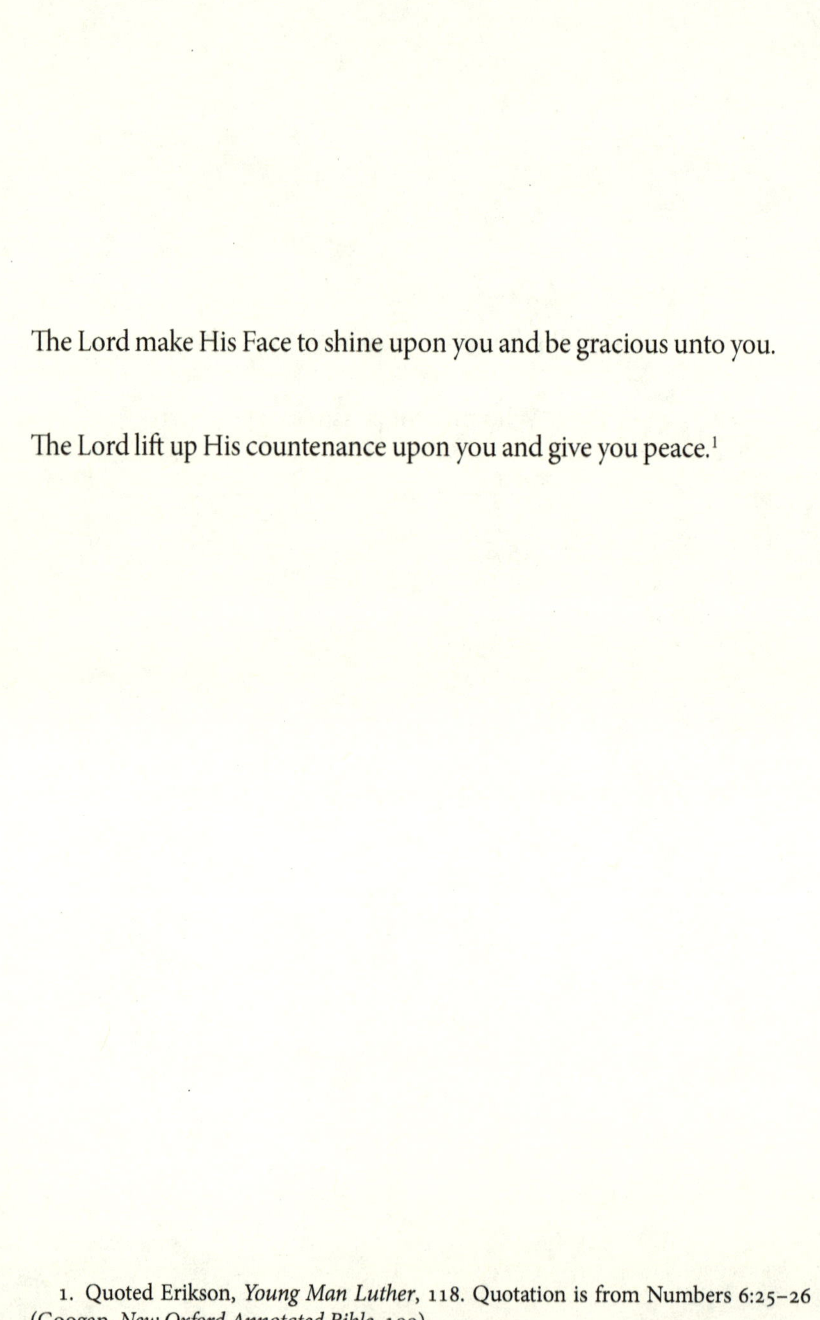

The Lord make His Face to shine upon you and be gracious unto you.

The Lord lift up His countenance upon you and give you peace.[1]

1. Quoted Erikson, *Young Man Luther*, 118. Quotation is from Numbers 6:25–26 (Coogan, *New Oxford Annotated Bible*, 199).

Contents

Acknowledgments

THIS BOOK WAS INSPIRED by and developed in conversation with two remarkable men, Philip Blumberg, my analyst, and the psychiatrist Dr. James Gilligan, with whom I have taught a seminar on retributivism and Shakespeare at New York University School of Law for several years and recently co-authored a book on Shakespeare. It could not have been written without their advice and support, as well as that of Carol Gilligan, with whom I have taught at New York University for the past twenty years and co-authored two books on feminism and democracy. Charles Strozier made quite illuminating suggestions about the role of psychoanalysis in the historical argument, including references to his own important works, for which I am very grateful. And several participants in a discussion group Strozier runs online made helpful and supportive suggestions when we discussed the manuscript, including Jim Gilligan, Carol Gilligan, Chuck Strozier, John Alderdice, Jill Gentile, John Riker, Michael Britton, David Lotto, David M. Terman, James Block, Marcia Dobson, Neil K. Aggarwall, Harriet Wolfe, and Michael Miller. Conversations with and bibliographical suggestions by my colleague Jeremy Waldron and my student Matt Lieberman were also helpful.

The book was researched and written during summers supported by research grants from the New York University School of Law Filomen D'Agostino and Max E. Greenberg Faculty Research Fund, and I am grateful to the research committee for its support, as well as the support of Dean Troy McKenzie.

A work of this sort, so rooted in my personal life, flourished in loving relationship to the person closest to me, Donald Levy, my beloved.

New York City, March 25, 2025

Introduction

How I Came to Write This Book Now: Winnicott on Psychoanalysis and on Jesus as "a Leading Psychotherapist"

THIS BOOK MAY SURPRISE those who know my works through the many books I have published on moral philosophy, constitutional law, feminism, gay rights, and Shakespeare.[1] It certainly surprised me in researching and writing it. I am not conventionally religious, and indeed, as a gay man living in a loving relationship to the Jewish man with whom I have shared my life for some fifty years, have been notably critical of the forms of Christianity that historically supported and still support the irrationalist prejudice I call homophobia as well as sexism and anti-Semitism.[2] I was raised in a remarkable Italian-American family, two loving parents in an egalitarian marriage and a sister, who was Roman Catholic but surprisingly liberal, in contrast to the Catholic Church, on matters of the arts as well as political issues like contraception and even abortion. But, the church's condemnation of homosexuality was, during the period of my youth, implicitly accepted though later my parents and sister came to understand, tolerate, and even embrace me and my partner. So, my own personal struggle to understand, accept, and embrace my sexual preference informed my passionate interests, as a scholar, in both moral philosophy and constitutional law, including my criticism of the form of Christianity, Roman Catholicism, in which I was born and brought up. So, why this book, and why now?

1. Richards, *Theory*; *Sex, Drugs*; *Toleration*; *Foundations*; *Conscience*; *Women, Gays*; *Free Speech*; "Patriarchal Religion"; *Fundamentalism*; *Rise of Gay Rights*; *Why Love*; *Revolution*; *Love and Violence*.

2. See, for example, Bamforth and Richards, *Patriarchal Religion*.

The explanation must begin with a notable feature of my Roman Catholic upbringing. Unlike Protestants, who closely read and study the Synoptic Gospels, what I knew of Jesus was nothing I learned at school (I went to public schools and then Harvard College), but was essentially the views I heard through the sermons of the priests, Capuchin monks, at the masses I attended every week with my parents and sister and what my humane and loving parents and sister made of it, in particular, my father's feminist humanism (notably condemning anti-Semitism and supporting my mother's career as a hospital pharmacist and my sister's ambitions) and his love of the arts (including developing his extraordinary gift singing opera, a remarkable voice I heard throughout my childhood, while he worked as a civil engineer for the Army Corps of Engineers); my beloved mother's moral independence, striving for excellence, and intense devotion to what she called the sacred heart of Jesus; and my sister's love of learning and the arts (her Harvard doctoral dissertation was on Walter Pater and T. S. Eliot), which we have shared over the years. I had during this period never read or studied the Gospels in the way I have recently, and thus my questioning of Catholic homophobia never took place, as it has for other Christians, within the framework of what I now call Christianities, namely, the many forms of Christianity that historically developed from their understanding of the life and teachings of Jesus of Nazareth.[3] I turned rather, like my teacher at Harvard College, John Rawls,[4] to secular moral philosophy, and indeed my first book, my DPhil dissertation from Oxford (working with H. L. A. Hart and G. J. Warnock), was an attempt to show how his approach to moral philosophy could justify a general theory of ethics inspired, as Rawls's work was, by a reconstruction and rethinking of Kant.[5] It was Rawls who, while I worked with him on my senior thesis, rebutted my own feeble defense of homophobia, suggesting a coherent and defensible moral and political philosophy might condemn homophobia as not only as morally wrong but inconsistent with liberal constitutionalism. That suggestion inspired my life's work as a teacher and scholar of criminal and constitutional law at the New York University School of Law.

3. See, for example, Scanzoni and Mollenkott, *Is the Homosexual*; Myers and Scanzoni, *What God*.

4. On Rawls's early religious views and the reasons for his turn to secular moral philosophy, see Rawls, *Brief Inquiry*.

5. Richards, *Theory*.

Many of my books have studied closely the role resistance of Christians within Christianity played in the development of constitutional democracy (Locke on toleration);[6] the criticism of slavery, racism, and sexism by the abolitionist feminists in the antebellum period in the United States;[7] the role radical Christian thought played in the criticism of slavery and racism before, during, and after the Civil War in the thought of Theodore Parker, Frederick Douglass, and Abraham Lincoln;[8] the role of radical Christian thought on nonviolence in both Gandhi's satyagraha in India and King's civil rights movement in the US;[9] and the recent development of forms of liberal Christianity and reactionary illiberal Christianity whose views were given expression by President Donald Trump in conservative appointments to the US Supreme Court and now in his second presidential administration.[10] My previous scholarly work thus puts me in a unique position to explore the connections of Christianity, including the internal debates among Christianities, to the development of democracy as well as a liberal ethics of human rights. No one has, I believe, done this in the ambitious and original way that this book does, written by an American constitutional lawyer, moral philosopher, and historian.

To be more specific, there are three other themes in my work that have led me to a closer study of Christianities. First, my books on the historical development of the American constitutional doctrine of toleration led me to two radical Protestant thinkers, both religious Protestants, namely, John Locke and Pierre Bayle. Both of them, Bayle quite explicitly, work within the Christian tradition, arguing that the Catholic endorsement of religious persecution by Augustine of Hippo misinterprets the Gospels, and endorses a conception of intolerance quite inconsistent with the central value of Christian liberty. Locke's argument for toleration is quite central to the arguments of both Thomas Jefferson and James Madison for the distinctively American constitutional doctrines of both free exercise and anti-establishment, the first liberties protected by the First Amendment of the US Bill of Rights.[11] Second, my collaborative teaching and writing with the developmental psychologist, Carol Gilligan, led us

6. Richards, *Toleration.*

7. Richards, *Women, Gays.*

8. Richards, *Foundations*; *Conscience.*

9. Richards, *Disarming Manhood.*

10. Richards, *Fundamentalism.*

11. See Richards, *Toleration.*

to write two books,[12] the first of which argued that patriarchy had corrupted not only psychology (Freud), the arts, and democracy, but also religion, including the Christianities that had endorsed anti-Semitism. Third, my collaborative teaching with the psychiatrist James Gilligan led not only to our co-authored book on what Shakespeare tells us about the psychology of violence in the framework of Jim's distinction between shame and guilt cultures,[13] but to my most recent book on Shakespeare, *Love and Violence*.[14] It was in that work that I came to see and explore the impact of my earlier work with Carol on patriarchy and my recent work with Jim on shame and guilt cultures to understanding the development of Christianities. This book is a development and deepening of this work as well as my earlier books.

Love and Violence develops a view of love, building on Plato and Freud's discovery of transference love, as central to the human psyche, what I call love's mirror central to the experience of the arts and through which developmentally we become human, supporting ethics and democracy. Our capacity for love is, however, compromised by the long-standing patriarchal cultures that condemn all forms of love across the barriers that patriarchy imposes on love across the boundaries of religion, race-ethnicity, gender, sexual orientation, and the like. In particular, the cultural psychology of patriarchy explains the role the shaming of manhood plays as an incentive to violence, so that violence is not, as Freud mistakenly thought, an inescapable fact of our biology, but an aspect of culture that can be addressed and changed. James Gilligan's pathbreaking work on violence, rooted in his close study of violent criminals, decisively shows that Freud's view, which never rested on empirical research, was, in fact, a mythological response to the anti-Semitic violence that had traumatized the life and work of Freud, a Viennese Jew in one of Europe's most anti-Semitic cultures—at least so I argue later in this book.

The great importance of Jim Gilligan's psychiatric work with violent criminals is that he brought to bear on his clinical work with them a psychoanalytically informed view of shame cultures, in which a rigid gender binary and hierarchy are imposed on gender roles and enforced by the shaming of those roles. Freud's view of the moral emotions was dominated by guilt, an emotion connected to morally culpable failures of

12. See Gilligan and Richards, *Deepening*; Gilligan and Richards, *Darkness*.

13. Gilligan and Richards, *Holding*.

14. Richards, *Love and Violence*.

love and empathy, and transference love made sense as a way of revealing the sources of such failures. It was no accident that Freud's approach did not work for the narcissistic disorders studied by the psychoanalyst Heinz Kohut, in which shame plays the central role,[15] and in which aggressive rage is seen as a response to the shaming of the self,[16] as seen, Kohut argues, in the narcissistic rage of men against women,[17] rooted in patriarchy.[18] What Jim Gilligan found in his work with violent criminals surprised him, for his background in psychiatry and psychoanalysis was that therapy for such men could not and would not work. The word that Gilligan uses for the therapy he discovered, to his surprise, could work with these violent men was respect, which meant listening respectfully to their stories, even though, sometimes, they physically attacked him. We need to keep in mind the unusual context for these discoveries, namely, men in detention whose violence was out of control and desperately required crisis intervention to bring it under control, including the high levels of violence in prison among criminals. Gilligan discovered, in and for that context, an alternative scientific method to transference love, namely, respectful listening.

What did he learn?

Though the men admitted they committed violent acts, their highly developed sense of retributive justice always claimed they were the victims of injustice and this was why they had turned to violence. There were no more committed advocates of strong retributivism than these violent men, but they were the victims, not the perpetrators. A memorable New Yorker cartoon of February 9, 1981, brings out their way of thinking. In the cartoon, there are three fish: one small, another medium size, and a third large fish, all about to devour one another. The small fish thinks: "there is no justice In the world"; the middle-sized fish reflects: "there is some justice in the world"; the large fish thinks: "the world is just." The shame morality of these violent men, among the worst off in American culture, is very much that of the victimized small fish.

These men experienced no guilt, and nothing in the American system of criminal justice, including prisons and the death penalty, brought them to any sense of responsibility and guilt for what they had done. The American love affair with the prison had been rationalized as "the

15. See Kohut, *Analysis*; Kohut, *Restoration*.

16. See Kohut, *Restoration*, 111–33.

17. See Kohut, *Restoration*, 232.

18. On this point, see Kohut, *Restoration*, 232.

penitentiary," an institution that would bring them to a sense of guilt. It did nothing of the kind, if anything, shaming them, and thus heightening their retributive rage and violence. Gilligan came to see their sense of retributive justice as itself an expression of having been brutally inducted into a still extant and flourishing shame culture and acting out its logic. It raised the question for him that the very idea of strong retributivism was itself an expression of a shame culture, and its continuing force showed the degree to which a shame culture still persisted uncritically in the midst of a guilt culture like that of the United States.

But, respectful listening by Jim Gilligan and his associates was something these men had never experienced in their lives. The consequence was that they had no voice, or rather violence had become their voice. To his surprise, Gilligan discovered what nothing in his psychiatric training would have led him to expect, namely, that respectful listening itself elicited voices from these men, narratives of both psychological and social injuries to their sense of self, injuries that shamed and insulted them, wounded their capacities for love and the basic competencies for living, and were perceived by them as unjust, calling for retributive violence, a continuing war not only on fellow prisoners but, when released, on everyone in the culture that had so disrespected them. These injuries took the form of lethal traumatic violence in their childhoods and youth, which arose not merely from an absence of loving care but from being attacked by violent abuse, physical and sexual, or from abandonment. In consequence, the men thought of themselves as unworthy of and incapable of love, clothed in what Wilhelm Reich has called body armor,[19] the armor of a narcissistic pride required by an invulnerable patriarchal manhood, a death of the relational self and its vulnerability to love. There was in their background not only no love, but also the infliction of social injuries to their sense of self, the injuries of racial and class prejudice, and no educational training in basic competencies of life in complex modern societies; many were illiterate, and some too ashamed to admit it and even to seek education when offered. Their lives were rigidly defined by the patriarchal culture of manhood they adopted or had been compelled to adopt as what defined manhood, and the rigid gender binary and hierarchy (men over other men—thus, their virulent homophobia[20]—and over boys, and all women) they accepted as in the nature of things meant

19. See, for further discussion, Reich, *Character*, 370–90.

20. See, on this point, Gilligan, *Violence*, 76, 81, 83–84, 156–57, 164, 171, 189.

any shaming of their armored patriarchal manhood elicited violence. Patriarchy had killed their capacity for love and a responsible sense of competence, which explained their lack of guilt for their violent crimes.

What Gilligan discovered (and it was a discovery) was, building on the work of the psychiatrist Jonathan Shay, that it was not only the demands of the American military in Vietnam that preserved a shame culture in the midst of a guilt culture and thus inflicted moral injury, but that some American children had been so unjustly treated, lacking not only love but even minimal education, that they had come to accept or been brought to accept a rigid shame culture, based on patriarchal manhood, and were thus vulnerable to violence when their manhood was insulted even by mere questioning. At the bottom of their psychological abyss was the shame of lovelessness and incompetence. What he also found is that a therapy of respectful listening (a form of love) could work, significantly reducing propensities to violence and even bringing men to a sense of guilt for what they had done. However, such guilt may lead to violence against the self—suicide. Such men, sensitized to their own violence, would ask to be restrained when they recognized in themselves their impulses to violence against self and others, coming to regard the restraints of prison life as a form of care they had never known and now craved. The key to recovery is programs, including restraint but prominently education as well, that foster both love of self and love of others. Only therapies of love addressed the absence of love, which had led to their propensities to violence. Violence was not, as Freud believed, a fixed biological instinct, but itself arose from the ways in which a patriarchal shame culture killed love and could, as a cultural psychology, be cured by a culture of love, a topic to which we return in chapter 8. Freud had correctly seen, as had Plato, the central role of love in the human psyche but had not extended his empirical researches to violence, shown by Gilligan to connect to culturally inflicted injuries to the capacity for love.

It was Ian Suttie who earlier made the same point about the inadequate, indeed mythological, basis of Freud's theory of violence (as an instinct, Thanatos),[21] which Jim Gilligan's work empirically confirms. In Suttie, patriarchy casts a dark shadow on both the experience and expression of love, "the 'taboo' of tenderness,"[22] which creates "an artificial mental differentiation and consequent emotional barrier between adult

21. Suttie, *Origins.*

22. Suttie, *Origins*, 80.

males on the one hand, and women and children on the other."[23] In effect, "a puritan intolerance of tenderness increases the unconscious regressiveness it hates, and interposes unnecessary moral obstacles in the way of the maturation it designs to accelerate . . . It does not produce really mature minds, but merely a hardness and cynicism with a core of anxious, angry, infantility,"[24] precisely what Gilligan observed in the violent criminals he studied—the anger of shamed manhood arising, not from human nature, but from a patriarchal culture that injures the core of our humanity—loving relationships of care and support.

It is in the concluding chapter of *Love and Violence* that I began to explore how my earlier argument in *Love and Violence* might extend understanding to the cultural psychology of Christianities, focusing there almost exclusively, on the basis of conversations with Carol Gilligan, on Augustine of Hippo. Augustine, so I argued, had himself developed a quasi-psychoanalytic argument in *Confessions*, one that deformed the Christian tradition, in particular his argument for intolerance that Locke and Bayle would later rebut but also his own moral condemnation of human sexuality through the doctrines of original sin and predestination as inconsistent with the love of God. When I wrote that chapter, my own understanding of psychoanalysis had not been closely informed by the works of the most important psychoanalyst after Freud, D. W. Winnicott, and thus had not yet explored how Winnicott's discoveries enabled me to develop a better understanding of not only the psychology of the deformation wrought by the Augustinian version of the Christianities, but the psychological and indeed ethical appeal of one of the versions of the Christianities that attended more closely, certainly than I had in my past life as a believing Catholic, to the historical figure of Jesus of Nazareth in so far as compelling recent work on the historical Jesus has more clearly revealed his remarkable moral personality, both his life and teachings, based, so I argue, on the antipatriarchal love of equals.

Winnicott's complete works are now available in twelve volumes published by Oxford University Press, and his work has decisively informed some of the most important psychoanalytic works since his death.[25] My interest in Winnicott arose from his empirically based clinical work with

23. Suttie, *Origins*, 95.

24. Suttie, *Origins*, 96.

25. See, for example, Phillips, *Winnicott*; Modell, *Private Self*; Modell, *Other Times*; Modell, *Object Love*; Modell, *Psychoanalysis*.

analysands suffering not only from neurotic disorders[26] but, in contrast to Freud, from psychotic disorders as well.[27] It was his work as well with mothers and children, including his work on child psychoanalysis (Winnicott, though himself childless, was famously remarkable in his ability to relate to children),[28] refocusing psychoanalysis in several ways, that illuminated my own developmental experience, including my struggles to accept my sexual orientation and live as a gay man in loving relationship to another man. Winnicott certainly included among his analysands gay men, one of whom he apparently persuaded to accept his homosexuality after three disastrous marriages,[29] and made a notable report to the Wolfenden Commission in Britain (considering the decriminalization of homosexuality, which the Commission supported in 1957 and Parliament enacted in 1967) that healthy emotional development included homosexuality, and less healthy compulsive homosexuality should be regarded not as crime, but as an illness and treated as such.[30] But, my interest in Winnicott's work and its implications for Christianities arose not only from his humane treatment of homosexuals, but from five of his central contributions to psychoanalysis.

First, under the impact of John Bowlby's work on attachment and loss[31] and the related development of an empirically based attachment theory developed by Mary Ainsworth and others,[32] showing the importance of early secure attachment (as opposed to insecure attachment in later life[33]), Winnicott came to see loving relational attachments among persons, not instinctual drives, as central to the human psyche, reflected in his remarkable paper, "The Capacity to Be Alone,"[34] in which the ability to be alone rests on the belief in secure attachments. It was Winnicott's observation that infants live in relationship that led to his famous observation "that there is no such thing as an infant because when we see an infant at this early stage we know that we will find infant-care with

26. See, for example, Winnicott, "Holding and Interpretation," 303–474. .

27. See, for example, Little, *Psychotic Anxieties*; Guntrip, "My Experience."

28. See Winnicott, "Therapeutic Consultations"; Winnicott, *Piggle.*

29. See Winnicott, "Further Clinical."

30. See Winnicott, "Memorandum."

31. See Bowlby, *Attachment.*

32. Ainsworth and Bowlby, "Ethnological"; Holmes, *John Bowlby*; Goldberg et al., *Attachment Theory*; Cassidy and Shaver, *Handbook.*

33. See, on this point, Way, *Rebels*, 37–42.

34. Winnicott, "Capacity to Be Alone."

the infant as part of that infant-care."[35] The centrality of attachment to the development of the human psyche, in the place of Freud's instincts (love and hate), led Winnicott to reject, like James Gilligan and many others as well,[36] the role of Thanatos in Freud as an ineliminable root of violence: for Winnicott, "Death only becomes meaningful in the infant's living processes when hate has arrived, that is at a late date, far removed from the phenomena which we can use to build a theory of the roots of aggression."[37] Winnicott thought of aggression as rooted not in a primal instinct, but in resistance as part of the primitive expression of love by the frustrated child that cannot yet distinguish objective from subjective as the child comes to a maturity that eventually recognizes its own responsibility,[38] and regarded Freud's view as resting on a misunderstanding of this process.[39] Winnicott came later to observe that this process continues later in human development as, in service of the reality principle, such resistance takes the form of unconscious imaginative destruction that leads to "love of a real object: that is, an object outside the area of the subject's omnipotent control."[40] Such destruction is of the child's projection of its own imagination on to another, coming to experience the other as a person, not an object. Winnicott's views were always based on the close observation of both young children and mothers, unlike many other psychoanalysts of his period, who had difficulty understanding his discovery of "an aspect of nondestructive aggression that is necessary for the creation of a true external object"[41] (a person, not an image of a person). Resistance, in this sense, may support the development of the moral competence to resist injustices that dehumanize on the unjust basis of stereotypical images.

Second, Winnicott came to understand human development in general and moral development in particular not in terms of Freud's focus on identification with the patriarchal father in the Oedipus Complex, but in terms of the "good-enough mother,"[42] and the roots of both neurosis and

35. Winnicott, "Fate of the Transitional Object," 524.

36. See, for example, Suttie, *Origins*; Sagan, *Freud, Women*; Carveth, *Still Small Voice.*

37. Winnicott, "Communicating and Not Communicating," 444.

38. See Winnicott, "Aggression."

39. See Winnicott, "Primary State."

40. Winnicott, "Use of an Object," 362.

41. Baudry, *Winnicott's 1968 Visit*, 1086.

42. Winnicott, "Ideas and Definition," 360. See also Winnicott, "Mother's Contribution."

psychosis in terms of traumatic losses or injuries in this and other early relationships. In this work, I will continue to use Winnicott's own terminology "the good-enough mother," but it is clear to me, as I believe it was to Winnicott, that men can and do perform this role, what George Lakoff calls "nurturant parent morality,"[43] a feature of my own family experience of *both* my parents. All my subsequent references to "the good-enough mother" should be interpreted accordingly. Sarah Hrdy has recently shown that in our evolutionary history and increasingly today men can and do perform this indispensable role in the development of human infants and children.[44]

Third, unlike the psychoanalyst Melanie Klein,[45] Winnicott observed that these traumas were not in the biological nature of things, but were framed by the personal, often culturally framed experience that mothers brought to their care for their child and the child's responsiveness, including resistance to such care. Recent empirical work studying babies shows such responsiveness occurs earlier than Winnicott supposed.[46]

Fourth, Winnicott came to see the struggles of the analysands he worked with, both children and adults, as a move from a false self they have developed in compliant response to parental demands to what he called a true self in which the analysand discovered and gave expression to the true self.[47] It was in clinical work with patients of this kind that he found one of his patients had been so trapped in the false self of her head that her rage expressed itself in a "violent head-banging [that] appeared as part of an attempt to produce a blackout."[48] Winnicott came to understand the true self as never fully revealed, resting on a right not to communicate,[49] a private self touched and seen often only through the arts (including music), all of which resonated with my own experience of resistance to patriarchal demands, demands Winnicott analogized to rape, a "sin against the self."[50]

43. Lakoff, *Moral Politics*, 108–40.

44. Hrdy, *Father Time*.

45. See Winnicott, "Letter to Melanie Klein."

46. See Stern, *Interpersonal World*; on Winnicott, 100–101, 229, 241. See also Gopnik, *Philosophical Baby*.

47. See Winnicott, "Ego Distortion,"

48. Winnicott, "Mind and Its Relation to the Psyche-Soma," 253. For illuminating discussion of Winnicott's work, see Cohen, *All the Rage*, xxxv, 88, 98, 146, 162.

49. See Winnicott, "Communicating and Not Communicating."

50. Winnicott, "Communicating and Not Communicating," 441.

Fifth, Winnicott came to a pathbreaking understanding of what he observed in the relationship of child to mother through play with transitional objects (for example, teddy bears):

> It is usual to refer to "reality-testing," and to make a clear distinction between apperception and perception. I am here staking a claim for an intermediate state between a baby's inability and growing ability to recognize and accept reality. I am therefore studying the substance of an *illusion,* that which is allowed to the infant and which in adult life is inherent in art and religion.[51]

Winnicott saw "the essential feature . . . of transitional objects" as "*the paradox, and the acceptance of the paradox:* the baby creates the object, but the object was there waiting to be created and to become an object"[52], and he brilliantly used play with symbols in his analyses of children.[53] As the earlier quote states, Winnicott came to see such imaginative play as a more general phenomenon in the development of human culture, something he came to believe Freud had ignored, that he connected not only to art and religion, but ethics itself[54]—a theme I shall explore later in my argument. Imaginative play may, as Huizinga argued, be crucial to the development of human culture,[55] and, as Plato apparently suggested in *The Laws*, to its support.[56] Indeed, such play—enabling us to imagine and explore new worlds[57]—is the origin of a human creativity that Winnicott saw as at the core of a personally meaningful, fulfilled human life[58] and an ethics based on "the universal right to be a free or an integrated autonomous individual."[59]

In his important study of animal play, Gordon Burghardt has shown that there are five criteria for play as a feature of human and non-human animal life: (i) not directly contributing to survival, (ii) its spontaneous, voluntary, autotelic character, (iii) its difference from serious behavior, (iv) its repeatable but nonstereotypical character, and (v) arising when

51. Winnicott, "Transitional Objects," 407.

52. Winnicott, "Use of an Object," 358.

53. See Winnicott, "Therapeutic Consultation"; Winnicott, *Piggle.*

54. See Winnicott, "Morals and Education."

55. See Huizinga, *Homo Ludens.*

56. See, on this point, Schofield, *How Plato Writes,* 275–89.

57. See, for an important development of this Winnicottian idea, Modell, *Other Times.*

58. See, on this point, Winnicott, "Creativity."

59. Winnicott, "Use of an Object," 35.

not under stress.[60] The importance of Winnicott's view of the role of play in human culture is how it clarifies, on the basis of empirical observation of child development, the role of imaginative play in the extended care and support required for our long human development (what ethologists like Burghardt call our highly altricial, as opposed to precocial, species[61]), the psychological basis of the crucial role of culture in human development. If anything, the best recent work on babies, like Alison Gopnik's *The Philosophical Baby*, confirms Winnicott's insight on the crucial importance of play in the imagination and culture central to human development, including moral imagination:

> Play is the signature of childhood. It's a living, visible manifestation of imagination and learning in action. It is also the most visible sign of the paradoxically useful uselessness of immaturity. By definition, play . . . has no obvious point or goal or function. It does nothing to advance the basic evolutionary goals of mating and predation, fleeing and fighting. And yet these useless actions—and the adult equivalents we squeeze into our workday—are distinctively, characteristically human and deeply valuable. Plays are play, and so are novels, paintings, and songs.[62]

Such play does not disable the child, as Freud and Piaget supposed, to distinguish fiction from truth; on the contrary, "children *know* they are pretending,"[63] and is not precausal, as Piaget supposed, because:

> children are also extremely good at counterfactual thinking. If counterfactual thinking depends on causal understanding and is a deep, evolved part of human nature, then even very young children should also be able to think causally. In fact, it turns out that they do already know a great deal about the causal structure of the world—about how one thing makes another happen. In fact, this is one of the most important, and more evolutionary, recent discoveries of developmental psychology.[64]

Nor is it true, as Piaget also supposed, that children lacked moral knowledge because they "couldn't take the perspective of others, infer

60. See Burghardt, *Genesis*, 70–82, 314.

61. See, for example, Burghardt, *Genesis* 85, 128. An altricial animal, like a young bird, is helpless at birth, requiring care; a precocial animal is born highly developed, not requiring care.

62. Gopnik, *Philosophical Baby*, 14.

63. Gopnik, *Philosohical Baby*, 30–31.

64. Gopnik, *Philosophical Baby*, 34.

intentions, and following abstract rules . . . Modern science shows that this just isn't true. Literally from the time they are born children are empathic . . . and three-year-olds understand rules and try to follow them."[65] Indeed,

> The new research shows that children have some of the foundations of morality from the time they're very young, even from the time they are born. But these foundations aren't just innate, unchanging "moral grammar" or a hardwired set of emotional reactions. Instead, children's moral thinking, and so our own, changes as we learn more about the world and ourselves. Just as children are born with theories about the world, but also with powerful capacities for changing those theories, they seem to be born with certain fundamental moral ideas, but also with powerful capacities to change their moral judgments and actions.[66]

The development of the capacity for play is, as R. W. White observed,[67] an intrinsically valuable and valued human competence in which humans take intrinsic pleasure in their mastery, the "joy of mastery, a mastery that is self generating" and "obviously extends to adult life."[68] As Arnold H. Modell put the point, quoting and commenting on White:

> "My thought is that the seeking of efficacy is a primate biological endowment as basic as the satisfactions that accompany feeding and sexual gratification." I would add that such joys can be experienced in solitude, when the other is absent or is merely a silent presence.[69]

Modell's observation about solitude echoes Winnicott's insight into the capacity to be alone. It also clarifies what Winnicott meant in his important observation of the aggression experienced by infants in resisting care, an anticipation of later resistance to the demands of the false self.

The insights psychoanalysts often draw from the arts, revealing truths otherwise difficult verbally to access, is evident in the work of Freud and many others, including my own work on Shakespeare with Jim Gilligan, but also in Winnicott. Winnicott thus mentions at one point

65. Gopnik, *Philosophical Baby*, 204. See, for further discussion of this view, Bruner, *Actual Minds*, 57–69.

66. Gopnik, *Philosophical Child*, 203–4.

67. See White, *Ego and Reality*.

68. Quoted in Modell, *Private Self*, 72,

69. Modell, *Private Self*, 52.

to an analysand that his struggles were earlier stated by the poet Wordsworth, commenting:

> Here I referred to Wordsworth's 'Ode on the Intimations of Immortality from Recollections of Childhood'—'Shades of the prison-house', etc., but to my surprise he was not acquainted with this.[70]

Wordsworth's "Ode" could not have been more illuminating about what Winnicott had discovered through psychoanalysis, as the following excerpt shows:

> Our birth is but a sleep and a forgetting:
> The Soul that rises with us, our life's Star,
> Hath had elsewhere its seeing,
> And cometh from afar:
> Not in entire forgetfulness,
> And not in utter nakedness,
> But trailing clouds of glory, do we come
> From God, who is our home:
> Heaven lies about us in our infancy!
> Shades of the prison-house begin to close
> Upon the growing Boy . . . [71]

In the development of my thinking about Christianities, it was not these five features of Winnicott's psychology alone that compelled me to rethink my earlier views, but two remarkable letters, one to his sister and close friend Violet, and the other to the psychoanalyst Wilfred R. Bion, that directly connect his work as a psychoanalyst to the religion (Methodism) in which he had been brought up,[72] and in both cases he invokes not theology, but the historical Jesus of Nazareth, as he had come to understand the historical Jesus.

The letter to his sister makes a claim about Jesus himself:

> I shall probably be accused if I say that Christ was a leading psychotherapist (I don't know why, but Violet is fond of saying that what I saw is blasphemy, when there is no connection whatever between what I have said and the term.). It is not less true that extreme acts and religious rituals and obsessions are an exact counterpart of these mind disorders, and by psychotherapy,

70. Winnicott, "Holding and Interpretation," 410.

71. Wordsworth, *Selected Poems*, 159.

72. See Parker, *Winnicott*.

> many fanatics or extremists in religion can be brought (if treated early) to a real understanding of religion and its use in setting a high ethical standard.[73]

What struck me is Winnicott's view that psychotherapy enabled "a real understanding of religion and its use in setting a high ethical standard."

The letter to Bion is about the historical Jesus, as Winnicott had now come to understand him:

> I, like you, was brought up in the Christian tradition (Wesleyan) and I have no desire to throw away all that I listened to over and over again and tried to digest and sort out.
>
> It is not possible for me to throw away religion just because the people who organize the religions of the world insist on belief in miracles. What I wanted to know is, have you met with the amazing book by Robert Graves and his friend Joshua Podro, called the Nazarene Gospel restored? It is not possible to buy this book but it is in most of the libraries. Naturally it is frowned upon by all the Christian churches because it deals with the reconstruction of the Jesus story which was current but not much recorded before an attempt was made to get accepted records somewhere in the first and second centuries. In other words, by a tremendous amount of erudition and research these authors have been able to make a reconstruction of the original story, and I find a study of this book absolutely fascinating and very important for the understanding of the Bible story that we came to know so well. I wish I could buy a copy of this book, and send it to you but unfortunately it is out of print.[74]

There are two questions I had when I read these letters. First, what could Winnicott have meant in calling Jesus "a leading psychotherapist." Second, why would the historical Jesus, in the view taken of him by Robert Graves and Joshua Podro's *The Nazarene Gospel Restored,* be "absolutely fascinating and very important for the understanding of the Bible story we know so well." Let me take the second question first.

I have had as much difficulty as Winnicott confesses to Bion in securing a copy of the book as on Amazon it sold for over $1,000, but now have one copy on interlibrary loan and another purchased at a not unreasonable price from another book seller. The edition I now own was

73. Winnicott, "Letter to His Sister," 55.

74. Winnicott, "Letter to Bion," 158.

published in 1953,[75] and I can well understand how it may have shocked established religious thought at the time, as Winnicott surmised (in contrast, today good work on the historical Jesus is easily available, as we shall later see). I will discuss later in my argument current work on the historical Jesus I have come to regard as reliable. Much of it regards Jesus as much more rooted in Jewish thought than had once been the conventional Christian view,[76] but none of it goes as far as Graves and Pordo do as Jesus taking "the contemporary Pharisaic attitude toward the Mosaic Law" and sponsored by "members of the religious aristocracy of Jerusalem,"[77] or anointed as king of Israel, or downplaying the role of women in the Synoptic Gospels, or regarding him and his followers as highly literate (John Dominic Crossan, for example, doubts this[78]). Graves also wrote a fictionalized version of the historical Jesus, *King Jesus: A Novel*[79] in which Jesus is regarded as an enemy of the female power[80] advocated by Graves in *The White Goddess*,[81] which explains the unjustified misogyny in his view of the historical Jesus. Winnicott would not have known of any of this. What presumably struck him is that the historical Jesus, in the account of Graves and Podro, is at all points human, not divine, indeed surviving the crucifixion, living, as Graves and Podro argue in another book, in Rome[82] and wandering as an outcast elsewhere. The entire development of Christianity by Paul in his gospel to the gentiles is thus heretical, having on their view no historical basis,[83] including the Pauline doctrines of original sin and predestination which were to play such an important role in later Christianities (both Roman Catholicism and various forms of Protestantism and sometimes sanguinary theological controversies between and among them), as well as features of Paul's epistles that liberal Christians today question and reject,

75. Graves and Podro, *Nazarene Gospel.*

76. See, on this point, Vermes, *Religion of Jesus*; Vermes, *Jesus and the World*; Vermes, *Jesus the Jew*; Vermes, *Authentic Gospel*; Vermes, *Changing Faces*; Klausner, *Jesus of Nazareth*; Sanders, *Jesus and Judaism*; Fredriksen, *When Christians Were Jews*; Fredriksen, *From Jesus to Christ.*

77. Graves and Podro, *Nazarene Gospel, xii.*

78. Crossan, *Jesus*, 28, 65.

79. Graves, *King Jesus.*

80. See, on this point, Seymour, *Robert Graves*, 289–90, 298–99, 308, 314–16.

81. Graves, *White Goddess.*

82. Graves and Podro, *Jesus in Rome.*

83. Graves and Podro, *Nazarene Gospel*, xvii–xxiii.

in particular, his sexism, homophobia, and anti-Semitism. Winnicott apparently found Grave and Podro's historical Jesus appealing precisely for such reasons.

Understanding the historical Jesus in this completely human way, what did Winnicott mean in his letter to his sister that "Christ was a leading psychotherapist"? I take this statement *quite* seriously despite myself having initial doubts about how an invention of psychoanalysis by Freud, a nineteenth-twentieth-century atheist and rather anti-clerical Jew, could have *anything* to say about the historical Jesus. But, Freud's discovery of psychoanalysis, and it was I believe a discovery, was itself inspired, as my argument shows, by a psychological mirroring he found in Plato's account of love, which has been true as long as we have loved one another. And Freud's discovery was by no means the last word on the truths to which the method would lead, as Winnicott's work shows. And if Winnicott did himself discover such further truths, they advance understanding of the importance of intimate relationships, which have existed as long as we have loved one another, including early relationships (the good-enough mother) on which Freud did not focus in the way Winnicott does. Since Winnicott's views of human nature are an advance over Freud's, those views may clarify and even advance understanding of loving human relationships, including forms of mirroring that have long existed, as Plato on love shows. It is from this perspective I argue, in chapters to follow, that Winnicott offers a defensible interpretive understanding of Jesus's teaching and life and indeed its enduring appeal. It does so in two ways. First, it clarifies, as I shall later argue, important features of the love and ethics Jesus both advocated and exemplified (see chapter 3), including the empathetic care and concern for the inner despairing life of the poor and the exploited, the sick and outcasts, and how that understanding was so moving and sometimes successful, but also, since antipatriarchal, so threatening. And second, it offers a psychoanalytic understanding of how later Christianities can have gotten Jesus so wrong, including his central teaching on love and nonviolence. Winnicott himself made observations on both points which I find quite suggestive, as my later argument will show.

On the first point, Winnicott's most extensive discussion of the psychology of religion is in "Morals and Education"[84]:

84. Winnicott, "Morals and Education."

> By experience of life and living the child in health becomes ready to believe in something can be handed over in terms of a personal god. But the personal god has no value to a child who has not had the experience of human beings, persons humanizing the terrifying superego formations that relate directly to the infantile impulse and to the fantasy that goes with the functioning and with crude excitements involving instinct.[85]

The persons in question are, for Winnicott, good-enough mothers: "[i]n individual development, *the precursor of the mirror is the mother's face,*"[86] coming to a sense of self through seeing himself in her loving eyes, what I call love's mirror in later chapters. But, the infant is subject not only to fears of but anger at mothers for frustrations the infant may not understand:

> The mother is needed over this time and is needed because of her survival value. She is an environment-mother and at the same time an object-mother, the object of excited loving. The child gradually comes to integrate these two aspects of the mother and to be able to love and to be affectionate with the surviving mother at the same time. This phase involves the child in a special kind of anxiety which is called a sense of guilt, guilt related to the idea of destruction where love is also operating.[87]

It is the power of love responding to destructive impulses with understanding and continuing support (marked in good mothering by the "absence of the talion reaction in the mother"[88]) that leads the child "towards constructive or actively loving behaviour in his limited world, reviving the object, making the loved object better again, rebuilding the damaged thing."[89] For Winnicott, the psychology of religion arises, as in Feuerbach's not dissimilar projection theory,[90] from such love, "as man continues to create and re-create God as a place to put that which is good in himself."[91] As Winnicott put it, "we can say that on the basis of what had been experienced as an individual, we may teach the concept of, say, everlasting arms. We may use the word 'God', we can make a specific

85. Winnicott, "Morals and Education," 384.
86. Winnicott, "Mirror-Role," 211.
87. Winnicott, "Morals and Education," 385.
88. Quoted in Modell, *Other Times*, 24.
89. Winnicott, "Morals and Education," 385.
90. See Feuerbach, *Essence of Christianity*.
91. Winnicott, "Morals and Education," 378.

link with the Christian church and doctrine, but it is a series of steps."[92] One of Winnicott's analysands directly linked psychoanalysis itself with religion in a way that is suggestive of his own view of the psychology of religion: "People use God like an analyst—someone to be there while you're playing."[93] And Winnicott himself observed: "Is it not from *being God* that human beings arrive at the humility proper to human individuality?"[94] I argue in later chapters that central figures in the development of Christianities, Augustine and Luther among others, engaged with God psychoanalytically as a loving analyst in precisely this way.

There is, finally, Winnicott's poem, "The Tree," written evidently from the perspective of Winnicott's identification with Jesus himself:

> Someone touched the hem of my garment
> Someone, someone and someone
> I had much virtue to give
> I was the source of the virtue
> the grape of the vine of the wine
> I could have loved a woman
> Mary, Mary, Mary
> There was not time for loving
> I must be about my father's business
> There were publicans and sinners
> The poor we had always with us
> There were those sick of the palsy
> and the blind and the maimed
> and widows bereft and grieving
> women wailing for their children
> fathers with prodigal sons
> prostitutes drawing their own water from deep wells in the hot
> sun
> Mother below is weeping
> weeping
> weeping
> Thus I knew her
> Once stretched out on her lap
> as now on a dead tree
> I learned to make her smile
> to stem her tears
> to undo her guilt

92. Winnicott, "Children Learning," 318.

93. Winnicott, "Playing," 177.

94. Winnicott, "Communication Between Infant and Mother," 234.

to cure her inward death
To enliven her was my living
So she became wife, mother, home
The carpenter enjoyed his craft
Children came and loved and were loved
Suffer little children to come unto me
Now mother is weeping
She must weep
The sins of the whole world weigh less that this
woman's heaviness
O Glastonbury[95]
Must I bring even these thorns to flower?
Even this dead tree to leaf?
How in agony
Held by dead wood that has no need of me
by the cruelty of the nail's hatred
of gravity's inexorable and heartless pull
I thirst
No garment now
No hem to be touched
It is I who need virtue
Eloi, Eloi, lama sabachthani?
It is I who die
I who die
I who die
I die
I[96]

What we know of Winnicott's early family life is what this intimate poem tells us: that his mother lived in a patriarchal marriage and "was a depressive woman, and that Donald took it as his task to provide her with relief. Donald's mother was clearly a background to her husband, whose

95. Author note: Glastonbury is thought to be the site of the oldest Christian church in England. See Wikipedia, "Glastonbury." The last abbot of Glastonbury, Richard Whiting, had signed the Act of Supremacy, acknowledging Henry VIII as supreme in matters of religion, but refused to hand over Glastonbury because he argued that 1535 Suppression of Religious Houses Act did not apply to large houses like Glastonbury. He was not tried, as he should have been by the House of Lords, but Cromwell tried him himself for treason and had the old man hanged, drawn, and quartered in 1539 at Glastonbury. Whiting's resistance and terrible death, albeit as a Catholic, may have been honored by Winnicott, himself a dissenter, in this poem. See Wikipedia, "Richard Whiting (abbot)."

96. Winnicott, "Tree." © Oxford University Press, 2017. Reproduced with permission of the Licensor through PLSclear.

career was brilliant and public."[97] His father, successful in business and politics and a deeply religious (Methodist) man, was "an overpowering, narcissistic presence for his son,"[98] who resisted following his father's way of life in business. Winnicott only ends his unhappy first marriage for his second marriage with a woman very much his equal and whom he loved sexually after his father's death. The highly personal poem clarifies what Winnicott meant in his letter to his sister, "that Christ was a leading psychotherapist": he had come to see his vocation for psychoanalysis as an expression of his love for his mother and those afflicted like his mother and even himself,[99] and psychoanalysis was crucial because Jesus exemplified what psychoanalysis brought to the care and cure of the afflicted, a matter we shall explore in later chapters. It is not surprising, as we shall later see, that Winnicott would come to see his work with the afflicted and his own afflictions deriving from a patriarchal family in terms of Jesus's life and work, nor that other psychoanalysts, often dealing with people from similar backgrounds, have sometimes offered compelling interpretations of the parables of Jesus.[100]

In "Some Thoughts on the Meaning of the Word Democracy,"[101] Winnicott connected his views of the importance of good-enough mothers to the defense of democracy, but also pointed to the dark side of such long dependence. As he put it,

> In psycho-analytical and allied work, it is found that all individuals have in reserve a certain fear of *woman.* Some individuals have this fear to a greater extent than others, but it can be said to be universal. This is quite different from saying that an individual fears a particular woman. This fear of *woman* is a powerful agent in social structure, and it is responsible for the fact that in very few societies does a woman hold the political reins. It is also responsible for the immense amount of cruelty to women, which can be found in customs that are accepted by almost all civilizations.[102]

97. Rodman, *Winnicott,* 13–14.

98. Rodman, *Winnicott,* 17.

99. On Winnicott's own personal struggles not only with his father and with the sexual problems in his first marriage, but with Melanie Klein and Anna Freud, see Rodman, *Winnicott.*

100. See, for example, Ford, *Parables.*

101. Winnicott, "Some Thoughts."

102. Winnicott, "Some Thoughts," 416.

Winnicott remarkably thus uses his view of good-enough mothering better to understand an unconscious misogyny rooted, so he argues, in the experience infants have of such one-sided dependence on women "when the infant is doubly dependent because totally unaware of dependence."[103] It is striking that Winnicott should thus have anticipated the insights of comparable psychoanalytically informed feminists, like Dorothy Dinnerstein,[104] Nancy Chodorow,[105] and Jessica Benjamin.[106] However, in contrast to these recent thinkers, Winnicott despairs, because of such deeply rooted unconscious misogyny, "that men or women would ever tolerate the general principle of women generally at the highest positions of political power,"[107] as good-enough mothering could never be shared with men. In contrast, Sarah Hrdy has recently argued such sharing not only enjoys the support of the sciences of primatology and cultural anthropology, but of increasing numbers of men, gay and straight, who now perform this caring role to their benefit, the benefit of society, and the more just treatment of women.[108] The development might have surprised Winnicott but it is consistent with his general view both of the role of Christian loving conscience, based on treating people as equals, and the imaginative play conscience makes possible in proposing and experimenting with cultural change, including ethical change and what Thomas Nagel has recently called authentic moral progress in the treatment of homosexuals.[109]

Winnicott also goes on to investigate psychoanalytically what can happen in religion when failures in mothering undermine trust, and he has clearly in mind the Christianities that "have made much of original sin."[110] It is at this point that he argues that psychoanalysis, which may clarify what love means in the historical Jesus, may also clarify what went wrong in historical Christianities:

> religion could learn something from psycho-analysis, something that would save religious practice from losing its place in the civilization process, and in the process of civilization.

103. Winnicott, "Some Thoughts," 416.
104. Dinnerstein, *Mermaid.*
105. Chodorow, *Reproduction.*
106. Benjamin, *Bonds.*
107. Benjamin, *Bonds,* 416–17.
108. See Hrdy, *Father Time.*
109. See, on this point, Nagel, *Moral Feelings.*
110. Winnicott, "Morals and Education," 379.

> Theology, by denying to the developing individual the creating of whatever is bound up in the concept of God and of goodness and of moral values, depletes the individual of an important aspect of creativeness.[111]

The question of original sin also arose in one of the records we have of one of his analyses, as, near the end of the analysis, Winnicott discusses the analysand's rejection of Freud's *Totem and Taboo*, pointing out to the analysand that the role of "original sin" in the book does not take seriously the love of the mother and the role of the analyst as both a mother-figure and father-figure.[112]

Inspired by much that seems to me true in Winnicott's pathbreaking understanding of psychoanalysis and its implications for interpreting Christianities, the argument of this book will proceed as follows.

Chapter 1 explores the value of what I call love's mirror in the development of the human psyche, first noted by Plato and the inspiration of Freud's discovery of the role of transference love in psychoanalysis, and explains as well the impact on me of James Gilligan's empirical work on the roots of violence, which will play a role later in understanding the roots of the role of nonviolence in the life and teaching of Jesus of Nazareth. I then offer a theory of guilt vs. shame cultures and their development in history, first suggested to me by Jim Gilligan, which will play a prominent role in the understanding of the life and teaching of Jesus Nazareth, as, like Socrates, advocating a guilt culture in transition from a shame culture. The distinction between shame and guilt cultures plays a central role in the argument to follow.

Chapter 2 shows how Roman patriarchy illustrates a shame culture perpetually at war; locates Jesus as working within the unique Jewish tradition of prophetic resistance to the surrounding imperialisms that subjugated Israel; and places Jesus's life and thought as a Jewish ethical prophet (modeled on Elijah among others) in the context of developing a guilt culture, based in loving egalitarian relationships, resisting Roman patriarchy, a resistance for which he died. The search for the historical Jesus was central to Winnicott's interest in his view of Jesus as "a leading psychotherapist," and thus I discuss this interest of his in the context of the development of this search in Soren Kierkegaard, Albert Schweitzer, Rudolf Bultmann, the Jesus Seminar, John Meier, John Dominic Crossan,

111. Winnicott, "Morals and Education," 379.

112. Winnicott, "Holding," 472–73.

and Elizabeth Schüssler Fiorenza, much of which confirms Winnicott's view of the historical Jesus, albeit on more historically reliable grounds.

Most surprisingly, Winnicott's psychoanalysis illuminates many of the most distinctive features of Jesus's teaching and life, as I try to show in the chapter on the antipatriarchal Jesus (chapter 3). Jesus, on my account, is more Jewish than many Christians realize and that Jewish scholars have long recognized, and the establishment of Christianity as the established church of the Roman Empire (making Christianities, in my view, more Roman than Christian) all the more tragic, requiring that even the Gospels themselves are sometimes framed and interpreted by their authors and leading theologians to exculpate the Romans and inculpate the Jews for the death of Jesus,[113] founding Christianities in a religious anti-Semitism and sexism false to the historical Jesus and disastrous for the Jews and women and gays as well as the development of democracies in future ostensibly Christian cultures.

Psychoanalytic argument, drawing on Winnicott's insights into human development, shows how and why Christianity, as developed by Augustine and Luther, became more Roman than Christian (chapter 4). My own work on Augustine and Erikson's brilliant psychoanalytic study of Luther make this case.

Chapter 5 examines and criticizes the role that a one-sided, nonreciprocal agape love and original sin played in their thought, as well as Anders Nygren and Soren Kierkegaard, and how twentieth-century moral theologians (Niebuhr and Tillich) have challenged these views, including Niebuhr's view of racism as original sin and how Christian nonviolence might work in the US as it worked in India (an argument that decisively influenced Martin Luther King Jr.) as well as Niebuhr's view of what I call political religions, including the corrupt role of religion in rationalizing the evils of racism and sexism.

Chapter 6 argues that the view of the antipatriarchal Jesus clarifies as well how his view of ethics was the inspiration for Kant's moral and constitutional philosophy of universal human rights, and discusses both the appeal and difficulties in Kant's views, including his view that ethics cannot be empirically explained, and his advocacy, for example, of the *lex talionis* in punishment, and his condemnation of homosexuality, both of which gave rise to Nietzsche's criticism of Kant. The chapter then argues that John Rawls's proposal of a constructivist contractualism reconstructs

113. See, on this point, Ruether, *Faith and Fratricide.*

Kant's views on a sound basis, and argues as well that a sound naturalistic basis for such ethics can be developed on the basis of relational love, leading to respect, as the central human need that explains Rawls's conception of basic human rights and the difference principle, all supported by contemporary work on the role of relational psychology in human development.

Chapter 7 explores the role resistance of radical heterodox Christians within Christianity played in the development of constitutional democracy (Locke on toleration); the criticism of slavery, racism, and sexism by the abolitionist feminists in the antebellum period in the United States; the role radical Christian thought played in the criticism of slavery and racism before, during, and after the Civil War in the thought of Theodore Parker, Frederick Douglass, and Abraham Lincoln; the role of radical Christian thought on nonviolence in both Gandhi's satyagraha in India and King's civil rights movement in the US; the role of psychoanalytic Christianity in the peacemaking in Northern Ireland; and the recent development of forms of liberal Christianity that seek common ground with other religious and philosophical traditions as well as scientific thought.

Finally, chapter 8 contrasts Freud's conservative psychoanalytic understanding of the relationship of religion and ethics, with that of Winnicott's view of religion, properly understood, as supporting and leading to an ethics and democratic politics that treats persons as equals, including resistance to injustice. Freud's views rest on a non-empirical mythological view of a death instinct (Thanatos) that regarded violence and indeed war as ineliminable features of human culture. Winnicott, in contrast, rejects this view on the ground that actual observation of human development shows that loving attachments, including the forms of resistance of the child as part of the ongoing relationship, are central to human development and it is culturally supported traumatic actions and omissions that injure such attachments that lead to violence (for example, the initiation into patriarchal gender roles, and the shaming of patriarchal manhood as a stimulus to violence). Winnicott's view of the antipatriarchal Jesus (including his advocacy of nonviolence against Roman patriarchy) explain how he came to see his work as a psychoanalyst as inspired by Jesus as "a leading psychotherapist," and how he came to see as well his discovery of the crucial role of play in human creativity in both the arts and sciences as clarifying the compelling appeal of creative ethical voice in both the life and teaching of Jesus, the antipatriarchal Jewish prophet.

1

Love and the Human Psyche

My perspective in this book starts with and then explores what most researchers in the human sciences now take to be central to the human psyche and its development: namely, attachment love, at the heart, as we have seen, of Winnicott's theory and practice of psychoanalysis. Then based on Jim Gilligan's work on shame and guilt, I show how violence arises from trauma, that is from injuries to love fostered and justified by the shame culture of patriarchy.

TRANSFERENCE LOVE IN PSYCHOANALYSIS

My understanding of the human psyche derives in part from an interpretation of Freud's discoveries, drawing on Plato, what the philosopher and psychoanalyst Jonathan Lear has called, "love and its place in nature."[1] Following very much along the lines of Erich Fromm's earlier interpretation and critique of Freud's discoveries,[2] Lear shows how Freud's theory of Eros arises from Plato's psychology of sexual love in the *Symposium* and *Phaedrus*. Plato's earlier theory of love in the *Symposium* aimed to show, contrary to the earlier speakers in the dialogue before Socrates, that not

1. See Lear, *Love*; Lear, *Open-Minded*; Lear, *Freud*; Lear, *Happiness*; Lear, *Radical Hope*.

2. See Fromm, *Escape*; Fromm, *Man for Himself*; Fromm, *Sane Society*; Fromm, *Art of Loving*.

all forms of sexual love were valuable, nor were all forms necessarily egoistic.[3] In the *Phaedrus*, Plato offers an astonishing *psychological* portrait of human love. Both Phaedrus, quoting the rhetorician Lysis, and Socrates himself had stated what may have been a conventional Athenian view of the love of men for boys, namely, that it was better if the lover did not love the boy. Socrates, however, abruptly abandons his earlier view, and offers in its place the tripartite theory of the soul later developed at length in the *Republic* (intellect, spirit, and appetite) stated in the *Phaedrus* in terms of the charioteer (the intellect) trying to control two horses (one courage or spirit, the other appetite, or lust). The moral power of love in the dialogue is precisely that the lover loves, indeed is devoted to the welfare of, the boy, and both the psychological and normative force of such love is that such love elicits love in the boy that takes the form of self-knowledge:

> Then the boy is in love, but has no idea what he loves. He does not understand, and cannot explain, what has happened to him. It is as if he had caught an eye disease from someone else, but could not identify the cause; he does not realize that he is seeing himself in the lover as in a mirror. So when the lover is near, the boy's pain is relieved just as the lover's is, and when they are apart he yearns as much as he is yearned for, because he has a mirror image of love in him—"backlove"—though he neither speaks nor thinks of it as love, but as friendship. Still his desire is nearly the same as the lover's, though weaker: he wants to see, touch, kiss, and lie down with him; and of course, as you might expect, he acts on these desires soon after they occur.[4]

Freud rediscovered in transference love what Plato had earlier seen in the psychology of human erotic love through what he discovered in the psychoanalysis of the dreams and free associations of a certain group of neurotics, namely, analysands whose neuroses could be reenacted and explored in their relationship to the analyst, as they saw in their "transference love for the analyst" a mirror of the archaic roots of their own problems in relationships and in life.[5] Freud follows Plato in regarding transference love using Plato's mirroring imagery: "The doctor should be

3. On these points, see Levy, "Definition of Love."

4. Plato, *Phaedrus*, 532. In her important recent study of Plato and his relationships in the context of the decline of the Athenian democracy, Carol Atack suggests that the conversations of Socrates and Phaedrus in *Phaedrus* "represented a version of Plato's own relationships—with Socrates, his teacher, and Dion, his favoured student," Atack, *Plato*, 156.

5. See Freud, for example, "Dynamics"; "Remembering"; "Observations."

opaque to his patients and, like a mirror, should show them nothing but what is shown to him."[6]

Jonathan Lear comments on Freud's discovery as a discovery about human love:

> Psychoanalysis, Freud once said, is a cure through love. On the manifest level, Freud meant that psychoanalytic therapy requires the analysand's emotional engagement with the analyst and the analyst's empathic understanding of his patient. But the latent content of this remark, which Freud only gradually discovered, and then through a glass darkly, is that psychoanalysis in its essence promotes individuation. In that sense, psychoanalysis is itself a manifestation of love. And the emergence of psychoanalysis onto the human scene must, from this perspective, be part of love's developmental history.[7]

Plato had made the same point in the *Phaedrus* when Socrates observes the way different individuals experience and make sense of love in their lives, some to their great good, others less so.[8]

Freud's discovery is twofold: the first rooted in Plato, the second beyond Plato. The first is that human erotic love unlike the periodicity of animal reproductive sexuality is not tied to reproduction but is factually and imaginatively quite independent of it (as Freud observed in the deep imaginative and sometimes creative lives of homosexuals such as Leonardo, or Winnicott observed in the role of imaginative creativity as such in a fulfilled human life). The second is that human love, as manifest in transference love, has not only an instrumental value in leading to abstract goodness, as Plato believed,[9] but the human value of self-knowledge as lovers see themselves, their development and lives, more clearly through the eyes or mirrors of their lovers, something Plato may also have believed (his conception of mirroring leads to self-knowledge and may be part of what he meant in regarding erotic love as leading to the ethical good). It was Freud, however, who saw this feature of human love, mirroring, as the basis of transference love in psychoanalytic therapy.

Transference love, as a form of love, leads or can lead to self-knowledge in therapy, understanding one's neurosis and even psychosis. Thus, for Freud, transference love is when the patient transfers onto the analyst

6. See Freud, "Recommendations," 118.

7. Lear, *Love*, 27–28.

8. See Plato, *Phaedrus*, 532–33.

9. On this point, see Levy, "Definition of Love."

or therapist feelings the patient has for significant people in their life (often a parent), ascribing to the analyst the behavior patterns or character of the parent or other emotionally central person from their past. Transference love thus can reveal the confusion between past and present which is the essence of neurosis, where the patient goes through life confusing and responding to people in the present (in this case the analyst) with important figures from their past. Thus examining or analyzing or interpreting transference love is a way of getting at the core of neurosis understood as the inhibition (in the present) of the capacity to love. For example, a form of this process may lead to the recognition, like that of Jim Gilligan, that shame and guilt ironically inhibit what they presumably are designed to sustain: namely our desire and capacity to love. Hence the inefficacy of both shame and guilt in efforts to prevent violence, as illustrated through the failure of our prison system. For Freud, transference love was, like dreams, a royal road to the unconscious, and hence to understanding neurosis. What Freud discovered in transference love is a deeper psychological truth about the role of love itself as distinctively human: we become human through loving relationships to other persons, and transference love, as a form of such love, rests on and advances the capacity to love.

It is for this reason that the psychoanalytic method that Freud discovered introduced into the distinctively human sciences the central role of the free associations of analysands and the web of relationships, past and present, that such associations reveal over time as the analysand discovers and explores the web of such relationships, past and present, in and through the relationship to the analyst. Psychoanalysis both nurtures and supports voice in the analysand, sometimes surprising voices and the thoughts and emotions they express. The free expression of voice expresses itself in narratives, narratives constantly examined and reexamined and always subject to change and revision as one story yields to another and yet another, fallible discoveries responsive to experience as approximations to the complexities of the layers of the human psyche as the analysand finds through self-knowledge better, less conflicted ways of living and loving, sometimes through coming to understand and resist what D. W. Winnicott explored as our captivity to false selves.[10] It was Freud himself early in his development of psychoanalysis who worried about how different his method was from what was generally taken to

10. See, on this point, Winnicott, *Through Paediatrics*, 71–72, 100, 225, 280–81, 286, 292, 296–99.

be science. Or, if you prefer, from the view of science that he previously had held.

> Like other neuropathologists I was trained to employ local diagnoses and electro-prognosis, and it still strikes me myself as strange that the case histories I write should read like short stories and that, as one might say, they lack the serious stamp of science. I must console myself with the reflection that the nature of the subject is evidently responsible for this, rather than any preference of my own.[11]

"The nature of the subject," as Freud puts it, is *human* psychology. It is for this reason that Freud came to see and to explore literature (including Shakespeare) in his work and to recognize in his use of literature the role of narrative in structuring human life.

It is a prominent feature of the development of psychoanalysis and psychiatry after Freud, reflected in the works of Jonathan Lear, Erich Fromm, and many others, including D. W. Winnicott, John Bowlby, Daniel N. Stern, Harry Stack Sullivan, Stephen A. Mitchell, Donnel B. Stern, and Carol Gilligan,[12] that the human psyche is formed in interpersonal relationships from the outset in the infant's relationship to a mother or caregiver, as the infant experiences itself as an emerging person in relationship to a mother's or caregiver's love for the child as well as the child's relationship to other caring persons over time, including eventually lovers. The distinctively human *mind*, as Charles Horton Cooley, the sociologist, brilliantly observed: "lives in perpetual conversation."[13] Erich Fromm gave, I believe, an accurate expression of love in human life, namely, "[c]are, responsibility, respect, and knowledge,"[14] Fromm's formulation includes but is not limited to forms of sexual love, but includes as well the role of loving attachments throughout distinctively

11. Freud, *Studies on Hysteria,* 160.

12. For Carol Gilligan's recent use of Bowlby's attachment theory to explain the persistence of patriarchy, see Gilligan and Snider, *Why Does Patriarchy.* For a recent study of the psychological roots of the limits in Freud's approach, see Whitebook, *Freud.* My conception of love as central to human personality and relationships uses and elaborates an interpersonal psychology of human relationships developed by a range of past and contemporary psychologists. Among the works that have inspired me are the following: Sullivan, *Interpersonal Theory*; Mitchell, *Relational Concepts*; Tronick, *Power of Discord*; Stern, *Interpersonal World*; Hrdy, *Morthers and Others*; Benjamin, *Shadow of the Other*; Beele et al., *Infant Research*; Murray, *Social Baby*; and Brajelton, *Neonatal.*

13. Cooley, *Human Nature,* 90. See also Mead, *Mind, Self.*

14. Fromm, *Art of Loving,* 30.

human lives in which so little is determined, in contrast to animals, by inborn patterns and instincts, and in which love itself is so connected to nurturing individuality and integrity—care, responsibility, respect, and knowledge. Thomas Merton made the same points:

> We do not become fully human until we give ourselves to each other in love. And this must not be confined only to sexual fulfillment: it embraces everything in the human person—the capacity for self-giving, for sharing, for creativity, for mutual care, for spiritual concern.[15]

> Love is a personal revolution.[16]

> Love is the revelation of our deepest personal meaning, value, and identity. But this revelation remains impossible as long as we are the prisoner of our own egoism. My true meaning and worth are shown to me not in my estimate of myself, but in the eyes of the one who loves me, and that one must love me as I am, with my faults and limitations, revealing to me the truth that these faults and limitations cannot destroy my worth in *their* eyes; and that I am therefore valuable as a person, in spite of my shortcomings, in spite of the imperfections of my exterior "package."[17]

Our species is the sociable interpersonal species par excellence in which we are born so fragile and so in need of care and so much must culturally be acquired from others, unlike the life of most animals. Interpersonal attachments, rooted in love, make us human. We are, as Michael Tomasello's works and the writings of Sarah Blaffer Hrdy make clear, the species in which the capacity for mutual understanding, for empathy, mind-reading and cooperation, are present in rudimentary form from the very beginning and integral to, in Tomasello's terms, becoming human.[18]

Erich Fromm's and D. W. Winnicott's pathbreaking importance lies in their view of love that, in contrast to Freud's, sees it as central to[19] what

15. Merton, *Love,* 27.

16. Merton, *Love,* 28.

17. Merton, *Love,* 35.

18. See, on all these points, Tomasello, *Becoming Human*; Tomasello, *Natural History of Human Thinking*; Tomasello, *Natural History of Morality*; Hrdy, *Mothers and Others*; Hrdy, *Father Time*.

19. See Fromm, *Escape*; Fromm, *Man for Himself.*

Michael Tomasello has called the "natural history of human morality."[20] Once we understand the force of love in this way, as constitutive of the human psyche,[21] the next question is what retards or stands in the way of its force in human life.

If Freud's pathbreaking insights into the role of neurosis in human life arose from his discovery of transference love in his work with analysands, his inability to make psychological sense of the forces of aggression and violence in the human psyche arose from his acknowledgment that the method of transference, which had been used so successfully with some analysands, did not work with others, in particular, those suffering from narcissistic disorders and the victims of war trauma. Freud and other early psychoanalysts were familiar with and tried to understand the war trauma of soldiers who fought in World War I, and indeed tried unsuccessfully to adapt what they had discovered about the therapies of transference love to disorders for whom such therapy did not work.[22] As Jonathan Lear observed, victims of war trauma "would live and relive with the most violent intensity the horrific experiences of war trauma" and Freud came to think "that these compulsive repetitions could not be understood as disguised and conflicted attempts at gratification" (as he believed about the analysands for which his method worked), and concluded "their explanation must be 'beyond the pleasure principle.'"[23] But, his argument at this point for a death drive (conflicting with the drive for love) was, unlike his earlier pathbreaking work, not based on clinical observation but on a mythological appeal to biology[24] undoubtedly shaped, as I shall later argue, by the traumatic experience of anti-Semitism he had endured throughout his life and that he saw as politically resurgent and even probably triumphant at the end of his despairing life.[25]

D. W. Winnicott had, in contrast to Freud, successfully used the psychoanalytic method in the treatment not only of neurotics but of psychotics and, for this reason, saw no empirical reason to introduce a drive for death when the issues, true vs. false self, could be explored as

20. See Tomasello, *Natural History of Morality.*

21. See, on this point, Levy, "Definition of Love."

22. See Ferenczi et al., *Psycho-Analysis and the War Neuroses*, originally published 1921, published by Forgotten Books, 2012.

23. Lear, *Open Minded*, 143.

24. See Lear, *Open Minded*, 143–147. For Freud's biologically based argument, see Freud, *Beyond the Pleasure Principle.*

25. See, for an investigation along these lines, Whitebook, *Freud.*

injuries in attachment that could, through psychoanalysis, be understood and sometimes repaired. Winnicott regarded attachments, not instincts, as the core of the human psyche and its development, and his view of the focal importance of good-enough mothering in attachment love quite realistically included what he had observed, that such mothering included not only the mother's love and the child's responsive pleasure in the mother's love, as Tronick's "still-face" experiment shows,[26] but also the mother's continuing love responding to the infant's anger when frustrated (marked by the "absence of the talion reaction in the mother"[27]) that supports the central importance of trust in child development.[28] When Winnicott criticizes, as we earlier saw, the belief in original sin in some Christianities as one of the ways Christianity went wrong, presumably he thought as well that the mothers and fathers during the relevant historical periods were not only not good enough, but in some way traumatically damaging to their children, giving rise to a sense of evil in the child that must be rendered consistent with a belief in God's goodness, a theme I will take up later in my argument considering Augustine and Luther.

Erich Fromm's psychological study of the aggressive violence of fascism, including his important study of both Hitler's psychology and its appeal to the German people,[29] came to reject Freud's theory of the death instinct precisely because it naturalized the psychology of aggressive violence and failed to take seriously its cultural framework and "the degree to which the unfolding of a person's capacities is blocked."[30] As he put his point elsewhere, "The person who has not freed himself from the ties to blood and soil is not yet fully born as a human being; his capacity for love and reason are crippled; he does not experience himself nor his fellow man in their—and his own—human reality."[31] In contrast, Freud traced the morality of fascism to groups, like the army and church whose members followed the orders of a leader,[32] ultimately transmitted intergenerationally through biology not culture in contrast to D. W.

26. In this experiment, the child's responses to the mother's changes in facial expression show both the pleasure in the mother's smile and despair when her face is still. See, for discussion, Stern, *Interpersonal World*, 132, 149.

27. Quoted in Modell, *Other Times*, 24.

28. See, on trust in human development, Erikson, *Childhood*, 247–51.

29. See Fromm, *Escape*.

30. Fromm, *Man for Himself*, 216.

31. Fromm, *Sane Society*, 58.

32. See Freud, *Group Psychology*, 93–99.

Winnicott's discoveries of the role of imaginative play in the formation and development of culture. The wrong turns in Freud's psychology, including his interpretation of the Oedipus Complex and the death instinct, arose, Fromm argued, from "the strictly patriarchal attitude which was so characteristic of Freud's time, and which he shared so completely."[33]

SHAME AND GUILT CULTURES

How should we understand the culture of patriarchy and its psychological connections to violence? The cultural anthropologist Ruth Benedict, writing at about the same time as Fromm's study of German fascism, invented the idea of a shame as opposed to a guilt culture. Americans were puzzled by the suicidal violence that Japanese soldiers showed in World War II, and Benedict, who had never been to Japan and did not read or write Japanese, had been asked to bring her cultural anthropology to bear on understanding Japanese violence. In response, she wrote her remarkable 1946 book, *The Chrysanthemum and the Sword: Patterns of Japanese Culture*.[34] Benedict, a lesbian, had experienced the injuries of patriarchy in her marriage. Once living outside such patriarchal structures in loving lesbian relationships based on mutual freedom and equality,[35] she came to an understanding of Japanese fascism as rooted in the shame culture of Japan in which men and women were defined in the terms of a rigid gender binary and a hierarchy privileging male honor, where any threat to that hierarchy elicited overwhelming shame and humiliation and thereby became a provocation for violence. The Japanese emperor cult was rigidly patriarchal with the emperor as a god-king, and the young men initiated into that system modeled themselves as men on allegiance to his commands or supposed commands, leading to a psychology acutely sensitive to any threat to their manhood, the shaming or dishonoring of manhood eliciting violence not only against others but against oneself.

Benedict is probably the first to establish what became the anthropologists' and others' use of the terms *shame cultures* and *guilt cultures*, and to develop the contrast between them, i.e., shame vs. guilt cultures:

> A society that inculcates absolute standards of morality and relies on men's developing a conscience is a guilt culture by

33. Fromm, *Sane Society*, 43.
34. Benedict, *Chrysanthemum*.
35. See, on this point, Richards, *Why Love*, 189–208.

> definition, but a man in such a society may, as in the United States, suffer in addition from shame when he accuses himself of gaucheries which are in no way sins. He may be exceedingly chagrined about not dressing appropriately for the occasion or about a slip of the tongue . . .
>
> True shame cultures rely on external sanctions for good behavior, not, as true guilt cultures do, on an internalized conviction of sin. Shame is a reaction to other people's criticism. A man is shamed either by being openly ridiculed and rejected or by fantasying to himself that he has been ridiculous. In either case it is a potent sanction. But it requires an audience or at least man's fantasy of an audience. Guilt does not.[36]

Benedict's pathbreaking argument in *The Chrysanthemum and the Sword: Patterns of Japanese Culture*[37] explained to Americans their puzzlement about the suicidal levels of violence in Japanese aggressiveness in World War II in terms of the contrast between a dominantly shame culture (Japan) and a guilt culture (the United States), in the latter of which respect for the value of the equal right to life played a more important role. The United States may have been a dominantly guilt culture when Benedict wrote, but, if so, it was not unambiguously so, as the dominant culture of the antebellum American South had been quite patriarchal,[38] and, even after defeat in the Civil War, these cultural patterns remained sufficiently intact to support a cultural racism that was allowed to continue there (lynchings) for a surprisingly long period. Distinctions must be made among different forms of shame and guilt cultures, including mixed cases like the United States and others.

Benedict had earlier developed an anthropological theory implicitly of shame cultures in her discussion, based on the earlier work of her teacher Franz Boas, of the Kwakiutl,[39] an Amerindian people, who used competitive conspicuous displays of wealth and power to support a rigidly defined order based on the gender binary and hierarchy, rationalizing violence,[40] and the anthropologist Michelle Rosaldo later found a similar shame-based cultural pattern in the cannibalistic cultural patterns of

36. Benedict, *Chrysanthemum*, 222–23.

37. Benedict, *Chrysanthemum*.

38. See Wyatt-Brown, *Southern Honor*.

39. See Boas, *Kwakiutl*; Boas, *Mind*.

40. See Benedict, *Patterns*, 173–222.

New Guinea tribes,[41] and the historian historian Bertram Wyatt-Brown found the same in the old South.[42]

Rosaldo in particular called for more attention among anthropologists to a coherent theory of shame in personality and culture. She argued that "of all themes in the literature on culture and personality the opposition between guilt and shame has probably proven most resilient."[43] Rosaldo's own description of the Ilongot, a tribe who periodically engage in group raids on neighboring tribes in which they murder and decapitate members of the other tribes, notes that

> In severing and tossing heads, Ilongot men recount, they could relieve hearts burdened with the "weight" of insult, envy, pain, and grief; and . . . achieve an "anger" that . . . makes shy and burdened youths . . . equal to their peers. . . . [44]
>
> Ilongot shame involves an "anger" born . . . in the contfrontation of a would-be-peer with facts of weakness and social inferiority. . . . "shame" is a thing that leads to striving and the shows of "anger" through which unacceptable imbalances are eventually overcome. . . . "shame" involves awareness of deficiency or slight, a weight one is enjoined to overcome in subsequent displays of one's capacity and "anger."[45]
>
> . . . as children learn to speak, the verbal challenges of adults are seen to "shame" them in a way that motivates the acquisition of new skill and knowledge. Verbal wit, fine dress, productive skill are all, Ilongots claim, things that the young acquire because they envy the accomplishments of peers and would not have their fellows' excellence stand to "shame" them. Growing up and learning to behave with competence and poise requires casting off youthful vulnerability to one's fellows' taunts, and doing this means one redresses "weighty" shame with "light" displays of energy and force [e.g., headhunting]. In fact, headhunting . . . is in large part an angry answer to the distressing "shame" of childhood.[46]

41. See Rosaldo, *Knowledge.*
42. See Wyatt-Brown, *Southern Honor.*
43. Rosaldo, "Shame," 135.
44. Rosaldo, "Shame," 137.
45. Rosaldo, "Shame," 143.
46. Rosaldo, "Shame," 144.

> Feelings of "weight"—whether one's grief at loss, or shame at insult, or envy at the headhunting accomplishments of peers—are what make all men think of killing. . . . Most youths declare that they are loathe to marry until they have taken heads for fear others will "shame" them. As novices, . . . they cannot work dependably, think clearly, or enjoy the company of kin because their "shame" brings sullenness, distraction, and ill-ease. But then, Ilongots claim, headhunting cures this. . . . raids are designed to turn the vulnerable, subordinate and awkward youth into an adult peer.[47]

It is equally clear, in Rosaldo's account, that the Ilongot did not experience feelings of guilt, either prior to or following these murders:

> . . . none appeared to feel remorse for prior violent deeds, or speak of moral right and wrong when telling why they killed.[48]

> . . . Ilongots never speak of guilt, require punishment for wrongs, or seek displays of suffering and remorse in making up for untoward violence. . . . My earlier question—Do not killers suffer guilt?—is shown [to be] of questionable relevance to the Ilongot moral world. . . . The fact that Ilongots never speak of "guilt" in their reports of raids does not itself decide the cultural (or psychological) irrelevance of such things as self-recrimination and remorse in the experience of killers. More telling, I suggest, is the fact that Ilongots but rarely discuss actions with reference to established normative codes or formal rules of wrong and right. . . . notions of "ought" and "obligation" appear lacking. . . .[49]

Thus, Rosaldo concludes, "Ilongots may not feel guilt taking heads."[50] Finally, she says, despite important differences that can be drawn between these cultures, "Ilongots . . . join ranks with Japanese . . . and Homeric Greeks as the enactors of shame morality.[51]"

In his brilliant book on the shame culture of the American South before the Civil War, Bertram Wyatt-Brown defines its demands of "primal honor," as follows: (1) "immortalizing valor," "particularly in the character of revenge against familial and community enemies," (2) "opinions of others, as an indispensable part of personal identity and gauge

47. Rosaldo, "Shame," 146.
48. Rosaldo, "Shame," 137.
49. Rosaldo, "Shame," 139–40.
50. Rosaldo, "Shame," 142.
51. Rosaldo, "Shame," 149.

of self-worth," (3) "physical appearance and ferocity of will as signs of inner merit," (4) "defense of male integrity and mingled fear and love of woman," and (5) "reliance upon oath-taking as a bond."[52] Southern patriarchal women, themselves rigidly confined to a code placing them on an asexual pedestal forbidding sex outside marriage and defining their roles in marriage as in service of the dynastic aims of their fathers, husbands, brothers, and sons, are, like the women of ancient Sparta, the enforcers of patriarchy, shaming the men (including their sons) who would not fight or fight well in wars.[53] In contrast, guilt cultures, like the Quakers, "directly challenged the tenets of honor . . . [c]ondemned as subversive for shattering custom, the Friends made themselves walking testaments of pious shamelessness." Appealing to an independent moral conscience of equal respect and nonviolence critical of dominant patriarchal hierarchies, "[t]hey adopted the Beatitudes and tried to live by them . . . Like the early Christians, Quakers appealed largely to the honorless—the servant and tenant classes, the cottagers of Wales, the small artisans of England,"[54] and, one should add, to women resisting not only slavery and racism, but sexism.[55] It is such guilt cultures whose later development leads to constitutional democracies based on the right of conscience and gender equality as a constitutional value, both critical of community values of racism, sexism, anti-Semitism, and homophobia based on the repression of conscience and speech.

By the time Ruth Benedict came to giving a name to a distinction that was already in wide use by her colleagues, the conceptual distinction itself (though expressed in different terminologies) had been around for a long time. Not just for centuries but millennia. In fact, probably the earliest extant description of the essential difference between a shame culture and a guilt culture was made by an early Christian thinker, Augustine, in contrasting the "earthly city" (Roman shame culture) with the "heavenly city" (Christian guilt culture):

> The glory with the desire of which the Romans burned is the judgment of men thinking well of men. [But] virtue is better, which is content with no human judgment save that of one's

52. Wyatt-Brown, *Southern Honor,* 34.
53. Wyatt-Brown, *Southern Honor,* 35, 39–40, 51.
54. Wyatt-Brown, *Southern Honor,* 75.
55. On this point, see Richards, *Women, Gays.*

> own conscience. Whence the apostle says. "For this is our glory, the testimony of our conscience."[56]

The fact that there is a long tradition of social thought, going back to Plato[57] and including Aristotle,[58] St. Augustine, and Nietzsche[59] (among others), that includes concepts more or less equivalent to the one Ruth Benedict denominated "shame cultures" and "guilt cultures," suggests that the neglect of this concept, and the distinctions it encapsulates, might represent an important lacuna in our current thinking about culture and psychology.

How, then, might it be possible to conceptualize shame and guilt cultures in a way that could be applied without undue over-simplification to any culture; that would not, in other words, limit the concept to an over-simplified, all-or-nothing, either/or dichotomy incapable of taking account of the enormous variability between cultures, the almost limitless complexity within each of them, and the uniqueness of each that renders all of them incommensurable, at least in some important respects, with any of the others? At the very least, to begin with, it seems clear that we need to recognize that shame and guilt cultures vary on continua that range along two different axes, pure or homogeneous vs. mixed or heterogeneous, and extreme v. mild.

With that in mind James Gilligan proposed that we distinguish between relatively pure, or homogeneous, shame or guilt cultures, in which only one of these sanctions is operative to a marked degree, and the predominant moral sanction is shame only or guilt only; and "mixed" or heterogeneous cultures (such as our own) in which there are significant admixtures of both sanctions. It would be useful also to distinguish between "extreme" (as opposed to "mild") shame and guilt cultures. The former would refer to societies in which exposure and sensitivity to

56. Augustine, *City* 5.12 (Bettenson, 199).

57. Plato introduced the concept in the *Republic*, coining the word *timokratia* (that is, timocracy, from time: honor, and *kratein*: to rule, *cratos*, authority), meaning a state in which love of honor and glory is the ruling motive. The particular state he used the term to characterize was, appropriately, Sparta. See Plato, *Republic*, 8.545b, 8.547, 8.548e, 8.549c.

58. Aristotle used the term oligarchy in a slightly different, though certainly not contradictory, sense to refer to a hypothetical state in which public honor is distributed according to wealth—that is, the more wealth, the more honor (and by implication, the more poverty, the more shame). See Aristotle, *Politics*, 2033.

59. On ancient Greece as a shame culture in contrast to Christian culture as a guilt culture, see Nietzsche, *On the Genealogy of Morals*.

experiences of shame or guilt, respectively, are relatively frequent, intense and irrevocable, as opposed to ones in which individuals are relatively protected from such experiences so that they are less likely to occur or to be overwhelming or permanent. It may be seen that exposure and sensitivity to experiences of shame and/or guilt must be a function of both personality and culture. In other words, individuals themselves may vary in their sensitivity or susceptibility to shame or guilt; and cultural institutions and mores may also affect the frequency and intensity with which individuals in a society are exposed to, or protected from, life experiences capable of triggering, in the sensitive person, shame or guilt.

The term "shame culture," then, would be used to refer to societies in which the source of moral sanctions and authority is perceived to reside in other people (be they real or imaginary), in their ridicule, criticism or contempt. "Guilt cultures," by contrast, would be those that rely on an internalized conscience and its resultant conviction of sin and absolute standards of morality.

For an example of a pure and extreme shame culture we can turn to the Kwakiutl Indians of Vancouver Island, as documented in a series of monographs by the founder of scientific American ethnography, Franz Boas (and paraphrased by his pupil Ruth Benedict).[60] Here, to give a brief illustration of the inordinate degree to which the individuals in a culture can be preoccupied with and sensitive to shame and pride, enshrining them in their central institutions, are excerpts from her summary:

> Behavior . . . was dominated at every point by the need to demonstrate the greatness of the individual and the inferiority of his rivals. It was carried out with uncensored self-glorification and with gibes and insults poured upon the opponents. . . . The Kwakiutl stressed equally the fear of ridicule, and the interpretation of experience in terms of insults. They recognized only one gamut of emotion, that which swings between victory and shame. . . . Even this, however, gives only a partial picture of the extent to which this preoccupation with shame dominated their behavior. The Northwest Coast carries out this same pattern of behavior also in relation to the external world and the forces of nature. All accidents were occasions upon which one was shamed.[61]

60. See Boas, *Kwakiutl*; Boas, *Mind*; Benedict, *Patterns*, 173–222.

61. Benedict, *Patterns*, 214–15.

Possibly the communities of early Christians who practiced primitive Christian communism before and during Augustine's time would have been among the best examples of guilt cultures. However, the most intensively studied guilt culture of today is in many respects similar to those communities, and in fact does practice primitive Christian communism. This is the society of the Hutterites, a Protestant (Anabaptist) religious sect numbering about 9,000 people and scattered throughout the norther Middle West and southern Canada in about ninety colonies of communal farms. One study reports that:

> religion is the major cohesive force in this folk culture. The Hutterites consider themselves to . . . live the only true form of Christianity, one which entails communal sharing of property and cooperative production and distribution of goods. The values of brotherliness, self-renunciation and passivity in the face of aggression are emphasized. The Hutterites speak often of their past martyrs and of their willingness to suffer for their faith at the present time.[62]

And another study points out that, along with the stress on religion and duty to God and society and nonviolence,

> there is a tendency in their entire thinking to orient members to internalize their aggressive drives. Children and adults alike are taught to look for guilt in themselves rather than in others.[63]

These authors concluded that although the Hutterites' strongly held Christian faith "gives many Hutterites a sense of great security," it "is also responsible for the high frequency of guilt feelings."[64] And an intensive study of a large number of Hutterites by means of projective tests and interviews made two relevant points. First, the tests revealed an unusually large burden of guilt (compared to American cultural norms). And second, "it clearly is aggressive impulses that seem to cause the most guilt in Hutterite society."[65] Such a propensity to guilt inhibits the violence to others characteristic of shame cultures, though it may express itself in more violence to the self (depression as a form of self-punishment).

The Hutterite culture rather clearly illustrates features in that interpersonal violence is almost wholly absent as a way of resolving conflict,

62. Kaplan and Plaut, *Personality*, 12.

63. Eaton and Weil, *Culture*, 86.

64. Eaton and Weil, *Culture*, 217.

65. Kaplan and Plaut, *Personality*, 80.

and a culture of equal respect supports a shared personal and communal responsibility for one another, as equals. The contrast between the high levels of violence in the United States and the much lower levels in Western Europe in general and the Scandinavian democracies in particular is connected to the degree to which, in contrast to the United States, the values of equal respect and communal responsibility and sharing support more highly developed guilt cultures in which their social democracies do not shame the dependencies of needing welfare so common in the United States and demonstrably linked to the degree to which America retains features of a shame culture and thus encourages violence.[66]

What does all this have to do with violence? Pure and extreme shame cultures place a positive value on aggressiveness toward others (war, murder, torture, theft, enslavement, social and economic inequities), and a negative value on self-punishment. The Kwakiutl, for example, engaged in headhunting, cannibalism, burning slaves alive, and undiscriminating, merciless war and murder against even totally innocent, unsuspecting, hospitable, sleeping friends, neighbors, relatives, or hosts—men, women, and children. Furthermore, it seems clear that the motive for this aggressiveness was the desire to minimize or wipe out feelings of shame, humiliation and "loss of face," and to maximize feelings of pride and social prestige, and that aggressive behavior was a recognized and honored way of doing this. For example, Benedict writes, in line with the interpretation that "all accidents were occasions upon which one was shamed," for the Kwakiutl "the great event which was dealt with in these terms was death. . . . Death was the paramount affront they recognized. . . . They took recognized means . . . to wipe out the shame." When a chief's son died, for example, he would kill a neighboring chief. "In this, according to their interpretation, he acted nobly because he had not been downed, but had struck back in return."[67]

Guilt cultures, by contrast, condemn aggression toward others, though they place a positive value on aggression directed toward the self. According to Eaton and Weil there has not been a single case of murder, assault, or rape among the Hutterites since their arrival in America in the 1870s.[68] Not only is physical aggressiveness banned, but even its verbal expression: "No fighting or verbal abuse is permitted. It is expected that

66. See Gilligan, *Why Some Politicians.*

67. Benedict, *Patterns,* 215–16.

68. Eaton and Weil, *Culture,* 141.

a Hutterite man will not get angry, swear, or lose his temper."[69] This is all the more remarkable when it is realized that the Hutterites have been constant victims of severe persecution by their neighbors everywhere they have lived. In Europe, "ghastly atrocities . . . during several periods brought the sect close to physical extinction";[70] nevertheless, their martyrs are looked up to as models of correct (saintly) behavior. The Hutterites are strict, absolute pacifists, which is why emigration to North America was their only alternative to complete extinction, and since coming here many have been punished and even imprisoned for their refusal to participate in the military. They internalize their own aggressiveness in the form of feelings of guilt and sin; frequent and severe depressions; actively provoking or passively submitting to martyrdom and persecution (what Freud called "moral masochism"); shaming themselves by publicly confessing their sins; punishing themselves as penance; and occasional suicides (but, as we have said, no homicides).

Statistical studies of pure and extreme guilt cultures have not been possible because there are so few of them; indeed, apart from the Hutterites and a few other Anabaptist sects (the Amish, the Mennonites), it would be difficult to find any, other than, perhaps, some small, highly religious groups or sects within Judaism or Christianity, such as monastic communities of monks and/or nuns. As Freud said, no one feels guiltier than the saints; but by the same token, no one is rarer than the saints—for a variety of reasons, including the fact that they tend to become victims of individual or collective martyrdom. However, at the risk of generalizing on the basis of many shame cultures and only a few guilt cultures, and also extrapolating from what appear to the characteristics of shame and guilt as they manifest themselves in individuals, Jim Gilligan and I believe we can also suggest the following differences between pure and extreme shame and guilt cultures:

1) Shame cultures have hierarchical, authoritarian social structures and values that divide people into superior versus inferior grades of socio-economic status, with wide variations of social class and caste, prestige, wealth and power, often with institutionalized aristocracies and slavery. Shame cultures thus enforce the gender binary and hierarchy of patriarchy, in effect naturalizing it. These hierarchies include those of class, caste (including race/ethnicity and religion), gender (underlying

69. Kaplan and Plaut, *Personality*, 19–20.

70. Kaplan and Plaut, *Personality*, 12.

sexism and homophobia), and, as Piaget saw,[71] age (gerontocracies). Its political psychology requires not only hierarchy but always a lowest class, often held in what Carol Gilligan and David Richards have called "moral slavery," a structural injustice that rationalizes violently irrational scapegoating.[72] For example, cultures in which "sensitivity to insult is extreme" are significantly more likely to have class stratification, castes, slavery, invidious displays of wealth, and possession and inheritance of private property. Guilt cultures, by contrast, are classless, democratic and communistic, with relatively equal distributions of prestige, power, and wealth. Competition, such as it is, is more likely to be for the highest degree of humility than of prestige and honor.

2) Guilt cultures institutionalize confession of sins as a means of relieving guilt (by increasing shame). In shame cultures, exposure of transgressions of social mores is avoided, and concealment of them is sought as a means of avoiding shame, thus motivating lying, deception and fraud.

3) Shame cultures place a negative value on needs to be loved and taken care of, and frustrate and discourage them (by one form or another of shaming); instead, they honor the development of self-reliance, activity and achievement. For example, cultures in which "sensitivity to insult is extreme" are significantly more likely to be those in which "initial indulgence of dependency is low," "early dependence satisfaction is low," "overall indulgence of the infant is low," "early oral satisfaction potential is low," "dependence socialization anxiety is high," and "the constancy of presence of the infant's nurturant agent is low." Other indices of shame, such as "boastfulness," "invidious display of wealth," and overall "narcissism" correlate significantly with those and other indices of negative valuation of passive dependent needs to be loved and taken care of, such as "total positive pressure toward developing both self-reliant behavior and achievement behavior in the child is high," "the child's inferred anxiety over non-performance of achievement behavior is high," "display of affection toward the infant is low," "immediacy, degree and consistency of reduction of the infant's drives is low," and so on.

Guilt cultures, by contrast, discourage aggressiveness in all forms, encourage submissiveness, patience, meekness and humility, and thus have the effect in many spheres of behavior of discouraging activity (i.e.,

71. See Piaget, *Moral Judgment.*

72. See Gilligan and Richards, *Deepening Darkness,* 10, 18–20, 72, 133–34, 197, 215.

wherever it becomes associated with aggressiveness or self-aggrandizement rather than with nurturance or care-taking). Independence can also be guilt-inducing, where it is perceived to have the meaning of abandoning those toward whom one has an obligation.

SHAME AND GUILT IN HISTORY

While the Kwakiutl and many others provide examples of shame cultures, only the study of the Western tradition provides us with the opportunity to observe the transition from a shame to a guilt culture within one society, and I believe the transition is crucial to understanding the historical Jesus of Nazareth and the Christianities ostensibly inspired by his life and teaching.

The classics scholar Eric Dodds, in *The Greeks and the Irrational*,[73] drawing on Ruth Benedict's definitions, has documented this transition in Greek history from an earlier shame culture, the society depicted in *The Iliad*, to a later guilt culture, classical Athens at the time of the tragedians and philosophers. Speaking of "the uninhibited boasting in which Homeric man indulges," Dodds says that "Homeric man's highest good is not the enjoyment of a quiet conscience, but the enjoyment of time, public esteem [honor]. . . . And the strongest moral force which Homeric man knows is not the fear of god, but respect for public opinion, aidos [shame or sense of shame, sense of honor]. In such a society, anything which exposes a man to the contempt or ridicule of his fellows, which causes him to 'lose face,' is felt as unbearable."[74]

By the time the Greeks became a guilt culture, however, they worried not about experiencing too little pride and prestige, but too much—overweening pride or arrogance, up to and including violence—for which they used the term hubris. Far from being the highest good, pride by this time was called the "prime evil" (*proton kakon*), as Theognis called it; the *hamartia*, or tragic flaw, for which, in Aristotle's analysis, Sophocles's Oedipus punished himself. It is significant that in the earlier shame culture's version of the Oedipus myth, Oedipus, far from feeling guilty and self-punitive, continued to reign in Thebes and was eventually buried with royal honors![75] Probably the individual who symbolized

73. Dodds, *Greeks.*
74. Dodds, *Greeks,* 17–18.
75. Dodds, *Greeks,* 36, 55.

this transition to a guilt culture most vividly was Socrates, who declared that it was better to suffer evil and injustice than to perpetrate it,[76] and who finally accepted suicide as a punishment (suffering injustice) even when he could easily have avoided doing so by leaving Athens, which he regarded as doing an injustice.

For the most extreme development of guilt in the ethos of a culture, however, we must turn to Judaeo-Christian culture. Many scholars have made this observation. Freud, for example, commented that "the people of Israel . . . out of their sense of guilt . . . created the over-strict commandments of their priestly religion."[77] And Nietzsche saw that "the arrival of the Christian God . . . has brought with it the phenomenon of the uttermost sense of guilt."[78] And we have already noticed that the earliest extant description of the difference between a shame and a guilt culture was written by one of the early Christian thinkers, St. Augustine. The greater intensity of guilt in Christian, as compared with Greek, culture is indicated by the growth in guilt-affective tone of the word *hamartia*, from "tragic flaw" (the usual translation of Aristotle's meaning) to "sin," the New Testament meaning of the word, including Augustine's doctrine of original sin that rendered sexuality itself a matter of guilt. And Jesus of Nazareth, like Socrates, became a personal symbol for the values of a guilt culture, becoming a victim rather than a perpetrator of violence (and severely chastising his followers when they were ready to defend him by means of violence). This does not necessarily indicate any great difference between early Christianity and the religious and moral values of major portions of the Jewish community at that same time, for Christianity was, after all, a Jewish sect, and 72 of the 77 verses of the "Sermon on the Mount" have rabbinical precedent.[79] In other words, Christianity was simply a sub-culture within the larger religious culture of the Judaism of its time.

It is worth noting, however, that the Judaeo-Christian tradition, like the Greek one, began as a shame culture and only later developed into an extreme guilt culture. The earliest moral emotion mentioned in the Bible, for example, in the description of Adam and Eve, is "shame." What is unique about Judaism, however, is how early and strongly the theme of guilt emerged. Nevertheless, throughout much of the Old Testament

76. See Plato, Crito 49a-d, 43–44; Gorgias 509 c, 853.

77. Freud, *Civilization and Its Discontents*, 127.

78. Nietzsche, *Genealogy*, 71.

79. Buttrick, *Speaking Jesus*.

the image of waging war successfully so as to humiliate the enemies of the Jewish people and put them to shame is a strong theme, alternating in a constant counterpoint with the guilt-dominated moral exhortations of the prophets who warn against the sinfulness of pride, violence, injustice and neglect of the poor, until the latter theme finally drowns out the former. The parallelism between Greek and Jewish culture—first a shame culture, then a guilt culture—together with the apparently much wider distribution of shame than of guilt cultures throughout the world, suggests the possibility that there is a general trend for cultures, like individuals, to be sensitive to shame before they are to guilt.

Sarah Hrdy's recent book on human evolution offers a compelling account of why this should be so.[80] It is, as Hrdy observes, remarkable, when there may once have been fewer than 20,000 breeding human adults,[81] how our species survived at all. What was evidently crucial, Hrdy argues, was our capacity, as Tomasello's work shows, for mutuality and shared intentionality, which extended to both hunting and gathering, sharing food, and the care of human infants who require constant care to survive, leading to cooperative breeding. Groups of humans during this early period were quite small hunter-gatherers and largely egalitarian, and shame, an emotion resting on what others in the group think of you, was the selectively appropriate moral emotion to support the solidarity of such small groups, living in isolation from other groups, required to survive.[82] As Robert Bellah has recently persuasively argued, during this period of what he calls tribal religion, religion, based on both mimesis and ritual, would have played a crucial role in forms of tribal solidarity beyond kin relationships.[83] However, when the agrarian revolution leads to the explosion of human populations often in competition with one another for limited resources, cultures are increasingly organized patriarchally on terms of political and religious autocracy,[84] what Bellah called the archaic religion of patriarchal god-kings based on mythology,[85] and the shaming of patriarchal manhood leads to devastating civil and imperialistic wars. Bellah argues that the axial age around 500 BCE, a

80. See Hrdy, *Father Time.*

81. Hrdy, *Father Time*, 68.

82. For a similar evolutionary argument based in both genetics and co-operative reciprocity, see Sauer, *Invention.*

83. See Bellah, *Religion in Human Evolution*, 117–74.

84. See Lerner, *Creation.*

85. See Bellah, *Religion in Human Evolution*, 175–264.

period classically discussed by Karl Jaspers,[86] arises in four cultures during this period, ancient Israel,[87] ancient Greece,[88] China in the late first millennium BCE,[89] and ancient India.[90] The thinkers of the axial age in these four cultures arise, for Bellah, as forms of criticism of dominant archaic tribal religions in light of universalistic ethical standards and what Merlin Donald calls external symbolic storage and theoretic culture.[91] My account here discusses two of them, ancient Jewish (and later Christian) culture and Greece, in the terms of the transition from shame to guilt cultures.

The emergence of guilt cultures takes the form of the developing ethical standards that question the dominant shame culture, and its leading advocates (Socrates and Jesus) are executed largely because of the offense taken at their criticism. The historical Jesus must be understood against this background—in particular, the patriarchal Roman culture that executed him. If Jesus is indeed centrally antipatriarchal, as I and others believe, it is not difficult to understand not only why he should be executed but why the Christianities allegedly inspired by his life and teaching have themselves been so uncritically in thrall to the patriarchies he deplored, including the hegemonic Roman patriarchy governing the gentile world in which early Christianity found its first audiences.

Indeed, the history of Christianity illustrates the regression of a culture from a guilt into a shame culture. During its first three centuries of existence, Christianity existed under conditions that would appeal to guilt-ridden people—namely, persecution and martyrdom. Early Christianity fit Nietzsche's description of slave morality, since it identified with slaves and the qualities necessary to be slaves, such as meekness, passivity, and submissiveness in the face of domination and exploitation (advice it gave to those who literally were slaves, as well as to the free). For example, Jesus said that "when you have done all that you were ordered to do, say, 'We are worthless slaves, we have done only what we ought to have done'" (Luke 17:10).[92]

86. Jaspers, *Origin*; See also Bellah and Joas, *Axial Age*.
87. Bellah, *Religion in Human Evolution*, 265–323.
88. Bellah, *Religion in Human Evolution*, 324–98.
89. Bellah, *Religion in Human Evolution*, 399–480.
90. Bellah, *Religion in Human Evolution*, 481–566.
91. See, on this point, Donald, *Origins*, 269–360. See also Donald, *Mind*.
92. Coogan, *New Oxford Bible*, 1902. See also Meeks, *Moral World*, 38.

However, with the conversion of the Emperor Constantine early in the fourth century, Christianity became the religion of the masters, not just the slaves; and the motives for becoming a Christian changed accordingly. Thus, Christianity changed from a relatively pure and extreme guilt culture to (at least) a mixed shame-and-guilt culture, capable of inspiring extremes not only of masochism, as formerly, but also of sadism; of martyrdom and murder, saintliness and savagery, piety and power, Francis of Assisi and Torquemada. The earlier self-sacrificing guilt culture of Christianity survived, or was revived, in only a few atypical pockets of extreme religious fervor, such as some monastic communities and sects such as the Hutterites.

Ruth Benedict's theory of shame versus guilt cultures was developed as an explanation of one culture, that of Japan. The role of what we call patriarchy—the gender binary and hierarchy—is implicit in her account, suggesting that historically shame cultures are dominantly patriarchal both in personal and political life. Later important works of historical psychology include, as we have seen, the work of E. R. Dodds,[93] but also that of Zevedei Barbu,[94] both of whom developed a diachronic dimension of the distinction between shame and guilt cultures. Both study, for example, the development from the dominantly shame culture of *The Iliad* (in which the shaming of manhood and violence are prominent) to the more inward guilt culture reflected in many of the Greek tragedies as well as in the emergence of Socratic philosophy (in which reflection on ethical responsibilities to self and others becomes central). Barbu prominently uses the rise and decline of patriarchy[95] as an important feature of his historical psychology, as well as the related idea of shame and guilt cultures,[96] both in his account of the development of ancient Greek culture and the development of what he calls "British national character."[97] The latter account focuses on the transition from the dominantly religious culture of medieval Britain and the growth of political absolutism, both patriarchal, to the shift to a questioning of the medieval consensus and its patriarchally hierarchical chains sponsored by the impact of both the Renaissance and Reformation on British culture.

93. Dodds, *Greeks*.

94. See Barbu, *Problems*.

95. See Barbu, *Problems*, 7, 52, 60, 83, 91, 92, 95, 98, 110, 119, 120, 123, 179.

96. See Barbu, *Problems*, 96–122.

97. See Barbu, *Problems*, 145–218.

Cross-cultural research indicates that manhood has always been psychologically conflicted and fragile,[98] but the question of psychological fragility takes a different form in cultures like ours (like that of ancient Athens and Britain) which, at certain points in their history, are more democratic though still patriarchal, and which are in transition from patriarchy to a more democratic culture.

It was the close study of the shame culture of ancient Greece in *The Iliad* that led the psychiatrist, Jonathan Shay, to develop, based (unlike Freud) on clinical observation of the PTSD of Vietnam War veterans, a diagnostic understanding of the effects of war trauma and a method of care and cure.[99] The American soldiers drafted to serve in Vietnam came from a fairly developed guilt culture in which not culpably harming, let alone killing, others plays a prominent role. Military service in Vietnam required American men to break this code, ostensibly justified by fighting a war just in its ends and means (just war theory being the way a guilt culture justifies war). But, military service in Vietnam was patriarchally organized in terms of obeying the orders of their superiors in the military hierarchy, and the shaming of manhood was in this shame culture the mode of enforcing such orders, as it was in the shame-driven violence of the Trojan War. But, the ancient Greece portrayed in *The Iliad* was a pervasively patriarchal shame culture in which the roles of both men and women were rigidly defined by the gender binary and hierarchy, and any deviation from those roles (whether women shaming their husbands by adultery, or men being shamed by such adultery) elicited illimitable violence, shame being the response to the humiliation of one's patriarchally defined womanhood or manhood. But, the American men, drafted to serve in Vietnam, came from a dominantly guilt culture, and thus, unlike the ancient Greeks and Trojans of *The Iliad*, brought to their military service ethical convictions in tension with the role the shame culture of military service demanded they play. In his diagnostic work with the soldiers afflicted by PTSD, Shay came to understand the character of their war trauma as the moral injury that the shame culture of military service inflicted on their moral characters. Their moral characters were formed by a sense of what was right, but their experience of military service in the Vietnam War was that the war was unjust both in its ends and means and yet they were compelled to obey such patriarchal authority, sometimes

98. See, on this point, Gilmore, *Manhood*.

99. See Shay, *Achilles*.

killing innocent people and seeing men they loved brutally killed in a conflict with no just end. It was this experience of moral injury to character in obedience to patriarchal authority that broke trust with soldiers (that the war would be and was just) and that required such obedience in a high stakes situation of life and death that injured their moral character. Only the communalization of such moral injury with one another enabled its victims to experience the grief they felt and repair.

2

The Search for the Historical Jesus

ANY SERIOUS CONSIDERATION OF the historical Jesus, including my view of him as the antipatriarchal Jesus, must begin with the patriarchal character of the Roman Empire to which his life and teaching are a response, and the long tradition of Jewish resistance to the various imperialisms (including the Romans, who ruled Israel at the time of Jesus and crucified him). I begin with the highly patriarchal character of Roman imperialism, and then turn to the long tradition of Jewish resistance to imperialism, including, of course, the prophets, on whom Jesus clearly depended.[1] I then turn to the search for the historical Jesus, in particular, relatively recent work on the historical Jesus whose critical historiographical methodologies I have come to regard as reliable. I discuss the Gospels that Christianities have regarded, even with all their internal inconsistencies, as embodying the best account we have of the life and teaching of Jesus—the Gospels of Mark, Matthew, Luke, and John.[2]

1. See, on this point, Buttrick, *Speaking Jesus*.

2. I do not consider the Gospel of Thomas. See Meyer, *Gospel of Thomas*. For the view that this Gospel depends on the other Gospels, and adds nothing historically reliable, see Meier, *Marginal Jew: Companions*, 199.

ROMAN PATRIARCHY

There is no culture more influential in supporting and sustaining patriarchy in Western culture than Roman patriarchy, including not only its legitimating impact on Western absolute monarchies (kaiser in Germany, czar in Russian, thus mean Caesar) but on Western imperialism and the form and substance of Christianity after Constantine made it the established church of the Roman Empire and even on American constitutionalism, as Founders argue among themselves in the names of Roman republican thinkers (for example, Publius) in *The Federalist*.[3] It is not therefore surprising that Shakespeare with his deep interest in the role patriarchy plays in male violence should have written so many plays situated in or about Rome, including *Titus Andronicus*, *Julius Caesar*, *Antony and Cleopatra*, *Cymbeline*, and *Coriolanus*. Shakespeare's source for *Coriolanus*, as it was for *Antony and Cleopatra*, was Plutarch, and Shakespeare's focus in this remarkable play is on the initiation into patriarchy of a Roman military leader, Coriolanus, by his patriarchal mother. There is no mother in *King Lear*, so the play turns entirely on a patriarchal father's relationship to his three daughters. In *Coriolanus*, Shakespeare centers our attention on the mother-son relationship, and a patriarchal mother is its focus. It is Shakespeare's almost clinical examination of how men are and can be initiated into patriarchy by patriarchal women. Its connections of Roman politics to the Roman family very much reflects everything we now know about the patriarchal Roman psychology of men and women, so the play is unusually close to historical fact, which it dramatizes quite brilliantly.

There are two important strands in the historical literature on ancient Rome. First is the literature on the public political and military life of Rome,[4] which started as a small city-state under the rule of elected kings and turned upon their expulsion into a form of aristocratic republic that aggressively expanded over the next four centuries to rule the entire Mediterranean basin and much more. Its success led, as we shall see, to internecine civil wars that discredited republican government, making

3. See, on all these points, Gilligan and Richards, *Deepening Darkness*.

4. For an illuminating overview and summary of this literature, see Walbank et al., *Cambridge Ancient History*; Astin et al., *Cambridge Ancient History Rome and Mediterranean*; Crook et al., *Cambridge Ancient History*; Bowman et al., *Cambridge Ancient History: Augustan Empire*; Bowman et al., *Cambridge Ancient History: High Empire*; Bowman et al., *Cambridge Ancient History: Crisis of Empire*; Cameron and Garnsey, *Cambridge Ancient History*.

possible the transition under Augustus to what Roman republicans traditionally despised, the rule of kings, to wit, autocratic imperial rule that was to endure for yet another four hundred years. (Its decline was given a still classical statement in Gibbon's masterpiece, *The Decline and Fall of the Roman Empire.*[5]) Second is the more recent literature on the Roman family.[6] These two literatures, with a few notable exceptions,[7] exist largely in isolation from one another: that on public life written largely by men, on family life largely by women. There is a link between these two literatures in the concept central to my inquiry—patriarchy.

Patriarchy, frequently misinterpreted to mean the unjust oppression of women by men, is an anthropological term denoting families or societies ruled by fathers. It sets up "a hierarchy—a rule of priests—in which the priest, the *hieros*, is a father (*pater*). As an order of living, it elevates some men over other men and all men over women; within the family, it separates fathers from sons (the men from the boys) and places both women and children under a father's authority."[8]

The Roman conception of authority was highly patriarchal. In both the public and private domains, and at the core of both, as our interpretation of patriarchy suggests, lay Roman religion. Roman politics, personal life, and religion were tightly integrated, a fact that has led astute students of ancient Rome from Polybius[9] to Niccolo Machiavelli[10] to think of Roman religion as easily manipulable by its leading politicians to serve their ends, including their aggressive imperialistic adventures. Except for the Vestal Virgins, the various orders of Roman priests, including the augurs required to signify that the gods were propitious to some proposed undertaking, were occupied by leading politicians (Julius Caesar, for example, was elected *pontifex maximus*, a leading priestly role).[11] Although the various priesthoods under the republic look to our eyes highly decentralized, the interpretation of all religious questions was in the hands

5. See Gibbon, *Decline and Fall.*

6. See, for example, Hallett, *Fathers and Daughters*; Treggiari, *Roman Marriage*; Saller, *Patriarchy*; Dixon, *Roman Mother*; Dixon, *Roman Family*; Rawson, *Marriage, Divorce*; Dixon, *Reading Roman*; Gardner, *Women*; Pomeroy, *Goddesses*; McDonnell, *Roman Manliness.*

7. See Hallett, *Fathers and Daughters*; Evans, *War, Women.*

8. Gilligan, *Birth of Pleasure*, 4–5.

9. See Polybius, *Rise*, 349.

10. See Machiavelli, *Prince and Discourses*, 145–58.

11. See Meier, *Caesar*, 160–62, 164, 169. See also Goldsworthy, *Caesar.*

of the Senate, as final arbiter, and the Senate was also the main body that conducted foreign policy, including Rome's wars.[12] The Senators, called the Fathers, thus exercised a patriarchal authority over the meaning of Roman religion.[13]

The transition from an elected monarchy to a republic in fifth-century BCE Rome led to the apparent increase in positions of political leadership (for both patrician and plebeian males), because under Rome's republican form of government, political responsibilities were much more broadly shared than under the monarchy. It was the duty of all male citizens who satisfied property requirements to leave their farms and serve in Rome's armies.[14] Correspondingly, it is under the republic that we see the beginning of Rome's apparent expansion of military operations.[15] What is historically remarkable is its extraordinary belligerence:

> The Roman's state bellicosity is indicated not only by the frequency with which it went to war, but also by the high proportion of its citizen manpower that was regularly committed to military service . . . . These figures [of military service] . . . represent a very high level of military involvement as Roman citizens, which as far as we know cannot be matched by any other pre-industrial state.[16]

The Roman view was that Rome fought just wars only,[17] but on close examination there is good reason to believe that their wars often cannot thus be justified,[18] resting, rather, on a militaristic ethos that led the leaders and people of the Roman Republic to regard imperialistic conquest as their mission. The Roman style of war, exemplified by two of its greatest generals, Julius Caesar and Pompey, was always highly aggressive,[19] and political power under the republic was tied to military leadership and success. An otherwise important Roman republican leader like Cicero, an orator, lawyer, and writer (but not a military leader), remained largely

12. See, on this point, Lintott, *Constitution*, 65–88.

13. See, on this point, Beard, "Priesthood," 19–48.

14. See Palmer, *Archaic Community*, 220,

15. See, on this point, Ogilvie, *Commentary*, 234, 283–89, 302, 307–9, 314–21, 353–66, 390–411, 521–25, 567–74, 584–89, 597–606, 620–32.

16. Walbank et al., *Cambridge Ancient History*, 383.

17. See Walbank et al.,*Cambridge Ancient History*, 384.

18. For a powerful questioning of the Roman view, shared by some historians, see Harris, *War and Imperialism*.

19. See, on this point, Goldsworthy, *Caesar*, 303.

on the periphery of political power during the civil war, and ultimately was murdered when it served the interests of Antony and Octavian.[20] Violence became a way of life for Romans, directed not only against its enemies but, increasingly, against one another.[21]

Roman patriarchy legitimated this militaristic ethos, imposing its hierarchical religious demands not only in public life but in private life as well. In the Roman home, fathers were the priests, having authority over rituals and lives in that domain. The remarkable powers of the Roman father, the *patria potestas*, gave him

> unlimited authority over all his legitimate children, irrespective of whether or not they were married, and of their offspring as long as he lived. Thus, for example, the *pater familias* has the right to expose his child, to scourge him, to sell him, to pawn him, to imprison him, and, *in extremis*, even to kill him.[22]

While exercising such patriarchal authority in their families, Roman fathers were in turn subject to the patriarchal authority exercised by the Fathers in the senate.

These interacting and reinforcing patterns of patriarchy both rest on and explain evidence of an underlying personal and political psychology in both the men and women who sustained the belligerent militarism of the Roman Republic and Empire. I am struck, in this connection, by the way Josephus, a close and respectful observer of the Roman army in action (in the imperial period), describes Roman men:

> [T]heir nation does not wait for the outbreak of war to give men their first lesson in arms; they do not sit with folded hands in peace time only to put them in motion in the hour of need. On the contrary, as though they had been born with weapons in their hand, they never have a truce from training, never wait for emergencies to arise. Moreover, their peace manoeuvres are not less strenuous than veritable warfare; each soldier daily throws all his energy into his drill, as though he were in action. Hence that perfect ease with which they sustain the shock of battle: no confusion breaks their customary formation, no panic paralyzes, no fatigue exhausts them; and as their opponents cannot

20. See, in general, Everitt, *Cicero*. On Cicero's limited role in Roman politics, see Everitt, *Augustus*, 67.

21. See Lintott, *Violence*.

22. Eyben, "Fathers and Sons," 115. Eyben notes that these powers were significantly limited by the time of the empire.

> match these qualities, victory is the invariable and certain consequence. Indeed, it would not be wrong to describe their manoeuvres as bloodless combats and their combats as sanguinary manoeuvres.[23]

Roman men, according to Josephus, are so deeply and consistently steeped in militarism that they appear "as though . . . born with weapons in their hand."

Of course, no baby is born this way. Quite the opposite; human babies are remarkable for their relationality, their ability to read and respond to the human world around them with sensitivity. Since Josephus's Romans are neither relational nor sensitive, these human capacities have been blunted or stamped out of them. Our question, then, is how Roman patriarchal culture could so structure both private and public life so as to render this outcome seemingly natural or inevitable.

We turn in this regard to the contemporary literature on trauma and its effects on human neurophysiology and psychology.[24] The now-well-documented consequence of trauma is a loss of voice and of memory, in particular, loss of the voice of intimate relationship. This loss or suppression of voice, however, is often covered by an identification with the voice of the person who imposed the trauma and an internalization of the demands that this more powerful person imposes on one's life. The crucial mechanism here is dissociation: the psychological process through which the surviving self separates itself from the self that was overwhelmed. A voice that speaks from experience is silenced in favor of a voice that carries more authority, leading to a replacement of one's personal sense of emotional presence and truth with what Sandor Ferenczi, the Hungarian psychoanalyst, describes as an "identification with the aggressor,"[25] the taking on as one's own the voice and demands of the oppressor. This process, leading to what Ferenczi observed as false compliance, is in itself largely unconscious, due in part to the loss of memory that follows the traumatic rupture of relationships.[26]

What Josephus's observations suggest is a personal and political psychology in which such traumatic breaks in intimate relationships are both normal and normative, justified by the demands of patriarchy, in

23. Josephus, *Jewish Wars, Books I–II*, 27.

24. See for example, van der Kolk et al. *Traumatic Stress*; Herman, *Trauma*; Herman, *Truth and Repair.*

25. See Laplanche and Pontalis, *Language*, 208–9.

26. Ferenczi, "Confusion of Tongues."

effect, an institutionalized trauma that supports and sustains the required militaristic ethos. In the case of Roman patriarchy, these demands took the form of a highly gendered code of honor, coupled with institutionalized practices of shaming. The honor of a Roman citizen rested on his being willing and able, with the complicity of women, to engage in both Roman politics and its expression in continual imperialistic wars. This involved not only military service with its risks of injury and loss of life but also a willingness to disrupt personal life.

A family living under the rule of the Roman *patria potestas* experienced a form of oppression at the center of intimate life, including control not only over inheritance and genealogy but also over the use of force to hold people in line.[27] Even if many Roman fathers declined to exercise these powers oppressively, the very legitimation of such power, as a model for what legitimate power is, makes the traumatic disruption of any intimate relationship, including that between fathers and sons, normative and in the nature of things. Polybius, a Greek whose home town had been damaged by Romans, noted in mixed horror and admiration that "there have been instances of [Roman] men in office who have put their own sons to death, contrary to every law or custom, because they valued the interest of their country more dearly than their natural ties to their own flesh and blood."[28] In place of intimate relationship, the son identifies with the honor of his father, and of his father before him, honor descending through a line of fathers.

The mechanism of such honor codes is again beautifully illustrated by Polybius, who portrays the ritual he describes as very much at the heart of the psychology of Roman imperialism:

> Whenever one of their celebrated men dies, in the course of the funeral procession his body is carried with every kind of honour into the Forum to the so-called Rostra . . . . The whole mass of the people stand round to watch, and his son, if he has left one of adult age who can be present, or if not some other relative, then mounts the Rostra and delivers an address which recounts the virtues and successes achieved by the dead man during his lifetime. By these means the whole populace . . . are so deeply engaged that the loss seems not to be confined to the mourners but to be a public one which affects the whole people. Then

27. See, for a good general treatment, Treggiari, *Roman Marriage*; Saller, *Patriarchy, Property.*

28. Polybius, *Rise*, 348.

> after the burial of the body . . . they place the image of the dead man in the most conspicuous position in the house . . . . This image consists of a mask, which is fashioned with extraordinary fidelity both in the modeling and its complexion to represents the features of the dead man . . . . And when any distinguished member of the family dies, the masks are taken to the funeral, and are there worn by men who are considered to bear the closest resemblance to the original. . . .
>
> They all ride in chariots . . . and when they arrive at the Rostra they all seat themselves in a row upon chairs of ivory. It would be hard to imagine a more impressive scene for a young man who aspires to win fame and practice virtue . . .
>
> [T]he most important consequence of the ceremony is that it inspires young men to endure the extremes of suffering for the common good in the hope of winning the glory that awaits upon the brave.[29]

Such rituals enacted the patriarchal relationship of fathers to sons, leading sons to identify with a sense of family honor, stretching into the past. Since fathers were often absent from family life (either through absence in war or death in war or, because of significant age differences from their wives, through natural death), Roman matrons, as wives and mothers, became crucial players in the patriarchal system.

Women, in the terms of this gender ideology, did not exist as persons with a mind and sexuality of their own, for the terms of Roman arranged marriage respected neither. Such powers of fathers or even of brothers (Augustus married his beloved sister, Octavia, to Antony) over their sisters were, under the republic, important means to social solidarity. This was particularly true among otherwise highly competitive Roman republican men, struggling for leadership and honor in politics and war. Such men often sought, by enlisting the power of fathers or brothers, to elevate their status and political appeal through marriage to a higher status woman, as Octavian did through his marriage to Livia.[30] Thus are new alliances formed. Pompey and Julius Caesar manage, for example, to cooperate politically as long as Pompey is married to Caesar's beloved sister; when she dies and Pompey refuses Caesar's request that a comparable marriage be arranged,[31] the cooperation collapses and civil war follows.

29. Polybius, *Rise*, 346–47.

30. See, in general, Hallett, *Fathers and Daughters*.

31. See, on this point, Goldsworthy, *Caesar*, 294.

This function of arranged marriage under Roman patriarchy led to the particular weight that Romans traditionally placed on the chastity and fidelity of women, for only such limitations on women's sexuality could assure their husbands that the women's children were his. An honor code of this sort invests men's sense of honor in control over women's sexuality that, of course, traumatically disrupts any relationships that real women might otherwise form or, as moral and sexual agents, want to form. Indeed, such control is an intimate perquisite of male identity in such a patriarchal system, and any attack upon it constitutes an insult that elicits and justifies violence. The link between traumatic disruption of intimate relationships and violence is thus reinforced.

Marriages in Rome were arranged by fathers, crucially to advance dynastic ends of the father in politics. Consequently, the relationships of Roman wives to their husbands could be emotionally quite shallow.[32] For example, Augustus married his daughter, Julia, successively, to Marcellus, Agrippa, and Tiberius, the last of whom she apparently deeply disliked. And at the order of Augustus, Tiberius divorced a beloved wife to marry Julia.[33] The political career of Augustus himself (then called Octavian) evidently took off only when he married Livia, whose father and then husband had both fought against Octavian and Antony at Philippi. Livia's father, upon defeat by Octavian and Antony, had committed suicide, an act that must have traumatized his daughter. Nonetheless, with the support of her husband (by whom she was then pregnant), she divorced him to marry Octavian.

While Augustus apparently loved Livia and their marriage had unusually egalitarian features (including consultations with his highly intelligent, astute wife on all matters public and private), Livia came to marry Augustus very much in the context of Roman patriarchal marriage. Not only was she, a higher status woman, chosen at least in part by Augustus to advance his status and career, but she also married him under the shadow of traumatic loss (her father's suicide) and, given the military and political failures of her husband, in order to preserve her own life and his, as well as the life of her son by her first husband, Tiberius. Livia's living out the idealized conception of a good Roman wife makes sense against this background; her profound influence on her husband is, consistent

32. See, on this point, Hallett, *Fathers and Daughters*, 69, 211–48, 235.

33. Suetonius, *Twelve Caesars*, 112–13.

with Roman patriarchy, never a public matter, always staying within the strict bounds of Roman patriarchal propriety.[34]

With Livia, his mother, very much in his corner, Tiberius was to succeed Augustus as emperor, even though he was not Augustus's child. Behind her willingness to live out such a life, as the wife of a man she could have seen as responsible for her father's suicide, were a series of strategic moves, and also traumatic loss, the breaking of intimate relationships that was so common a feature of the psychology of Roman patriarchal womanhood and manhood.[35] Such powers of fathers and even husbands to inflict traumatic losses on both men and women gives rise to an armored psychology in both sexes that is consistent with the gender roles the patriarchal system requires of them, including violence against women triggered by violations of the chastity required by their gender roles.

Within these structures of Roman patriarchy lay the relationship of mothers to their sons. Such relationships were rigidly controlled by the duty of mothers to educate their sons into assuming their patriarchal roles. At least two of Rome's most remarkable leaders (Julius Caesar and Octavian, later Augustus) were unusually close to their mothers, both actively involved in advancing their son's careers.[36] Tacitus, writing in the late first or early second century CE, discussed the mother's role in raising children in a passage that presented Caesar's mother, Aurelia, as an ideal:

> In the good old days, every man's son, born in wedlock, was brought up not in the chamber of some hireling nurse, but in his mother's lap, and at her knee. And that mother could have no higher praise than that she managed the house and gave herself to her children . . . . In the presence of such a one no base word could be uttered without grave offence, and no wrong deed done. Religiously and with the utmost diligence she regulated not only the serious tasks of her youthful charges, but the recreations also and their games. It was in this spirit, we are told, that

34. See, for fuller discussion, Barrett, *Livia*; Wood, *Imperial Women*.

35. Herod's wife, Mariamne (as told in Josephus), is a good contrast. Herod killed her brother and grandfather, but loves her, so he gives her too much license, and she insults and betrays him, leading to her own execution—a patriarchal horror story. See Josephus, *Jewish Wars Books I–II*, 205–11.

36. On Julius Caesar's relationship to this mother, see Goldsworthy, *Caesar*, at 33, 35, 36, 49–50, 52, 59, 87, 100, 125–26*A*, 146, 148, 293–94; on Octavian's relationship, see Everitt, *Augustus*, 32, 45.

> Cornelia, the mother of the Gracchi, directed their upbringing, Aurelia that of Caesar, Atia of Augustus: thus it was that these mothers trained their princely children.[37]

Roman mothers of the elite, however, other than giving birth often had little to do with babies, who were cared for by nurses, often slaves, endearingly addressed by the young charges as "tatae."[38] Indeed, sometimes a Roman mother like Agrippina the Younger, mother of Nero, was through the vagaries of Roman politics absent entirely from her son's life in some of his earliest years.[39] At later stages, however, as Tacitus observes, the patriarchal system enlisted Roman matrons, often in collaboration with their brothers, into playing important roles in the inculcation in their sons of the required sense of patriarchally defined responsibilities, roles characterized by "disciplinarian skills rather than indulgence or over-protectiveness, even towards small children."[40]

The model here for Roman mothers was Coriolanus's mother (Venturia, in Livy's history), who persuaded her son, who had been unjustly exiled from Rome, not to fight against the city of his birth, thus saving Rome at the expense of his life.[41] The consequence was an anger directed toward mothers, so that even when a woman like Livia played a supportive and evidently very important role in her husband's political life and success, she was, as mother to Tiberius, "that feminine bully, his mother."[42] Livia, clearly ambitious that her son would become emperor, certainly supported Augustus's order that Tiberius divorce his wife to marry Julia (Augustus's daughter), a separation that was for Tiberius traumatic. And against this backdrop, we can make sense of Tiberius's rather rigid identification with Roman gender ideology, in terms of which he would later criticize his mother whenever she exercised political responsibilities inconsistent with Tiberius's view of the proper role and station of women.[43] Similarly, and more drastically, Nero, who would certainly never have become emperor without his mother's strenuous efforts on his behalf, when challenged by his imperious mother to disrupt both his

37. Tacitus, *Dialogue*, 307.

38. See, Dixon, *Roman Mother*, 146–49.

39. Agrippina was exiled by Caligula, her brother, to the Pontian isles, during which time Nero was brought up by his aunt Domitia. See Barrett, *Agrippina*, 69–70.

40. Dixon, *Roman Mother*, 145.

41. Livy, *Early History*, 156–57.

42. Tacitus, *Annals*, 34.

43. See, on this point, Tacitus, *Annals*, 41.

intimate sexual liaisons and his artistic interests, turned to homicidal violence against her.[44]

The action of *Coriolanus* is set at a time of transition in the history of the Roman Republic from its early rule by kings and later by an aristocratic senate to a republic in which the plebeians had secured much stronger representation in its politics by the election of two tribunes of the people who had veto power over the appointment each year of the consul, the leader of the republic for that year. Shakespeare's tragedies often study periods of transition from shame to guilt cultures; indeed, the whole enterprise was apparently inspired by Shakespeare's own intimacy with shame-driven military leaders like Essex and others and their catastrophic falls from power in a period that was giving rise to a new kind of entrepreneurial British man and woman less bound by patriarchal codes of honor. Two of Shakespeare's most important Roman tragedies, *Julius Caesar* and *Antony and Cleopatra*, are set at a later period of transition in Roman culture from the republic of the civil wars to the autocracy of the Roman Empire, culminating in the rule of Octavian, later Augustus Caesar, a nephew of the assassinated Julius Caesar.

Julius Caesar studies an idealistic republican, Brutus, in conspiracy with a much less idealistic group of co-conspirators (notably, Cassius), who kill Caesar, an action Brutus, whom Caesar loved, comes to regret, even feel guilty about. Whereas the other conspirators bridle at Caesar's move to become the apex of the patriarchal hierarchy, Brutus is persuaded by Cassius and comes to believe that Caesar will compromise the Roman republic itself, grounded in an elite of competing aristocrats of equals in the Senate, which played the central initiating role in Roman politics, including going to war. Antony in *Julius Caesar* is portrayed as Caesar's close friend and ally, who experiences his murder as traumatic and unjust, calling for retribution:

> Woe to the hand that shed this costly blood.
> Over thy wounds now I do prophesy
> (Which like dumb mouths do ope their ruby lips
> To beg the voice and utterance of my tongue)
> A curse shall light upon the limbs of men:
> Domestic fury and fierce civil strife
> Shall cumber all the parts of Italy:
> Blood and destruction shall be so in use,
> And dreadful objects so familiar,

44. See, in general, Barrett, *Agrippina*; Champlin, *Nero*.

That mothers shall but smile when they behold
Their infants quartered with the hands of war:
All pity choked with custom of fell deeds,
And Caesar's spirit, ranging for revenge,
With Ate by his side come hot from hell,
Shall in these confines, with a monarch's voice,
Cry havoc and let slip the dogs of war,
That this foul deed shall smell above the earth
With carrion men, groaning for burial.[45]

Shakespeare's portrayal of the Roman people in *Julius Caesar*, mobilized into mob violence and bloody civil war by Antony's brilliant "Friends, Romans, countrymen," is of a people not in love with the republican institutions Brutus cherishes, and easily manipulated by a populist demagogue like Antony into a civil war that will, in fact, end the Roman Republic, exactly what the idealistic Brutus had meant to prevent. And Antony, who appears earlier in the play as genuinely grieving the injustice of Caesar's murder, later becomes as ruthless in his political assassinations (including killing Cicero) as most of Caesar's assassins had been. So much, Shakespeare suggests, for republican or democratic enthusiasms, which, within forty years of his death, led to the English Civil War and the execution of Charles I. Shakespeare would hardly have approved, but his extraordinarily powerful and popular tragedies prophetically suggest what was coming.

THE HEBREW BIBLE AS RESPONSE AND RESISTANCE TO IMPERIALISMS

All the best recent work on the historical Jesus confirms both his life and teaching must be understood in the context of the Jewish tradition on which he depends and that he elaborates so creatively.[46] The demands of Roman imperialism, which ruled Israel during the life of Jesus and crucified him, were yet another seminal context for understanding the historical Jesus. Jacob L. Wright in his important recent book, *Why the*

45. Shakespeare, *Julius Caesar*, 3.1.258–275.

46. See, for example, among many others that I have consulted, Vermes, *Religion of Jesus*; Vermes, *Jesus the Jew*; Vermes, *Authentic Gospel*; Vermes, *Changing Faces*; Klausner, *Jesus of Nazareth*; Sanders, *Jesus and Judaism*; Fredriksen, *From Jesus to Christ*; *When Christians Were Jews*.

Bible Began,[47] has powerfully drawn together both the Jewish tradition and its response to imperialism in a way no one can reasonably ignore. His book shows convincingly, I believe, that the entire tradition of the Hebrew Bible arose from and must be understood against the background of the powerful imperialisms that had, for very long periods in the history of the Jewish people, defeated and subjugated them, including the Egyptians, Assyrians, Babylonians, Persians, Greeks (the Hellenistic kings who succeeded Alexander the Great), and the Romans, the last of whom conquer Jewish resistance twice, destroying not only the temple (the center of the Jewish religious tradition) but requiring the dispersion of the Jewish people elsewhere. Such subjugations included the Assyrians transporting ten of the twelve tribes of Israel to Assyria, the Babylonian conquest and transporting Jews to Babylonia (the Babylonian exile) followed by their return allowed by the Persian king, Cyrus, and, after the death of Jesus, the exile elsewhere of the Jewish people for two millennia. Resistance to the imperialisms that afflicted them distinctively defines the Jewish people.

Wright shows that the formation of the Bible draws on two narratives, the Family Story of Israel and the Palace History of Judah (after the ten tribes are relocated by the Assyrians). The writings of the Family History "include the Family Story in Genesis and the Exodus Conquest Account."[48] The Palace History, which "would eventually grow to significant proportions, comprising much of the books of Samuel and Kings" has "at its core . . . the synthesized story of Saul and David in which David mounts the throne of Israel that Saul had first occupied."

> The history has a clear political message. It argues that David and his line are the rightful rulers of all Israel, and that the nation's deity approved of David's decision to make Jerusalem the place where he was to be worshipped. Following YHWH's instructions, the same prophet who had previously anointed Saul now anoints David, and later YHWH promises to never take his love from his descendants, as he did from Saul . . .
>
> The tales represent some of the fiercest story telling in the entire Bible, and they continue to attract many readers and retellings. The intended audience would have discerned parables of Israel's and Judah's history.[49]

47. Wright, *Why the Bible Began*.
48. Wright, *Why the Bible Began*, 110.
49. Wright, *Why the Bible Began*, 111.

Wright shows how the two narratives are melded into one, in which their defeats by imperialistic powers and how to understand such defeats are the central theme:

> [T]he National Narrative, which begins in Genesis and ends in Kings, does not have a happy ending. Its conclusion describes Judah's downfall and exile, and it has nothing to say about the period of reconstruction that followed. The narrative begins with auspicious promises and great triumphs: the creation of the world, the birth of a family, liberation from bondage, the formation of a nation, the rapid conquest of Canaan, the hope-filled establishment of a mighty United Monarchy under David, and the completion of a glorious temple under Solomon. Yet things go awry thereafter. The United Monarchy cleaves into two competing states, which wage war with each other for generations. Eventually the Assyrian and Babylonian armies conquer these two states and deport their inhabitants. In the end, nothing remains.
>
> Such is the biblical version of Israel's and Judah's history, and this National Narrative comprises the first half of the Hebrew Bible, encompassing the Torah and the Former Prophets (Joshua, Judges, Samuel, and Kings) . . . [T]he account of a people's past is distinctive in the ancient world, not only in its length and subject matter, but also in its basic structure. The pattern of most monarchic inscriptions begins with defeat and ends in triumph. The biblical narrative presents the opposite, with the liberation and success at the beginning, and destruction and downfall at the end.
>
> The Latter Prophets (Isaiah, Jeremiah, Ezekiel, and the Twelve 'Minor' Prophets) not only make defeat the focus of their penetrating discourses, but also place responsibility squarely on the nation. By identifying the sins of the past, they lay out survival strategies for the future . . .
>
> Defeat, life in exile, and national restoration are also formative themes for much of the 'Writings,' the third and final section of the Hebrew canon . . . The works in this section depict the consequences of defeat and the means of surviving in a new age of foreign rule. Daniel and Esther relate to life in exile. The book of Chronicles retells the story of the nation's rise and fall . . . Ezra-Nehemiah depicts exiles returning to Judah and rebuilding the ruins of Jerusalem; this restoration proceeds, however, in the shadow of foreign hegemony. The order of the Psalms follows the nation's history; with the final ones offering thanksgiving for return and restoration. The book of Job describes trauma

> inflicted on an individual in a manner that mirrors the nation's collective experience.
>
> The only three books that do not relate explicitly to defeat are Proverbs, Ecclesiastes, and the Song of Solomon . . .
>
> With its unusual attention to loss, biblical literature lends itself as an exceptionally rich resource for studying what the cultural historian Wolfgang Schivelbusch calls 'an empathetic philosophy of defeat [that] seeks to identify and appreciate the significance of defeat itself.'[50]

Wright argues that the National History combines what he calls the People's History and the Palace History, the former being tied to the Jewish people, the latter to the history of the Israeli rulers:[51]

> The Palace History has a clear agenda. Focussing on the political unification of the two kingdoms under the Davidic dynasty in Jerusalem, its authors created a momentous even if short-lived, memory of a 'United Monarchy.' In this way, they identified the status quo—the existence of the two kingdoms—as the tragic rupture of an earlier unity. This political division is the nation's 'original sin' . . .
>
> The People's history goes much further. In the place of a political union forming a United Monarchy, it posits a national unity of one people . . . Later supplements expand the sense of kinship with a written pact (i.e., the covenant that YHWH ratifies with the Israelites at Sinai), making it the foundation and framework for the nation's existence. If the 'original sin' in the Palace History is a political division that results in two competing kingdoms, in the People's History it is when the Israelites breach the covenant by worshipping a golden calf. This was a dissolution of the direct bond between YHWH and the nation. When YHWH threatens to destroy the nation and replace It with another, Moses mediates on Israel's behalf and convinces YHWH to restore a relationship with Israel.[52]

The prophets, appealing to a direct relationship to YHWH, criticize both political leaders and the people themselves. Jeremiah, for example, "paints an intimate portrait of Judean politics directly before and after

50. Wright, *Why the Bible Began*, 145–46.
51. Wright, *Why the Bible Began*, 189.
52. Wright, *Why the Bible Began*, 288–89.

the destruction"[53] by the Babylonians and the Babylonian captivity.[54] And "[t]he breathtaking poetry of Second Isaiah features the major themes of the biblical narrative: creation, the patriarchs and matriarchs, the exodus, and so on. Many of the poems date to the time of the Persian Empire which conquered Babylon in 539 BCE, reversed many of its imperial policies, and cleared the way of Judah's new beginning." Indeed,

> Second Isaiah identifies the messianic rule with the Persian ruler, Cyrus, who liberates the exiles ('sets the captives free') and permits them to return to their homeland in the 'new exodus' . . . This liberation is very different from the first exodus: the Persian kings are still in control; the returning exiles do not reconquer their homeland; and a Davidic ruler does not mount the throne . . .
>
> These efforts to both postpone and redefine national liberation are closely connected to how the final authors of the Palace History subordinated their work to the People's History.[55]

They did so in two ways: "1) humanizing of kingship, and 2) the framing of the nation's experience with the monarchy as just one, later chapter in a much longer story."[56]

In contrast to the idealization of rulers by the imperialisms that defeated and subordinated Israel, David's personal flaws are prominent in the biblical narrative,[57] as are critiques of kingship itself.[58] And, "the prophets frequently pronounce judgment on the throne. When David seizes Bathsheba and has her husband killed, the prophet Nathan boldly stands before the king and—in one of the Bible's most stirring scenes—proclaims 'You are the guilty one!' . . . The ideal prophet in the Bible stands at a distance from the throne and is often isolated from society . . . YHWH's prophet Elijah camps out in solitude by a wadi in the desert, where he relies on ravens to feed him."[59]

"The Palace History refers frequently to prophets in the reigns of the first kings. Thus, the book of Kings features lengthy accounts of two

53. Wright, *Why the Bible Began*, 131.
54. Wright, *Why the Bible Began*, 156.
55. Wright, *Why the Bible Began*, 292.
56. Wright, *Why the Bible Began*, 292.
57. Wright, *Why the Bible Began*, 295, 394.
58. Wright, *Why the Bible Began*, 297, 299, 320, 342, 394.
59. Wright, *Why the Bible Began*, 411–12.

prophets, Elijah and Elisha."[60] However, "[l]ater generations augmented the older oracles"[61]:

> In contrast, the biblical books of Amos, Hosea, Isaiah, Jeremiah, and so on are *system transcendent*. By pronouncing the end of YHWH's relationship with his people, these writings declare the demise of statehood, along with its ancient ideological foundation.[62]

Previously, "[t]he system was designed to weather many storms. But what it could not cope with was unmitigated defeat and destruction,"[63] which was the trauma the Jewish people now faced. Out of this,

> [s]omething completely new emerges after this rupture: history becomes relevant and important. The relationship between the nation and its deity is now said to have been established at a particular point in the past in a formal way and with written terms clearly defining the terms of the partnership. This is the pact that the people ratify with YHWH after their exodus from Egypt, and its terms are found in the laws of the Pentateuch . . . Now instead of pointing to basic moral principles, the prophets sally forth as prosecutors, cataloguing direct infractions of the written contract that YHWH made with the nation at the beginning of history. Of course, one did not need the Ten Commandments to know that robbery, murder, and adultery were wrong. Yet now a defeated nation should understand it not only acted wickedly but had also breached a written arrangement. The contractual violation made them doubly culpable for their demise and YHWH doubly just for his judgment.[64]

Wright analogizes the experience of the people of Israel with the literature of the survival from trauma and testimony.

> The same can be said for much of the biblical corpus, not least the prophetic writings: they are both survivors and witnesses. They dealt with the death that overwhelmed Israel and Judah by transforming it into concrete evidence for the veracity and reliability of the words YHWH spoke to 'my servants, the prophets' . . . As a result, these writings were preserved from the flames of

60. Wright, *Why the Bible Began*, 319.
61. Wright, *Why the Bible Began*, 320.
62. Wright, *Why the Bible Began*, 323.
63. Wright, *Why the Bible Began*, 322.
64. Wright, *Why the Bible Began*, 323–25.

> destruction, and now they bear trustworthy testimony to future generations who would otherwise make the mistakes of their ancestors. The nation is culpable, and its only hope is that the relationship with YHWH might be restored. But when it is restored, it will have to be established on a different foundation.[65]

THE SEARCH FOR THE HISTORICAL JESUS

Both my discussion of Roman patriarchy and of the Hebrew Bible frame my own understanding of the historical Jesus—Roman patriarchy because the antipatriarchal Jesus resisted and challenged patriarchy, the Hebrew Bible because Jesus regarded himself, in my view, as a prophet in the Jewish tradition, and sought to establish on a new foundation the covenantal relationship to YHWH on the basis of a conception of love and egalitarian personal relationships that, I shall later argue, can plausibly be illuminated by a psychoanalytically informed view of love as the mirror for human relationships and the basis for both ethics and democracy. But, my understanding of the historical Jesus has been informed by the search for the historical Jesus among Christianities, and my own view, to be plausible, must take seriously the search for the historical Jesus and those views of it that have come to seem to me historically reliable.

It is a real question among the Christianities that were inspired by the life and teaching of Jesus of Nazareth what weight should be given to historical research on Jesus beyond the Gospels themselves. The Protestant Reformation initiated by Martin Luther, among others, appealed directly to the Gospels themselves as more authoritative than what the complex theology and philosophy (influenced, in particular, by Aristotle) of Roman Catholicism had, in Thomism, made of them. And even among Protestants, there are important differences, none more starkly different than the view of Søren Kierkegaard and Albert Schweitzer.

Kierkegaard on the Historical Jesus

Kierkegaard repudiated any appeal to history as inconsistent with his own highly individualistic interpretation of the life and teaching of Jesus.[66] Most of Kierkegaard's works were written under pseudonyms, and

65. Wright, *Why the Bible Began*, 329.

66. See Kierkegaard, *Concluding Unscientific*, 23–49.

he thought of himself as an ironist, very much admiring the irony of Socrates,[67] and notoriously explored the negative emotions of his own guilt-ridden struggle to an authentic Christianity, based on a freedom acknowledging guilt, including anxiety,[68] fear and trembling,[69] and sickness unto death.[70] But, in one of the few of his works written under his own name, *Works of Love*,[71] Kierkegaard writes with unusual clarity and directness about his interpretation of a radical ethics and life of impartial love for all persons, repudiating any form of "caste"[72] and any system of "honor"[73] like that of a shame culture that exposes one's conscience to control by the views of a community. Kierkegaard's view of the demands of ethical impartiality is extraordinary, excluding apparently even marital love because it is selective and not impartial.[74] And it is his view that all established churches, including Christian churches, use shame in their practices, which justifies his attack on all established churches,[75] all to protect the radical individualism that Christian ethics requires, an argument that the separation of church and state protects religion from the state (not the state from religion) at the heart, as we shall later see, of the arguments for the separation of church and state of Jefferson and Madison that culminate in the First Amendment of the US Bill of Rights. What makes his arguments so striking is that they depend entirely on Kierkegaard's interpretation of the Gospels, repudiating any historical inquiry precisely because, as I understand his argument, it would compromise his conviction, based on his interpretation of the Gospels, that a moral individualism of ethical impartiality, precisely because it is so demanding (requiring so much sacrifice of personal life), is the heart of an authentic Christianity.

67. See Kierkegaard, *Concept of Irony.* On Socrates as ironist, see Vlastos, *Socrates.*
68. Kierkegaard, *Concept of Anxiety.*
69. Kierkegaard, *Fear.*
70. Kierkegaard, *Sickness.*
71. Kierkegaard, *Works of Love.*
72. Kierkegaard, *Works of Love*, 80.
73. Kierkegaard, *Works* of *Love*, 130.
74. Kierkegaard, *Works of Love*, 115, 117–18.
75. See, for example, Kierkegaard, *Moment*; *Kierkegaard, Practice.*

Schweitzer on the Historical Jesus

In contrast, Albert Schweitzer in his *The Quest for the Historical Jesus*[76] takes quite seriously the search for the historical Jesus, thus reviewing the existing literature at the time he wrote (including, among many others, Ernest Renan's *The Life of Jesus*,[77] who regarded Jesus as a self-deluded fanatic man who had repudiated all his Jewish roots and was an Aryan, and David Friedrich Strauss's *The Life of Jesus Critically Examined*,[78] which did not deny Jesus's divine nature, but regarded the miracles as myths). Schweitzer took his own view of what was reliable, namely, that Jesus was an eschatological prophet in the Jewish tradition of prophecy and must be understood in that context. The eschatology he expected did not, however, occur, and Jesus dies tragically in Schweitzer's chilling words:

> The Baptist appears, and cries: 'Repent, for the Kingdom of Heaven is at hand.' Soon after that comes Jesus, and in the knowledge that He is the coming Son of Man lays hold of the wheel to set it moving on that last revolution which is to bring all ordinary history to a close. It refuses to turn, and He throws Himself upon it. Then it does turn; and crushes him. Instead of bringing in the eschatological conditions, He has destroyed them. The wheel rolls onward, and the mangled body of the one immeasurably great Man, who was to bend history to His purpose, is hanging upon it still. That is His victory and His reign.[79]

Nonetheless, the life and teaching of Jesus move Schweitzer as a model for both ethics and an ethical life:

> He comes to us as One unknown, without a name, as of old, by the lake-side, He came to those men who knew Him not. He speaks to us the same word: 'Follow thou me!' and sets us to the tasks which He has to fulfill for our time. He commands. And to those who obey him, whether they be wise or simple, He will reveal Himself in the toils, the conflicts, the sufferings which they shall pass through in His fellowship, and, as an ineffable mystery, they shall learn in their own experience Who He is.[80]

76. Schweitzer, *Quest.*
77. Renan, *Life of Jesus.*
78. Strauss, *Life of Jesus.*
79. Schweitzer, *Quest*, 368–69.
80. Schweitzer, *Quest*, 401.

Unlike Kierkegaard who repudiates history to identify with the Jesus he finds in the Gospels, Schweitzer searches for the historical Jesus, criticizes earlier historians like Strauss who, in his view, domesticate his teaching to express contemporary German liberal values, and discovers through his study of the historical Jesus the compelling moral personality with whom, following Paul's identification with Jesus,[81] he identifies as closely as did Kierkegaard, finding in his life and teaching an ethics quite as radical and as demanding as Kierkegaard. On the basis of his placing Jesus in the tradition of Jewish prophecy, Schweitzer debunks arguments of psychiatrists that Jesus was mentally ill, suffering from paranoid fears of persecution and delusions of grandeur.[82] He grants that Jesus may have suffered from some hallucinations, but denies, for example, that either Jesus's criticism of the family or his favorable treatment of eunuchs (Matt 19:3–9) can be regarded as insane: the first, because the criticism may be valid; the second, because Jesus clearly accepted marriage as an institution, and his view of eunuchs may be understood as including them among the despised whom he welcomed and to whom he ministered (which would clearly today include gays):

> Jesus sees in the eunuchs the despised one who like the children are destined to honor in the Kingdom of God because formerly they had been among the rejected ones.[83]

Schweitzer interprets Jesus's ministry as to the Jews only, attributing to him on this ground a "predestinarian view [that] goes along with the eschatology."[84]

So, Schweitzer did not find through his study of the historical Jesus what Kierkegaard feared, not taking Jesus the person seriously, but, like many later historians of Jesus, whom I shall shortly discuss, a transformative understanding of his remarkable moral personality through a historically rigorous study of his life and teaching against the background of his cultural context in the Jewish prophetic tradition and, I would add, the imperialist subjugation of Israel with whom all Jews were familiar and many of them resisted, some of them, unlike Jesus, violently.

What makes Schweitzer's seminal work on the historical Jesus so important, anticipating more recent developments in this historical

81. See Schweitzer, *Mysticism of Paul.*

82. See Schweitzer, *Psychiatric Study of Jesus.*

83. See Schweitzer, *Psychiatric Study of Jesus*, 70.

84. Schweitzer, *Quest*, 352.

scholarship, is how he connects his version of the imitation of Jesus, unlike Kierkegaard, with a demanding life of action in the world. Think, by way of comparison, of Thomas Jefferson's redaction of the Gospels, excluding everything miraculous,[85] and the life Jefferson led in giving effect to a constitutionalism that aspired to protect human rights. Like Jefferson, Schweitzer was moved by the moral personality of Jesus and an active love he believed, following Jesus, was the basis of ethics and an ethical life.[86]

Schweitzer was a pathbreaking scholar of the music of J. S. Bach and performer of Bach's organ music[87] and a Lutheran minister and a distinguished scholar of the history of religion. His interpretation of the demands of Christian ethics led to a critique of the "ignoble patriotism"[88] of German fascist nationalism and the failure of supposedly progressive "civilization" to take seriously what he called reverence for life.[89] His interpretation of the demands of Christian ethics was at least as demanding as, perhaps more demanding than, Kierkegaard's: Schweitzer gave up a promising career in German academic life to become a physician, and to work as a physician with his wife Helen Bresslau, who had trained as a nurse to assist him, working as a physician to natives in Lambarene in the Gabon province of French Equatorial Africa.[90] Becoming a physician and working as a physician were clearly inspired by his sense of Jesus himself as a physician ministering to the ills of outcasts.

Rudolf Bultmann on the Historical Jesus

Schweitzer's *Quest for the Historical Jesus* is published in 1906 and is followed by the later influential historical studies of the Gospels of Rudolf Bultmann whose "form-criticism" construes the Gospels in terms of the "life situation" (*Sitz im Leben*) not as "an individual historical event, but a typical situation or occupation in the life of a community," "a sociological concept," in particular the rationalizing needs of the Christian churches

85. See Jefferson, *Jefferson Bible*. For Schweitzer's skepticism about the miracles, see Schweitzer, *Quest*, 111, 115.

86. See Schweitzer, *Out of My Life*, 46–52.

87. See Schweitzer, *J. S. Bach*.

88. Schweitzer, *Philosophy*, 29.

89. See, for his argument to this effect, Schweitzer, *Philosophy*.

90. See, for Schweitzer's account, Schweitzer, *Out of My Life*.

to justify their authority after the crucifixion of Jesus of Nazareth.[91] This allows him to explore the contradictions of the synoptic Gospels (Mark, Matthew, and Luke) not only with one another, but with John,[92] using the term "mythology" to question the historicity of various claims in the Gospels (for example, the virgin birth). For Bultmann, such questioning as "mythology" leads not to ultimate religious skepticism, but makes room for the role of faith in the teaching of the Gospels (John, in particular) he regards as most compelling.[93] His historical approach importantly anticipates the more recent work by historians on the historical Jesus, to which we now turn.

The Jesus Seminar and John Meier on the Historical Jesus

There are two recent developments in the study of the historical Jesus that I have found compelling: first, the published works of the Jesus Seminar itself;[94] and second, the multivolume work of John P. Meier.[95]

Both these historical projects take quite seriously the two central accusations in 1953 of Graves and Podro in *The Nazarene Gospel Restored* to the treatment of the historical Jesus by the then dominant Christianities. First, they failed to take seriously that Jesus was a Jew working within the Jewish tradition. Second, "the whole rationale of the quest for the historical Jesus is that one may not without further ado cite a Christian Gospel written in A.D. 70 or 90 to establish that Jesus of Nazareth actually said or did in A.D. 28–30."[96] The Gospels were written in Greek at least 40 years after the death of Jesus when the authors had to depend on largely oral sources probably in the language Jesus spoke, Aramaic. Its authors wrote, based on such sources (in particular, on a source containing Jesus's central teaching, Q, on which Matthew and Luke depend) in, during, and after the period of the Jewish war with Rome, leading to the

91. Bultmann, *History*, 4.

92. Bultmann, *Gospel*.

93. Bultmann, *Theology*. On "mythology" in Bultmann's thought, see Bultmann, *Jesus Christ*; Congdon, *Rudolph Bultmann*.

94. See Funk et al., *Five Gospels*; Funk and the Jesus Seminar, *Acts of Jesus*; Funk et al., *Gospel of Jesus*; Funk et al., *Parables*. For commentary, see Miller, *Jesus Seminar*; Johnson, *Real Jesus*; Witherington, *Jesus Quest*.

95. Meier, *Marginal Jew: Roots*; *Marginal Jew: Mentor*; Meier, *Marginal Jew: Companions*; Meier, *Marginal Jew: Law and Love*; Meier, *Marginal Jew: Parables*.

96. Meier, *Marginal Jew: Law and Love*, 4.

destruction of the temple in 70 CE and the end of any possibility of a Jewish Christianity centered in Jerusalem (led by Jesus's brother, James, who was executed). Each of the Gospels reflects the situation of the author writing as well as his audience, which differ from author to author. The Gospels thus reflect the views of authors and their prospective audiences during a period of crisis for both Judaism and Christianity when a Jewish Christianity (which would have preserved Jewish religious practices like circumcision and the dietary laws) no longer had an audience or much of an audience, and the appeal of Christianity was, under the leadership of Paul who never knew Jesus, a gospel to the gentiles who were, in Paul's view, no longer bound by Jewish religious practices. Paul's epistles were written well before the Gospels and contain little that is historically reliable about Jesus but much that later Christianities would take quite seriously (including doctrines of original sin and predestination), in particular his Epistle to the Romans, a central text for the Catholic Augustine and the Protestant Luther.

Both accusations of Graves and Podro are valid, in particular requiring a rethinking of the historical Jesus that takes seriously the Jewish tradition he assumes and elaborates.[97] Much of their force rests on the role Christian anti-Semitism had grotesquely played, in the thought of both Augustine and Luther and others, as Rosemary Ruether has powerfully shown,[98] in rationalizing the forms of violent political anti-Semitism (culminating in the Holocaust) that were, undoubtedly, the context for the historical arguments of Graves and Podro. Both the Gospels themselves and the later thought of Augustine, Luther, and others did not take seriously, as an audience, Jewish Christianity, but, under the impact of Paul's increasingly hegemonic gospel to the gentiles, took as its audience gentiles who lived and worked within the structure of Roman patriarchal imperialism. The early Christians, persecuted by Roman authorities, certainly resisted the demands of the imperialism, but, once Constantine makes Christianity the established church of the Roman Empire, Christianity itself became more Roman than Christian, as we shall later see. It is in this context that the Gospels themselves, reflecting the views of their gentile audiences, frame a narrative that does not take seriously that Jesus

97. See, for example, among many others that I will later discuss, Vermes, *Religion of Jesus*; Vermes, *Jesus*; Vermes, *Jesus the Jew*; Vermes, *Authentic Gospel*; Vermes, *Changing Faces*; Klausner, *Jesus of Nazareth*; Sanders, *Jesus and Judaism*; Fredriksen, *From Jesus to Christ*; Fredriksen, *When Christians Were Jews*.

98. See Ruether, *Faith and Fratricide*.

is crucified by Roman political authority and that the Jews who may have been involved, the Sadducees,[99] were themselves a small minority and subordinate to Roman authority, which gave them any power they had over Jewish religious life. If anything, the historical Jesus as a Jew was probably closer to the Pharisees in his thinking, on which Graves and Podro build their argument entirely, but not taking seriously, as more contemporary historians argue, his significant disagreements with the views of Pharisees of the period, as well as his originality in interpreting these and other Jewish sources.[100]

It is an important feature of the historical criteria adopted by both the Jesus Seminar and John Meier that they prominently include what Meier calls "the criterion of embarrasment"[101]and the "criterion of discontinuity,"[102] the first of which grounds authenticity in the fact that the later church would have been embarrassed by such a view, and the second of which turns on the fact that the "words or deeds of Jesus . . . cannot be derived either from Judaism or from the early Church after him."[103] Others include "multiple attestation,"[104] and a criterion of "coherence"[105] that validates only sayings and deeds consistent with the first three criteria, and "the criterion of rejection and execution"[106] that material must be consistent with what all the historical sources point to, "the historical fact that Jesus met a violent end . . . and then asks what historical words and deeds can explain his trial and execution as 'King of the Jews.'"[107] Meier's multivolume historical study is a particularly illuminating and judicious application of these criteria to the historical materials, from which I have learned much.

99. On the Sadducees, see Meier, *Marginal Jew: Companions*, 389–444.

100. See, for example, the first of the Jewish scholars to write about Jesus, Klausner,Jesus of Nazareth. On the contentious disagreements of the historical Jesus with the Pharisees on many points (including divorce, eating or curing on the sabbath, washing one's hands before eating, etc.), see Meier, *Marginal Jesus: Companions*, 289–340, 643–45.

101. Meier, *Marginal Jew: Roots*, 168.

102. Meier, *Marginal Jew: Roots*, 171.

103. Meier, *Marginal Jew: Roots*, 171.

104. Meier, *Marginal Jew: Roots*, 174.

105. Meier, *Marginal Jew: Roots*, 176.

106. Meier, *Marginal Jew: Roots*, 177.

107. Meier, *Marginal Jew: Roots*, 177.

All of these historians as well as others I have consulted[108] do not always agree on the historicity of certain words and deeds, but they concur on much, and their disagreements are themselves of interest. The work of the Jesus Seminar, some thirty distinguished scholars working as an independent group over a period of six years, is, I believe, especially compelling from this perspective because the color-coded system they use to indicate whether, how, and why they agree or disagree, as well as the strength of their disagreements, bespeaks the remarkable intellectual integrity as individual scholars they bring to their common project.

> They came to the following basic facts:
>
> 1. Jesus was a real person.
> 2. Jesus was a follower of John the Baptist; he quit John and returned to Galilee where he began eating and drinking in profane style.
> 3. Jesus talked about the Empire of God in parables and aphorisms.
> 4. Jesus was a charismatic healer and exorcist.
> 5. Jesus was executed by the Romans around 30 C.E.
> 6. Paul of Tarsus claimed the risen Jesus appeared to him ca. 34 CE.
>
> It was said that the risen Jesus appeared to Simon Peter (date and locale unknown).[109]

In reviewing the historicity of the sayings and deeds of Jesus, the seminar came to appreciate that Jesus was a creative wordsmith. They concluded:

> 1. Jesus was an artisan of words.
> 2. Jesus created stories for his audience to interpret on their own.
> 3. The parables and aphorisms of Jesus can be said to play provocatively against the assumptions of the first-century imagination.
> 4. Insights from Jesus's parables and sayings provide the listener with new images of the Empire of God.

108. These sources include Vermes, *Religion of Jesus*; Vermes, *Jesus*; Vermes, *Jesus the Jew*; Vermes, *Authentic Gospel*; Vermes, *Changing Faces*; Klausner, *Jesus of Nazareth*; Sanders, *Jesus and Judaism*; Fredriksen, *From Jesus to Christ*; Fredriksen, *When Christians Were Jews;* Ehrman, *Jesus.*

109. Funk et al., *Gospel of Jesus,* 4.

> The Empire of God becomes discerned when the listener actively works out the parables and sayings.[110]

All of these scholars note the differences and even inconsistencies even among the Synoptic Gospels (Mark, Matthew, Luke). The central teaching of Jesus, deriving from Q, is only in Matthew and Luke, and in somewhat different forms. Both depend on Mark, as well as Q and independent sources accessible to each of them. The Gospel of John is an independent work dependent on different sources.[111] Its chronology of the events of the life of Jesus is quite different, and apparently more historically accurate;[112] its anti-Semitism is quite virulent, "You are from your father the devil," John 8: 45[113] (probably reflecting conflicts between Jewish and gentile Christians), and its christological theology (Jesus as the son of God) powerfully stated.[114] These features, however, clarify the growing chasm between the historical Jesus and the Christian tradition that developed after his death, a tradition that, in the view of these historians, shaped the Gospels themselves in ways foreign to the historical Jesus, including, among them, Albert Schweitzer's interpretation that Jesus precipitated his own death.[115] The Jesus Seminar thus concludes: "the scattered facts we can muster do not of themselves produce a Jesus who is the Christ of the Christian faith. The authors of traditional Christian faith are Peter and Paul."[116]

Among the claims in the Gospels, not historically supported, are the birth and infancy narratives (including the virgin birth) of Jesus;[117] "the veracity of any of the later appearance narratives"[118] after Jesus; that Jesus spoke of a kingdom to come,[119] rather than a kingdom now coming into

110. Funk et al., *Gospel of Jesus*, 4–5.

111. On the sources of the Gospels, see Coogan, *New Oxford Bible*, 1777–82, On the independence of the Gospel of John, see Meier, *Marginal Jew: Mentor*, 724.

112. See, on this point, Meier, *Marginal Jew: Roots*, 395–401, 403–6; Coogan, *New Oxford Bible*, 1918–19.

113. Coogan, *New Oxford Bible*, 1935.

114. See, on this point, Meier, *Marginal Jew: Mentor*, 810.

115. See, on this point, Meier, *Marginal Jew: Mentor*, 340–41.

116. Funk and the Jesus Seminar, *Acts of Jesus*, 534.

117. Funk and the Jesus Seminar, *Acts of Jesus*, 497–526. See also Meier, *Marginal Jew: Roots*, 208–30.

118. Funk and the Jesus Seminar, *Acts of Jesus*, 533.

119. Funk et al., *Five Gospels*, 40–41.

existence[120] (Meier once believed in the claim of a future kingdom, but found it unsupported by historical research[121]); that he had any specific knowledge of his coming death;[122] that he speculated about the coming of the messiah;[123] that he believed in an apocalypse;[124] that he was tried by temple authorities ("the Fellows [of the Jesus Seminar] were virtually unanimous in their judgment that the account of the Judean trials was mostly a fabrication of the Christian imagination"[125]); and many others.

These historians have, however, much to say about two important features of Jesus's life and teaching. First, Jesus worked within and appealed to the long Jewish tradition, earlier discussed, of prophetic resistance, including resistance to the imperialisms that subjugated them. Second, much of what is distinctive in Jesus's life and teaching is his resistance to the patriarchal assumptions not only of Israel's Roman rulers (earlier discussed), but to the patriarchal assumptions his own Jewish culture apparently accepted. I begin with the first, and then turn to the second, which will be the basis of the central argument of this book: that psychoanalysis illuminates the life and teaching of the antipatriarchal historical Jesus.

We earlier examined the very development of the Bible, as a distinctive form of literature in contrast to that of the imperialisms that subjugated the Jews. What makes it distinctive is the central largely oral role of the prophets, appealing directly to and from God, speaking both to the leaders of Israel and to the Jewish people themselves in ethical criticism of their morally culpable failures of both action and omission that both explain how a just God could have permitted their subjugation, and show what must be done both to satisfy their just God and lead God once again to support his chosen people.

Both the life and teaching of the historical Jesus draw upon the prophetic tradition, most notably Jesus self-consciously modeling himself on the prophet Elijah,[126] a miracle worker and itinerant prophet calling the leaders and people of Israel to accountability for their ethical lapses at the end time. Meier, however, observes:

120. Funk et al., *Five Gospels,* 364–65.

121. Meier, *Marginal Jew: Mentor*, 6.

122. Funk et al., *Five Gospels,* 208, 212.

123. Funk et al., *Five Gospels,* 249.

124. Funk et al., *Five Gospels,* 531–32.

125. Funk et al., *Five Gospels,* 121.

126. See, on this point, Meier, *Marginal Jew: Companions,* 4, 48, 495, 922–26.

> By "end time" or "eschatology" one should not understand some phantasmagoric destruction of heaven and earth or the complete end of human history in the manner of Jewish apocalypses . . . Rather, Jesus was announcing the end of the present state of things, the end of sacred history as Israel had known it up until now, and the definitive beginning of a new, permanent state of affairs. God would soon rule Israel directed as its king, and his holy will would be done by his repentant and forgiven people, who would experience the full peace and joy that God had intended for them from the beginning.[127]

But,

> What this would mean in detail Jesus did not say. He is not a political leader in the sense of someone enunciating a detailed political and social program that was to be implemented by particular practical measures. Rather, the transformation of Israel in the end time was to be the work of God coming as king. As the prophet of this kingdom, it was Jesus' task to prophesy this world-changing advent of God and to begin the preparation of Israel by calling it to repentance, baptism, and a renewed moral life within a loving, compassionate society. By such attention-grabbing actions as his miracles, his table fellowship with religiously or socially disreputable Jews, and the sending of the twelve disciples to their fellow Israelites, Jesus intended both to anticipate and to set in motion what God alone would fully accomplish at his coming. All these symbolic-prophetic acts of Jesus were understood by him to unleash the powers of the kingdom that they foreshadowed.
>
> At the same time, though, these acts were *only* symbolic and prophetic. They were not pragmatic programs intended to set up a new political regime in Palestine. Jesus spoke not in terms of practical agendas to be carried out by bureaucratic committees or rebellious troops. He spoke in parables, in allusive, riddle-like speech that meant to evoke, challenge, and change people's perceptions of themselves, their neighbors, and their God, not to describe the way they were to restructure the system of tax collection or reapportion plots of land. To be sure, Jesus spoke in bold and even hyperbolic fashion of great-hearted forgiveness (including the remission of debts), selfless almsgiving, and generosity to assisting others in need. None of this—nor all of it

127. Meier, *Marginal Jew: Companions*, 624.

> together—added up to a clear and detailed political or economic program.[128]

On the response to Jesus's life and teaching:

> one can see how tension and confrontation would inevitably arise from Jesus' words and actions. On the one hand, what Jesus said and did had ramifications for the present order of things political, social, and economic. On the other hand, Jesus himself had no detailed plan for setting up some new rival political or economic order. Jesus was not laying out some practical strategy for restoring autonomy to the kingdom of Israel as it had previously existed in the Davidic, Hasmonean or Herodian form. As the eschatological prophet, Jesus announced and symbolized a totally different order of things, one created by God alone. That Caiaphas or Pilate, immersed in the task of running Judea day to day, did not appreciate the fine eschatological nuances of Jesus' particular understanding of the kingdom of God is hardly surprising. What they saw out of the windows of their Jerusalem palaces was a popular Jewish prophet stirring up an enthusiastic Jewish populace during the great pilgrim feasts. Not only did he harangue the crowds surging around the temple complex with visions of an imminent new kingdom, he backed up his heady message with supposed miracles that anticipated the coming transformation.
>
> After all, John the Baptist has made no overt political claims or moves, but Antipas had decided anyway that an ounce of prevention by way of execution was worth a pound of cure by way of military action. A single execution—we hear nothing of subsequent persecution, let alone execution, of John's disciples—forestalled a possible uprising at a later date. At a certain point, after increasing tensions each time Jesus visited Jerusalem during the feasts, and especially after Jesus staged provocative, prophetic acts by his entry into Jerusalem and by his 'cleansing of the temple' just before the Passover of A.D. 30, Caiaphas and Pilate adopted the 'Antipas solution': cut off the head of the movement with one swift, preemptive bow. The headless movement, so completely centered and dependent on one charismatic prophet who wielded all authority within the group, would quickly dissolve. In the famous words of many a politician: it seemed like a good idea at the time.[129]

128. Meier, *Marginal Jew: Companions*, 624.

129. Meier, *Marginal Jew: Companions*, 624–25.

Josephus, initially a leader of the Jewish revolt who later joins the Romans (whose success was read by Josephus as shifting God's endorsement from the Jews to the Romans), writes of the execution of John in precisely such terms:

> For Herod killed him, although he was a good man and [simply] bade the Jews to join him in baptism and practicing justice toward one another and piety toward God . . . Herod began to fear that John's ability to persuade people might lead to some sort of revolt, for they seemed likely to do whatever he counseled. So [Herod] decided to do away with John by a preemptive strike, before he sparked a revolt.[130]

Josephus also wrote of Jesus:

> At this time [i.e., the role of Pontius Pilate as prefect of Judea] there appeared Jesus, a wise man. For he was a doer of startling deeds, a teacher of people who receive the truth with pleasure. And he gains a following both among many Jews and among many of Gentile origin.[131]

And Josephus writes of why Pilate executed Jesus in similar terms to the reasons of Herod for executing John the Baptist:

> . . . Pilate, because of an accusation made [or possibly an indictment brought] by the leading men among us, condemned him to the cross.[132]

Meier explains:

> That is to say, Pilate, who as the Roman prefect of Judea had supreme power over life and death over provincials, exercised it by crucifying Jesus. He did so after 'the leading men [literally: the first men] among us,' no doubt the high priest and other officials around him, including perhaps some of the lay aristocrats, brought some charge or indictment against Jesus to Pilate's attention.[133]

The death of John the Baptist, whom Jesus had once followed and several of whose disciples joined Jesus, undoubtedly shocked Jesus: "when Jesus heard this, he withdrew from there to a boat to a deserted

130. Quoted in Meier, *Marginal Jew: Roots*, 20.

131. Quoted in Meier, *Marginal Jew: Mentor*, 621.

132. Quoted in Meier, *Marginal Jew: Mentor*, 627.

133. Quoted in Meier, *Marginal Jew: Mentor*, 627.

place by himself" (Matt 15:3),[134] and, when it is suggested to him that Herod Antipas might intend the same for him, he responds:

> "Go and tell that fox for me." Listen, "I am casting out demons and performing cures today and tomorrow, and the next day I must be on my way, because it is impossible for a prophet to be killed outside Jerusalem." Jerusalem, Jerusalem, the city that kills prophets and stones those who are sent to it!"[135]

And the matter of such violence by those in authority is referred to by Jesus in terms associated with the death of John:

> From the days of John the Baptist until now the kingdom of heaven has suffered violence, and the violent take it by force.[136]

The connection of violence against Jesus's teaching is usually in the Gospels attributed to the Jews (Herod Antipas, for example, was himself a Jew), no doubt reflecting the attempt of its writers—writing for a largely gentile audience—to exculpate the Romans and inculpate the Jews. Only the Gospel of John, written independently from the Synoptic Gospels from different, sometimes more reliable historical sources, expressly shows us how the reasoning of Caiaphas, the chief priest, and others about why Jesus must be killed, reveals the grisly realpolik of temple leaders protecting Jews from the violence of their Roman masters:

> "What are we to do? This man is performing many signs. If we let him go on like this, everyone will come and destroy both our holy place and our nation." But one of them, Caiaphas, who was high priest that year, said to them, "You know nothing at all. You do not understand that it is better for you to have one man die for the people than to have the whole nation destroyed." He did not say this on his own, but being high priest that year he prophesied that Jesus was to die for the nation and not for the nation only, but to gather into one the dispersed children of God. So from that day they planned to put him to death.[137]

Caiaphas was at least right to worry about Roman violence. Rome, as we already saw, was a deeply patriarchal shame culture, and its propensity to violence was culturally supported by its patriarchal institutions both

134. Coogan, *Oxford, New Oxford Bible*, 1804.

135. Coogan, *New Oxford Bible*, 1896.

136. Coogan, *New Oxford Bible*, 1798, Matt 11:12.

137. Coogan, *New Oxford Bible*, 1939, John 11:48–54.

in personal and political life and are the key to understanding both its success as an imperial power, and the role of violence in its imperialism, including its rule over the Jews. After the death of Jesus, there were to be two disastrous Jewish wars against the Romans—the First Jewish-Roman War (66–74 CE) and the Bar Kokhba revolt (132–136 CE), ending in the diaspora of the Jews for some two millenia. The zealots, a group committed to violence, may possibly have been known to Jesus: one of his disciples, Simon the Cananean, has been called a zealot,[138] though the zealots "did not emerge as a distinct group until the First Jewish Revolt."[139] Zealots appealed to recent Jewish history: the Jews had earlier successfully used violence to resist their Ptolemaic rulers for Hellenizing Jewish culture in violation of Jewish law, and had established a Hasmonean dynasty from 140 BCE to 37 BCE, a history recounted in 1 Maccabees and 2 Maccabees. The forces of the Roman Republic intervened in the Hasmonean Civil War in 63 BCE and made it into a client state, marking the decline of the Hasmonean dynasty; Herod the Great, a Jew and himself a client of Rome, displaced the last reigning Hasmonean client-ruler in 37 BCE.[140] Herod's son, Herod Antipas, another client of Rome, ruled in Galilee during the life of Jesus. Rome ruled directly in Judaea through its prefect, Pontius Pilate.

What Caiaphas or the Romans for that matter did not take seriously was Jesus's quite remarkable teachings about nonviolence in the Sermon on the Mount:

> You heard that it was said, "An eye for an eye and a tooth for a tooth." But I say to you. Do not resist an evildoer. But if anyone strikes you on the right cheek, turn the other also; and if anyone wants to sue you and take your coat, give your cloak as well; and if anyone forces you to go one mile, go also the second mile. Give to everyone who begs from you, and do not refuse anyone who wants to borrow from you.
>
> You have heard that it was said, "You shall love your neighbor and hate your enemy." But I say to you, Love your enemies and pray for those who persecute you; for he makes his sun rise on the evil and the good, and sends rain on the righteous and unrighteous. For if you love those who love you, what reward to you have? And if you greet only your brothers and sisters, what more are you doing than others? Do not even the Gentiles

138. See, on this point Coogan, *New Oxford Bible*, 205–8.

139. Meier, *Marginal Jew: Companions*, 565.

140. See Wikipedia, "Hasmonean Dynasty."

> do that same? Be perfect, therefore, as you heavenly Father is perfect.[141]

Jesus famously answered the query about paying taxes to Rome by acknowledging their legitimacy,[142] but, as we earlier saw, he recognized the unjust violence directed against John the Baptist by Herod Antipas. He also rebuked an attempt by his disciples to establish a hierarchy among them in terms that show he clearly questioned and rejected Roman patriarchy:

> You know that the rulers of the Gentiles lord it over them, and their great ones are tyrants over them. It will not be so among you; but whoever wishes to be great among you must be your servant, and whoever wishes to be first among you must be your slave; just as the Son of Man came not to be served but to serve, and to give his life a ransom for many.[143]

It is thus quite clear what Jesus thought of the patriarchal hierarchies of the gentiles ("tyrants") or the compliance of Jewish temple authority with the use of violence against him, rebuking his followers for using violence against the violence of his unjust arrest, and questioning why the authorities use violence in secret when he taught openly in the temple.[144]

Meier argues at some length that Jesus's command to love enemies is one of his most original and distinctive claims, not anticipated, unlike the Golden Rule,[145] by anyone in either the religious or secular writings of the period.[146] Both his life and teaching illustrate how central nonviolence was to his teaching, which leads us finally to explore why the antipatriarchal Jesus is the way to understand not only him but the appeal of his life and teaching to so many, including the psychoanalyst Winnicott.

John Dominic Crossan on the Historical Jesus

Two of the scholars who were among the fellows of the Jesus Seminar have made the critique of patriarchy among the central claims they find

141. Coogan, *New Oxford Bible,* 1790, Matt 6:38–48.

142. See Luke 20:20–27.

143. Coogan, *New Oxford Bible,* 1812, Matt 21:21–29.

144. See Matt 26:47–57.

145. For his contrasting argument about the Golden Rule, see Meier, *Marginal Jew: Law and Love,* 551–57.

146. See Meier, *Marginal Jew: Law and Love,* 528–51.

in the historical Jesus, namely, John Dominic Crossan and Marcus J. Borg. One of them, Borg, has argued that "the emergence of feminist theology seems to me to be the single most important development in theology in my lifetime."[147] After I consider the work of Crossan (I will turn to discuss Borg's work in later chapters), I shall explore the contribution of feminist historians Borg has in mind, as it brings out the remarkable sensitivity to issues of gender of the historical Jesus.

In his three remarkable books on the historical Jesus,[148] Crossan affirms many of the findings of the Jesus Seminar. There is doubt, for example, whether Jesus could read or write; his genius was essentially oral in a tradition still large oral;[149] he did not speak of the kingdom to come, but of the kingdom coming to existence now through his life and teaching;[150] he explicitly objected to any precedence among his disciples, rejecting the model of "how those who supposedly rule over foreigners lord it over them, and how their strong men tyrannize them. 'It's not going to be like that with you! With you, whoever wants to become great must be your servant, and whoever among you wants to be 'number one' must be everybody's slave. After all, the son of Adam didn't come to be served, but to serve, even to give his life as a ransom for many'";[151] Jesus "engaged in some anti-temple act and made some statement against the temple, or against customary practices within its precincts";[152] Jesus's sayings and parables "cut against the social and religious grain," "they characteristically call for a reversal of roles or frustrate everyday expectations," and "are often characterized by exaggeration, humor, and paradox";[153] children are valued by Jesus in a way that points "to Jesus' dramatic reversal of the child's traditional status in ancient societies as a silent nonparticipant";[154] Jesus not only rejects his family (including his mother) who regard him as out of his mind,[155] but expressly calls for relationships that reject the family roles of father, mother, sister, brother, and the like, and his statement "I did not come to bring peace but a sword" is made to

147. Borg, *God We Never Knew*, 70.

148. Crossan, *Historical Jesus*; Crossan, *Jesus*; Crossan, *God and Empire*.

149. Funk and the Jesus Seminar, *Acts of Jesus*, 27.

150. Funk and the Jesus Seminar, *Acts of Jesus*, 40–41.

151. Funk and the Jesus Seminar, *Acts of Jesus*, 95.

152. Funk and the Jesus Seminar, *Acts of Jesus*, 67.

153. Funk and the Jesus Seminar, *Acts of Jesus*, 31.

154. Funk and the Jesus Seminar, *Acts of Jesus*, 89.

155. Funk and the Jesus Seminar, *Acts of Jesus*, 190.

illustrate how critical of the family his teaching is;[156] Jesus contrasts the asceticism of his teacher, John the Baptist, with the condemnation of him for living so differently: "'He is demented.' The son of Adam came both eating and drinking, and they saw, 'There's a glutton and a drunk, a crony of toll collectors and sinners'";[157] and Jesus, whose teaching calls for nonviolence, refers to John's prophetic message of repentance to prepare for God's rule as now "breaking in violently and violent men are attempting to gain it by force."[158]

But, for purposes of my own argument about the antipatriarchal Jesus, Crossan's works tower above other historians because he brings to his argument in these books about the historical Jesus precisely the interdisciplinary perspectives (for example, perspectives of historical anthropology, including the shame culture of both the Romans and Jews, as well as the views on illness and disease of the period) which contextually illuminate both why the life and teaching of Jesus had the broad popular appeal it had, in particular, for the often impoverished and exploited peasants who were largely his audience. For example, there can be no doubt that, as Meier has made clear at some length,[159] Jesus's healings were widely believed at the time to be marks of his miraculous powers, including exorcisms, healings of the paralyzed and the crippled, the blind, raising the dead, and the so-called nature miracles (for example, feeding of the multitude). And these healings or actions or the belief in them were enormously appealing to his audiences. To make sense of the force of such acts and beliefs Crossan appeals to the findings of historically informed medical anthropology and its findings that the work of shamans and others deal not with diseases, but with illnesses, and some of Jesus's healings and their appeal must be understood as dealing with illnesses that shamans and others cure.[160] There is also, of course, psychosomatic illness that psychoanalysis integrated with new knowledge in developmental biology and the neurosciences and biomedical sciences can and has addressed,[161] and, if I am right about Jesus's psychoanalytic powers (see next chapter), his very care for and empathy with those otherwise

156. Funk and the Jesus Seminar, *Acts of Jesus*, 173–74.

157. Funk and the Jesus Seminar, *Acts of Jesus*, 180.

158. Funk and the Jesus Seminar, *Acts of Jesus*, 179.

159. See Meier, *Marginal Jew: Mentor*, 509–1038.

160. See, on this point, Crossan, *Historical Jesus*, 336–37.

161. See, on this point, Taylor, "Psychoanalysis"; Aisenstein and de Aisenberg, *Psychosomatics*.

abandoned may have had similar curative powers, as an analysand may come through transference love to understand the dehumanizing traumas patriarchy has afflicted on her or him.

There is another quite salient feature of Jesus's life and teaching which bears on this matter. On Crossan's view, what was quite central to Jesus's quite original life and teaching were what he calls "open commensality,"[162] the willingness of Jesus to dine with anyone, violating all the constraints shame cultures (including Jewish culture) impose on such open dining. If such commensality was the central symbolic expression of Jesus's universalism instead of the Eucharist, in which later Christianities believed, the Jews questioning Jesus's authority in the Gospel of John would not have been as repelled as they apparently were when Jesus insists that salvation requires that they must "eat the flesh of the son of Man and drink his blood"[163] (Jewish dietary laws forbade the consumption of blood). In fact, the Gospel of John strikingly does not include the Eucharist in his narrative of the last supper that appears in the three Synoptic Gospels, but include Jesus washing the feet of his disciples, an expression of the equal discipleship that eschews master and servant. If I am right that the Gospel of John is often historically accurate, it would make open commensality the central symbol of Christianity, rather than the grisly Eucharist as Jesus poses it to the revolted Pharisees. What is, however, most striking is how Jesus answers the condemnation of such dining:

> And as he sat at dinner in the house, many tax collectors and sinners came and were sitting with him and his disciples. When the Pharisees saw this, they said to his disciples, "Why does your teacher eat with tax collectors and sinners?" but when he heard this he said, "Those who are well have no need of a physician, but those who are sick. Go and learn what this means. I desire mercy, not sacrifice. For I have come to call not the righteous but sinners."[164]

In understanding the role of healing in Jesus's life and teaching, we should take quite seriously his sense of himself as a physician, not a moral judge, and there is a revelatory exchange with the Pharisees when they query

162. Crossan, *Historical Jesus*, 261.

163. Coogan, *New Oxford Bible*, 1931, John 6:53–54.

164. Coogan, *New Oxford Bible*, 1795, Matt 9:19–14.

Jesus about a man born blind (whom Jesus cures) whom the Pharisees assumed must have:

> "sinned, this man or his parents, that he was born blind?" Jesus answered, "Neither this man nor his parents sinned; he was born blind so that God's works might be revealed in him. We must work the works of him who sent me while it is day, night is coming when no one can work."[165]

What makes this exchange revelatory is that it is the only place in the Gospels that Jesus quite expressly denies that the illnesses he cures reflect sin or even demonic possession, a recurrent charge made against Jesus himself. Jesus refuses to see himself as a moral judge, a view stated with great power in the central expression of his teaching, the Sermon on the Mount:

> Do not judge, so that you may not be judged. For with the judgment you make you will be judged, and the measure you give will be the measure you get. Why do you see the speck in your neighbor's eye, but do not notice the log in your own eye. Or how can you say to your neighbor, "Let me take the speck out of your eye." While the log is your own eye? You hypocrite, first take the log our of your own eye, and then you will see clearly to take the speck of your neighbor's eye.[166]

Jesus was quite clear that the audience of the Sermon on the Mount should "not think I have come to abolish the law or the prophets; I have come not to abolish but to fulfill."[167] And Jesus has no doubt about the content of our moral duties based on the Ten Commandments. When asked about this, his answer is unequivocal:

> Then someone came to him and said, "Teacher, what good deed must I do to have eternal life?" And he said to him, "Why do you ask me about what is good? There is only one who is good. If you wish to enter into life, keep the commandments." He said to him, "Which ones?" And Jesus said, "You shall not murder. You shall not commit adultery; You shall not steal; You shall not bear false witness. Honor your father and mother; also, You shall love your neighbor as yourself." The young man said to him, "I have kept all these, what do I still lack?" Jesus said to him, "If you

165. Coogan, *New Oxford Bible*, 1935, John 8:4–5.
166. Coogan, *New Oxford Bible*, 1792, Matt 7:1–6.
167. Coogan, *New Oxford Bible*, 1788, Matt 6:17–18.

> wish to be perfect, go sell your possessions, and give the money to poor, and you will have treasure in heaven; then come, follow me." When the young man heard this word, he went away grieving, for he had many possessions.[168]

What Jesus may have questioned in his exchange with the young man was what he clearly condemned in those who peacock their self-righteous compliance with the Ten Commandments:

> He also told them this parable to some who trusted in themselves that they were righteous and regarded others with contempt: "Two men went up to the temple to pray, one a Pharisee and the other a tax collector. The Pharisee, standing by himself, was praying thus, 'God, I thank you that I am not like other people: thieves, rogues, adulterers, and even like this tax collector. I fast twice a week; I give a tenth of all my income.' But the tax collector, standing far off, would not even look up to heaven, but was beating his breast and saying, 'God, be merciful to me, a sinner!' I tell you this man went down to his home justified rather than the other; for all who exalt themselves will be humbled, but all who humble themselves will be exalted."[169]

Wealth was in the context of the inequalities of wealth and status of this period so problematic for Jesus because it was associated with a self-righteous peacocking of the few wealthy and their contempt for the quite numerous poor (Jesus's primary audience), as the rather harrowing and starkly moving parable of the rich man illustrates:

> There was a rich man who was dressed in purple and fine linen and who feasted sumptuously every day. And at his gate lay a poor man named Lazarus, covered with sores, who longed to satisfy his hunger with what fell from the rich man's table, even the dogs would come and lick his sores. The poor man dies and was carried away by the angels to be with Abraham. The rich man also died and was buried. In Hades, where he was being tormented, he looked up and saw Abraham far away with Lazarus by his side. He called out, "Father Abraham, have mercy on me, and send Lazarus to dip the tip of his finger in water and cool my tongue; for I am in agony in these flames." But Abraham said, "Child, remember that during your lifetime you received you good things, and Lazarus in like manner evil things; but now he is comforted here, and you are in agony. Besides all this, between you and us a

168. Coogan, *New Oxford Bible*, 1810, Matt 19:16–23.

169. Coogan, *New Oxford Bible*, 1903, Luke 18:9–15.

> great chasm has been fixed, so that those who might want to pass from here to you cannot do so, and no one can cross from there to us." He said, "Then, father, I beg you to send him to my father's house—for I have five brothers—that he may warn them, so that they will not come into this place of torment." Abraham replies "They have Moses and the prophets; they should listen to them." He said, "No, father Abraham; but if someone goes to them from the dead, they will repent." He said to him, "If they do not listen to Moses and the prophets, neither will they be convinced even if someone rises from the dead."[170]

Jesus accepted the same Ten Commandments that the Pharisees and other Jews did, but his startling originality is in display in his many arguments with them throughout the Gospels about the proper interpretation of them, including even Jesus's denial that the teaching of Moses on divorce was any longer authoritative. These disagreements are most brilliantly posed in the Gospel of John when the Pharisees come back again and again to their collective pride as learned men in their interpretation of the Bible, "How does this man have such learning, when he has never been taught."[171] Jesus's response is always in terms of a moral individualism based on his relationship to God, a loving father, whom he calls "abba,"[172] an intimate term like "daddy." The ultimate basis of the Ten Commandments is, Jesus insists, in answering the scribes, the "first of all," the Love Commandments:

> Jesus answered, "The first is 'Hear, O Israel: the Lord our God, the Lord is one; you shall love the Lord your God with all your heart, and with all your soul, and with all your mind, and with all your strength.' The second is this, 'You shall love your neighbor as yourself.' There is no other commandment greater than these."[173]

As Meier observes,[174] the Love Commandments are taken from Deuteronomy and Leviticus, and are thus rooted in the Pentateuch, the Torah, itself. Jesus's appeal to love in his relationship to God the loving father is the ultimate basis of the ground for his disagreements with the Pharisees in the Gospel of John, who are so infuriated with him that they are moved to

170. Coogan, *New Oxford Bible,* 1900, Luke 16:19–31.
171. Coogan, *New Oxford Bible,* 1932, John 7:15–16.
172. Coogan, *New Oxford Bible,* 1858, Mark 14:36.
173. Coogan, *New Oxford Bible,* 1854, Mark 12:28–32.
174. See Meier, *Marginal Jew: Law and Love,* 488–99, 570–71.

stone him. Jesus, as a prophet in the Jewish tradition of prophets, speaks to and from God with an authority above that of both politicians and priests, which explains why the lives and teachings of prophets, including Jesus, infuriated both politicians and priests, leading often to their deaths.

The appeal directly to God by Jesus is thus quite conventional in the tradition of Jewish prophets, but there is a feature of both his life and prophetic teaching that, as Crossan observes, is quite original, his resistance to the shame culture not only of the Roman imperialists, but the shame culture Jesus condemned in what he argued was the misinterpretation of the Hebrew Bible by the Pharisees and others:

> Then Jesus said to the crowds and his disciples, "The scribes and the Pharisees sit on Moses' seat; therefore, do whatever they teach you and follow it; but do not do as they do, for they do not practice what they teach. They tie up heavy burdens, hard to bear, and lay them on the shoulders of others; but they themselves are unwilling to lift a finger to move them. They do all their deeds to be seen by others; for they make their phylacteries broad and their fringes long, and to be greeted with respect in the marketplaces, and to have people call them rabbi. But you are not to be called rabbi, for you have one teacher, and you are all students. And call no one your father on earth, but you have one Father, the one in heaven . . . All who exalt themselves will be humbled, and all who humble themselves will be exalted."[175]

As I suggested earlier in my discussion of the transition from shame to guilt cultures, the life and teaching of Jesus marks, like the teaching of Socrates and his student Plato, such a transition, and both of them (Jesus and Socrates), in resisting the patriarchal shame culture around them with its propensity to violence, are killed precisely because of their teaching centering on an emerging conception of reflective moral individualism both in religion (Jesus) and in philosophy (Socrates). In my discussion of the antipatriarchal Jesus in the next chapter, I will propose an understanding of both Jesus's life and teaching, including his view of the primacy of a relational love of persons (including the love of God for us, persons made in his image) in understanding ethics, that draws on psychoanalytic insights. Jesus is, like Socrates, a moral individualist, indeed inventing the idea of centering an ethical life in a conscience based in personal conviction, the moral foundation of the idea of inalienable human rights. But, in both the case of Jesus and Socrates, their views

175. Coogan, *New Oxford Bible*, 1816–1817, Matt 23:1–13.

developed always in interpersonal argument with others, as both the Platonic dialogues and the Gospels make quite clear, and resisting the dominant patriarchal values of the culture around them, including, in the case of Socrates, the ways in which the dominant shame culture had undermined the ethical legitimacy of democracy, which could not make a place for a voice, like his, critical of its mistakes.

In the case of Jesus, his resistance to the patriarchal values around him (both Roman and Jewish) takes a more radical form. Shame cultures, as we saw in our earlier discussion, arise from patriarchal conceptions of the honor of tribal groups, requiring hierarchies that, when challenged, elicit violence. As Carol Gilligan and I put in it our co-authored book, *The Deepening Darkness*, "[p]atriarchy is an anthropological term denoting families or societies ruled by fathers. It sets up a hierarchy—a rule of priests—in which the priest, the *hieros*, is a father, *pater.* As an order of living, it elevates some men over other men and all men over women; within the family, it separates fathers from sons (the men from the boys) and places women under a father's authority."[176] Jesus came to believe, beginning with his role as a disciple of John the Baptist and developing in his own ministry when he left John, that the Jewish tradition itself, perhaps imitating the success of Roman patriarchy in subjugating them, had become a dominantly shame culture of patriarchal priestly authority betraying the earlier resisting voices of the prophets, whom he took as models. His arguments with the Pharisees and others reveal, again and again, his view that "[t]hey do all their deeds to be seen by others," the mark of a shame culture, and it is through the priestly patriarchal authority they collectively exercise that they have betrayed the ethical core of Jesus's view of equality and his leading what Ernest Renan called an "exalted democratic movement,"[177] the Jesus movement.

What makes Jesus's life and teaching so antipatriarchal is that it challenges and resists the interpretation of the Jewish tradition by a patriarchal priesthood that shames any dissenter as an outcast and, precisely because patriarchal manhood is challenged, is humiliated by any resistance, and wrecks homicidal violence on his dissent. What is thus so ethically revolutionary in the Sermon on the Mount is that Jesus, as prophet, reinterprets all the commands of the Ten Commandments in an antipatriarchal way: the prohibition of murder becomes a prohibition of

176. Gilligan and Richards, *Deepening Darkness,* 22.

177. Quoted in Crossan, *Historical Jesus,* 265.

the role anger plays in patriarchal insults to manhood; the prohibition of adultery becomes a prohibition of lust for a married person; the allowance of divorce becomes a prohibition (presumably, because it enforces the patriarchal authority of men to divorce wives at will); the prohibition of swearing falsely becomes a prohibition of swearing itself; the endorsement of the lex talionis of retributive justice becomes not resisting an evildoer; loving your friends and hating your enemies becomes loving your enemies; practicing piety becomes not doing so in public; giving alms, not trumpeting publicly one's virtue; praying but not as hypocrite; praying in the terms of the Lord's prayer forgiving trespasses against one; whenever fasting, to not look dismal and to keep it secret "so that your fasting may be seen not by others but by your Father who is in secret; and your Father will reward you."[178] These antitheses, as they are called, call for an ethical inwardness based in a guilt arising from hurting others one loves, the second of the Love Commandments, a guilt that is universal in its scope. It was, for Jesus, all the better, more compelling if actions motivated by love and guilt were private, even "secret," not playing, as shame does, to a collective patriarchal tribal audience.

The antitheses are in their nature, in claiming to "fulfill" the law, in fact a probing attack on and inversion of the psychology of patriarchy. Patriarchy requires rigid gender roles of manhood and womanhood governing both public and private life held in place by a shaming of patriarchal manhood that calls for and indeed celebrates violence in war, as we earlier saw in the Roman imperialistic wars that led to the collapse of the Roman Republic and establishment of the Roman Empire under an autocratic emperor, Caesar (all Roman emperors were given this name). Any insult to one's patriarchal manhood elicits violence, and the antitheses condemning anger as a response to insult, retribution in dealing with perceived evil doers, as well as hating enemies invert what patriarchal manhood requires, calling for lenity, as well as not resisting and loving enemies. Woman under patriarchy do not exist as persons, but in roles that advance patriarchal aims of supporting and indeed rearing patriarchal men, including their virginity before and their fidelity in marriage. In contrast, men enjoy a sexual freedom both before and in marriage that is shocking in women. Jesus's concern with limiting divorce arises, I believe, from limiting the degree to which predatory husbands abandon

178. Coogan, *New Oxford Bible*, 1791, Matt 6:18–19.

them on a whim. And, as we shall shortly see, Jesus treats women in a remarkably antipatriarchal way.

One of the most important and quite credible claims Crossan makes about Jesus is that his very conception of the kingdom of God was directed against the Roman Empire's conception of the divinity of its emperors.[179] It was Jesus's point, as a prophet speaking to and from God, that no patriarchal priesthood could have ethical authority when, as Jesus showed in his arguments with them, they had demonstrably flawed interpretations of their own tradition. The same point applies *a fortiori* against the Roman patriarchy that rationalized its violent imperialism under the empire in terms of the divinity of the emperor as a god. Jesus's life and teaching fundamentally contested that conception, and he apparently died for it (the Romans quite misunderstanding his teaching about nonviolent democratic equality, compulsively *insisting* any authority he claimed must be patriarchal, claiming to be a king of the Jews, thus challenging the autocratic authority of the only king Romans patriarchally accepted, the god-king emperor—for the Romans, treason).

There are other equally striking antipatriarchal features of the life and teaching of Jesus, some of which I will explore in the next chapter, in particular, his attacks on the whole structure of the family, calling for his followers to leave their families, and indeed abandon the roles of family life:

> Do not think that I have come to bring peace to the earth; I have not come to bring peace, but a sword.
> For I have come to set a man against his father,
> and a daughter against her mother,
> and a daughter-in-law against her mother-in-law;
> and one's foes will be members of one's own household
> Whoever loves father or mother more than me is not worthy of me; and whoever loves son or daughter more than me is not worthy of me . . .[180]

And, there is the deep interest of his ministry, as a self-proclaimed physician, in care and even cure for the sick and maimed, and his love for outcasts like tax collectors and prostitutes and others, and his remarkable interest not only in children, but in infants, an interest I will explore in the next chapter.

179. See, in particular, Crossan, *God and Empire*, Crossan, *Jesus Against Rome.*

180. Coogan, *New Oxford Bible*, 1797, Matt 10:34–36.

Elisabeth Schüssler Fiorenza on the Historical Jesus

We come finally to Jesus's treatment of women, and Borg's claim that "the emergence of feminist theology seems to me to be the single most important development in theology in my lifetime."[181]

Borg has in mind the relatively recent works on the historical Jesus by Rosemary Radford Ruether[182] and Elisabeth Schüssler Fiorenza,[183] anticipated by the somewhat earlier works of Mary Daly.[184] Rosemary Ruether, in particular, not only contributed to feminist theology, but authored as well her quite brilliant and transformative *Faith and Fratricide: The Theological Roots of Anti-Semitism*, the best study to date of the roots of anti-Semitism both in the New Testament and in the thought of early Christian theologians.[185] Nineteenth-century feminists also pioneered much earlier attempts to interpret the Bible as indicting both racism and sexism in ways that anticipate more contemporary work (notably, the Grimke sisters, Angelina and, in particular, Sarah[186]) and in the leading nineteenth-century feminist Elizabeth Cady Stanton's *The Woman's Bible*,[187] indicting the Bible itself on independent ethical grounds. Her bible was published in 1895 and 1898, a book so shocking to women in the suffrage movement that, over the objections of Susan B. Anthony, it was repudiated in 1896 by the National-American Woman Suffrage Association. Stanton confesses that she had tried to get Greek and Hebrew scholars to participate in her study of the Bible but "they are afraid that their high reputations and scholarly attainments might be compromised by taking part in an enterprise that for a time may prove unpopular."[188] Her own view is "that I do not believe that any man ever saw or talked with God,"[189] and accepts only those teachings that comport with her own ethical views, for example, "the wisdom of the golden rule and the fifth

181. Borg, *God We Never Knew*, 70.

182. See Ruether, *Sexism*.

183. See Schüssler Fiorenza, *In Memory of Her*; Schüssler Fiorenza, *Searching the Scriptures: Feminist Introduction*; Schüssler Fiorenza, *Searching the Scriptures: Feminist Commentary*; Schüssler Fiorenza, *Discipleship*; Schüssler Fiorenza, *Congress*.

184. Daly, *Church*; *Beyond God the Father*.

185. Ruether, *Faith and Fratricide*.

186. See, for fuller discussion, Richards, *Women, Gays*, 81–124.

187. See Stanton, *Woman's Bible*.

188. Stanton, *Woman's Bible*, 4.

189. Stanton, *Woman's Bible*, 6.

commandment"[190] (honor thy father and mother). One wonders what she would have made of recent historical feminist work, to be shortly discussed, on Jesus's repudiation of the patriarchal family.

These recent historically minded scholars have all the relevant languages that their nineteenth-century sisters had, but, unlike them, bring their training powerfully and collaboratively to bear on the search for the historical Jesus with the same integrity as the Jesus Seminar and Meier. The best of their work has, however, added something revelatory to the work of scholars of the historical Jesus, who in the light of the role Christian anti-Semitism played in the writing of the Gospels, have framed the search for the historical Jesus to free it of the hatred of the Jews that Jesus, a Jew, could not and would not have endorsed. Certainly, some of these scholars have, for example, discussed Jesus's indictment of the patriarchal family (Crossan[191]) and the role of women not only among his followers but as disciples (Meier[192]). But, the feminist scholars have introduced into the search for the historical Jesus an interpretive framework that moves beyond the focus on anti-Semitism in the formation of the Gospels to the role of misogyny. To this extent, their work deepens the understanding of the prominence Crossan and others found in the role resistance to patriarchy plays in the life and teaching of the historical Jesus because, as we have seen, the very definition of patriarchy uses gender in its mandate of hierarchy: "[p]atriarchy is an anthropological term denoting families or societies ruled by fathers. It sets up a hierarchy—a rule of priests—in which the priest, the *hieros*, is a father, *pater.* As an order of living, it elevates some men over other men and all men over women; within the family, it separates fathers from sons (the men from the boys) and places women under a father's authority."[193] Accordingly, an interpretive lens that takes seriously both the anti-Semitism and misogyny of the Gospel writers deepens our understanding of the antipatriarchal Jesus, as I will now try to show, drawing on the work of the contemporary feminist scholars referenced earlier.

Elisabeth Schüssler Fiorenza has articulated the dimensions of the problem in rethinking the role of misogyny in the Christianities after Jesus both in the Gospels themselves and later works based allegedly on

190. Stanton, *Woman's Bible,* 7. For an illuminating discussion of Stanton's work on *The Woman's Bible*, see Gifford, "Politicizing," 52–63.

191. See Crossan, *Historical Jesus,* 299–302.

192. See Meier, *Marginal Jew: Companions,* 73–81, 248.

193. Gilligan and Richards, *Deepening Darkness,* 22.

the historical Jesus in pointing to perhaps the best historical study of Christianities after Jesus, Ernst Troeltsch's monumental *Social Teaching of the Christian Churches.*[194] Troeltsch ascribes the views on sexuality and gender of Christianities, both in the Catholic and Protestant traditions, to its "grotesque exaltation of sexual restraints" leading to "well-known ideas about the danger inherent in the female sex."[195] And he ascribes the problem to the uncritical "conception of the Patriarchalism of love,"[196] an idea quite foreign to the life and teachings of the historical Jesus, including, as Schüssler Fiorenza points out, Jesus's women disciples in general, the central importance of Mary Magdalene among them, and the prominence of women in the Gospel of John,[197] as well as Jesus's quite clear critique of patriarchal marriage, the hostility to him of his own family, and the stark instruction to his own disciples, that, in her historically informed view of the original text, reads:

> Call no one father
> For you have one father
> (and you are all siblings).[198]

By interpreting the Gospels in this and other ways, Schüssler Fiorenza calls for a new paradigm for the historical search for Jesus, one not only free of the interpretive lens of anti-Semitism but of the lens of the patriarchal conception of gender. What makes her argument for this new paradigm so compelling is that it brings out how foreign to the historical Jesus is both anti-Semitism and misogyny and, as we shall now see, homophobia.

In her important book, *Love Between Women,*[199] Bernadette Brooten shows, for example, that the Pauline homophobia of the Christian tradition reflects nothing in the remarkably antipatriarchal life and teaching of the historical Jesus, but rather sexist conceptions of gender roles that Paul and others uncritically parrot in their virulent screeds against lesbians and homosexuality more generally. Brooten shows, for example,

194. See Troeltsch, *Social Teaching.* For Elisabeth Schüssler Fiorenza's discussion of Troeltsch, see Schüssler Fiorenza, *Memory of Her,* 75, 78–79.

195. Troeltsch, *Social Teaching,* 1:131.

196. Troeltsch, *Social Teaching,* 1:285.

197. See, on this point, Fiorenza, *In Memory of Her,* 315–33.

198. Schüssler Fiorenza, *In Memory of Her,* 150. Schüssler Fiorenza's interpretive argument is of Matt 23:8–10.

199. Brooten, *Love Between Women.*

that homophobic arguments in Paul essentially assume as authoritative and depend on the gendered codes of honor of the patriarchal culture around him and was, given the dominance in the development of Christianities of Paul's mission to the gentiles, his main audience. It is, as we have seen, a feature of patriarchy that deviation from prescribed gender roles by men shames men, but deviation by women also brings shame on men (adultery is the high crime and misdemeanor of patriarchy because women break out of their prescribed role as wives and fall in love). Paul's homophobia thus parrots the patriarchal conceptions of women in the cultures that were his audience, and it is because lesbians—or, for that matter, any women—do not conform to those roles (for example, not obeying the commands of their patriarchal husbands or, as slaves, their masters) and thus shame men that he condemns them. As we saw earlier in our discussion of shame and guilt cultures, this development in Christianities illustrates what was to become unfortunately dominant in the inquisitions and wars and violent anti-Semitism of later Christianities, the regression from a guilt to a shame culture. None of it has anything to do with the historical Jesus of Nazareth.

Jesus's teaching limiting divorce, challenging the view of Moses, is justified by him because men "were so hard hearted," and his disciples then suggest "it is better not to marry." Jesus does not accept this view. Rather,

> he said to them, "Not everyone can accept this teaching, but only those to whom it is given. For there are eunuchs who have been so from birth, and there are eunuchs who have made eunuchs by others, and there are eunuchs for the sake of the kingdom of heaven. Let anyone accept this who can."[200]

Meier regards Jesus as "a male celibate,"[201] and notes that Jesus, as a prophet, may be following the celibacy of some of the prophets, for example, Jeremiah.[202] The idea appears to be that a prophet, speaking from and to God, was bound in an exclusive love. But, in light of Jesus's critique of the family as such, he may have thought sexuality in patriarchal marriage was itself not unproblematic. The fact that he responds, when Sadducees attempt to tangle him in contradiction over who would be the wife of seven brothers at the resurrection, by denying marriage would exist at the resurrection, suggests patriarchal marriage is no longer required when

200. Coogan, *New Oxford Bible,* 1810, Matt 19:6–13.

201. Meier, *Marginal Jew: Companions,* 621.

202. Meier, *Marginal Jew: Companions,* 622. See also 504–5, 507, 621–22.

God's love is directly available, which would not be an issue at the time of the resurrection when we would be released from patriarchy. At no point, unlike Paul, does he reject marriage as such, but makes attempts better to protect women from divorce without cause from wayward husbands. And his view of those eunuchs "who have been so from birth" certainly would encompass homosexuals. Schweitzer, we earlier saw, embraces the idea, regarding homosexuals as one among those unjustly denigrated, whom Jesus would embrace among the other outcasts he embraced. Jesus's discussion of eunuchs confirms this reading.

Jesus not only apparently dined with prostitutes, but, though he clearly regarded adultery as condemned by the Ten Commandments, took a very different view of the ways shame cultures violently attacked adulterers, for example, by stoning. The parable of the woman taken in adultery is illustrative and worth taking quite seriously:

> The scribes and pharisees brought to him a woman who had been caught in adultery, and making her stand before all of them, they said to him, "Teacher, this woman was caught in the very act of committing adultery. Now in the law Moses commanded us to stone such women. Now what do you say?" They said this to test him, so that they might have some charge to bring against him. Jesus bent does and wrote with his finger on the ground. When they kept on questioning him, he straightened up and said to them, "Let anyone among you who is without sin be the first to throw a stone at her." And once again he bent down and wrote on the ground. When they heard it, they went away, one by one, beginning with the elders, and Jesus was left alone with the woman standing before him. Jesus straightened up and said to her. "Women, where are they? Has no one condemned you?" She said, "No one, sir." And Jesus said, "Neither do I condemn you. Go your way, and from now on do not sin again."[203]

Jesus in the Sermon the Mount had endorsed the Ten Commandments, including the commandment condemning adultery, but he also cautioned about hypocritical moral condemnation based on the failure to reflect on one's own competence to apply to oneself the standards one applied to others. The parable of the adulterous woman clearly regards stoning for adultery as violating this ethical standard, and, implicitly, the shame culture that rationalized such political violence. The appeal to apply standards to themselves elicits from the men a sense of guilt, marking

203. Coogan, *New Oxford Bible*, 1933–34, John 8:3–12.

Jesus's role as a crucial figure in the development of a guilt culture based on individual moral responsibility and culpability from a shame culture, based on tribal patriarchal violence.

The woman taken in adultery is silent, and clearly brought into public to shame her, and speaks only briefly in her own voice in response to Jesus's query of what had happened to her accusers. There is, however, an earlier narrative in the Gospel of John that even more powerfully illustrates how antipatriarchal Jesus was when relating directly to women; it also illustrates, as I will argue in the next chapter, how exactly Jesus works as a physician, perhaps even, as Winnicott believed, a psychotherapist. The narrative, Jesus talking to a Samaritan women at a well (John 4:4–30) is illustrative on two counts: that the interlocutor is not a Jew but a Samaritan, for whom Jews had contempt; and that Jesus not only speaks with but listens to the woman, interprets her plight in a way that surprises even her, and indeed brings her to believe in him and his message.

On the first point, there is no doubt that Jesus thought of both his life and thought as directed at Jews, not gentiles, referring to the latter in an exchange with a gentile women who asks that he cure her little daughter possessed by an unclean spirit as "dogs."[204] Jesus, however, characteristically listens to her rebuke ("Sir, even the dogs under the table eat the children's crumbs"[205]), and, moved by her rebuke, cures her daughter. And the quite moving parable of the Good Samaritan, in which answering to the query, "And who is my neighbor?"[206] Jesus clearly responds that the response of a non-Jew (a Samaritan), "moved by pity,"[207] caring for a man robbed and stripped and paying for an innkeeper to care for him, was, in contrast to two Jews who passed by, the real neighbor because moved by mercy for the robbed man. The others pass by, feeling nothing for such unjust suffering.

It is, however, illustrative of the antipatriarchal relationship of Jesus to women that he even talks to a woman, let alone a Samaritan woman, in the way he does—listening to and interpreting her responses in the way he does (more on this in the next chapter). The narrative is as follows:

> Jacob's well was there, and Jesus, tired out by his journey, was sitting by the well. It was about noon.

204. Coogan, *New Oxford Bible*, 1844, Mark 8:27.
205. Coogan, *New Oxford Bible*, 1844, Mark 8:28.
206. Coogan, *New Oxford Bible*, 1889, Luke 10:29.
207. Coogan, *New Oxford Bible*, 1889–90, Luke 10:23.

A Samaritan woman came to draw water, and Jesus said to her. "Give me a drink." (His disciples had gone to the city to buy food.) The Samaritan woman said to him, "How is it that you, a Jew, ask a drink of me, a woman of Samaria?" (Jews do not share things in common with Samaritans.) Jesus answered her, "If you knew the gift of God, and who it is that is saying to you, 'Give me a drink,' You would have asked him, and he would have given you living water." The woman said to him, "Sir, you have no bucket, and the well is deep. Where do you get that living water? Are you greater than our ancestor Jacob, who gave us the well, and with his sons and his flocks drank from it?" Jesus said to her, "Everyone who drinks of this water will be thirsty again, but those who drink of the water that I will give them will never be thirsty, but those who drink of the water that I will give them will never be thirsty. The water that I will give them will become in them a spring of water gushing up to eternal life." The woman said to him, "Sir, give me this water, so that I may never be thirsty or have to keep coming her to draw water."

Jesus said to her, "Go, call your husband, and come back." The woman answered him, "I have no husband." Jesus said to her "You are right in saying, 'I have no husband'; for you have had five husbands, and one you have now is not your husband. What you say is true!" The woman said to him. "Sir, I see that you are a prophet. Our ancestors worshiped on this mountain, but you say that the place where people must worship is in Jerusalem." Jesus said to her, "Woman, believe me, the hour is coming when you will worship the Father neither on this mountain nor in Jerusalem. You worship what you do not know; we worship what we know, for salvation is from the Jews. But the hour is coming, and is now, here, when the true worshipers will worship the Father in spirit and truth, for the Father seeks such as these to worship him. God is spirit, and those who worship him must worship in spirit and truth." The woman said to him, "I know the Messiah is coming" (who is called Christ). "When he comes, he will proclaim all things to us." Jesus said to her, "I am he," the one who is speaking to you.

Just then his disciples came. They were astonished that he was speaking with a woman, but no one said, "What do you want?" or, "Why are you speaking with her?" Then the woman left her water and went back to the city. She said to the people, "Come and see a man who told me everything I have ever done!

> He cannot be the Messiah, can he?" They left the city and were on their way to him.[208]

It is equally striking how Jesus speaks and listens to Jewish women, bound, as they are, to patriarchal roles in both family and religious life. He has no problem dealing with uniquely female suffering, for example, "a woman who had been suffering from hemorrhages for twelve years,"[209] whose trust in him leads to cure. And, in his exchange with the sisters Mary and Martha, he defends Mary's listening to Jesus against Martha's more conventional understanding of a woman's role:

> Now as they were on their way, he entered a certain village, where a woman named Martha welcomed him into her home. She had a sister named Mary, who sat at the Lord's feet and listened to what he was saying. But Martha was distracted by her many tasks, so she came to him and asked, "Lord, do you not care that my sister has left me to do all the work by myself? Tell her then to help me." But the Lord answered her. "Martha, Martha, you are worried and distracted by many things; there is need of only one thing. Mary has chosen the better part, which will not be taken away from her."[210]

The historical work of Elisabeth Schüssler Fiorenza and the scholars who have elaborated her perspective have brought to bear on the interpretation of the Gospels an antipatriarchal lens, found also in Crossan and others, but now centered on the role gender plays in upholding patriarchal hierarchies: patriarchy "is an order of living, it elevates some men over other men and all men over women; within the family, it separates fathers from sons (the men from the boys) and places women under a father's authority."[211] Bringing this lens to bear on the interpretation of the Gospels leads to extensive and often revelatory discussions of the whole range of places in the Gospels where the antipatriarchal Jesus relates to women in ways patriarchy forbids.[212] We have already discussed several of them, but several others are worth discussion here.

208. Coogan, *New Oxford Bible*, 1926, John 4:6–31.

209. Coogan, *New Oxford Bible*, 1838, Mark 5:25–26.

210. Coogan, *New Oxford Bible*, 1890, Luke 10:38–42.

211. Gilligan and Richards, *Deepening Darkness*, 22.

212. See Schüssler Fiorenza, *In Memory of Her*; Schüssler Fiorenza, *Searching the Scriptures: Feminist Introduction*; Schüssler Fiorenza, *Searching the Scriptures: Feminist Commentary*.

There is a scene in all four Gospels in which a woman, clearly devoted to Jesus, anoints with a precious substance either his head (Mark 14:3; Matt 26:7) or his feet (Luke 7:36–50; John 12:1–8) which Jesus accepts with gratitude and to which others (probably men) object. There are two defenses of her by Jesus that are particularly striking. In the one when they object that the costly ointment could have been sold and the money given to the poor, Jesus responds:

> [Y]ou always have the poor with you, and you can show kindness to them whenever you wish; but you will not always have me. She has done what she could; and she has anointed my body beforehand for its burial. Truly, I tell you, wherever the good news is proclaimed in the whole world, what she has done will be told in remembrance of her.[213]

The other response in a narrative where the woman is a sinner and the Pharisee to whose house he has been invited for dinner objects because of her having sinned and because of her emotional outburst and overwrought anointing of Jesus's feet:

> And a woman of the city, who was a sinner, having learned that he was eating in the Pharisee's house, brought an alabaster jar of anointment. She stood behind him at his feet, weeping, and began to bathe his feet with her tears and to dry them with her hair and anointing them with ointment. Now when the Pharisee who had invited him saw it, he said to himself. "If this man were a prophet, he would have known who and what kind of woman this is who is touching him—that she is a sinner." Jesus spoke up and said to him, "Simon, I have something to say to you." "Teacher," he replied, "speak." "A certain creditor had two debtors; one owed three hundred denarii, and the other fifty. When they could not pay, he canceled the debts of both of them. Now which of them did he love more?" "I suppose the one for whom he canceled the greater debt." And Jesus said to him, "You have judged right." Then turning toward the woman, he said to Simon, "Do you see this woman? I entered your house; you gave me no water for my feet, but she has bathed my feet with her tears and dried them with her hair. Therefore, I tell you, her sins, which were many, have been forgiven; hence she has shown great love. But the one to whom little is forgiven, loves little." Then he said to her, "Your sins are forgiven." But those who were at the table with him began to say among themselves, "Who is

213. Coogan, *New Oxford Bible*, 1857, Mark 14:7–10.

> this who even forgives sins?" And he said to the woman, "your faith has saved you: go in peace."[214]

Forgiveness of sinners is one of the most striking features of both Jesus's life and teaching, and one neither understood nor valued by the patriarchal men who, in the Gospel of John, are moved to stone him, as they would have stoned the woman taken in adultery. Such forgiveness is called for not only for women but for men, as in perhaps the most well-known of his parables, the prodigal son, in Luke 15:11–32. The antipatriarchal lens Jesus brings to his life and teaching is thus in play not only in his treatment of women whom patriarchal culture condemned even unto stoning when they deviate from their patriarchal gender roles, but also for men who, as the Sermon on the Mount tells us, are locked into patriarchal roles requiring violence or even self-destructive predatory narcissism, as in the prodigal son.

His relationship to Mary Magdala or Mary Magdalene stands out among his other relationships to women. The Gospels distinguish her from the "disciples," but she enters the narrative in connection with them, her cure by Jesus, and her presence with the disciples among his followers:

> [H]e went on through the cities and villages, proclaiming and bringing the good news of the kingdom. The twelve were with him, as well as some women who had been cured of evil spirits and infirmities. Mary, called Magdalene, from whom seven demons had gone out, and Joanna, the wife of Herod's steward Chuza, and Susanna, and many others, who provided for them out of their own resources.[215]

Meier observes:

> If Jesus' hobnobbing with tax collectors and sinners upset the stringently pious, Jesus' traveling entourage of women followers, notably Mary Magdalene, probably disturbed them even more—especially some, if not all, of the women apparently followed Jesus without benefit of husbands or chaperones.[216]

214. Coogan, *New Oxford Bible*, 1881–82, Luke 8:37–50.

215. Coogan, *New Oxford Bible*, 1882, Luke 8:1–4.

216. Meier, *Marginal Jew: Companions*, 247.

Meier, after carefully reviewing the evidence,[217] concludes, of Mary Magdalene and the other women followers of Jesus, "the most probable conclusion is that Jesus viewed and treated these women as disciples."[218]

But, if Mary Magdalene should be regarded as a disciple of the historical Jesus, her loving devotion is of a qualitatively different order from the other disciples, who often do not understand him and abandon him at the time of the crucifixion, terrified by what happened to him and undoubtedly what might happen to them (in fact, as with the death of John the Baptist, followers are not punished, suggesting that the fear of the authorities of both John the Baptist and Jesus, both nonviolent, extended only to the leaders, whose criticism of them was the object of their homicidal fury). It is surely notable that, at the depiction of the scene of the crucifixion in the three Synoptic Gospels, only Mary Magdalene and a few other women are mentioned, not Mary, his mother; Mary the mother of Jesus appears with the disciple John as well as these women at the crucifixion only in the Gospel of John. And even in this Gospel, at the wedding at Cana, Jesus refers to her when she points out there is no wine in a way that hardly suggests intimacy: "Woman, what concern is that to you and to me?"[219] And there is, as we have already noted, the hostility of his family, including his mother, to his ministry, their attempts to stop him, and his refusal to meet with them, observing that only his disciples now have a call on him:

> Then his mother and his brothers came; and standing outside, they sent to him and called him. A crowd was sitting around them, and they said to him, "Your mothers and your brother and sisters are outside, asking for you." And he replied, "Who are my mother and my brothers?" And looking at those who sat around him, he said, "Here are my mothers and my brothers! Whoever does the will of God is my brother and sister and mother."[220]

The idealization of Mary is very much part of the Catholic tradition among Christianities,[221] but appears in the Gospel of Luke, in his unhistorical birth narrative and attempt to connect Jesus to biblical messianic

217. Meier, *Marginal Jew: Companions*, 73–80.

218. Meier, *Marginal Jew: Companions*, 80.

219. Coogan, *New Oxford Bible*, 1922.

220. Coogan, *New Oxford Bible*, 1835, Mark 3:21–35.

221. See, for fuller discussion, Warner, *Alone*.

prophecy of a virgin birth and his setting of Mary's Magnificat in Luke 1:46–56, the subject of musical masterpieces by Monteverdi and Bach. It may be that the gay writer, Colm Toibin, affords a more historically accurate portrayal of Mary in his *The Testament of Mary*, a mother appalled by what happens to her son, but early struck that "he could look at a woman as though she were his equal, and he was grateful, good-mannered, intelligent."[222]

But it is Mary Magdalene who not only was a longstanding disciple of Jesus but, in contrast to his male disciples, neither betrays (as Peter does three times) nor abandons him—not only present at the crucifixion but the crucial figure in the rather starkly terrifying Gospel of Mark, but who goes with other women to the now empty tomb. In one version,

> as they entered the tomb, they saw a young man, dressed in a white robe, sitting on the right side; and they were alarmed. But he said to them, "Do not be alarmed; you are looking for Jesus of Nazareth, who was crucified. He has been raised; here is not here. Look, there is the place they laid. But go, tell his disciples and Peter that he is going ahead of you to Galilee; there you will see him, just as he told you."[223]

In another even starker version:

> Now after he rose early on the first day of the week, he appeared first to Mary Magdalen, from whom he had cast out seven demons. She went out and told those who had been with him, while they were mourning and weeping. But when they heard that he was alive and had been seen by her, they would not believe it.

After this he appeared in another form to two of them, as they were walking into the country. And they went back and told the rest, but they did not believe him.

> Later he appeared to the eleven themselves as they were sitting at the table; and he upbraided them for their lack of faith and stubbornness, because they had not believed those who saw him after he had risen.[224]

222. Toibin, *Testament of Mary*, 6.
223. Coogan, *New Oxford Bible*, 1862, Mark 16:5–8.
224. Coogan, *New Oxford Bible*, 1863, Mark 16:9–14.

Strikingly, in another version Mary Magdalene does not recognize Jesus when he appears to her after the resurrection, in John:20:14. He no longer appears as he did, and Mary assumes he is a gardener, and weeps, begging help to find the body of Jesus. He responds:

> Jesus said to her, "Mary!" She turns and said to him in Hebrew, "Rabbouni!" (which means Teacher). Jesus said to her, "Do not hold on to me, because I have not yet ascended to the father. But go to my brothers and say to them, 'I am ascending to my Father and your Father, to my God and your God.'" Mary Magdalene went and announced to the disciples. "I have seen the Lord"; and she told them that he said these things to her.[225]

In all these versions, it is Mary Magdalen who first believes in the resurrection. The very idea of the resurrection, so central to Christianities, arises from her experience of a man she deeply loved, and her experience of how such traumatic loss might, consistent with his life and teaching of love, be redeemed. It we take seriously what the historical Jesus tells us in defending the love of women for him (the woman, for example, who anoints him), and defends her because, in contrast to the men who condemn them, "she has shown great love," we need better to understand why, as Fiorenza puts it, "The woman-identified man, Jesus, called forth a discipleship of equals that still needs to be discovered by women and men today."[226] It is the love of Mary Magdalen for Jesus, a man who may have loved her as an equal in a way she had never experienced love and thus brought her to a new transformative understanding of love's redemptive curative power over patriarchal idealization, denigration, and despair, that refuses to accept that such love could or should ever be lost or destroyed, but held tenaciously as a deep and universal truth of human psychology that redeems us from a dehumanizing despair and thus sustains life itself. Here, Mary is not

> the fallen woman lifted up to be closest to Christ, a stereotype of medieval iconography and devotion. Rather, Mary is the first witness to the Jesus event, to the Resurrection, the one who brings the news to the apostles, the apostle to the apostles. She is equal to Peter and the apostles and, if one hearkens to

225. Coogan, *New Oxford Bible*, 1951–52, John 20:16–19.

226. Schüssler Fiorenza, *In Memory of Her*, 154.

> the non-canonical gospels found at Nag Hammadi in Egypt in 1945, she may indeed enjoy the highest status of all Christ's followers.[227]

Indeed, the gnostic Gospel of Mary among these non-canonical Gospels may be closer to the enduring significance of Mary's refusal to believe that Jesus and his teaching were dead, namely, that the resurrection, "was not a unique event in the past," but "symbolized how Christ's presence could be experienced in the present. . . . What mattered was not literal seeing, but spiritual vision."[228] In chapter 8, we shall consider whether a psychoanalytic understanding of Jesus's life and teaching may offer along these lines, as Elaine Pagels has suggested based on the gnostic Gospels, a better because more psychoanalytic understanding of the continuing appeal and value of the antipatriarchal Jesus.[229]

Why women? In the Gospel of John, an answer is suggested: Jesus, appealing to the experience of women and women alone, explains to his disciples as he faces his death how terrible pain like the traumatic loss of a beloved man and loving prophet like Jesus should be understood:

> When a woman is in labor, she has pain, because her hour has come. But when the child is born, she no longer remembers the anguish because of the joy of having a human being in the world.[230]

The antipatriarchal Jesus arises from his antipatriarchal relationships to both women and men, and we know the response of his audiences to his teaching:

> They were astounded at his teaching, for he taught them as one having authority, but not as the scribes.[231]

It was essentially an oral teaching, based on the interpretation of Jewish scriptures but contesting how the scribes and pharisees interpreted them, challenging his audiences: "And why do you not judge for yourselves what is right?"[232] Both his life and teaching clearly moved men and women, but, at the end, women did not betray him, and those like Mary Magdalen,

227. Critchley, *Mysticism*, 279–80.
228. Pagels, *Gnostic Gospels*, 11.
229. Pagels, *Gnostic Gospels*, 122–41.
230. Coogan, *New Oxford Bible*, 1946, John 12:21–22.
231. Coogan, *New Oxford Bible*, 1831, Mark 1:22–23.
232. Coogan, *New Oxford Bible*, 1895, Luke 12:57–58.

cured by his teaching, saw something both in his life and teaching men did not, something truer to human psychology.

I have learned much from the search for the historical Jesus we have now discussed at some length. But, there is, I think, something missing, something about both the life and teaching of Jesus of Nazareth that modern developments in psychology in general and psychoanalysis in particular help us to understand.

3

The Antipatriarchal Jesus

In the Introduction, I explained the project for this book as trying to understand what the most important psychoanalyst after Freud, D. W. Winnicott, could have meant in a letter to his sister at the beginning of his interest in psychoanalysis:

> I shall probably be accused if I say that Christ was a leading psychotherapist (I don't know why, but Violet is fond of saying that what I saw is blasphemy, when there is no connection whatever between what I have said and the term). It is not less true that extreme acts and religious rituals and obsessions are an exact counterpart of these mind disorders, and by psychotherapy, many fanatics or extremists in religion can be brought (if treated early) to a real understanding of religion and its use in setting a high ethical standard.[1]

And why did Winnicott, in a letter to the psychoanalyst Bion, write:

> I, like you, was brought up in the Christian tradition (Wesleyan) and I have no desire to throw away all that I listened to over and over again and tried to digest and sort out.
>
> It is not possible for me to throw away religion just because the people who organize the religions of the world insist on belief in miracles. What I wanted to know is, have you met with the amazing book by Robert Graves and his friend Joshua

1. Winnicott, "Letter to His Sister," 55.

> Podro, called the Nazarene Gospel Restored? It is not possible to buy this book but it is in most of the libraries. Naturally it is frowned upon by all the Christian churches because it deals with the reconstruction of the Jesus which was current but not much recorded before an attempt was made to get accepted records somewhere in the first and second centuries. In other words, by a tremendous amount of erudition and research these authors have been able to make a reconstruction of the original story, and I find a study of this book absolutely fascinating and very important for the understanding of the Bible story that we came to know so well. I wish I could buy a copy of this book, and send it to you but unfortunately it is out of print.[2]

The book's exploration of the search for the historical Jesus arose from Winnicott's excitement about the Graves and Podro book, and we have now seen that Winnicott was clearly right that the search for the historical Jesus enabled us better to understand what is true and what is false in the Gospels, at least as understood by the best historians of the historical Jesus. Certainly, Winnicott was correct in disengaging the historical Jesus from what Paul and Peter made of him and their crucial roles in the development of Christianities. But, Graves and Podro cannot be relied on in the ways they regard Jesus as essentially and only a Pharisee, as the anointed king of Israel tied lineally to David, and as a person who survived the crucifixion. But once we see the historical Jesus freed from these erroneous historical assumptions, we discover something Graves and Prodro do not see and thus cannot acknowledge in the life and teaching of the historical Jesus, that he would have protested and repudiated the anti-Semitism of the Christianities that claimed to follow his teaching, but that he would have repudiated as well the misogyny that Graves, in particular, makes a spectacular mistake in ascribing to Jesus. It was in the effort to clear away these misunderstandings and reveal the antipatriarchal Jesus, as the historical Jesus, that I examined the search for the historical Jesus in the way I have.

Now, however, we turn to something missing, so I have come to think, even in the best work of the historians I have discussed (Crossan, Meier, Schüssler Fiorenza), namely, how Winnicott may have been correct in discovering in his own quite revolutionary rethinking of psychoanalysis a way of making sense of the historical Jesus as a psychologist, even a psychoanalyst or perhaps a proto-psychoanalyst. It is important

2. Winnicott, "Letter to Bion," 158.

to be quite clear that the ways in which I use Winnicott's view of psychoanalysis to make sense of the historical Jesus are not expressly made by him. I have certainly learned from some of his rather brief remarks on how the Christianities he had come to deplore went wrong (original sin, in particular) and indeed in the next chapter suggest how psychoanalysis can clarify what went wrong in the Christianities that made Christianity, as I put it, more Roman than Christian (discussing both Augustine and Luther). I also have come to believe both religion and ethics share a common psychological role in what Winnicott called creative symbolic play (the root, for him, of human culture and ethics), and will explore this insight in the argument to follow. Winnicott was certainly a progressive political liberal based in universal human rights, as am I, but he was not a moral philosopher and constitutional lawyer, the perspectives that I bring to this study. Winnicott certainly saw that psychoanalysis might lead to "a real understanding of religion and its use in setting a high ethical standard." I have come to agree with him, and regard this book as both supporting and even justifying this very strong claim about both religion and ethics. Thus in later chapters, I will explore how his views clarify not only the psychology of ethics, but of democracy—a connection he explored in suggestive ways I will develop in later chapters.

Psychoanalysis has not, of course, historically been a friend of religion. The subject was of course discovered, as we saw in chapter 1, by Sigmund Freud, an iconic secular Jew, indeed an atheist (*The Future of an Illusion*), whose life and work were framed by the virulent political anti-Semitism of the nation and city where he worked, Austria and Vienna. It would have been, I believe, psychologically difficult for Freud not to have been, to say the least, skeptical of the Christianities (in particular, the Catholicism of most Austrians) whose anti-Semitism was, at least in part, responsible for the genocidal political anti-Semitism of Adolf Hitler, also an Austrian. Some students of Freud's thought have tried to connect his discovery and invention of psychoanalysis to earlier Jewish mystical thought,[3] but even they concede how tenuous the connection is (Freud did not read one of the central texts of Jewish mysticism[4]). But, Joel Whitebook has now decisively shown that Freud was very much an enlightenment thinker along the lines of Voltaire ("ecrisez l'infame," Voltaire on the Catholic Church, "crush the infamous thing"),[5] and one can

3. Bakan, *Sigmund Freud.*

4. See Bakan, *Sigmund Freud,* 298.

5. See Whitebook, *Freud.*

see, given the Catholic anti-Semitism of Austria, why. There are, of course, important cultural works by Freud that draw explicitly on the Jewish tradition (*Totem and Taboo*, 1913; *The Moses of Michelangelo*, 1914; *Moses and Monotheism*, 1939), but always in the context of Freud's mistaken Lamarckianism, as examples of how facts, as Freud regarded them, of human psychology (like the Oedipus Complex) are not transmitted culturally but biologically (so the parricide of Moses, the father, by his sons, expressed in the Oedipus Complex, has been inherited from the original parricide of Moses). Freud's misreading of the Jewish tradition is evident in *Moses and Monotheism*, a late work written at the end of his life after he had finally fled Vienna for London and against the background of the apparent political success of Hitler's politically aggressive anti-Semitism, where, as Yerushalmi has acidly noted,[6] Freud attributes Jewish neurosis to unconscious trauma about wrongs done to the Jewish people when, in fact, no people was more aware or conscious of the unjust traumas they suffered at the hands of their imperialist conquerors than the Jews in the biblical narratives, as Jacob Wright has shown.[7]

By the time he wrote *Civilization and Its Discontents*,[8] Freud had come to accept Thanatos (the death drive), which gave rise to aggressiveness and war, as the basic drive in competition with the other basic drive Eros, and he regards not only ethics as such, but Christian ethics, "Love thy neighbor as thy self," as unavailing. Freud acknowledges Jesus, as poised between Thanatos and Eros:

> The most arresting example of this fateful conjunction is to be seen in the figure of Jesus Christ—if, indeed, that figure is not a part of mythology, which called it into being from an obscure memory of that primal event.[9]

By primal event, Freud means the parricidal killing of Moses by his sons, which he takes the killing of Jesus to repeat (unconsciously, of course). Ethics is, against Thanatos, unavailing:

> Ethics is thus to be regarded as a therapeutic attempt—as an endeavour to achieve, by means of a command of the superego,

6. See Yerushalmi, *Freud's Moses*, 84–85.
7. See Wright, *Why the Bible Began*.
8. Freud, *Civilization and Its Discontents*.
9. Freud, *Civilization and Its Discontents*, 142.

> something which has so far not been achieved by means of any other cultural activities.[10]

And the demands of Christian ethics are even more unrealistic and thus unavailing:

> [I]t assumes that a man's ego is psychologically capable of anything that is required of it, that his ego has unlimited mastery over his id. This is a mistake; and even in what are known as normal people the id cannot be controlled beyond certain limits. If more is demanded of a man, a revolt will be produced in him or a neurosis, or he will be made unhappy. The commandment, "Love thy neighbor as thyself," is the strongest defence against human aggressiveness and an excellent example of the unpsychological proceedings of the cultural super-ego. The commandment is impossible to fulfill; such an enormous inflation of love can only lower its value, not get rid of the difficulty. Civilization pays no attention to all this; it merely admonishes us that the harder it is to obey the precept the more meritorious it is to do. But anyone who follows such a precept in the present-day civilization puts himself at a disadvantage *vis-à-vis* the person who disregards it. What a potent obstacle to civilization aggressiveness must be, if the defence against it can cause as much unhappiness as aggressiveness itself! "Natural" ethics, as it is called, has nothing to offer except the narcissistic satisfaction of being able to think oneself better than others.[11]

In discussing how and why Winnicott could have come to such a different understanding than Freud of the relation of psychoanalysis to ethics and religion in general and Christianity in particular, we must begin with what they share and do not share. Winnicott always honored Freud and tended to downplay and even understate his disagreements with Freud. Freud remains for him the discoverer and creative pioneer of psychology: his central discovery of transference love, on reading Plato, placed love at the center of our human nature; and Freud's uses of transference love in free association and resistance are the methods Winnicott both used and adapted. Winnicott successfully extended analysis to psychosis beyond Freud's focus on neurosis, but his most important creative contribution to psychoanalysis arose from his psychoanalytic work with women as mothers and with children, including innovating therapies

10. Freud, *Civilization and Its Discontents*, 142.

11. Freud, *Civilization and Its Discontents*, 143.

based on the play of children with transitional objects. Joel Whitebook in his pathbreaking study of Freud[12] explores at some length how someone as perceptive as Freud could have centered his work on the relation of fathers to sons in the Oedipus Complex, the center of Freud's work since his *The Interpretation of Dreams*, ignoring what Winnicott and others discovered and made central to the psychoanalytic understanding of human development, the relationship of mothers to their children.

Whitebook's explanation is that Freud, by placing central weight on his own self-analysis in *The Interpretation of Dreams*, himself deviated from the professional ethics of analysts that they must themselves be analyzed but by other analysts, which Freud failed to do (analyzing himself), narcissistically locking himself to own experience, or what he imagined his experience to be. This explains how Freud could have generalized his own neurotic Oedipal relation to his own father as the model for all human development, and failed to see the importance in his own life and the life of others of the relation to mothers, the earliest child-parent relationship. It is this failure that explains how Freud, who himself worked closely with intelligent women as analysts and as analysands,[13] could develop views on the psychology of women as morally inferior that are, to say the least, problematic. In effect, Freud is reading psychoanalysis through a patriarchal lens, which Whitebook connects to Freud's distaste for abstract music in a city, Vienna, where composers of the status of Mozart and Beethoven had brilliantly flourished, and where Mahler had worked during Freud's life. Such blindness clarifies how long it took Freud to appreciate the dimensions of the violent political anti-Semitism that nearly killed him and did kill several members of his family. Freud, in discovering the unconscious, was blinded by the patriarchal lens of his own version of psychoanalysis, unconscious for this reason of his own misogyny, and thus could not see facts inconsistent with his patriarchal assumptions.

If for Freud the human psyche was organized around the two primal drives, Eros and Thanatos, Winnicott found in his psychoanalytic work that the central organizing fact of the human psyche was human relationships, through which, beginning with what he called "good enough mothers," we become human through what I called in chapter 1 the mirroring of oneself, from infancy on forward and throughout our lives, through our relationships to those we love, who enable us to see ourselves as Plato saw

12. Whitebook, *Freud*.

13. See Appignanesi and Forrester, *Freud's Women*.

in the role of eros between lovers in the *Phaedrus*. Winnicott, like James Gilligan and many others, found no empirical justification for Thanatos, as a biological drive. Violence is certainly a fact of our human experience, but Winnicott saw violence as more connected to culturally framed traumas of commission or omission in early relationships, failures of loving relationship, a psychology that patriarchy both encourages and sometimes requires as part of the initiation into patriarchy.[14] So, shame plays the role it does as the psychological trigger of violence when patriarchal men experience humiliation of their manhood as defined by patriarchy.

Winnicott found that aggression played an important role in human development in general as a way that both the infant and growing child resist what they take to be failures of care, and assert their burgeoning sense of independence while still in relationship. Good-enough mothers, as he put it, understand and support such aggressive independence assuring the child they are not abandoning him, marked in good mothering by the "absence of the talion reaction in the mother."[15] Aggression in this sense is an expression of resistance associated with the developing competences of the child as an independent person.

The empirical study of such resistance has now become a central subject for the human sciences, which no longer limit their study to men only.[16] Along these lines, Carol Gilligan, the developmental psychologist, has recently argued, on the basis of her own empirical work with girls and young women and the work of her and her students with boys and young men, that there is a rather different cultural initiation into patriarchy for girls and boys, later for girls and earlier for boys, that call in both cases for traumatic breaks in relationship, losses that lead to the acceptance of the patriarchal stereotypes of manhood and womanhood.[17] Resistance to such stereotypes expresses itself in the freeing of voices otherwise repressed or silenced by the violence of patriarchy under threat, and the nonviolence of such voices is a crucial feature of how they operate, often in new forms of associations, breaking the disassociation and accommodation on which patriarchy depends. The initiation into patriarchy has for this reason becoming a prominent feature of studies of human development.[18]

14. See, for a powerfully explanatory exploration of the impact of patriarchy on men, Real, *I Don't Want to Talk About It.*

15. Quoted in Modell, *Other Times*, 24.

16. On this point, see Gilligan, *In a Human Voice.*

17. See Gilligan, "Moral Injury."

18. On this point, see Rogers and Way, "Child Development."

The pathbreaking importance of Freud's discovery of psychoanalysis was, as we have seen, transference love and how, in the analytic situation, it made possible an experience of love of the analysand for the analyst, a trust that allows the analysand through free association and resistance to understand how deficits in earlier relationships with parents and others may have detrimentally impacted both love and work in their later lives and how they may repair any damage done. The revolutionary importance of Winnicott in the development of psychoanalysis based on transference love is that he did not limit such love to relationships of fathers to sons, but saw the significance of such transference love in the earliest relationships of mothers to their infants as well as all later relationships in the role mirroring plays in such relationships as we see ourselves through the eyes of those who love. Freud discovered transference love in Plato's discussion of the mirroring of male lovers in the *Phaedrus*, and, like Plato, focused on the love of two men, fathers and sons. As we earlier saw, what he did not see was that such relationships were themselves structured by patriarchy and this led to his elaboration of psychoanalysis through a patriarchal lens, which compromised the empirical basis for his findings shown in his mythology of Thanatos. Thus, by reading transference love modeled on the patriarchal relationships of fathers to son, he failed to see how patriarchy itself structures manhood along the patriarchal lines of a shame culture, and the role that insults to such manhood play in violence. It is, for Freud, unconscious guilt over parricide that explains the punitiveness of the superego, not, as Winnicott argues, the experience of interpersonal love that leads to conscience, giving rise to guilt in breaking such relationships and the repair of relationships through love.

Winnicott's revolution in psychoanalysis was to discover and develop transference love through an antipatriarchal lens, which explains his attention to both mothers and children. Understanding psychoanalysis in this way (see Introduction), Winnicott's claim to his sister "that Christ was a leading psychotherapist" not only makes a great deal of sense, but illuminates the life and teaching of the historical Jesus, in particular what it was in his life and largely oral teaching to "the whole crowd that was spellbound by his teaching"—an appeal that terrified "the chief priests and the scribes," "looking for a way to kill him."[19]

The appeal was, I believe, that Jesus appealed to a truth of our human nature that Winnicott called good-enough mothering that he

19. Coogan, *New Oxford Bible*, 1852, Mark 11:18–19.

argued occurred both at the beginning and throughout human life, what we today call an ethics of care. In his book, *Moral Politics*,[20] George Lakoff offers two quite different conceptual schemes to account for conservative as opposed to liberal politics in the United States, strict-father morality as opposed to nurturant-parent morality. There is no doubt that Winnicott's evidence-based view of human nature, based on his work as a psychoanalyst, brought to attention a nurturant-parent morality whose importance had previously not been given attention. It was, for him, as deep a truth of human nature and its development as we now have on the empirical basis not only of psychoanalysis but other studies of infant and human development that we discussed in the Introduction. We are the mind-reading species, a fact that makes possible the cooperation and cultural developments (both scientific and artistic) which have brought us to where we are, sometimes called the Anthropocene, in which human activity has become the dominant force in climate and the environment, both for good and for ill.

The cultural form we call patriarchy, discussed at length in earlier chapters, is a strict father morality, one which, as we seen, supported the violence of Roman imperialism in which Roman boys are initiated into a patriarchal manhood that supports and indeed valorizes such violence against both men and women. What made Jesus's teaching so deeply appealing was that it resonated with the experience of his audience of a human nature requiring care especially for those most needing such care, attending precisely to those on the lowest rung of the gender hierarchy enforced by patriarchy. Jesus cares and calls for care for those patriarchy would marginalize and even deny and denigrate and persecute.

Keep in mind the audience for his teaching, whom he addresses in the beatitudes that begin the Sermon on the Mount:

> Blessed are the poor in spirit, for theirs is the kingdom of heaven.
> Blessed are those who mourn, for they will be comforted.
> Blessed are the meek, for they will inherit the earth.
> Blessed are those who hunger and thirst for righteousness, for they will be filled.
> Blessed are the merciful, for they will receive mercy.
> Blessed are the pure in heart, for they will see God.
> Blessed are the peacemakers, for they will be called the children of God.

20. Lakoff, *Moral Politics*.

> Blessed are those who are persecuted for righteousness' sake, for theirs if the kingdom of heaven.
> Blessed are you when people revile you and persecute you and utter all kinds of evil against you falsely on my account. Rejoice and be glad, for your reward is great in heaven, for in the same they persecuted the prophets who were before you.[21]

Or, in the cognate Sermon on the Plain:

> Blessed are you who are poor,
> for yours is the kingdom of God.
> Blessed are you who are hungry now,
> for you will be filled.
> Blessed are those who weep now,
> for you will laugh.
> Blessed are you when people hate you, and when they exclude you, revile you, and defame you on account of the Son of Man. Rejoice you in that day and leap for joy, for surely your reward is great in heaven: for that is what their ancestors did to the prophets.[22]

We can see such an ethics of care in the way Jesus grounds what he takes to be core ethical demands (the Ten Commandments) in the two Love Commandments: "the first is . . . 'you shall love the Lord your God with all your heart, and with all your soul, and with all your mind, and with all your strength.' The second is: 'You shall love your neighbor as your self.' There is no other commandment greater than these."[23] Nurturant parental morality is, for Jesus, what the relationship to God is and how and why we love or come to love such nurturant persons in our lives both early and throughout our lives, and come through such nurturance to love ourselves (the basis of the First Love Commandment). It is also the experience of such nurturant love, the basis of love for self, that expresses itself in love for others (the basis of the Second Love Commandment).

In fact, while the historical Jesus certainly has a view of the content of the ethical commandments ultimately grounded in the two Love Commandments, he is, if anything, expressly skeptical of the way people make moral judgments, "Do not judge, so that you may not be judged,"[24] illustrated, vividly, in his treatment of the proposed stoning

21. Coogan, *New Oxford Bible*, 1788, Matt 5:1–13.

22. Coogan, *New Oxford Bible*, 1879, Luke 6:20–24.

23. Coogan, *New Oxford Bible*, 1854, Mark 12:30–32

24. Coogan, *New Oxford Bible*, 1792, Matt 7:1.

of the woman taken in adultery, bringing the men to a sense of their own guilt in holding her to standards they could not comply with. All forms of self-righteousness are suspect for him, including the attempt to impute righteousness to him, "Why do you call me good? No one is good but God alone."[25] Jesus's sense of his human frailty, including sinning, does not comport with the christological view of him, conspicuous in the Gospel of John, as the divine son of God. He is human, all too human. It is this very *man's* life and teaching that has compelled so many, as it did Winnicott and does me.[26]

The Love Commandments are phrased, of course, as commandments, but, if Winnicott's view of the centrality of loving relationship to our becoming human is a feature of human nature, it is always there as a feature of our deepest psychological *needs*, our nature as human. In quieting the fears and anxieties he saw in his audiences, Jesus appeals to nature in the same way:

> Therefore I tell you, do not worry about your life, what you will eat or what you will drink, or about your body, what you will wear. Is not life more than food, and the body more than clothing? Look at the birds of the air: they neither sow nor reap nor gather into barns, and yet your heavenly Father feeds them. Are you not of more value than they? And can any of you by worrying add a single hour to your span of life? And why do you worry about clothing? Consider the lilies of the field, how they grow; they neither toil nor spin, yet I tell you, even Solomon in his glory was not clothed like these. But if God so clothes the grass of the field, which is alive today, and tomorrow is thrown into the oven, will he not much more clothe you—you of little faith? Therefore do not worry, saying, "What shall we eat?" or "What will we drink?" or "What will we wear?" For it is the Gentiles who strive for all these things; and indeed your heavenly Father knows that you need all these things. But strive first for the kingdom of God and his righteousness, and all these things will be given to you as well.
>
> So do not worry about tomorrow, for tomorrow will bring worries of its own. Tomorrow's trouble is enough for today.[27]

The kingdom of heaven, as Jesus conceives it, is defined by egalitarian loving relationships, relationships that alone were a need of our human

25. Coogan, *New Oxford Bible*, 1849, Mark 10:18.

26. See, on this point, Schillebeeckx, *Jesus*.

27. Coogan, *New Oxford Bible*, 1791–92, Matt 6:25–34.

nature. What interested Winnicott and seems to have interested Jesus is the ways in which injuries to this need, inflicted by traumatic acts or omissions by parents in a patriarchal culture, can be repaired through love or, more precisely, transference love. Thus, Jesus is not interested in the moral condemnation of outcasts, but regards himself more as a physician to them than a moral judge:

> And as he sat at dinner in the house many tax collectors and sinners came and were sitting with him and his disciples. When the Pharisees saw this, they saw to his disciples, "Why does your teacher eat with tax collectors and sinners." But when he heard this, he said, "Those who are well have no need of a physician, but those who are sick. Go and learn what that means. I desire mercy, not sacrifice. For I have come to call not the righteous but sinners."[28]

Jesus, thus conceiving himself as a physician not a moral judge, works as psychoanalysts like Winnicott did, using a technique, psychoanalysis, that its inventor, Freud, regarded as a therapy of love, very like Jesus's therapies.

Much of Jesus's extraordinary appeal was not only to his teaching, but to his view of himself as a physician and his powers of care and cure, in which the crowds in Galilee came to believe, a belief historians now accept. Winnicott came to believe that what he had found in analysis, both of himself and of others, was a kind of trust like that Erik Erikson regarded as fundamental to the development of infants and children[29] and that Erikson himself had observed, in his important study of Jesus, based on Norman Perrin's historical Jesus:[30] "one cannot help noticing, on Jesus' part, an unobtrusive integration of maternal and paternal tenderness,"[31] very much in line with Winnicott's own views both on a psychoanalysis of good-enough mothering and Jesus. Jesus's care may plausibly be understood psychoanalytically as Jesus's transference love for the maimed and afflicted he cured, a love they had never experienced from a culture that often denigrated and demonized any sickness as a kind of demonic possession (Jesus was himself accused by Pharisees of being demonically

28. Coogan, *New Oxford Bible*, 1795, Matt 9:10–14.

29. See Erikson, *Childhood*, 247–51.

30. Perrin, *Rediscovering*. See, on this point, Capps, *Erik Erikson's Verbal Portraits*, 101–33.

31. Erikson, "Galilean Sayings," 322.

possessed[32]). Such love and concern may have relieved suffering and even cured people, just as psychoanalysis sometimes does (for example, psychosomatic illnesses rooted in anxieties, losses, deprivations, and the like that cripple self-regulating capacities[33]). The Gospels repeatedly describe Jesus's motivations as "compassion":

> When the Lord saw her [a widow grieving over the death of her son], he had compassion for her and said to her, "Do not weep."[34]

> When he saw the crowds, he had compassion for them, because they were harassed and helpless, like sheep without a shepherd.[35]

> Moved with compassion [for two blind men], Jesus touched their eyes. Immediately, they regained their sight and followed him.[36]

And when he visits the grieving Mary, whose brother Lazarus had died, he expresses a compassionate, indeed empathetic grief:

> When Mary came where Jesus was and saw him, she knelt at his feet and said to him, "Lord, if you had been here, my brother would not have died." When Jesus saw her weeping, and the Jews who came with her also weeping, he was greatly disturbed in spirit and deeply moved. He said, "Where have you laid him?" They said to him, "Lord, come and see." Jesus began to weep. So the Jews said, "See how he loved him!" But some of them said, "Could not he who opened the eyes of the blind man have kept this man from dying?"[37]

Martin Buber in his *Two Types of Faith*[38] contrasts the faith of a people, like the Jews, already in a covenantal relation to God, with the faith of a person brought to faith as an individual. The people cured by Jesus are largely Jews, and Jesus, regarded as a prophet, brings them faith or trust

32. See Matt 12: 22–50.

33. On this point, Taylor, "Psychoanalysis"; Aisenstein and de Aisenberg, *Psychosomatics*..

34. Coogan, *New Oxford Bible,* 1880, Luke 7:13.

35. Coogan, *New Oxford Bible,* 1796, Matt 9:36.

36. Coogan, *New Oxford Bible,* 1812, Matt 20:34.

37. Coogan, *New Oxford Bible,* 1939, John 11:34–38, Jesus raises Lazarus from the dead.

38. Buber, *Two Types of Faith.*

in him as Jews; but he also cures non-Jews (for example, the Syrophoenician woman, indeed honoring her faith[39]). Jesus's care across boundaries most would not cross was evident throughout his ministry, but clear here in his care for the afflicted, so bringing to faith, as it is put in the Gospels, may plausibly be regarded, as I believe it was by Winnicott, as an experience of trust responsive to a transference love they had not heretofore experienced. This is the kingdom of God coming into existence.

There are two places in the Gospel of John that support this analysis. First, there is his refusal to accept the view of Pharisees that a blind man since birth must have sinned. Jesus views his condition as a matter of fact and how we and he deal with it is up to us. In fact, his care for the blind man cures him. Second, even more strikingly, there is the long conversation with the Samaritan woman, someone with whom (as a woman, and as a Samaritan) a more conventional Jewish man would not have spoken, let alone listened to. Jesus does both in the closest thing to an analytic session that appears in the Gospels. In the process of talk with and listening to his woman, Jesus offers what analysts would call an interpretation of the free associations of an analysand, a kind of mind reading of the unconscious revealed through free association. Jesus, in fact, correctly observes that the woman has been married before, had had a number of husbands, and is not married now. The astonished woman regards him as a prophet and urges her people to take him seriously: he might be the messiah (a shocking thought that the messiah should be a Jew, as opposed to a Samaritan).

There are other features of Jesus's life and work clarified by psychoanalysis.

There is the recurrent claim in the Gospels that Jesus reads minds, not only the unconscious of the Samaritan woman at the well, but the minds of those who disagree with him.[40] Like any good analyst, he listens not only to words but to gestures, actions, levels of affect, emotions, and the like, and he thus reads their minds, as a trained analyst does and as clinicians in general do,[41] often more correctly than not.

More importantly, there is something quite remarkable in any man of this period—Jesus's interest in childhood and in children, even infants. The discovery of childhood is one of the great psychological discoveries of psychoanalysis, and no one explored the discovery more expertly and

39. Mark 7:24–30.

40. See, for example, Matt 12:15; Matt 12:18; Mark 2:8; Luke 6:8: Luke 11:17.

41. See, on this point, Donald, *Mind So Rare*, 59–70; see also 129–30, 143–44.

creatively than Winnicott both in his work with mothers and his psychoanalysis of children. Nothing would have struck Winnicott as more psychoanalytic than Jesus's interest in children, including infants, and the way he justified this interest:

> [H]e asked them [the disciples], "What were you talking about on the way?" But they were silent, for on the way they had argued with one another who was the greatest. He sat down, called the twelve and said to them, "Whoever wants to be first must be last of all, and servant of all." Then he took a little child and put it among them; and taking it in his arms, he said to them, "Whoever welcomes one such child in my name welcomes me, and whoever welcomes me welcomes not me but the one who sent me."[42]

> People were bringing little children to him in order that he might touch them; and the disciples spoke sternly to them. But when Jesus saw this, he was indignant and said to them, "Let the little children come to me; do not stop them; for it is to such as these that the kingdom of God belongs. Truly I tell you, whoever does not receive the kingdom of God as a little child will never enter it." And he took them up in his arms, laid his hands on them, and blessed them.[43]

> At that time the disciples came to Jesus and asked. "Who is the greatest in the kingdom of heaven?" He called a child, whom he put among them, and said, "Truly I tell you, unless you change and become like children, you will never enter the kingdom of heaven. Whoever becomes humble like this child is the greatest in the kingdom of heaven. Whoever welcomes one such child in my name welcomes me."[44]

> Take care that you do not despise one of these little ones; for, I tell you in heaven their angels continually see the face of my Father in heaven.[45]

> At that same hour, Jesus rejoiced in the Holy Spirit and said, "I think you, Father, Lord of heaven and earth, because you have

42. Coogan, *New Oxford Bible*, 1847–48, Mark 9:36–37.
43. Coogan, *New Oxford Bible*, 1849, Mark 10:13–17.
44. Coogan, *New Oxford Bible*, 1808, Matt 18:1–6.
45. Coogan, *New Oxford Bible*, 1809, Matt 18:10–12.

> hidden these things from the wise and the intelligent and have revealed them to infants."[46]

I quote these passages (there are others) because they reveal what would have struck Winnicott about the historical Jesus: that Jesus himself undertakes good-enough mothering (taking a child in his arms) in a way that shocks his disciples, as it would many patriarchal men even today. In her recent important book, *Father Time: A Natural History of Men and Babies,*[47] Sarah Hrdy, an evolutionary psychologist, shows that men nurturing babies was very much part of our evolutionary history; that patriarchal norms, when they became dominant in human cultures, marginalized or even denigrated such care; and that men today, including gay men having and raising children, increasingly display such care to their benefit, the benefit of babies, and people (including women) generally. The antipatriarchal Jesus himself undertakes the nurturant role men can and do take, rebukes his disciples for trying to stop him, and finally tells them that such caring relationships are a model for the kingdom of heaven: acceptance of an ethics of care and all that means in egalitarian loving relationships of care as the core of a life worth living (rejecting, as he insists, hierarchy in their relationships to one another). The initiation into patriarchy takes place after infancy, and infants and young children thus experience the importance of a mirroring love kept "from the wise and the intelligent and . . . revealed to infants," indeed, in a phrase about mirroring, "continually see the face of my Father in heaven."

There is also, as we discussed at some length in the previous chapter, Jesus's speaking to and listening to women, including non-Jewish women, in ways quite unconventional in this period, very much Winnicott's own experience as an analyst in the seriousness with which he takes good-enough mothering as the core of a well-lived life. But, it is precisely the seriousness with which Jesus takes these women and their experience, including that several of them (Mary Magdalene, certainly) are disciples, and it is Mary's love for Jesus that allows her to act on her love when the male disciples flee and betray. Indeed, the idea and experience of the resurrection arises, so I have argued, from Mary's love. Winnicott correctly sees in the historical Jesus an antipatriarchal interest in women that he shares.

46. Coogan, *New Oxford Bible,* 1889, Luke 10:21–22.

47. Hrdy, *Father Time.*

Winnicott framed what he found in his analytic work in terms of the true and false self and the related idea of an incommunicable secret self. The idea is that, often in psychoanalytic work of an analyst with an analysand, the free associations and resistances revealed through transference love take the form of an analysand discovering that his or her sense of a life not worth living was an accommodation to acts or omissions of a parental or other figures requiring the analysand to accommodate to the figure's often patriarchal demands in matters of love or vocation, at the expense of what the analysand comes to regard as his or her true buried self. The true self remains incommunicable because of its sense of a vulnerability as threat, as it has been by the pressure of past accommodations to the false self. It seems to me not unlikely that Winnicott, a close reader of the Gospels, may have been struck by finding a not dissimilar or perhaps even the same idea in the remark at the end of the Sermon on the Mount that a loving relationship to God should not take the form of fasting "seen by others but by your Father who is in secret; and your Father who sees in secret will reward you."[48] Jesus was, as we have seen, always a critic of the shame culture that continued to be present in Jewish religious practice, peacocking, for example, one's piety so it is seen by others. Jesus always calls for an inward conscience rooted in one's relationship to a loving God, what Winnicott calls the secret self,[49] or perhaps the soul, a relationship when broken that leads to guilt and the move to reparation.

In the Gospel of John, the debates of Jesus with the Pharisees often take the form of their appealing to the probably literate learning of their group in contrast to Jesus's oral claim to speak, as prophets did, directly to and from God. Jesus refuses to accept the deliverances of the priestly community as the final arbiter of the interpretation of Jewish law because his antipatriarchal stance appeals not to a patriarchal priesthood, but directly to a loving God who calls for an egalitarian love. For Jesus, as for Winnicott, one is never alone in thus questioning conventional views, but always in a trustful personal relationship that sustains one—enduring love. Winnicott saw loving attachments among persons, not instinctual drives, as central to the human psyche, reflected in his remarkable paper, "The Capacity to Be Alone,"[50] in which the ability to be alone rests on the belief in secure attachments. Similarly, it is Jesus's sense of an ongoing

48. Coogan, *New Oxford Bible*, 1791, Matt 6:18–19.

49. See, for an excellent exploration of this insight originating with Winnicott, Modell, *Private Self*.

50. Winnicott, "Capacity to Be Alone."

relationship to a nurturant loving parent that sustains him: he is not, as the Pharisees claim, alone.

There is one further view of Winnicott that bears upon how psychoanalysis or at least Winnicott's form of psychoanalysis illuminates, as Winnicott believed, the life and teaching of the historical Jesus ("Christ was a leading psychotherapist"), namely, the role of transitional objects and play both in child development and cultural development. Winnicott's discovery of transitional objects in child development was one of his most important and acclaimed discoveries as an analyst of children both in the squiggles he used in his therapy with children (a squiggle is some representation proposed initially either by analyst or analysand, and then responded to by the other, a process then repeated and repeated, leading to therapeutic discussion and often revelation), including his comparable work with a young girl called Piggle. The therapeutic role of squiggles with children allowed a psychoanalysis of analysands not yet fully literate, and yet capable of creating and responding to depictions that often revealed free associations and resistance and the unconscious.

Winnicott came to believe that the role of transitional objects in the play of young children that he came successfully to use in his psychoanalysis of children enabled psychoanalysis finally to move beyond Freud's Lamarckian mythology rooted in biology, to take seriously the independent role of culture and cultural development in human development, including our evolutionary developments as a symbol-making species. Play in human culture, on his view, was the key to understanding the role in human life of both the sciences and arts, but also philosophy and religion. His general theory of culture along these lines was never fully developed because of his early death, but he made many suggestive remarks about how cultural play could advance understanding of both ethics and religion, which he regarded as closely connected. His suggestion about religion, in particular, was that the psychology of religion can be understood, along the lines of Feuerbach's argument, influential on Marx, among others, that the psychology of Christianity, in particular, was a projection of our deeply human interests in love, a view I will explore shortly.

Joseph Klausner, one of the earliest Jewish scholars investigating Jesus the Jew,[51] concludes his study of Jesus as a figure that cannot be reduced to his Jewish parts:

51. See Klausner, *Jesus of Nazareth*.

> [I]n his ethical code there is a sublimity, distinctiveness and originality in form unparalleled in any other Hebrew ethical code; neither is there any parallel to the remarkable art of the parables. The shrewdness and sharpness of his proverbs and his forceful epigrams serve, in an exceptional degree, to make ethical ideas a popular possession. If ever the day should come and this ethical code be stripped of its wrapping of miracles and mysticism, the Book of the Ethics of Jesus will be one of the choicest treasures in the literature of Israel for all time.[52]

Winnicott's interest in the historical Jesus ("Christ was a leading psychotherapist") was very much along the lines of Klausner's hope for discovering the historical Jesus. The miracles or many of them, Winnicott believed, could be understood in terms of psychoanalytic transference love and care, which was, for Winnicott, a science. And the "mysticism," Jesus as God or the son of God, is not required to understand or value either his life or teaching which rest both on a defensible psychology and the appeal of the antipatriarchal egalitarian ethics of interpersonal love, rooted in human nature, he expressed.

What would particularly have interested Winnicott, from the point of view of his discovery of transitional objects, is, as Klausner points out, Jesus's "remarkable art of the parables." The parables have now been widely studied as ways of bringing home to a largely non-literate audience the ethical meaning of both his life and teaching.[53] Jesus, the ethical teacher, was also, it appears, a great artist, as the storytelling of the parables shows. Winnicott would, I believe, also have seen them psychoanalytically as transitional objects, as works of art often are, enabling an artist with a radical vision that would be difficult for his audience to understand and imagine and to communicate through a work of art, the storytelling of the parables, creative imaginative play with which his audience could join in imaginative play, in effect, imagining something that was otherwise unimaginable. The kingdom of God, which Jesus regarded both his acts (his cures) and teaching as breaking into a fallen world, could not have been more distant from the world of first-century Galilee and Judaea, subjugated by Roman patriarchy and by at least some Jewish leaders whose authority was always in service to their Roman masters. If Jesus was as antipatriarchal as our argument shows he was, his life and teaching could not have been more in conflict with the violent patriarchy

52. Klausner, *Jesus of Nazareth*, 414.

53. See, for example Jeremias, *Parables*; Jeremias, *Rediscovering*; Dodd, *Parables*.

that ruled Israel (see earlier discussion of Roman patriarchy) and that would murder an innocent man committed to nonviolence, who would have agreed though on different grounds with Socrates who in a similar situation said, better to suffer injustice than to commit injustice[54] (for Socrates, disobeying Athenian law, for Jesus, using violence to resist). His nonviolence may have saved his followers from crucifixion, as it did the followers of John the Baptist from beheading (John was beheaded by Herod Antipas). Both the leaders and followers of more violent resisters were executed. But nonviolence did not save Jesus, because his teaching challenged and was thus an ideological threat to the whole patriarchal world. Jesus's advice to his disciples on this point shows awareness of the interpersonal skills required for their nonviolent resistance to patriarchy: "See, I am sending you out like sheep into the midst of wolves; so be wise as serpents and innocent as doves."[55] These are, I believe, the interpersonal skills of a Gandhi and Martin Luther King Jr., leaders of social movements grounded at least in part on the teaching on nonviolence, as we shall later observe, of the antipatriarchal Jesus.

The parables are thus plausibly understood, as I believe Winnicott would have understood them, as transitional objects, and a number of them remain today both appealing and moving, the Good Samaritan and the Prodigal Son, among others. It would have confirmed Winnicott's belief that psychoanalysis had much to contribute to understanding the historical Jesus that a psychoanalyst, Richard Q. Ford, has offered plausible, sometimes compelling, readings of the parables, which, in his view, "can be understood as exploring the effects of various levels of coercion and the ways in which power over others stifles empathy."[56]

I earlier noted that Winnicott's suggestive writings on religion and its connection to ethics use a projection theory, like Feuerbach's, to explore how a psychoanalytic view like his own, in which loving attachment relationships are quite central, might offer a way of understanding religion and ethics as symbolic imaginative play on the model of his view of transitional objects. Winnicott was also quite critical of the way Christianities appealing to Jesus's life and teaching had developed doctrines that compromised and indeed undermined what Winnicott had come to regard as the life and teaching of the historical Jesus—in particular, the doctrines of original sin and predestination. Presumably, in line with his

54. See Plato, *Crito* 49a-d, 43–44; *Gorgias* 509 c, 853.

55. Coogan, *New Oxford Bible*, 1796, Matt 10:16–17.

56. Ford, *Jesus' Parables*, 145. See also Ford, *Parables of Jesus*.

projection view of the relation of psychoanalysis to religion, there would be a psychoanalytically illuminating way of understanding how this could have happened. If Jesus himself thinks and acts psychoanalytically (based on his relationship to a nurturant parent), then those who develop the Christian tradition often think and act in ways that are, I believe, strikingly psychoanalytic and may be understood in such psychoanalytic terms in their relationship to their nurturant or nonnurturant parents. My argument in the next chapter, dealing with Augustine and Luther, will be along these lines.

But, as I end my discussion of why Winnicott seems to me quite right in finding in the historical Jesus "a leading psychotherapist," it will be illuminating of the whole project of this book to regard the historical Jesus, as we have come now to understand him, as himself a great creative figure in the cultural play of the tradition of both religion and ethics as he found it in the Jewish tradition that was the basis of his sense of himself as a prophet on the model of Elijah. Our entire exploration of the historical Jesus—framed by our discussions of Roman patriarchy, shame and guilt cultures, and the Jewish tradition of resisting subjugation by patriarchal imperialist cultures, including Rome—sets the stage for understanding Jesus as very much a creative figure, indeed a culturally revolutionary figure, playing within the tradition he assumed. What moved the crowds who were stunned by his oral performances and his work as a physician with outcasts was his voice as a creative prophet speaking to and from a loving God more authoritatively than the patriarchal priesthood whose teaching he sometimes challenged.[57]

It is the historical Jesus himself who thus gave us a model of prophetic Christianity that moved Winnicott and many others today, a prophetic Christianity that, like Jesus, challenges patriarchal priesthoods because no longer in relationship to a God who is love. The view of the historical Jesus I have defended is, obviously, ethically revolutionary, as other recent historians have argued, notably, Crossan,[58] Borg,[59] and Walter Wink.[60] It is no accident, I believe, that historically, as I later argue, it has been only the most heterodox among Christianities, like the Quakers, who protested slavery, racism, and sexism; among American Quakers, it was Quaker women, notably the Grimke sisters (Angelina and Grimke)

57. See, on this point, Hengel, *Charismatic Leader.*

58. Crossan, *Historical Jesus.*

59. Borg, *Meeting Jesus Again*; Borg, *God We Never Knew..*

60. Wink, *Engaging the Powers.*

who played roles in antebellum abolitionist feminism. And Matthew Stewart has cogently argued in his recent book, *The Emancipation of the Mind*,[61] that it was only the most radical Christians, like Theodore Parker, and the anti-Christianity deriving from influential historical critiques of Christianity coming from Germany (Feuerbach) that enabled Frederick Douglass and even Lincoln to come to the views of the radical evil of slavery they shared and on this ground played the central roles they did against the dominant pro-slavery Christianity in the South and even the North.

As I observed in a previous chapter, Jesus was not a political or legal thinker, but a radical ethical thinker whose antipatriarchal egalitarian ethics is in advance of the major moral and political philosophers of the ancient world. Socrates was a citizen of the Athenian democracy, and certainly questioned its moral mistakes; but he fought in its imperialistic wars, and never questioned the institutions of slavery and the subjection of women central to Athenian life and thought. Plato, as we have seen in chapter 1, offered a theory of the mirror of love he believed made ethics possible, and through neo-Platonism was influential on Augustine. He takes a remarkably enlightened view of the abilities of women in the *Republic*, allowing women to be Guardians, but the ideal stated there is hierarchical, and slavery is not questioned. And Aristotle blatantly endorses both slavery and the subjection of women, the latter of which influenced Thomist misogyny. In contrast, the core of Jesus's ethics is egalitarian and, as I have argued, antipatriarchal. Though he has no developed political theory, his constant criticism of any hierarchy among the disciples inchoately suggests democracy. As we shall see in later chapters, Protestant Christianity will give rise to the first argument for toleration and indeed some form of democratic constitutionalism, but that is not until the seventeenth century, all of which we shall later discuss.

61. Stewart, *Emancipation of the Mind*.

4

How Christianities Became More Roman Than Christian

It was the great German scholar Ernst Troeltsch who offered, in my view, the most compelling analysis of what happened to the tradition of Christianities based on the life and teaching of Jesus of Nazareth. Troeltsch, like me, was struck by how the historical Jesus along the general lines of my earlier analysis could have given rise to a tradition that in so many ways did not reflect this life and teaching, focusing, in particular, on the conception of "the Patriarchalism of love"[1] and what he called the "grotesque exaltation of sexual restraint."[2] Troeltsch's more general point, with which I agree, is that from Paul to Augustine to Luther and even in the anti-Semitic way the Gospels were written when it comes to the trial and death of Jesus (exculpating the Romans, inculpating the Jews), the tradition of Christianities assumed axiomatically the patriarchal perspective that was most genial to the Roman world of their audience once Paul's gospel to the gentiles was the hegemonic way Christian practice and teaching was understood. It could be and indeed was understood in different ways, as Elaine Pagels's study of the gnostic Gospels clearly shows, Gospels which were later rejected as heretical.[3]

1. Troeltsch, *Social Teaching*, 1:285.
2. Troeltsche, *Social Teaching*, 1:131.
3. See Pagels, *Gnostic Gospels*.

While the early Christian movement took seriously some of Jesus's teaching, we see already in the epistles of Paul (written before the Gospels) doctrines of asceticism as well as an anti-Semitism, sexism, and homophobia, none of which can reasonably be attributed to the historical Jesus. The problem was, if anything, aggravated when Theodosius by edict in 380 CE makes Christianity the established church of the Roman Empire, and took on many of the features of Roman patriarchy, including a religio-political hierarchy with the Emperor at the top, and a religious hierarchy subordinate to his authority. As Troeltsch shows with great care, the pattern continues in and after the Reformation. While Luther marries, abandoning the celibacy of his monkhood, his views in both private and public life remain highly patriarchal, endorsing violence against Jews and the peasants who question the political authority of Luther's sponsors, and Calvin and other reformers support the burning of heretics. As we shall see later, Calvin and other reformers introduce more democratic elements into Christian practice, leading eventually, as we shall later see, to forms of Protestantism (in Locke and Bayle) that appeal to ideas of human rights and universal toleration, the foundations of liberal political constitutionalism. Troeltsch correctly identifies the center of the problem in the way in which antipatriarchal love, so central to the life and teaching of the historical Jesus, was seen and understood and repudiated and indeed denigrated by Christianities through the prism of a patriarchal conception of love. If love is so central to Christianity, as it appears to be, nothing could more distort, disfigure, and even repudiate its value than a view that does not take seriously the antihierarchical love lived and taught by the historical Jesus.

I will discuss many features of these later developments in chapters to follow, but here I want to explore these developments from a psychological perspective, as William James did in his pathbreaking *The Varieties of Religious Experience*.[4] James was not a conventional religious believer,[5] but, himself crippled by depression, closely examines the testimony of those who have experienced what he called the two kinds of religious experience, that of the healthy-minded and the sick-minded. It is the psychological role that religious experience plays in the sick minded that particularly interests James. James, a central figure in American pragmatism, takes no interest in the tradition of philosophical arguments for

4. James, *Varieties*.

5. See James, *Varieties*, xxiv.

the existence of God,[6] but, as a pragmatist, explores its "cash values,"[7] for example, bringing a relief to neurotic suffering. As one would expect in a philosopher of James's stature, he in fact believed that faith should play a role in religion only within certain guidelines.[8] But, in *Varieties*, his interest, as a psychologist, is in the psychology of religion, not its origin or truth, and he thus insists that nothing he documents, for example, in the psychological role of crisis and conversion in Methodism (Winnicott's religion of origin) should reasonably be interpreted as questioning its truth, but only pointing to its psychological value empirically.[9]

Winnicott's interest as a psychoanalyst in religion is, I believe, consistent with this program, including James's considered view in *Varieties* that religious experience was an aspect of the unconscious, what he called the "subconscious self"[10] or the "[o]ver belief."[11] James had critiqued the idea of the unconscious in his earlier work, *The Principles of Psychology*, but Donald Levy has shown that parts of his argument do not work and other parts accept a form of unconscious.[12] In *Varieties*, James quite clearly accepts the unconscious, citing Freud among others,[13] and sees that it plays a role in religious experience (arising, as Winnicott believed, from good-enough mothering). He also saw something that Winnicott certainly saw in the historical Jesus: that it is through religion that "in communion with the Ideal new force comes into the world,"[14] namely, an antipatriarchal conception of ethics and politics.

Winnicott's psychoanalysis of religious experience enables us to go further than James was able to do in understanding religious experience in general and of Christianities in particular. This is, I believe, quite appropriate since our argument in the previous chapter shows that the life and teaching of the historical Jesus uses a form of psychoanalysis, and I believe it remained central in the life and work of two of the main figures shaping the direction of Christianities, Augustine and Luther. For Winnicott, the psychoanalysis of religious experience begins with the

6. See, for example, James, *Varieties*, 63, 73–74.

7. James, *Varieties*, 443.

8. See, for example, James, "Will to Believe."

9. See, on this point, James, *Varieties*, 237.

10. James, *Varieties*, 511.

11. James, *Varieties*, 518.

12. See, on this point, Levy, *Freud Among the Philosophers*, 64–82.

13. James, *Varieties*, 233–36, 478–84.

14. James, *Varieties*, 521.

experience of love, either a strict parent morality or a nurturant morality, or some mixture of them. It is aspects of such early experience, including acts and omissions of what he called generically the good mother, that explain how love, which is the center of Christianity, is understood or misunderstood.

AUGUSTINE

The mirror of love, as we saw in chapter 1, was introduced by Plato in the *Phaedrus* and used by Freud as the basis for his discovery of transference love and its role in psychoanalysis. Augustine developed a Neoplatonic view of love in his understanding of the trinity, modeled on the unity of the human person, divided into memory, understanding, and love (will).[15] For Augustine, the very experience of God's presence in our lives is shown in the proto-psychoanalytic argument of his pathbreaking autobiography, *The Confessions*, which begins in his desire "simply to love and to be loved"[16] and ends in a theology based on "My weight is my love."[17] God is the addressee of *The Confessions*, "physician of my most intimate self,"[18] expressing, for Augustine, a transference love through which he comes to imagined self-knowledge of his life and loves, including his conversion to the only reliable lover, God, and the ethics, "righteousness,"[19] that expresses God's love (empathy). There is a striking analogy between the self-analysis of Freud and what is, in effect, the self-analysis of Augustine, both of which are confined to the imaginative life of the person alone, not in interpersonal relationship to another human person. In such cases, the imaginative life of even such creative thinkers as Freud and Augustine remains within the confines of their own limited experience, an experience in both cases framed by the patriarchal prism that they bring to their self-analysis, and thus do not question.[20]

It confirms the crucial role that the mirror of love plays in Augustine's Neoplatonic argument that he ultimately uses the Pauline formulation, "For now we see in a mirror, dimly, but then we will see face to

15. See Augustine, *On the Trinity* 14.1–19.

16. Augustine, *Confessions* 2.2.2 (Chadwick, 24).

17. Augustine, *Confessions* 13.10.10 (Chadwick, 278).

18. Augustine, *Confessions* 10.3.4 (Chadwick, 180).

19. Augustine, *On the Trinity* 13.13 (Haddan, 428).

20. For a criticism along these lines of Freud's naturalization of patriarchy, see Gilligan and Richards, *Deepening Darkness*, 159–97.

face,"[21] to make the point of how even his analogies between the trinity and the human person are not as clear as we might reasonably want them to be, requiring faith in an afterlife when we may experience God face to face.[22] But, for Augustine like Plato, the lover (whether divine or human) expresses love as a mirror for the beloved, an empathy that makes possible self-knowledge and both love for self and for others. The difference, of course, is that Plato's love grows from interpersonal erotic relationships of persons into empathy as such, but paradoxically Augustine not only denies such a connection, but condemns erotic sexual desire as such (conversion requiring celibacy), betraying, so I believe, the love of equals that was his deepest understanding of Jesus's teaching, thus a betrayal of that teaching, a betrayal shown by Augustine's historical role in justifying patriarchy in public and private life, including misogyny and state coercion of heretics and Jews, and all forms of nonprocreational sex (heterosexual and homosexual), all of which unjustly degrade persons, not treating them as equals. From my point of view, "we see in a mirror, dimly," as Paul puts the point, because the uncritical naturalization of patriarchy, by Paul and Augustine, among others, makes it difficult fully to see or take seriously the meaning of the love of equals, because the prism of patriarchy requires the inequalities of the patriarchal hierarchies. To illustrate, compare the appeal to the love of equals in 1 Corinthians 13 ("If I speak in the tongues of mortals and angels, but do not have love, I am a noisy gong or a clanging cymbal . . . Love is patient; love is kind . . . It does not insist on its own way; it is not irritable or resentful; it does not rejoice in wrongdoing"[23]) and Galatians 3 ("There is no longer Jew or Greek, there is no longer slave or free, there is no longer male and female, for all of you are on in Christ Jesus"[24]) with Paul's silencing of women in 1 Cor 14:34–36 ("women should be silent in the churches. They are not permitted to speak, but should be subordinate"[25]) and his paradoxically "irritable" and "resentful" (in the terms of 1 Cor 13) intemperate screed against homosexuals, among others, in 1 Cor 6:9–10. ("Fornicators, idolaters, adulterers, male prostitutes, sodomites"[26]). Contrast Jesus in Luke 7:36–50, on "a woman in the city, who was a sinner" whose anointing

21. Coogan, *New Oxford Bible*, 2054, 1 Cor 13:12.

22. See Augustine, *On the Trinity* 15.8 (Haddan, 497–98).

23. Coogan, *New Oxford Bible*, 2053–54.

24. Coogan, *New Oxford Bible*, 2084.

25. Coogan, *New Oxford Bible*, 2055.

26. Coogan, *New Oxford Bible*, 2043.

and kissing his feet Jesus defends as "she has shown great love,"[27] or his questioning of the self-righteous Pharisees in John 8 who would stone "a woman who had been caught in adultery" asking "Let anyone among you who is without sin be the first to throw a stone at her."[28] None can. Jesus here, as elsewhere, displays empathetic ethical powers of mind-reading and humane insight that disturb and surprise others ("When Jesus perceived their questionings, he answered them, 'Why do you raise such questions in your hearts'" ". . . Amazement seized all of them"[29]; "But, Jesus, perceiving their thoughts, said, 'Why do you think evil in your hearts'"[30]).

I earlier observed in the discussion of shame versus guilt cultures that probably the earliest extant description of the essential difference between a shame culture and a guilt culture was made by Augustine, in contrasting the "earthly city" (Roman shame culture) with the "heavenly city," the "city of God" (Christian guilt culture):

> Glory, the object of the Romans' burning ambition, is the judgement of men when they think well of others. That is why virtue is superior to glory, since it is not content with the testimony of men, with the witness of a man's own conscience. Hence the Apostle says, "This is our glory: the testimony of our own conscience."[31]

But, there are two features of Augustine's seminal articulation of a Christian guilt culture that were to be contested by later Christians and others, and indeed rejected as problematic: his theory of the coercive persecution of heretics, and his conception of sexual morality.

A radical shift separates the Christianity of the second century from that of the end of the fourth century, and no figure was more powerful in engineering this shift than Augustine of Hippo. The backdrop, decisively influential on the thought and life of Augustine, was the political decline of the Roman Empire itself, marked not only by bloody civil wars over the succession but also by the decisive political power of the Roman armies. As the armies proved increasingly unable to contain the barbarians on the borders of the empire,

27. Coogan, *New Oxford Bible,* 1881–82, Luke 7–8.

28. Coogan, New Oxford Bible, 1933, Matt 9:4–5.

29. Coogan, *New Oxford Bible,* 1877, Luke 5:22, 26.

30. Coogan, *New Oxford Bible,* 1794, Matt 9:5.

31. Augustine, *City of God* 5.12 (Bettenson, 199).

Rome was sacked in 410. This event shocked the Roman world and led to Augustine's work on *The City of God*, explaining why the Catholic Church (now the established church of the Roman Empire) was not responsible for this catastrophe.[32]

Christianity had been a distinctly minority religious preference in the second century. While it grew steadily after that,[33] its dominance in the fourth century was due to two remarkable developments: first, the decision of Constantine that Christianity was to be the established church of the Roman Empire, receiving massive state support and patronage continuously from then onward (except for the brief three-year reign of Julian the Apostate); and second, the decision of Theodosius in 391 that all pagan practices were to be repressed and that the state would use its coercive powers to support orthodox Christian views over heresies.[34] When Augustine converted to Christianity in 386, he was not sacrificing his earlier ambitions for success in the Roman political world, for he had learned from the example of Bishop Ambrose of Milan that a bishop exercised significant powers over the emperors and that the church could use the power of the state to enforce its orthodoxy.[35]

When he became Bishop of Hippo, Augustine was often successful in appealing to imperial power to enforce his views over his enemies, including the heretical Donatists early in his career and later the heretical Pelagians, the latter of whom denied the doctrine of original sin.[36] The great importance of Augustine in the history of church–state relations was his justification of the use of state power in such ways on religious grounds, thus rationalizing what Peter Heather has recently called "the Romanization of Christianity,"[37] retooling "itself to become a religion for warriors, against all the recorded commands of its founder in the Gospels."[38] In effect, as Heather convincingly shows, the *military* success of the Roman empire, once Christian, becomes the basis for the authority of secular rulers over Christianity, and later the military success of the papacy-inspired Crusades became the basis for the authority of the

32. See Stark, *Rise of Christianity.*

33. MacMullen, *Christianizing the Roman Empire*; Fox, *Pagans and Christians*; Fredriksen, *Ancient Christianties.*

34. See MacMullen, *Christianizing the Roman Empire.*

35. See McLynn, *Ambrose of Milan.*

36. See, on all these points, Brown, *Augustine of Hippo.*

37. See Heather, *Christendom*, xviii.

38. Heather, *Christendom*, 357.

papacy. Indeed, apparently Constantine's success in war was among his reasons for conversion.[39] The teaching of Jesus of Nazareth had nothing to do with it; quite the contrary, exemplifying the corruption of religion by politics, whatever the religion's ostensible non-violence, whether Christian or Buddhist or whatever. Augustine's theory of persecution would justify the inquisitorial powers of the Catholic Church in the Middle Ages and later, a view that was only fundamentally reexamined and repudiated by Vatican II in 1967.[40] And it was the refutation of this theory by Pierre Bayle and John Locke, among others, that was decisively important in the development of the institutions of constitutional democracy in which the argument for toleration has been of fundamental importance.[41]

At the heart of Augustine's theory of persecution lies his distinctive contribution to Christian theology, his doctrine of original sin, an inherited corruption of the will that corrupted human rationality and could be combatted as a way of securing human rationality, the rationale both for his theory of the persecution of heretics, his denigration of human sexuality, and his endorsement of autocracy, both secular and religious. The entire history of Christianity—both Catholicism and Protestantism—can be understood in terms of the ways in which Christians adopt or question the Augustinian view, including Augustine's defense of Roman imperialism and autocracy (supporting the divine right of kings) and the later impact of Protestantism on the development of human rights and constitutional democracy.[42]

Augustine's views on this matter can be freshly understood by counterposing his conversion to Christianity to Apuleius's conversion to the religion of Isis. Apuleius, author of *Metamorphoses* or *The Golden Ass*,[43] and Augustine were contemporaries, both North African Romans, and shared an education in classical philosophy as well as common ambitions and achievements as rhetoricians/lawyers. They also shared a common sense of crisis about the lives they had once led as privileged Roman men, both highly sexual. They took quite different paths, however—Apuleius into a new kind of loving relationship with an older woman (a devotee of the Isis religion, which prominently argued for the equality of women),

39. See, on this point, Fredriksen, *Ancient Christianities*, 203.

40. See, on this history, Regan, *Conflict and Consensus*.

41. See, on this point, Richards, *Toleration*.

42. See, for a brilliant general treatment, Troeltsche, *Social Teaching*.

43. For further discussion of Apuleius, see Gilligan and Richards, *Deepening Darkness*, 82–101.

Augustine into celibacy. At the center of Augustine's different path lie his views of women, women this highly sexual man had always desired and now came to regard as demonic precisely because they inspired sexual desire (the mark of original sin).

In this connection, a Catholic nun, Karol Jackowski, recently traced the "Catholic Church's obsession with legislating sexual morality" to

> the thinking of Augustine. His most famous prayer appears to be the tormented prayer of the Catholic priesthood still: "Lord, make me chaste, but not yet." And while some church historians tend to minimize and even deny Augustine's obsession with sex, I find that his teachings prove otherwise. One has only to look at Augustine's writings (especially on original sin and the seductive nature of woman) to see that this is clearly a man who could not, without anguish, stop thinking of sex, and could not stop blaming women for his misery.[44]

Jackowski points to Augustine's quite remarkable, highly mythologized reading of the Adam and Eve narrative, a narrative that is "[t]he cornerstone of current Catholic moral theology on sex and the subordinate nature of woman."[45]

There are two roads into Augustine's pivotally important thought on this matter: first, his interpretation of the Adam and Eve narrative in *The City of God*, which links a negative view of sexuality with misogyny (as Jackowski observes); and second, his highly introspective exploration of his psychological development from boy to sexual man to celibate priest and bishop in *The Confessions*. Both accounts support Jackowski's diagnosis of the close linkage between a negative view of sexuality and a misogyny that Thomas Aquinas assumed and codified as natural law.

Augustine's interpretation of the Adam and Eve narrative places Eve in the more responsible position and in essence holds her inferiority responsible for Adam's disobedience, the Fall, exile, and the taint of original sin. In Augustine's telling, the serpent "had a deceitful conversation with the woman—no doubt starting with the inferior of the human pair so as to arrive at the whole by stages, supposing that the man would not be so easily gullible, and could not be trapped by a false move on his own part, but only if he yielded to another's mistake."[46] It is this misogynist view of

44. Jackowski, *Silence We Keep*, 43.

45. Jackowski, *Silence We Keep*, 43.

46. Augustine, *City of God*, XIV.11 (Bettenson, 570).

women's intrinsic inferiority to which the Fall is attributed. Prior to this moment, Adam and Eve had not, for Augustine, experienced sexuality in the way humans now do, but a man could will erections for procreation (when needed), without any lust, just as some extraordinary people now can wiggle their ears at will or even pass air musically "without any stink."[47] The mark of the Fall, indeed its punishment, is the way sexuality now operates: "[T]otally opposed to the mind's control, it is quite often divided against itself,"[48] that is, feeling sexual desire when one does not want to feel it, and not feeling such desire when one wants to feel it. Indeed, Augustine points to the intensity of our sexual experience as a mark of our loss of rationality:

> This lust assumes power not only over the whole body, and not only from the outside, but also internally; it disturbs the whole man, when the mental emotion combines and mingles with the physical craving, resulting in a pleasure surpassing all physical delights. So intense is the pleasure that when it reaches its climax there is an almost total extinction of mental alertness; the intellectual sentries, as it were, are overwhelmed.[49]

Thus sexuality and the experience of pleasure per se become demonized.

Augustine rests his case on an experience he assumes to be universal: sexuality as a natural object of shame because it involves such loss of control, including control of our rational faculties:

> In fact, this lust we are now examining is something to be the more ashamed of because the soul, when dealing with it, neither has command of itself so as to be entirely free from lust, nor does it rule the body so completely that the organs of shame are moved by the will instead of by lust. Indeed if they were so ruled they would not be *pudenda*—parts of shame.[50]

Accordingly, the only proper form of sex is that which is done with the controlled intention to procreate. Sexuality without procreation or independent of such intention was, for Augustine, intrinsically degrading—a view he bequeathed to later Christianities.

This argument, naturalistically interpreted, rests on a rather remarkable fallacy. Augustine cites two observations about human sexual

47. Augustine, *City of God*, XIV.24 (Bettenson, 588).

48. Augustine, *City of God*, XIV.16 (Bettenson, 577).

49. Augustine, *City of God*, XIV.24 (Bettenson, 577).

50. Augustine, *City of God*, XIV.23 (Bettenson, 586).

experience: first, humans insist on having sex alone, unobserved by others, and second, humans cover their genitals in public. He argues that the only plausible explanation is that humans experience sex as degrading. The pleasure of sex thus becomes shameful, something to be avoided or hidden.

Assuming, for the purposes of argument, the truth of Augustine's anthropological assumptions,[51] it does not follow that humans find sex intrinsically shameful. These facts are equally well explained by the fact that people experience embarrassment in others witnessing their pleasure, not shame in the experience of sex itself. Shame is an emotion distinguishable from embarrassment, signifying a wound to one's pride or self-esteem. Embarrassment is experienced when a matter is made public that properly is regarded as private.[52] The twin facts adduced by Augustine are, indeed, better explained by the hypothesis of embarrassment, not shame. Surely, many people experience no negative self-evaluations when they engage in sex in private, which is what the hypothesis of embarrassment, not shame, would lead us to expect. For example, people may experience pride in knowing that other people know or believe that they are having sex (the recently married young couple). There is no shame here, but there would be embarrassment if the sex act were actually observed.

That people would experience such embarrassment reveals something important about human sexual experience, but it is not Augustine's contempt for the loss of control of sexual passion. Sexual experience can be a profoundly personal, spontaneous, and absorbing experience in which people expose fantasies and vulnerabilities that cannot brook the presence of an external observer. That humans require privacy for sex relates to the nature of the experience; its pleasure is not intrinsically degrading.

Augustine's view, as Jackowski argues, can be explained by the patriarchal misogynist assumptions he brings to his interpretation of the Adam and Eve story. To Augustine, women's inferiority accounts for the

51. A leading anthropological study of cross-cultural sexual practices reports that, universally, sexual intercourse occurs in private. See Ford and Beach, *Patterns of Sexual Behavior*, 68–72. This is not a characteristic of animal sexual behavior. "A desire for privacy during sexual intercourse seems confined to human beings. Male-female pairs of other animal species appear to be unaffected by the presence of other individuals and mate quite as readily in a crowd as when they are alone." Ford and Beach, *Patterns of Sexual Behavior*, at 71.

52. See, on this point, Richards, *Theory of Reasons*, 254.

Fall, and our sexuality is tainted by its association with woman as temptress. Indeed, our sexuality is, on this view, punishment for the Fall, the lapse of control reminding us of our primal disobedience. There is nothing interpretively inevitable in the approach to the Bible that Augustine takes, as Elaine Pagels has made quite clear.[53] There is, for example, the approach of Irenaean theodicy, which, in order to deal with the problem of evil, does not construe an original state of perfection and then fall but interprets the Adam and Eve story in terms of humankind's gradually growing into a sense of adult ethical responsibilities, learning from mistakes and developing over time new progressive insights into ethical demands.[54] Augustine brings to the narrative a misogyny that he then finds confirmed by his interpretation of it.

The psychological roots of this misogyny can, following Winnicott, be understood psychoanalytically in the terms in which Augustine narrates his own move from sexually active man to celibate priest, a move in which his mother Monica (a pious Catholic) plays a decisive role. He tells us in *The Confessions* that he had a loving affair with a woman with whom he had a son, Adeodatus: "she was the only girl for me, and I was faithful to her."[55] She was not, however, a woman of a class Augustine could marry, and he separated from her at his mother's insistence so that he could marry within the terms of the patriarchal order of the time. Monica had arranged a suitable marriage for her son, but since the girl in question would only be of age in two years, he had taken another woman as his mistress. Augustine's words for the separation from the woman he loved convey the traumatic nature of this break: "My heart which was deeply attached was cut and wounded, and left a trail of blood."[56] It is the psychology of traumatic loss that expresses itself in Augustine's idealization of celibacy, deriving from a competitive pride that, in contrast to his mother, he has gone beyond even her in taking what for him was the indispensable psychological route to the love of God, celibacy.

The psychoanalyst, Jessica Benjamin, clarifies the underlying psychology:

> It is a maxim of psychoanalysis that idealization is a defense against aggression and so emerges when hate cannot be

53. See Pagels, *Adam, Eve*, 98–126.

54. See Hick, "Irenaean Theodicy." I am grateful to Donald Levy for this reference.

55. Augustine, *Confessions* 4.2.2 (Chadwick, 53).

56. Augustine, *Confessions* 6.15.25 (Chadwick, 109).

> integrated with love; this failure of integration is the essential element in splitting. What determines whether hatred becomes the destruction that dispels idealization or, instead, goes inside where it requires idealization as a defense is, finally, *what happens in real life.*[57]

What happened in Augustine's real life is that he lost not only his beloved son Adeodatus (who died) but the two woman (the concubine and his mother) he loved, one of whom (his mother) had condemned the role sexuality played in Augustine's life and perhaps in the life of all men,[58] and Augustine—experiencing what probably was unconscious anger, and even hatred at her demands (including that he give up his beloved concubine)—resolves his ambivalence through an idealization of his mother and her view of sexuality (carried further than his mother might have carried it, as she always wanted her son to marry but in an arranged marriage she sponsored), an ambivalence acted out in anger and hatred of women (misogyny) and self-punishment of his own sexuality. It is the psychological mark of such ambivalence that the anger remains unconscious—consciously, even extravagantly professing love while acting out anger against oneself and others. Monica, certainly not a good-enough mother in Winnicott's sense, is idealized by her son, idealization covering loss and contempt and rage at women as such and the sexuality women provoke in men.

Augustine in *The Confessions* writes of his grief at his mother's death, shortly after his conversion, in a striking way that confirms this analysis: "I had lost the immense support she gave, my soul was wounded, and my life, as it were, torn to pieces, since my life and hers had become a single thing."[59] In light of Monica's rejection of her husband's delight in their son's sexual development (in contrast, "she shook with a pious trepidation and a holy fear"[60]) and her insistence to her son "that you, my God, were my father rather than he, and in this endeavour you helped her to gain victory over her husband,"[61] the psychoanalytic analysis of Margaret Mahler of such mother-son relations is relevant here:

57. Benjamin, *Bonds of Love,* 214.

58. Monica's response to the sexual development of her son, in which her husband rejoices, was radically different: "she shook with a pious trepidation and a holy fear" (Augustine, *Confessions* 2.3.6 [Chadwick, 27]).

59. Augustine, *Confessions* 9.12.30 (Chadwick, 174–75).

60. Augustine, *Confessions* 2.3.6 (Chadwick, 27).

61. Augustine, *Confessions* 1.11.17 (Chadwick, 14).

> If, however, the mother is too intrusive and consistently interferes directly or indirectly with the boy's phallic strivings, the ambitendent struggles in the case of girls may ensue in the boy as well and may even give way to passive surrender. The latter is particularly harmful if the father image does not lend itself to idealization and to true ego-identification.[62]

"[M]y life and hers had become a single thing," Augustine writes, a symbiotic fusion, the grieving son, Augustine, internalizing his mother's own misogyny about sexuality in women, and sexuality generally, as "a single thing."

It confirms such misogyny that Augustine models friendship as always between or among men, arguing that the biblical description of Eve as "a helper of his partner"[63] cannot mean friendship, but only her role in procreation:

> Now, if the woman was not made for the man to be his helper in begetting children, in what was she to help him? She was not to till the earth with him, for there was not yet any toil to make help necessary. If there were any such need, a male helper would be better, and the same could be said of the comfort of another's presence if Adam were perhaps weary of solitude. How much more agreeably could two male friends, rather than a man and woman, enjoy companionship and conversation in a life shared together.[64]

Correspondingly, the same idea that a woman's relationship to men is solely her role in procreation appears in Augustine's interpretation of the biblical text: "So God created humankind in his image, in the image of God he created them, male and female he created them."[65] Women is the image of God only in her relationship to men, "but when she is referred separately to her quality of help-meet, which regards the women herself alone, then she is not the image of God."[66] Women are thus persons only in patriarchal hierarchy to men, otherwise they are effectively dehumanized.

What we see in Augustine's formulation of a guilt morality is, in fact, what we earlier saw in Bernadette Brooten's critique of Christian

62. Mahler et al., *Psychological Birth,* 215.

63. Genesis 2 in Coogan, *New Oxford Bible,* 14.

64. Augustine, *Literal Meaning* 5 (Taylor, 65).

65. Genesis 1 in Coogan, *Oxford New Bible,* 13.

66. Augustine, *On the Trinity* 12.7 (Haddan, 389).

homophobia as based on pagan gender stereotypes deviation from which is shaming, namely, the distortion of a guilt morality by Augustine's uncritical carrying forward of Roman patriarchal shame morality (built on the gender binary and hierarchy), rationalized by a uniquely Augustinian reading of a biblical narrative that sexuality itself is intrinsically wrong and shaming, the just subject of punishing violence elicited by any challenge to or deviation from such imagined wrongness, including experiencing such sexual feeling (including, for Augustine, the "sense of shame at night-emissions"[67]) or, for heterosexual men like Augustine, the women who, in imagination or in fact, provoke such feelings. (Augustine for this reason "imposed strict codes of sexual avoidance on himself and his own clergy. He would never visit a woman unchaperoned, and did not allow even his own female relatives to enter the bishop's place. He expelled a young clergyman who has been speaking with a nun 'at an inappropriate hour of the day.'"[68]) So, it is the shaming of a conception of patriarchal manhood, thus understood, that elicits the violent repression of heretics and similar violence against sexual violations of patriarchal morality, for example, adultery. It is a crucial feature of leading liberal thinkers in the Protestant tradition that they come to reject both the theory of persecution (Bayle and Locke) and, as we see in Hawthorne's *Scarlet Letter*, the condemnation of all forms of adultery and later consensual homosexuality.

As we earlier saw, no one was more insistent than Augustine that God was love, and love was central to understanding our ethical lives. Consider the following:

> Once for all, then, a short precept is given thee: "*Love, and do what thou wilt*:" whether thou hold thy peace, through love hold thy peace; whether thou cry out, through love cry out; whether thou correct, through love correct; whether thou spare, through love do thou spare: *let the root of love be within, of this root can nothing spring but what is good.*[69]

The propensity to guilt, arising in loving relationships when the beloved is hurt or betrayed, has, however, been deformed by Augustine's patriarchal assumptions not only as rationalizing violence against others,

67. Brown, *Augustine of Hippo*, 391.

68. Brown, *Body*, 396.

69. Augustine, "Homily 7 on the First Epistle of John," para. 8. See also Augustine, *Homilies on the Gospel of John*.

but also, if a person rejected in his own life Augustine's political and personal morality, violence against the self, quite apparent, I believe, in his idealization of celibacy and implicit denigration of consensual adult nonprocreational sexuality (including homosexuality). It was such denigration that explains why Augustine took the sharpest objection to the Jewish view of sexuality as a good: he made this point in terms of "carnal Israel," explaining that "the Jews . . . prove themselves to be indisputably carnal,"[70] and thus worthy of denigration, a rationalization for Christian anti-Semitism.[71]

Consider Augustine's idealization of his own celibacy, as the "true and perfect sacrifice," a kind of heroism, so "does the soul itself become a sacrifice when it offers itself to God, so that it may be kindled by the fire of love and may lose the 'form' of worldly desire."[72] The violence of the punishing self-sacrifice of one's sexuality, including having sexual feelings, is thus idealized, reflected in Thomas A Kempis's later ascetic Augustinian call for a relationship exclusively to Jesus, "Love Him and cling to him for your friend because He will not abandon you,"[73] otherwise without friends, because "[t]he world is despicable,"[74] and thus one "ought to live like a dying man,"[75] with grisly in kind punishments in prospect when "you spare yourself and follow the flesh," "[t]he slothful . . . pricked forward with burning pokers,"[76] and the like. Contrast such Augustinian asceticism with Jesus's words in Matt 9:13: "I desire mercy, not sacrifice,"[77] and his comments on the lack of understanding of his fellowship dining with outcasts, "the Son of Man has come eating and drinking, and you say, 'Look, a glutton and drunkard, a friend of tax collectors and sinners!'"[78]

70. Cited in Boyarin, *Carnal Israel*, 1.

71. See, for further discussion, Gilligan and Richards, *Deepening Darkness*, 129–37.

72. Augustine, *City of God* 10.7 (Bettenson, 379).

73. à Kempis, *Imitation*, 47

74. à Kempis, *Imitation*, 81.

75. à Kempis, *Imitation*, 55.

76. à Kempis, 35.

77. Coogan, *New Oxford Bible*, 1795, Matt 9:13.

78. Coogan, *New Oxford Bible*, 1881, Luke 7:34.

LUTHER

If Augustine played a central role in the formation of Roman Catholicism, the comparable figure in Protestantism is Martin Luther: but their conversions move in opposite directions, in Augustine from sexual love to celibacy; in Luther, from celibacy to a sexually loving marriage.

For purposes of advancing my argument to explore psychoanalytically these towering figures in the history of Christianities, along the lines of Winnicott's views, there is happily for me at hand a superlative work of psychobiography, indeed of psychoanalytic biography, Erik Erikson's *Young Man Luther*.[79] It was a work familiar to me in college, where I took a course with Erikson at Harvard College, but it was in the context of the research project for this book that I reread it and found precisely the kind of psychoanalytic exploration that I believed Winnicott called for. Erikson studied Luther in the larger context of Erikson's work on identity in the life crisis, as no one better exemplifies such a life crisis than Luther. It was his relation to his parents which set the stage for his crisis:

> Luther's parents *were* simple folk, to be sure: hard, thrifty, and superstitious—but most of all, Hans Luder [the father] was an ambitious man. This ex-peasant, who had to yield his father's farm and fortune, who made his wife go and gather firewood in the forest—one of the items which has impressed biographer . . . He also made his son go to Latin school and to a university, and expected to become a jurist . . . For this, no price was too high, and money was available. In this family framework—a past to be lived down and a future to be started then and there at any cost—we must view the scant data on Luther's upbring, sometimes surer of the forces than of the facts.[80]

There was corporal punishment by both parents, and he wrote that the mother beat him "until the blood came" and this was for "one nut" which he presumably stole, and that such discipline "drove him into the monastery."[81] However:

> whatever resentment he felt against her was never expressed as dramatically was his fatherhate, which took the form of a burning doubt of divine righteousness.[82]

79. Erikson, *Young Man*.
80. Erikson, *Young Man*, 54.
81. Quoted in Erikson, *Young Man*, 67.
82. Erikson, *Young Man*, 65.

On Luther's relation to his mother, Erikson observes:

> [F]rom what burst forth later that which must have forced to lie dormant in childhood; this may well have included some communality of experience with the mother, whose spontaneity and imagination are said to have suffered at the side of Hans Luder.[83]

Nonetheless,

> The double role of the mother as one of the powerless victims of the father's brutality and also as one of his dutiful assistants in meeting out punishment to the children may well account for a peculiar split in the mother image. The mother was perhaps cruel only because she had to be, but the father because he wanted to be.[84]

Luther saw a direct impact of his view of religion: "From childhood on, I knew I had to turn pale and be terror-striken when I heard the name of Christ; for I was taught only to perceive him as a strict and wrathful judge."[85] To protect himself, Erikson points, echoing Winnicott's view of the need for a secret self, to Luther's "quite inarticulate stubbornness, a secret furious inviolacy, a gathering of impressions for eventual use within some as yet dormant new configuration of thought,"[86] but "[l]ike many an inhibited and deep-down sad youth, Martin utilized his musical gifts, his lute-playing and singing, to remain a welcome fellow among a circle of friends."[87] Erikson, reflecting on Luther's relation to this mother, states:

> as a clinician's judgment, that nobody could speak and sing as Luther did if his mother's voice has not sung to him of some heaven; that nobody could be as torn between his masculine and his feminine sides, nor have such a range of both, who did not at one time feel that he was like his mother; but also, that nobody would discuss women and marriage in the way he often did who had not been deeply disappointed by his mother—and had become loath to succumb the way she did to the father, to fate.[88]

The consequence was that, for Luther,

83. Erikson, *Young Man*, 65.
84. Erikson, *Young Man*, 70.
85. Quoted in Erikson, *Young Man*, 71.
86. Erikson, *Young Man*, 83.
87. Erikson, *Young Man*, 83.
88. Erikson, *Young Man*, 72–73.

> the Mother of God (that focus of women's natural religion-by-being-and-letting be) was dethroned. Luther refers to her almost sneeringly as one of the female saints who might induce a man to "hang on their necks" or "hold on to their skirts": "And because we would never do enough and holy works, and in spite of all remained full of fear and terror of [God's] anger, they told us to look to the saints in heaven who should be the mediators between Christ and us . . . "[89]

Luther's friends gave him "the nickname of Philosophicus,"[90] showing that, even at an early age, he was passionately serious, argumentative, and thoughtful about his reading in "elegant scholastic attempts to reconcile Aristotelian physics and the Last Judgement,"[91] a scholastic Aristotelian teaching he would come to reject before and after his conversion and becoming a celibate monk.

Erikson quotes a revelatory comment by Luther on his conversion: "I became a monk against the wishes of my father, of my mother, of God, and the Devil."[92] Throughout his struggles, Luther was transfixed by Augustine's similar attempt to answer "the question of man's identity in the hidden fact of God, and God's in the revealed face of man; it includes the possibility of ever receiving an inkling of mutual recognition as through a glass darkly, or the shadow of a smile."[93] What is so strikingly common in the experience leading to conversion of Augustine and Luther is their seeking a deeper love than any they had theretofore experienced, what Erikson calls: "[t]he search for mutual recognition, the *meeting face to face*, . . . in his [Luther's] religion which we must consider if we are to understand the deepest nostalgia of lonely youth."[94] What is so radically different is that Luther's struggles led him to reject "the suicide of celibacy"[95] and to marry a former nun and have children with her, whereas for Augustine rejecting sexual love and becoming celibate is central to the only way he came to believe he could achieve the only love worth having, the love of and for God.

89. Erikson, *Young Man*, 71.

90. Erikson, *Young Man*, 83.

91. Erikson, *Young Man*, 83–84.

92. Quoted at Erikson, *Young Man*, 72.

93. Erikson, *Young Man*, 182. For fuller discussion of Luther on Augustine, see Erikson, *Young Man*, 182–84, 204.

94. Erikson, *Young Man*, 115.

95. Erikson, *Young Man*, 161.

Luther's conversion leads to becoming a monk, but, as a monk and learned scholar and increasingly renowned preacher, Erikson sees his coming over time to his revolutionary views on Christianity (rejecting the authority of the Roman Catholic Church) in a series of lectures he gave while still a monk, including *Lectures on the Psalms,*[96] *Commentary on Galatians,*[97] and, finally, *Lectures on Romans*[98] (it was, strikingly, reading Romans that led to Augustine's conversion). He said of his preaching "You must preach as a mother suckles her child,"[99] appealing, as Erikson suggested, to his experience of his mother and that, as preacher, he was a good mother. These lectures culminate in his leaving monkhood and celibacy, marrying and having children, and espousing the doctrine of salvation through faith alone, abandoning the authority of the Catholic Church on what he called works and its commitment to scholastic philosophy, and becoming the leading figure in the Reformation. In a remarkable letter to his father, which he published as a preface to a pamphlet explaining why he gave up his monastic vows, Luther confesses that his father was always right that he could and should not give up sexuality for celibacy, but goes on say his views came from a loving God, not his father.[100] He continued to believe, however, "that concupiscence, *i.e.*, our drive endowment, is a leftover of original sin,"[101] and followed Augustine in regarding Eve as responsible for the fall.[102]

Luther's search for identity culminates in a conscience made possible by a direct relationship to the love of Jesus, not unlike the historical Jesus's appeal to his direct relationship to a loving father. But, understandably in light of Luther's traumatic relationship to his own father, there is no appeal in Luther to God the father, but to the love Luther found in Jesus himself. Luther's repudiation of the Law, the commands of God the father, is that the Law elicits sin:

> The Law is a mirror to show a person what he is like, a sinner who is guilty of death, and worthy of everlasting punishment. What is this bruising and beating by the hand of the Law to accomplish? This that we may find the way to grace. The Law is an

96. See Luther, *First Lectures on Psalms I*; Luther, *First Lectures on Psalms II.*
97. See Luther, *Commentary on Galatians*; Luther, *Saint Paul's Epistle.*
98. Luther, *Lectures on Romans*; Luther, *Commentary on Romans.*
99. Erikson, *Young Man,* 198.
100. Erikson, *Young Man,* 222–23.
101. Erikson, *Young Man,* 163.
102. See Luther, *Commentary on Genesis.*

> usher to lead the way to grace. God is the God of the humble, the miserable, the afflicted. It is His nature to exalt the humble, to comfort the sorrowing, to heal the broken-hearted, to justify the sinners, and to save the condemned. The fatuous idea that a person can be holy by himself denies God the hammer of the Law in His fist and smash the beast of self-righteousness and its brood of self-confidence, self-wisdom, self-righteousness, and self-help. When the conscience has been thoroughly frightened by the Law it welcomes the Gospel of grace with its message of a Savior who came into the world, not to break the bruised reed, nor to quench the smoking flax, but to preach glad tidings to the poor, to heal the broken-hearted, and to grant forgiveness of sins to all the captives.[103]

Thinking surely of his own father, Luther contrasts "the old man" to a personal relationship to Jesus, a passionate and fulfilling love:

> Meanwhile, the old man lives on the outside and is subject to the law. But insofar as justification is concerned, Christ and I need to be connected so that He can live in me and I in Him. This is a wonderful way of speaking. Now, since Christ lives in me, take a look at the type of grace, righteousness, life, peace, and salvation that there is in me. It is His, and yet it is also mine due to that inseparable union and adherence that comes through faith. By this faith, Christ and I are as if we were one in body and spirit. Inasmuch as Christ lives in me, it follows that together with Him, I am a participant of grace, righteousness, life, and eternal salvation. Thus the law, sin, and death have no place in me. The law has been crucified and devoured by the law, sin by sin, and death by death. In this way, Paul drags us away from self-inspections, from the law and its works, and brings us within Christ Himself where we are transplanted into the faith of Jesus. Therefore, we should not think there is some other reason for our justification except grace alone. That is why we should separate grace far apart from the law and works, for in this matter, they have nothing to do with one another.[104]

The speculations of scholastic philosophy are thus dismissed: "I do not bother my head with speculations about the nature of Christ. I simply

103. Luther, *Commentary on Galatians*, 90.

104. Luther, *Commentary on St. Paul's Epistle*, 143.

attach myself to the human Christ, and I find joy and peace, and wisdom of God in Him."[105] In contrast to his relationship to "the human Christ":

> the divine law—which ought to help to righteousness, if anything can—has not only helped, but has even increased sin; for the reason that the more the law forbids, the more our evil nature hates is, and the more it wants to give rein to its own lust. Thus the law makes Christ all the more necessary, and more grace is needed to help our nature.[106]

Luther was not only responsive to music, but himself a creative musical artist, writing a number of hymns for Lutheran services,[107] including "A Mighty Fortress Is Our God." In his two-volume study of J. S. Bach, Schweitzer observes, "Luther was not only a reformer but an artist," and regarded "artistic music as one of the most perfect manifestations of the Deity," particularly admiring contrapuntal polyphony, "a song adorned with many voices,"[108] most notably, the works of the Flemish composer, Josquin des Pres ("He is the master of the notes; they have to do as he wills; other composers have to do as the notes will"[109]). Schweitzer observes: "had Luther not been an artist, Bach would never have been able to write his sacred concert music for church purposes and as part of the church service"[110] (Bach used several hymns by Luther in his works[111]).

Bach was, in fact, a devout orthodox Lutheran, having a complete set of Luther's works in his library,[112] and Schweitzer regards Bach's work as largely in service of his Lutheran piety: "[f]or him, art was religion, and so had no concern with the world or with worldly success."[113] In his cantatas and passions, Bach creates extraordinary musical portraits of what he would have taken to be the historical Jesus (including the now notorious and historically discredited anti-Semitism of the Gospels—Luther was himself a virulent anti-Semite—that he sets in the two passions). My interest here is how these works—the Matthew Passion and one of the

105. Luther, *Commentary on Galatians*, 16.

106. Luther, *Commentary on Romans*, xxi.

107. See Wikipedia, "List of Hymns by Martin Luther."

108. Quoted in Schweitzer, *J. S. Bach*, 1:29.

109. Quoted in Schweitzer, *J.S. Bach*, 1:30.

110. Schweitzer, *J.S. Bach*, 1:30.

111. Schweitzer, *J.S. Bach*, 1:9–10.

112. Schweitzer, *J.S. Bach*, 2:168.

113. Schweitzer, *J.S. Bach*, 2:168.

cantatas—bring out the personal intimacy of Lutheran religiosity, from Luther to Bach on forward, to the human Jesus, and the identification of the believer with Jesus portrayed with extraordinary, dramatic musical power in several of these works, which literally bring the audience in relationship to Jesus as a person, a lover.

Consider, for example, two remarkable arias in the Matthew Passion. The first is the alto aria bringing the audience into identification with the bitter cry for mercy of Peter after his betrayal of Jesus, in German, "Erbarme dich, mein Gott," in English as follows:

> Have mercy, Lord on me,
> Regard my bitter weeping,
> Look at me, heart and eyes
> Both weep to Thee bitterly
> Have mercy, Lord![114]

The second is the soprano aria bringing the audience into identification with the love of Jesus dying for us and how his love frees us from guilt, in German, "Aus Liebe will mein Heiland sterben," in English as follows:

> For love my Saviour now is dying,
> Of sin and guilt He knoweth naught,
> So eternal desolation
> And the sinner's righteous doom
> Shall not rest upon my spirit.[115]

The cantata, "Ich habe genug" ("It is enough") has death for its theme, but the voice of the singer reflects "the heavenly home-sickness of the old man who is already detached from all the things of this world," in an aria in which, as Schweitzer puts it: "Inexpressible joy wells forth from the semiquaver passage with which the orchestra, in the first aria, accompanies the arabesques of the oboe."[116] The oboe and the voice portray a love for one another, or even making love, the believer and Jesus.

What Bach portrays in these and others works is an art portraying the intimacy of Luther's personal connection to Jesus, the human Jesus, as he and Bach experienced the connection, which certainly clarifies why it is Protestantism that gave rise to the search for the historical Jesus. Even though Luther and others had an imperfect understanding of the historical Jesus (attributing to him an anti-Semitism and sexism and even

114. Bach, *Matthaus-Passion*, 84.

115. Bach, *Matthaus-Passion*, 94.

116. Schweitzer, *J. S. Bach*, 2:256.

homophobia foreign to both his life and teaching), it is remarkable in the over-all history of the development of Christianities how much Luther made a quite personal conception of conscience based on an intimate relationship to a loving Jesus more central than it had ever been, and on this basis contested, as Erikson argues, very much in the spirit of the Renaissance:

> the Church's systematic and terroristic exploitation of man's proclivity for a negative conscience. Latin Christianity in Martin's time tended to promote freedom from the body as the price of the absolute power of negative external conscience: negative in that it was based on a sense of sin, and external in that it was defined and redefined by a punitive agency which alone was aware of the rationale of morality and the consequences of disobedience.[117]

The psychoanalytic brilliance of Erikson's exploration of Luther's crisis of identity is that it reveals, in the spirit of Winnicott's psychology of religion, Luther's own divided conscience, the positive conscience rooted in loving relationship, the negative conscience of his father's wrathful, punitive domination—the image of everything Luther came to hate in the Law and its works. What Erikson shows us in Luther's development is what Augustine showed us in *The Confessions* and what led Winnicott to regard Jesus as "a leading psychotherapist," namely, a struggle to find and stay in relationship to someone who could meet the psyche's need for a sustaining mirror of love and to bring into the world a way of being that the antipatriarchal Jesus called "the kingdom of heaven." Augustine's *Confessions* is, so I have come to believe, written intrapsychically to God, the loving therapist, and Erikson's Luther is in an intrapsychic relationship to a loving Jesus. But, in both cases, what disfigures their self-psychoanalysis is precisely that it is intra-psychic, and their identification, in Augustine's case with a mother he unconsciously hated, and, in Luther's case, with a mother he unconsciously loved more than hated and a father he unconsciously both loved and hated. In both cases, the consequence of such unconscious hate is that it works its will, projecting onto God the divided conscience, including the negative conscience's irrational hatreds—in Augustine for heretics and Jews, legitimating persecution; in Luther, virulent anti-Semitism and endorsement of violence against peasants resisting their exploitation.

117. Erikson, *Young Man*, 192.

What Augustine and Luther also share are the important roles they occupy in the creative play, in Winnicott's sense, in developing the tradition of Christianities, just as the historical Jesus did in his play as a prophet in the Jewish tradition that he assumed and elaborated. Creative play is the appropriate way to understand how in all these cases there is remarkable creativity in transforming a tradition and yet working within its parameters in which the relations of religion to ethics play an important part, and love is always a central value.

What remains of lasting value in Luther in the development of Christianities is the striking inwardness and subjectivity his appeal to conscience unleashed, in particular by his abandonment (calling it "the suicide of celibacy"[118]) of the celibacy that Augustine had believed was the only route to God's love. When Luther married

> he married, he said, because his father wanted him to, a statement so incomprehensible to some that they think it must have been a joke; yet his father, when he heard of Luther's hesitation, urged him to continue the family name which was endangered by the death of his brothers. And marriage was part of the belatedly manifest identification with his father which at this time, openly and secretly, began to determine much of Luther's life . . . A superior resiliency is suggested by the fact that despite having been a captive after years of monastic abstinence and a virginal youth, he could at the age of forty-five enter an apparently happy marriage . . . In 1526, his son was born, and christened, Hans [the name of his father].[119]

Ernst Troeltsch has persuasively shown that Luther and the other reformers defined "the Christian social idea" in terms of "the conception of the Patriarchalism of love,"[120] pointing, in particular, to Luther's authoritarianism and patriarchalism,[121] but notes:

> the sex ethic of Protestantism was very different from that of Catholicism. Luther's own marriage meant more than a very manifest and concrete attempt to overthrow the idea of the celibacy of the priesthood; it was also that proclamation of a principle of sex ethics which regarded the sex-life as something normal, and which gave it an ethical character, making it a means of the most

118. Erikson, *Young Man*, 161.
119. Erikson, *Young Man*, 237.
120. Troeltsch, *Social Teaching*, 1:285.
121. Troeltsch, *Social Teaching*, 2:528–29.

> vital ethical and religious functions for all believers. Luther did not conceive the purpose of marriage solely from the point of view of the procreation and nurture of children, as so frequently happens when a fundamentally ascetic spirit is softened and adjusted to other ideals, as, for instance, in Puritanism.[122]

Even within what Troeltsch calls the new sex ethic of Protestantism, there are, as he point out, differences, and the dominant pattern for sexual relations is still heterosexual patriarchal marriage. Nonetheless, the very inwardness and subjectivity of the role conscience now played among Protestant Christianities opened up the question of the legitimacy of patriarchy as the lens through which Christianity should be understood.

122. Troeltsch, *Social Teaching*, 2:545.

5

Agape Love in Christianities

THE HISTORICAL JESUS PLACES love at the center of both his life and teaching, but there is controversy among Christianities about how it should be understood as a religious and ethical ideal, including its connections, if any, to the forms of love in friendship, families, and erotic sexual love.

NYGREN AND KIERKEGAARD ON AGAPE LOVE

The issue has been dramatically posed by Anders Nygren in *Agape and Eros*, Nygren offers a detailed account of what he takes to be the distinctive Christian conception of agape love, which he regards as not in the Gospels, but starts with Paul and the tradition of Christianities that appealed to Paul, including both Augustine and Luther. Nygren is anxious to distinguish the development of agape love, which for him culminates in Martin Luther's "Copernican Revolution,"[1] from any form of erotic love, as stated and defended by Plato. The marks of agape love, in contrast to human love, is that it is a one-sided spontaneous outpouring of love for us on God's part[2] (whereas human love is "human motivated," extending its scope "to embrace benefactors to the self"[3]) and does not

1. Nygren, *Agape*, 681.
2. Nygren, *Agape*, 94–95.
3. Nygren, *Agape*, 96–97.

extend to self-love.[4] Nygren discusses Augustine as a central figure in the development of the idea of Christian love, but finds his account contaminated by its too close connection to Neoplatonic love and thus to Plato's erotic love.[5] Augustine's synthesis thus culminates in what Nygren calls Caritas, but it too is contaminated because, "for Augustine, . . . *all love is acquisitive love*."[6] Luther's importance, indeed his "Copernican Revolution," is his statement, for Nygren, of the true conception of agape love in Christianities:

> Against the egocentric attitudes, which had come to mark the Catholic conception of love, Luther sets a thoroughly theocentric idea of love.[7]

The marks of such true Christian love are that it is (1) "spontaneous in contrast to all activity with a eudaemonistic motive";[8] (2) "spontaneous in contrast to all legalism";[9] (3) "overflowing love,"[10] as Luther put it; (4) unlimited by man's "worth or worthlessness";[11] and (5) "poured out upon those who reward it with ingratitude."[12]

A view of this sort clearly assumes or defends, as Augustine did, original sin, that human nature is fundamentally flawed, even depraved, and that any possibility of overcoming these defects requires what various Christianities called agape love, a one-sided pouring out of love on us, shown, as they believed, in the sacrifice of Jesus, the model for the emphasis of most Christianities on self-sacrifice. There is a wide range of opinion among Christianities today about which interpretation of agape love is to be preferred,[13] but its features and difficulties are best studied, in my opinion, in the works of Søren Kierkegaard, which defend a Lutheran conception of agape very much along the lines of Nygren, and yet portrays, in several of his works, a kind of proto-psychoanalytic psychology

4. Nygren, *Agape*, 100–101.

5. Nygren, *Agape*, 449–75.

6. Nygren, *Agape*, 476.

7. Nygren, *Agape*, 683; italics in original removed.

8. Nygren, *Agape*, 726; italics in original removed.

9. Nygren, *Agape*, 727; italics in original removed.

10. Nygren, *Agape*, 730.

11. Nygren, *Agape*, 731.

12. Nygren, *Agape*, 732.

13. See, for illuminating discussions, Outka, *Agape*; Saturri and Werpehowski, *Love Commandments*.

of its development in stages: erotic love, ethics along Kantian lines, and finally religion: agape love of Jesus for us, the only true lover, and yet for Kierkegaard the most demanding of lovers, as his conception of agape love required.[14]

Kierkegaard is a notoriously difficult author, usually writing in pseudonyms. He celebrated, for example, the irony of Socrates, as a way to protect oneself from possible or probable persecution for one's true views.[15] But it is illuminating to regard both his life and prodigious writings (many of them self-published) in Winnicott's terms of the search for a true self in contrast to the false selves on offer in Danish culture. The search originates in a secret self he expresses enigmatically in his writings, precisely to protect his very human vulnerabilities from the kinds of domination he apparently experienced from a domineering, rigid and conventionally religious father, not unlike Luther's (the wealthy father's legacy, however, left his son sufficiently well off that he could pursue rather obsessively his writing and publication).[16] Kierkegaard was later to complain "that he never had a childhood,"[17] and a friend "recalled how his mother repeatedly told him that 'never in her life (and she had no little experience) had she seen a human being as deeply distressed as S. Kierkegaard by the death of his mother.'"[18] His mother, with whom he was quite close, is never mentioned, however, in his writings. Her loss was, for him, unspeakable.

The central event of Kierkegaard's life, about which he felt bottomless guilt to the end of his life, was his abrupt breaking off of his planned marriage to Regine Olsen, sending back the ring with a letter saying

> "So as not to go through more rehearsals of what must happen in any case, something that when it does happen will surely give strength let it be done. Above all forget the one who writes this: forgive someone who whatever else he was capable of could not make a girl happy." The letter was later reproduced in *Stages on Life's Way.*
>
> The strength Kierkegaard's letter produced in Regine was not of the kind he hoped. Instead of inspiring stoic fortitude it energized her into a frenzied defence of the engagement. On

14. Kierkegaard, *Either/Or*; Kierkegaard, *Stages on Life's Way.*
15. See, for example, Kierkegaard, *Concept of Irony.*
16. See, for illuminating biographies, Hannay, *Kierkegaard*; Garff, *Soren Kierkegaard.*
17. Hannay, *Kierkegaard*, 59.
18. Hannay, *Kierkegaard*, 51.

> receiving the letter she went immediately to Kierkegaard's apartment, but finding him away sat down there and wrote him what was, according to Kierkegaard, an "altogether despairing letter" in which she begged him "with tears and prayers (for the sake of Jesus Christ, in memory of my dead father") not to desert her. He could do "anything with her, absolutely anything" and she would "still thank [him] all her life for the greatest of blessings."
>
> The two months to come before the final break he called a period of "deceit." The deception was . . . putting on of indifference that he hoped would induce her to end it herself, or at least to go their separate ways. Apart from provoking Regine to do the opposite, the result was in a strange way to bind her to him forever. Paradoxically, by the time Kierkegaard recorded these thoughts Regine had become engaged to someone else . . . In his own case Kierkegaard found that the infinite in love was possible only in the pain of recollection and regret. Here he says that even though they are parted, his thought had been—"and it was love"—"either I become yours or you will be allowed to wound me so deeply, wound me in my melancholy and my relationship to God, so deeply that, although parted from you, I will yet remain yours."[19]

At the end of his life, Kierkegaard left his estate to Regine, which she refused, "asking that her letters be returned along with a few personal items."[20]

Kierkegaard complains to Regine, a woman he himself wounded, that she wounded him, "so deeply, wound[ed] me in my and my relationship to God." What is alive for Kierkegaard, in a way love for Regine was never alive, was his relationship to Jesus, modeled on Augustine's and Luther's passionately personal relationship to Jesus, their only true lover. For Augustine, this love required celibacy. For Luther, abandoning monasticism and celibacy because they stood in the way of his personal relationship to God's limitless agape love, who could alone minister to his wretchedness as a flawed human, as all humans were, in Luther's view. Kierkegaard, like Augustine and Luther, only becomes his true self in relationship to God's agape love, which, like them, he believes to be asymmetrical: spontaneously pouring out on us, wretched creatures otherwise damned to despair. Kierkegaard writes from and out of despair, a despair of human love forever lost and irremediable, in terms that a

19. Hannay, *Kierkegaard*, 156.

20. Hannay, *Kierkegaard*, 419.

psychoanalyst like Winnicott would immediately recognize in the titles of Kierkegaard's works, *The Concept of Anxiety: A Simple Psychologically Oriented Deliberation in View of the Dogmatic Problem of Hereditary Sin,*[21] *Fear and Trembling,*[22] *The Sickness Unto Death.*[23]

Kierkegaard's sense of his own bottomless guilt was, I believe, what his secret self gave creative expression to in his remarkable works, and his ultimate addressee was, I believe, the loving Jesus with whom Augustine and Luther were also in relationship. But, the conception of agape love that their Christianities share requires that the relationship be asymmetrical, a relationship always in its nature, because of the fall, imperfect, seeing God's face through a glass darkly. The clearest book Kierkegaard ever wrote on this point, and one of the very few he wrote in his own name, was *Works of Love.*[24] The book is written as an interpretation of Jesus's Love Commandments (love God, and love your neighbors as you love yourself). Kierkegaard draws, however, as the view taken of agape love by Christianities requires, a sharp psychological distinction between the ethical demands of God's love (the antipatriarchal idea of treating persons as equals) and human love, which, precisely because it is selective and intensely personal, is assumed to violate or be in tension with these ethical demands. So, Kierkegaard can understand his own guilt in terms of the tension between his love or assumed love for Regine and the demands of agape love, to which he sacrificed his love for Regine.

It is at this point that we can see the truth and value of Winnicott's psychoanalytic interpretation of the historical Jesus ("a leading psychotherapist"). Winnicott, on the basis of his understanding of the historical Jesus, distinguishes his antipatriarchal life and teaching from the Pauline tradition, all of which assumes a patriarchal lens, as we earlier saw. Winnicott takes Freud's central discovery, transference love, as what Jesus extended to all, in particular, the sick and infirm as well as the outcasts he listened to and took so seriously, including them in his open table fellowship. But, as we saw (chapter 1), Freud's theory of Eros arises from Plato's psychology of sexual love in the *Symposium* and *Phaedrus*. Plato's earlier theory of love in the *Symposium* aimed to show, contrary to the earlier speakers in the dialogue before Socrates, that not all forms of sexual love were valuable, nor were all forms necessarily egoistic, as Donald Levy

21. Kierkegaard, *Concept of Anxiety.*

22. Kierkegaard, *Fear and Trembling.*

23. Kierkegaard, *Sickness unto Death.*

24. Kierkegaard, *Works of Love.*

has shown.[25] In the *Phaedrus*, Plato offers an astonishing *psychological* portrait of human love. Both Phaedrus, quoting the rhetorician Lysis, and Socrates himself had stated what may have been a conventional Athenian view of the love of men for boys, namely, that it was better if the lover did not love the boy. Socrates, however, abruptly abandons his earlier view, and offers in its place the tripartite theory of the soul later developed at length in the *Republic* (intellect, spirit, and appetite) stated in the *Phaedrus* in terms of the charioteer (the intellect) trying to control two horses (one, courage or spirit; the other, appetite, or lust). The moral power of love in the dialogue is precisely that the lover loves, indeed is devoted to the welfare of, the boy, and both the psychological and normative force of such love is that it elicits love in the boy that takes the form of self-knowledge:

> Then the boy is in love, but has no idea what he loves. He does not understand, and cannot explain, what has happened to him. It is as if he had caught an eye disease from someone else, but could not identify the cause; he does not realize that he is seeing himself in the lover as in a mirror. So when the lover is near, the boy's pain is relieved just as the lover's is, and when they are apart he yearns as much as he is yearned for, because he has a mirror image of love in him—"backlove"—though he neither speaks nor thinks of it as love, but as friendship. Still his desire is nearly the same as the lover's, though weaker: he wants to see, touch, kiss, and lie down with him; and of course, as you might expect, he acts on these desires soon after they occur.[26]

Freud rediscovered in transference love what Plato had earlier seen in the psychology of human erotic love through what he discovered in the psychoanalysis of the dreams and free associations of a certain group of neurotics, namely, analysands whose neuroses could be reenacted and explored in their relationship to the analyst, as they saw in their "transference love for the analyst" a mirror of the archaic roots of their own problems in relationships and in life.[27] Freud follows Plato in regarding transference love using Plato's mirroring imagery: "The doctor should be

25. On these points, see Levy, "Definition of Love."

26. Plato, *Phaedrus*, 532.

27. See, for example, Freud, "Dynamics of Transference"; Freud, "Remembering, Repeating and Working-through"; and Freud, "Observations on Transference-Love."

opaque to his patients and, like a mirror, should show them nothing but what is shown to him."[28]

For Plato, of course, it is eros as transference love that leads to the good, or ethical truth. For Winnicott, transference love is central to psychoanalysis, and central to what he saw in the life and teaching of the antipatriarchal historical Jesus. There is, from his perspective, no psychological reason to distinguish human love from the love he calls for and practices in his life as a teacher and physician. Human love, of which transference love is an expression, takes the form of love's mirror, starting in what Winnicott called the good-enough mother enabling the loved child to see herself or himself as a valued person and growing over time through loving support of resistance into a sense of being a person centered in the secret self (the basis of the true as opposed to the false self), which continues in the other relationships in his life, including those to friends and lovers and teachers and others, aspiring to the love of equals both in personal and public life. The relationship of Jesus to God, on which agape love is modeled, is not asymmetrical, but, as Martin Buber puts it, an I-Thou relationship, through which "we are drawn to and full of love for the intimate person,"[29] "that which in the heart of God is looked for in men."[30] It is such an I-Thou relationship that distinguishes the role of God's love in the life and teaching of the antipatriarchal Jesus and Judaism generally:

> "Thou shalt love the Lord thy God . . . ";—is completely missing in Greece. Aristotle said: "For it would be strange for one to say that he loved Zeus," and held that *philia* (love, friendship) was impossible between man and God.[31]

Paul, in adopting an asymmetrical conception, abandoned, Buber argues, Jesus, because he fails to take seriously the human loves of Jesus, including for his disciples (including Mary) and others, always calling for equality, never hierarchy.[32] It was this asymmetrical and nonreciprocal conception of God's agape love that Baudelaire, in his Manichean bitterness about Christianities, was to analogize to that of a prostitute: "The

28. See Freud, "Recommendations to Physicians Practising Psycho-Analysis," 118.

29. Buber, *I and Thou*, 108.

30. Buber, *Two Types of Faith*, 79.

31. Bellah, *Religion in Human Evolution*, 326. See Dodds, *Greeks*, 35, 54, citing Aristotle's *Magna Moralia* 1208B.30 and *Nicomachean Ethics* 1159A.5.

32. See, on this point, Buber, *Two Types of Faith*, 78–80, 89, 96–97.

most prostituted being, who is Being par excellence, is God, because he is the supreme friend for each individual, because he is the common and inexhaustible reservoir of love."[33]

We earlier observed that Winnicott came to believe that what he had found in analysis, both of himself and of others, was a kind of trust like that Erik Erikson regarded as fundamental to the development of infants and children[34] and that Erikson himself had observed, in his important study of Jesus, based on Norman Perrin's historical Jesus,[35] "one cannot help noticing, on Jesus's part, an unobtrusive integration of maternal and paternal tenderness."[36] Even Erikson qualifies this observation about Jesus's "simply revolutionary" call for "an adult condition in which childlikeness has not been destroyed, and in which a potential return to childlike trust has not been forestalled. What is suggested, then, is a preservation and reenactment of the wonder of childhood: the 'innocent and ear,'" but noting "the patriarchal days in which this was said."[37] Why the qualification? No such qualification is needed if patriarchy does not define loving human relationships, including those of men to women, as I believe it did not for Jesus, who was, in this respect, *ethically* revolutionary, a challenge to patriarchy for which, as I believe, he was murdered. Taking seriously how antipatriarchal Jesus was both in his life and teaching explains precisely why for many, including me, "the gender of Jesus," like the tradition of later Christian mystics (often women) interpreting him, "is fluid, at once masculine and feminine, neither and both, a most queer God."[38] On this view:

> Christ is not a phallic God, but a very queer divinity, who is not just a father, but also a mother, and in all cases a lover. Christ's humanity is both man–ity and woman–ity, and much that is in between or neither.[39]

It also explains the secret self in Jesus's relationship to God, as he withdraws from others to commune with God (in contrast to the peacocking pharisees he condemned). Winnicott explains the secret self as a

33. Quoted in Taylor, *Cosmic Connections*, 216.

34. See Erikson, *Childhood*, 247–51.

35. Perrin, *Rediscovering*. See, on this point, Capps, *Erik Erikson's Verbal*, 101–33.

36. Erikson, "Galilean Sayings," 322.

37. Erikson, "Galilean Sayings," 322.

38. Critchley, *Mysticism*, 84.

39. Critchley, *Mysticism*, 250.

way of protecting the psyche from the unjust demands that conventional practices, like patriarchy, would otherwise demand. It is because Jesus's relationship to God is (as Buber saw) not patriarchal but an intimate loving relationship between equals (I and Thou), a view evidently central to the theology of love of the Christian mystic Meister Eckhart,[40] calling for "an equality between God and man"[41] (a teaching condemned by the pope a year after Eckhart's death[42]). Another mystic, Marguerite Porete, earlier wrote of love in not dissimilar terms, using "mirroring" to make her point,[43] leading to "[t]he first known case of an inquisitorial procedure ending with the burning of both a book and the accused author."[44] The Church had learned patriarchal violence from the Romans, and it is not surprising that the antipatriarchal Jesus himself—working in a culture as violently patriarchal as Roman Judaea—should have developed a secret self to protect his psyche from a Roman culture, like the later Catholic Church, so hostile to nonpatriarchal loving intimate relationships. Roman patriarchy killed Jesus, which makes the point about how threatening to patriarchy the life and teaching of Jesus were.

Once one takes the point about the antipatriarchal Jesus seriously, the entire project of asymmetrical agape love, as an interpretation of a Christian love rooted in Plato and neo-Platonism, lacks psychological and ethical support. Psychologically, it fails to take seriously Plato's pathbreaking naturalistic insight into human love and the role of mirroring in such love in all its forms. And ethically, it repudiates Jesus's central ethical teaching, treating persons as equals, as if God was a tyrannical patriarchal despot, requiring hierarchy, which Jesus expressly condemns in the request by his disciples to define hierarchies among them. Indeed, Winnicott came to see a central problem in Christianities that their misunderstanding of the role of love in Jesus's life and teaching had led to doctrines of the fall and predestination that had rationalized how and why Christianities had become more Roman than Christian, rationalizing violence against Jews, ethnic groups, women, and gays and lesbians. The problem was reading the historical Jesus through the prism of patriarchy, which distorted the link of his teaching to both ethics and democracy, as I shall later argue.

40. Critchley, *Mysticism*, 103–5, 108, 248–49.

41. Critchley, *Mysticism*, 108.

42. Critchley, *Mysticism*, 25, 49.

43. Critchley, *Mysticism*, 24, 108.

44. Critchley, *Mysticism*, 24.

TILLICH AND NIEBUHR ON REINTERPRETING AGAPE LOVE

There are two notable twentieth-century theologians and moral philosophers, both Lutheran, Paul Tillich and Reinhold Niebuhr, who have developed the Christian tradition in ways that depart from the defects in the Christianities we have so far studied, and suggest to me the continuing value and even truths that Christianity brings to contemporary debates about ethics, politics, and law. Why Lutherans? Luther was, I think, to the Catholic tradition he deplored a prophet in the historical tradition of Christianity in the same way Jesus was a prophet in the Jewish tradition he assumed and elaborated. He thus appealed, as the historical Jesus did, to a relationship to a loving father in forming the Protestant conscience and identity that was, in the same way Jesus had done, in Luther's view more authoritative than the patriarchal priesthood with whom he often disagreed. Both Tillich and Niebuhr work in Luther's tradition of Protestant conscience, but come to quite different conceptions of agape love and, correlatively, of its implications both for ethics and politics.

Paul Tillich was born in Germany and fled to the United States to escape the forces of German aggressive nationalism and to defend a conception of conscience as "ultimate concern,"[45] arguing that "[m]orality does not depend on any concrete religion; it is religious in its nature,"[46] even while ostensibly secular. Tillich departs from the orthodox understanding of a sharp distinction between eros and agape love,[47] and embraces a role for psychoanalysis in understanding how persons suffer a "pathological loss of power to respond to moral commands,"[48] and defends the idea, central to Winnicott's understanding of psychoanalysis, of God as a good mother.[49] Tillich thus eschews the Augustinian repression of sexuality as such as "injustice against oneself, and it has the consequence of all injustice: it is self-destructive because of the elements which are excluded."[50] In Tillich, the appeal to psychoanalysis in better understanding and realizing Christianity is quite explicit.

45. Tillich, *Love, Power,* 109.

46. Tillich, *Morality and Beyond,* 64.

47. Tillich, *Morality and Beyond,* 40–42, 93; Tillich, *Systematic Theology*, 3:272–73; *Love, Power,* 116–19.

48. Tillich, *Morality and Beyond*, 50. See also 42–53, 50–51, 58–59, 93.

49. Tillich, *Love, Power,* 112–13.

50. Tillich, *Love, Power,* 70.

Reinhold Niebuhr's conception of Christian conscience was formed in the period of the rise and triumph of fascist nationalism in Germany, Italy, Spain, and Japan, leading to the aggressive violence of these nations in World War II, as well as the period after World War II when religious leaders, like Niebuhr and others, questioned how this could have happened, including the role of Christian anti-Semitism in Germany leading to the Holocaust. Both his monumental *The Nature and Destiny of Man*[51] and his influential *Moral Man and Immoral Society*[52] question the Augustinian condemnation of erotic sensuality as evil in itself[53] as well as his doctrine of original sin,[54] and indeed endorse human love, "fully effective only in intimate and personal relations," as "the way of love may be the only way to justice."[55] And Luther's conception of human nature as intrinsically sinful is now given by Niebuhr an empirical interpretation no longer indicting human nature as such, but following empirical arguments of James Madison[56] and David Hume,[57] pointing to what happens to human psychology in political group psychology, in which individual conscience is often overridden by group antipathy to outsiders to the group, including the corruptions of religion in service of unjust wars, which he illustrates by the injustice of America's Spanish-American War and the like.[58]

It is against such propensities of group psychology (illustrated as well, for Niebuhr, by aggressive political nationalism in the totalitarianisms of fascist Germany and the communist Soviet Union, as forms of corrupt political religions) that Niebuhr understands the role of the individuality of moral conscience, rooted for him in the Christian idea of agape love but convergent with the role of conscience in Renaissance humanism (Niebuhr calls for a synthesis between these two conceptions of conscience[59]). Thus, moral man and immoral society.

The malign role of this political psychology is illustrated for Niebuhr not only by the genocidal anti-Semitism of Nazi Germany, but also by

51. Niebuhr, *Nature and Destiny of Man.*

52. Niebuhr, *Moral Man.*

53. Niebuhr, *Nature and Destiny of Man,* 1:228–40

54. Niebuhr, *Nature and Destiny of Man,* 2:260–62.

55. Niebuhr, *Moral Man,* 266.

56. Niebuhr, *Moral Man,* 113–14.

57. Niebuhr, *Moral Man,* 141.

58. Niebuhr, *Moral Man,* 96–112.

59. Niebuhr, *Nature and Destiny of Man,* 2:204–12.

British and American racism. Here, however, Niebuhr points to how nonviolent appeals to conscience, including Christian conscience, can be and have been effective, as in Gandhi's successful movement of satyagraha against British racist colonialism in India, appealing to contradictions within British culture between their ostensible Christianity and democratic constitutionalism and both the violence and anti-democratic colonialism of the British in India.[60] If the forces of conscience (whether based on Christian agape or Renaissance humanism) can have this force through nonviolence effectively resisting and ending British colonialism in India, Niebuhr argues—in a passage that inspired Martin Luther King Jr.[61]—the same might be true if nonviolence was used by the forces of humanist Christian or secular conscience in the United States exposing the contradictions of racist violence and subjugation of people of color with both American Christianity and democratic constitutionalism.[62]

Niebuhr's work on moral man and immoral societies is an early exploration of what I call political religions, and is notable for its insights into the role even Christianities have sometimes played in such religions. I turn to this subject next.

POLITICAL RELIGIONS

By political religion,[63] I mean, following Jim Gilligan, to identity the political ideology and psychology that historically motivated the great evils wrought long after Shakespeare wrote his tragedies, namely, nationalism, imperialism, totalitarianism (Hitler's fascism and Stalin's communism), and resurgent ethnic nationalism and religious fundamentalism today. Gilligan's understanding of political religion was inspired by Burke's astonishing analysis of the political psychology of the French revolutionaries, an analysis I have further developed in my most recent book on Burke and Madison and their contemporary legacies.[64] The psychological force of this political ideology is that it reinstates a fixed and certain political expression of patriarchy in reaction to the collapse in belief in the conventional sources of patriarchal authority (for example, patriarchal

60. Niebuhr, *Moral Man*, 241–43.

61. See, on this point, Richards, *Disarming Manhood*, 146–49.

62. Niebuhr, *Moral Man*, 238–56.

63. See Gilligan, *Terrorism, Fundamentalism and Nihilism.*

64. See Richards, *Revolution and Constitutionalism.*

religion—the death of God), leading to psychologically intolerable forms of moral nihilism. All of these political religions are in their nature both anti-democratic and anti-liberal, and have for this reason given expression to the monstrous evils of racism, anti-Semitism, sexism, and homophobia that they express and mobilize against innocent scapegoats. Jim Gilligan, a leading psychiatrist of violence, has powerfully analyzed the propensities to aggressive violence of political religions as an expression of the hegemonic shame cultures that typify political religions, covering over and marginalizing the moral emotion of guilt that arises from a sense of culpable harm to other persons, one's equals, rooted in love and humane fellow-feeling. What Shakespeare shows us in *Hamlet*, *Macbeth*, *Coriolanus*, and *Timon of Athens* is the role the shaming of patriarchal manhood plays in the forms of violence, including political violence, that political religions exemplify today.

Carol Gilligan and I thus argued in *The Deepening Darkness* that the political fascism of Mussolini in Italy and Hitler in Germany is best understood as a reactionary political psychology arising from the shaming of patriarchal nationalist manhood after the experience, as defined by Mussolini and Hitler, of the defeats of World War I.[65] Both opposed what they took to be the effeminacy of political liberalism, which called for treating persons as equals. Their rage centered on the attack on patriarchy's gender binary and hierarchy, implicit in democratic liberalism, and their violence targeted as scapegoats those they took to question patriarchy. As an ideology, fascism was empty of serious political theory. Rather, as quoted by Robert O. Paxton, "'The fist,' asserted a fascist militant in 1920, 'is the synthesis of our theory.'"[66] What made Hitler's political fascism so psychologically remarkable is that, rooted in what he called the shaming of German manhood by the Treaty of Versailles, his sense of shame so resonated with the German people who elected him that it overrode and suppressed the religious and philosophical culture of guilt of German culture, perhaps most brilliantly expressed in the moral philosophy of Immanuel Kant and was, in contrast to Japan, to reassert itself powerfully after the war.[67]

Hitler himself, a deeply narcissistic and shame-ridden man, mobilized Germans, as Captain Ahab did in Melville's *Moby-Dick*, aggressively and genocidally to war on his version of the white whale, the unjust

65. See Gilligan and Richards, *Deepening Darkness*, 232–38.

66. Quoted in Paxton, *Anatomy of Fascism*, 17.

67. See, on these points, Buruma, *Wages of Guilt*.

scapegoats of his rage, European Jewry, and Germans, like the mindless crew of Ahab's Pequod, surrendered to him any sense of ethical conscience.[68] Hitler made reference to the Versailles Treaty as early as 1925 in *Mein Kampf* as "a shame and disgrace"[69] and "this instrument of... abject humiliation" which should arouse the German people to "a common sense of shame and common hatred" in a "spirit of proud self-reliance, manly defiance, and wrathful hatred."[70] It was the failure of the Germans to respond in that spirit that "for five years now has been drowning the very last remnant of respect for us on the part of the rest of the world" and had brought "the nation [to] its time of deepest humiliation and disgrace."[71] Lest there appear to be no relation between the morality of *The Iliad* (whose subject is "the wrath of Achilles" over his humiliation by Agamemnon) and that of *Mein Kampf* (whose subject, correspondingly, is Hitler's wrath over the Germans' humiliation by Versailles), it is worth remembering that from the beginning of his career, "Hitler had let himself be represented grandiloquently as 'the man who would rather be a dead Achilles than a living dog.'"[72] If this could happen in one of the most advanced cultures of Europe (populated by the best and the brightest), Jim Gilligan argues it can happen anywhere, and we must understand how vulnerable any people may be to such political religions if they do not take seriously the threat of patriarchy not only to democracy but to ethics itself.

Undoubtedly, the most brilliant psychological analysis of such reactionary politics is Hannah Arendt's *Origins of Totalitarianism*.[73] What Arendt, who had observed the rise of fascism at first hand as a German student of both Heidegger and Jaspers, found in common in both German fascism and Soviet communism was the anti-scientific certitude of, in Hitler's case, racist science[74] and, in Stalin's case, the laws of history, both of which rationalized the patriarchal authority of Hitler and Stalin as a kind of priest-god, uniquely attuned to apodictic scientific and political truth, including whatever murders of the innocent such truth required.[75]

68. See Melville, *Moby-Dick*, 3–35, 174–212, 580–625.

69. Hitler, *Mein Kampf*, 464.

70. Hitler, *Mein Kampf*, 632.

71. Hitler, *Mein Kampf*, 231.

72. Frst, *Hitler*, 749.

73. See Arendt, *Origins*.

74. See Lifton, *Nazi Doctors*.

75. See, on these points, Arendt, *Origins*, 341–88.

It is a feature of this political psychology that, like other forms of patriarchy, it requires the violent suppression of any voice of persons that might reasonably challenge its authority, a challenge all the more threatening because its claims were so unreasonable, both scientifically and ethically. Arendt regarded this feature as central to totalitarian politics:

> The ideal subject of totalitarian rule is not the convinced Nazi or the convinced Communist, but people for whom the distinction between fact and fiction (*i.e.*, the reality of experience) and the distinction between true and false (*i.e.*, the standards of thought) no longer exist.[76]

The analogy to Trump's politics is striking (see Gilligan and Richards, *Darkness Now Visible)*. Such moral slavery, as we called it, dehumanizes its critics, and makes of them sometimes genocidally murdered scapegoats of that gnawing reasonable doubt of its ideology. Thus, the connection of totalitarianism (both fascism and Stalinist communism) to the evils of racism, anti-Semitism, sexism, and homophobia.

There is a comparably illuminating analysis of the underlying psychology of the political religion of fascism in the study by T. W. Adorno and his colleagues of the authoritarian personality.[77] Adorno's work was inspired by the conception of the authoritarian personality introduced by the psychoanalyst, Erich Fromm, to understand how fascism could have arisen from and taken over the German democracy.[78] Like Arendt and Adorno, Fromm—a Jew—had fled his homeland, and now tried to make sense of what had happened. Why had Germans come to fear the freedoms of democracy, in particular, its respect for the inalienable right to conscience, ceding ethical judgment to "irrational overestimation and admiration"[79] of a totalitarian leader? Fromm acutely observes the role of gender in Hitler's rhetoric: "the satisfaction the masses have in domination"[80]; as Hitler puts it, "[l]ike a woman . . . who will submit to the strong man rather than dominate the weakling."[81] There is a

76. Arendt, *Origins*, 474.

77. Adorno, *Authoritarian Personality.*

78. See Fromm, *Escape*,161–63, 167–68.

79. Fromm, *Escape*, 164.

80. Fromm, *Escape*, 220.

81. Quoted at Fromm, *Escape*, 220.

psychological disorder here, Fromm argues, a disorder in love: "Love is based on equality and freedom."[82]

Adorno's study, unlike Fromm's, is of the American authoritarian personality. Like Hannah Arendt, Adorno's study does not explicitly use patriarchy in his analysis; but, in fact, the F-scale describes, like Fromm's earlier view, what we have called patriarchal psychology—rigid conventionalism, authoritarian submission and aggression, opposition to the subjective, stereotypying power and "toughness," destructiveness and cynicism, projection of dangerous impulses on others, and exaggerated concern with sex (including homophobia).[83] Authoritarian psychology is thus marked by hierarchy (as opposed to equality),[84] by a rigid gender binary,[85] authoritarian moralism,[86] as well as by an intolerance of ambiguity[87] and associated belief in pseudo-science.[88] Bob Altemeyer's more recent confirmation and elaboration of this psychology identifies three features of "right-wing authoritarianism," namely, authoritarian submission, authoritarian aggression, and conventionalism,[89] which Karen Stenner's empirical work confirms and deepens.[90]

What neither Arendt nor Adorno see is how their arguments of political psychology clearly assume and are best understood in terms of the connection between patriarchy and fascism earlier stated by Virginia Woolf in *Three Guineas*.[91] What makes the analysis of *Three Guineas* so astonishing is not only Woolf's pathbreaking analysis of the patriarchal roots of fascist violence but also her larger call for a resistance in which women join with men (resistance to war was, for Woolf, an issue for both men and women, collaboratively). The issue, she argued, was what Josephine Butler called "the great principles of Justice and Equality and Liberty." Addressing men, Woolf comments:

82. Fromm, *Escape*, 159.

83. See Adorno, *Authoritarian Personality*, 228. On homophobia, see 240.

84. Adorno, *Authoritarian Personality*, 413–14.

85. Adorno, Authoritarian Personality, 428–29.

86. Adorno, *Authoritarian Personality*, 458.

87. Adorno, *Authoritarian Personality*, 461–64, 479–82.

88. Adorno, *Authoritarian Personality*, 464–65.

89. See Altemeyer, *Authoritarian Specter*, 6. For the relationship of Altemeyer's work to Adorno's, see 45–47. See also Altemeyer, *Right-Wing Authoritarianism*; Hunsberger and Altemeyer, *Atheists*.

90. See Stenner, *Authoritarian Dynamic*.

91. Woolf, *Three Guineas*.

> The words are the same as yours; the claim is the same as yours. The daughters of educated men who were called, to their resentment, "feminists" were in fact the advance guard of your own movement. They were fighting the same enemy that you are fighting and for the same reason. They were fighting the tyranny of the patriarchal state as you are fighting the tyranny of the Fascist state.[92]

Neither Arendt nor Adorno, among the very best human scientists of their time, can see, let alone acknowledge, the role gender plays in the phenomena they otherwise investigate so trenchantly. We need to understand how democratic peoples sometimes espouse what William James called in his own time American "stupidity and injustice," arising from what he called an ethical "blindness with which we all are afflicted in regard to the feelings of creatures and people different from ourselves."[93] When James wrote, as in the later period of Arendt and Adorno, gender was, as it largely remains today, marginalized in serious intellectual discourse, and he does not investigate the role gender plays in our "blindness."

Woolf sees it because, as her novel *Mrs. Dalloway* make quite clear, she connects the suicidality of Septimius and the thoughts of suicide of Mrs. Dalloway to the experience of trauma, in Septimius's case to what we would today call post-traumatic stress order, in Mrs. Dalloway's to being a good woman, not following her heart.[94] Woolf had herself been the victim of traumatic sexual abuse by her half-brother, which explains her understanding of the issue in both men's and women's experience and why she connects them. The psychological importance of trauma, in understanding the pivotal importance of gender in supporting a range of irrational prejudices, is that patriarchy rests on the infliction of traumatic initiations, and that thus the psyches of men and women, morally injured by such initiations, enact the gender binary and hierarchy in their lives, the model for the scapegoating stereotypes that rationalize irrationalist prejudices (men vs. women, race vs. race, religion v. religion, straight vs. gay, class vs. class, tribe vs. tribe, et al.). Unreal divisions between thought (male) and emotion (female) feed into unreal hierarchies, attacking, as Arendt saw,[95] the psyche itself. Such mandated divisions and hierarchies

92 Woolf, *Three Guineas*, 121.

93. See James, "On a Certain Blindness," 841.

94. See, for further discussion, Gilligan and Richards, *Deepening Darkness*, 213–14.

95. See, on this point, Young-Bruehl, *Why Arendt Matters*.

are not based in experience but in false authority, thus undermining democracy and, at the worst, rationalizing totalitarianism and genocidal murder of the innocent, as fascist German politics shows so starkly and so unforgettably to people of good will who refuse to deny what reality now shows us. The heart of its darkness is not merely falsifying but killing ethical experience, which rests on empathy for the equal dignity of all persons. And patriarchy is what motors this evil dynamic, this "blindness," in our personal and political lives.

The fascism of Hitler and Mussolini was an extreme form of the ethnic nationalism that took the form of a racism that rationalized the imperialism of many nation-states long before fascism. Indeed, World War I may be plausibly understood as a war among the competing racist imperialisms of Britain, Germany, France, Italy, Austria-Hungary, Russia, and the Ottomans, all based on a conception of patriarchal manhood that enforced a gender binary and hierarchy in which the imperialisms competed for the top of the hierarchy and were shamed by any supposed insult to their manly supremacy into the illimitable violence of World War I.

Some of these competing imperial states, notably Britain and France, had democratic and liberal traditions and some gave rise accordingly, as in the case of John Stuart Mill's *The Subjection of Women*, to feminist arguments based on criticism of the degree to which patriarchal gender stereotypes had corrupted liberal values of freedom and equality for all. But, whatever such liberal and feminist impulses there may have been in the French Revolution had been quashed by a Napoleonic despotism rationalized by imperialist aggressive violence against the other nations of Europe, including Britain. Such a degradation of liberal democracy by Napoleonic aggression and its defeat set back any genuine liberal democracy in Europe for much of the nineteenth and early twentieth centuries. What many of these nation states did agree upon after Napoleon was European racist supremacy over other peoples, which rationalized their imperialisms. At the bottom of it lay the conception of patriarchal manhood that Napoleon had successfully displayed in his imperialist conquests, and which Europeans did not question but aggressively acted out in their imperialisms in Africa, Asia, and elsewhere.

It was, strikingly, the defeat of the more autocratic forms of such European imperialisms (Germany, Austria-Hungary, and Russia) in World War I, all giving expression to patriarchal conceptions of nationalism, that set the stage for a shaming defeat that, as we have seen, gave rise to the even worse forms of ethnic nationalism in Italian, German, and Japanese fascism. Patriarchy, as Shakespeare's tragedies so clearly show, thus feeds on itself endlessly repeating the cycle of violence to which it gives expression. What Shakespeare's tragedies show us is the underlying psychology of humiliated patriarchal manhood, as in Richard III or Shylock or Macbeth or Iago and Othello or Edmund, that gives rise to illimitable forms of psychopathic violence, including the anti-Semitism inflicted on Shylock, the racism on Othello, the sexism on Edmund, all of which continue to persist in our personal and political psychology today.

The United States is predominantly a guilt culture, but there are both in its history and its contemporary politics powerful shame cultures that compromise and degrade its liberal democracy. The most prominent example historically is the role the Southern patriarchal shame culture played not only in supporting American slavery and racism in the antebellum period, but, when its hegemonic political and constitutional power was challenged by abolitionists like Lincoln, exploded in the incendiary violence of the American Civil War.[96] After the Reconstruction Amendments, which, among other things, extended federal protection of human rights to the states, condemned state racism, and extended the right to vote to men of color, both the shame culture and its incendiary violence persisted, leading to lynchings and the deplorable *Plessy v. Ferguson*, which constitutionally justified racist doctrines of separate but equal that perpetuated racism both in the South and nationally long into the twentieth century, and their legacy persists.[97]

Racism has also played an important role in America's unjust imperialist wars, including the Spanish-American War, World War II, the Vietnam War, and the incursion into Iraq. In particular, the Vietnam War, conducted by "the best and the brightest," illustrates yet again how powerful a patriarchal conception of manhood played in leading men who should have known better into a war unjust in its ends and means because, in their view, the very resistance to the war as unjust shamed us, as Nixon insisted long after he had promised to end the war.[98]

I see the same persisting dangers in the role fundamentalist patriarchal religion has played both here and abroad in a reactionary politics,

96. Wyatt-Brown, *Southern Honor.*

97. See *Plessy v. Ferguson*, 163 U.S. 537 (1896), overruled by *Brown v. Board of Education*, 347 U.S. 483 (1954).

98. See, on these points, Gilligan and Richards, *Darkness Now Visible*, 80–94; Immerwahr, *How To Hide an Empire.*

based on America First or Britain First or Russia First or Hungary First, shamed by the advances that have been made here and elsewhere in resisting the continuing cultural and political power of the patriarchal gender binary and hierarchy. The patriarchal religion may be fundamentalist Christians in the United States or theocratic Orthodox Catholics in Russia or the theocratic Muslims of Isis or of Buddhists in Myanmar, shamed by the challenges to patriarchy that they experience as moral nihilism, exploding sometimes into illimitable terroristic violence.

It is time for Americans to see and acknowledge that their politics is not now, nor has ever been, immune from this dynamic (Trump).[99] It should inspire Americans, always drawn to the authority of our Founders, that James Madison, the leading Founder, so clearly saw this evil in democratic group psychology, what he called "faction," as the central challenge to constructing a constitutional democracy that would respect human rights.[100] It is extraordinary that a form of constitutional originalism, which fails even to see this challenge and its significance, should now, in former President Trump's abject admiration for Justice Scalia, be the standard for appointment of justices to the Supreme Court of the United States,[101] leading to the appointment of three ideologically sectarian judges who have joined with other conservatives on the court to overrule *Roe v. Wade.*[102]

99. See, for cogent argument on this point, Whitman, *Hitler's American Model.*

100. See, for argument on this point, Richards, *Foundations.*

101. For further discussion of this point, see Gilligan and Richards, *Darkness Now Visible*, 85–88. See, for supporting historical and textual argument on the critique of originalism, Richards, *Foundations*; Richards, *Fundamentalism.*

102. See, on this point, Richards, *Revolution and Constitutionalism*, ch. 7: "Patriarchal Religion in U.S. Constitutional Law."

6

An Antipatriarchal Ethics

Kant and Rawls

WHY HAS THE INTERPRETATION of Kant played such an important role in recent moral and political philosophy, and how, if at all, can his ethics of universal human rights be understood from the perspective of the antipatriarchal historical Jesus? Many of Kant's concrete moral views (on women, race, homosexuality, the death penalty and the like) do not comport, as I shall show, with this perspective, and he is, if anything, rather critical of love as a basis for ethics. Certainly, Kant is quite clear in *Groundwork of the Metaphysics of Morals*[1] that Jesus exemplifies the person of good will, "the Holy one of the Gospels," because "when compared with our ideal of moral perfection . . . he is recognized as one," albeit saying of himself "why do you call me (whom you see) good but one, that is, God (whom you do not see)."[2] And one of his formulations of the Categorical Imperative, the kingdom of ends, plays a role in his thought very like the kingdom of God in Jesus's life and teaching. I have myself no doubt of the inspiration of Kant's secular moral philosophy by Jesus, but, in light of some of the difficulties in understanding the connection, what in the life and teaching of Jesus could have led to a secular Enlightenment moral philosophy, which tests the authority of Jesus himself by whether he meets the tests of that moral philosophy? And how should we understand and resolve the difficulties already mentioned?

1. Kant, *Groundwork*.
2. Kant, *Groundwork*, 23.

KANT ON DIGNITY AS THE BASIS OF UNIVERSAL HUMAN RIGHTS: APPEAL AND DIFFICULTIES

The key, I believe, to understanding the connection for Kant of his version of moral philosophy to Jesus is precisely the radical moral individualism of Jesus's conception of the authority of conscience informed by its source, his antipatriarchal relationship to a loving parent, and all the other such loving relationships both in his life and teaching. For Jesus, as for Kant, the authority of such conscience required each and every person to resist and indeed cross the patriarchal hierarchies that demanded outcasts of all sorts, and indeed denigrated and demeaned them as subhuman, and to treat each and every person as one's equal. It is this understanding of ethics that explains the laser focus of Jesus's ministry on compassion for such outcasts as *individual* persons, crossing the hierarchical boundaries patriarchy imposed separating poor from rich, women from men, sick from healthy, the peacocking self-righteous from the inwardness of care and concern for human suffering, and the like. The shame culture that sustains such hierarchies, which enforces its patriarchal demands, is always resisted and defied by Jesus, appealing to an inward ethics of guilt at harming or demeaning others. Nothing is more indicative of what Jesus meant by the coming through his ministry of the kingdom of heaven than his indictment of the culture of violence, enforcing transgression or questioning hierarchies, that enforced patriarchy, exemplified by Roman patriarchy and its subjugation of Israel and so many others. Jesus always refuses violence against injustice, calling rather for a resisting voice, and it was this voice that apparently led to his Roman execution by the brutality of crucifixion, the penalty for political dissenters, and the Romans regarded him as one. If I am right, he was the most radical critic of Roman patriarchy they had ever encountered, and his criticism in and of itself shamed them, eliciting barbaric and unspeakable violence on an innocent and good man.

It was, I believe, this radical moral individualism, calling for each and every person to treat other persons as equals, irrespective of the consequences, that led Kant to his moral philosophy of the Categorical Imperative, requiring each and every person to test their actions in terms that each and every other person could impose on themselves consistent what he called universalizability, a test of noncontradiction for ethical truth similar to the test of noncontradiction for epistemic truth. For Kant, ethics turns on this test being addressed to the conscience of each person, and why conscience is, for Kant, the most inalienable of human rights, indeed the foundation of our regarding persons as bearers and subject of universal human rights. The primacy of conscience in Kant is very much Luther's Protestant conscience, albeit secularized by him into a conscience available to everyone irrespective of religious convictions (including, of course, Jews). It is a conception of conscience much beyond Luther's and most of the other Protestant reformers (only the Jewish philosopher Spinoza offers a comparably expansive understanding[3]) but can and should be regarded as the best understanding of the Christian humanism of the historical Jesus of Nazareth.

What moved Kant to a deontological conception of ethics (right action determined independent of the good) was certainly that it offered the most philosophically defensible conception of Christian conscience (though it was no longer specifically Christian, but universal), but that its conception of human rights was foundational and defended the protection of human rights from compromise by utilitarian calculations of the greatest happiness of the greatest number, familiar to Kant from the works of David Hume. Kant's entire critical philosophy was constructed as an alternative to Hume, and nothing was more important to Kant than defending the conception of universal human rights he defended from any compromise because the balance of aggregate utility of large numbers over small minorities might require it. The very point of the protection of human rights is that they apply even when democratic majorities would flout them. His views are the foundation of the contemporary understanding of universal human rights that have since World War II been espoused by many constitutional democracies and international organizations.

One of the main difficulties Kant's arguments faced was his insistence that, unlike utilitarianism, it had no naturalistic basis, but was based mysteriously on our membership of the noumenal world and a radical moral freedom that could not be understood in the terms of the categories (including causation) required to understand the empirical world. It was this difficulty that led John Stuart Mill ultimately to defend utilitarianism as the best theory of political liberalism, and led both Hegel and Marx and others (Merleau-Ponty) to turn to history to fill what for them was the intolerable non-empirical foundations of Kant's ethics.

We can, I believe, address this problem if we bring into play our earlier discussion in chapter 1 of what we now know about human

3. See, on this point, Gilligan and Richards, *Deepening Darkness*, 139–40.

development, and the centrality of loving relationships in such development, as Winnicott clearly saw in religion and ethics. There is a naturalistic basis in our humanity for love and empathy, as the work of the evolutionary psychologist Michael Tomasello, among others, has clearly shown.[4] Our species has distinctive capacities of mind reading and shared intentionality that we display as babies that make possible the collective intentionality of human culture and the crucial role that teaching plays among humans in communicating and transforming and critically examining culture, including, as Tomasello argues, both science and ethics. Tomasello argues that the attempts by Rawls and other contractualists to reinterpret Kant are in line with the empirical facts of the human moral development of our capacities for empathy.[5] As a Kantian recently put the point, a contemporary Kantian ethics refuses to follow Kant to understand either science or ethics metaphysically (as grounded in a truth inaccessible to experience—what Kant called the noumenal world), but rather naturalistically "in the sense that it explains the existence of value in terms of valuing, and it explains the existence of valuing as something that is inherent in a sentient creatures's relation to herself. Value is a perspectival notion that arises within the point of view of two forms of conscious life."[6] Empathy is, as the psychoanalyst Heinz Kohut put the point, "the capacity to think and feel oneself into the inner life of another person,"[7] the basis of transference love in psychoanalysis and, if I am right, of ethics, a development from what Kohut called "the nuclear self"[8] or what Arnold Modell has called "the private self,"[9] a basis of the sense of ethical authenticity and self-esteem. What Jim Gilligan discovered about love arose thus empirically from within the point of view of his conscious life and the conscious life of the violent men he worked with, as a psychoanalyst, so closely. And love as empathy was key, in particular, a love across the patriarchal boundaries that divide us.

Ethics is not, as Kant mistakenly believed, empirically mysterious, but the naturalistic expression of our distinctive humanity, namely, empathy, our capacity to read and take seriously other minds and to develop the thoughts and feelings of universalistic ethical thought, treating others

4. See Tomasello, *Becoming Human*.

5. See Tomasello, *Becoming Human* on this point, 192, 200, 247, 285.

6. Korsgaard, *Fellow Creatures*, 168.

7. Kohut, *How Does Analysis*, 82.

8. For illuminating commentary, see Strozier et al., *New World of Self*, 42–58.

9. See Modell, *Private Self*, 46–55.

as equals.[10] Kant, of course, sharply distinguished what he called the basis of ethics, respect, from anything like love, and indeed argued that we cannot understand literally "the passages from Scripture that contain the command to love one's neighbor, even our enemy. For love as inclination cannot be commanded."[11] But, Jesus's appeal to the two Love Commandments (love God, and your neighbor as yourself) is precisely not an appeal to the Law of the Pentateuch, but to the human competences and propensities that made possible embracing the Law in its true meaning in antipatriarchal human relationships. Loving God comes first, for Jesus, because only the experience of being loved and loving in a nurturant parental morality (Winnicott's good mother), including the mirroring of parent and child, makes possible coming to trust others and understand what it is to be human in relationship, a process continuing throughout human life. In thus making love real for the child including the nurturance of the competences central to human development, such love fosters the development of the capacity both for self-respect and respect for others in the exercise of those competences, among which is the competence to respect others as one's equals. Kant called this competence human dignity. What Jesus saw that Kant did not is the crucial link between nurturant care (love) and competence (respect) in human development, because, I am inclined to think, Jesus thought psychoanalytically in a way Kant did not.

If Kant had been able to do so, he would have avoided a number of his concrete moral judgments which are at war with his ethics. We can see this quite clearly in the way, as Thomas McCarthy has shown, Kant's condemnation normatively of European colonialism is in tension, if not contradiction, with his treatment of alleged racial differences in his anthropological works explaining, even rationalizing, colonialism and slavery,[12] and his similar treatment of gender differences,[13] excluding women from citizenship.[14] Consider his view of a mandatory death penalty, and his condemnation of homosexuality.

Some of Kant's substantive moral arguments, including his moral defense in his theory of right of strong retributivism (including advocacy

10. See Darwall, *Second-Person Standpoint* on this point.

11. Kant, *Groundwork*, 15.

12. See, on this point, McCarthy, *Race, Empire*, 26, 42–68, 169–71, 186–91, 224–25, 234, 237–43.

13. See, on this point, McCarthy, *Race, Empire*, 52.

14. See, on this point, Okin, *Women*, 6.

of the death penalty as the only just punishment for murder), are themselves philosophically problematic. Kant's defense of these views is striking:

> whatever undeserved evil you inflict upon another within the people, that you inflict upon yourself. If you insult him, you insult yourself; if you steal from him, you steal from yourselves; if you strike him, you strike yourself; if you kill him, you kill yourself. But only the *law of retribution (ius talionis)*. . . . can specify definitely the quality and quantity of punishment . . . [15]

Kant's argument for the *ius talionis* is not consistently pursued[16] which itself suggests its problematic character since avoiding contradiction is central to universalizability; it is applied forcefully only to the death penalty for murder and to be pursued there even if we knew that civil society no longer existed (so it could have no deterrent effect).[17] Why? Ethics is, for Kant, autonomous from the empirical world of Newtonian causal laws, a realm of noumenal freedom in which we impose ethics on ourselves and others through the Categorical Imperative mysteriously in abstraction from our causal background and concrete appetitive selves, prefiguring Rawls's original position (Rawls, however, regards moral development as something any plausible ethical form must take seriously). It is this perspective without any attention to the empirical world or empirical consequences that leads Kant to argue, as he does, that an ethical person, if he or she murdered and was appropriately guilty, would impose on herself or himself death as the only just punishment for culpable wrongdoing. We are commanded to do this, as he puts the point in *The Critique of Practical Reason*, because it expresses "the spontaneity of the subject as a thing in itself, for the determination of which no physical explanation can be given,"[18] shown by our morally blaming people even if "born villains quite incapable of improvement."[19] We are thus to ignore any deterrent or reformative effects, punishing even if it

15. Kant, *Metaphysics of Morals*, 473

16. Kant has problems finding the appropriate penalty for verbal injury, violence by the upper to the lower classes, for stealing, for killing from different motives, for crimes involving too many accessories, and even for killings of infanticide and dueling, introducing considerations of "honor" as reasons for regarding these latter two crimes as not punishable by death. See Kant, *Metaphysics of Morals*, 474–76.

17. See Kant, *Metaphysics of Morals*, 474.

18. Kant, *Critique of Practical Reason*, 219.

19. Kant, *Critique of Practical Reason*, 220.

has no empirical effects in the world in reducing levels of violent crime. But there is compelling empirical evidence that people's culpability varies in precisely the way Kant denies, and that retributive punishment of the sort he contemplates does not, and may even incentivize criminality, and there is also growing evidence that forms of violent criminality are in fact not freely chosen, as Kant supposed, but reflect causal histories of unjust treatment, including traumatic abuse and shaming forms of economic and social inequality.[20] Once one insists that ethics is as much grounded in the empirical world as anything else in the natural world (including ethics, which is part of nature and of human nature) Kant's argument for strong retributivism loses appeal even within the framework of Kantian universalizability. Rather, a more reasonable principle would be to universalize a principle that would allow any form of detention only within the limits of H. L. A. Hart's constraints of justice,[21] taking seriously real harms and causal histories and unjust inequalities that require forms of therapy and treatment as more appropriate ways to lower crimes rates and advance reform.

Kant's strong retributivism rests on an indefensible conception of freedom from causal law that reflects not reasoning but the deliverances of a rather guilt-ridden conscience with a highly punitive superego, which is shown by the intrapsychic way he tests his views, namely, the experience of one's own sense of deserved self-punishment in imagining oneself as a murderer, as if guilt-ridden impulses of self-punishment are *simpliciter* the measure of reasonable punishment of others, which does not follow. Kantian universalizability is a plausible test today for the ethics of maxims of action if it takes seriously whether a proposed maxim would be accepted by all reasonable persons including a reasonable understanding of the natural and human world, as we now understand those worlds as closely interconnected.[22] But, Kant's strong retributivism fails even to engage the considerations that would make such a principle acceptable to persons who reasonably would require any such detention to reflect not only a defensible theory of harms but the lessened culpability of those whose development has been marked by an injustice, including trauma, and, in light of those considerations, empirically validated

20. See Gilligan, *Violence*; Gilligan, *Preventing Violence*; Gilligan, *Why Some Politicians.*

21. See Hart, *Punishment and Responsibility*, 1–17.

22. For a recent example of such a plausible contemporary Kantian theory whose method I endorse, see Korsgaard, *Fellow Creatures.*

forms of effective prevention, deterrence, and reform. What Kant gives us is his own highly personal sense of how he, a morally sensitive product of a guilt culture that does not accept the harm principle but embraces unjust Augustinian Puritanical patriarchal sexual repression, would, in consequence, want to self-punish himself as the measure of justice to others. But why should such a Puritan superego, like Angelo's in Shakespeare's *Measure for Measure*, anachronistically today be the measure of humane conscience universally? I argue elsewhere how and why today American criminal justice embraces Kantian strong retributivism, but I argue it reflects not a reasonable empirically grounded view of guilt but the unjust expression of a still-powerful shame culture that alone makes sense of the unjust cruelties American law endorses.[23]

And Kant's moral condemnation of any consensual sex outside marriage is, to say the least, problematic,[24] and his condemnation of consensual homosexuality as "contrary to natural instinct and to animal nature"[25] has no empirical basis (homosexuality is for many the only natural expression of loving and is, in fact, common in the animal world). When he later makes reference to Greek homosexuality as "originally a praiseworthy thing, for one picked out a promising youth to rear and educate, as was the case with Socrates and Xenophon" (Plato's linking of love—indeed, homoerotic love—to ethics strikingly is unmentioned), he goes on to observe "it came in the end to be an impermissible association," which "demeans man below the beasts."[26] How did it come to be "an impermissible association"? What happened between Plato and Kant? Kant, whose ethics is defined by its independence of religion, here uncritically endorses Augustinian Christian homophobia in a way that many Christians now themselves repudiate on internal religious grounds. Yet here an ostensibly secular ethical theory parrots quite rhetorically repressive anachronistic views. It bespeaks the contradiction internal to Kant's claims here that they are put in the terms of the shame morality (demeaning) that his guilt morality (based on harms to others) usually eschews, suggesting the uncritical role in his thinking of the

23. See Richards, *Love and Violence*, 212–26. There are suggestions even in Kant's argument for strong retributivism that a shame culture may be at work. See, for example, how he appeals to "honor" in discussing verbal injuries and violence between the upper and lower classes as well as a reason for not punishing dueling and infanticide by death. See Kant, *Metaphysics of Morals*, 473–74, 476–77.

24. Seel Kant, *Lectures on Ethics*, 155–62, 377–81.

25. Kant, *Lectures on Ethics*, 161.

26. Kant, *Lectures on Ethics*, 380–81.

quite patriarchal religious views of this period, views that can be traced to Augustine of Hippo.

NIETZSCHE'S CRITIQUE OF KANT

These difficulties in Kant's ethical theory led Friedrich Nietzsche to argue in his most philosophically important work, *On the Genealogy of Morals*,[27] that Kant's strong retributivism reflected a long history of repellent Christian thought in Aquinas and Tertullian that took pleasure in the punishment of the damned and that "even with old Kant; the categorical imperative gives off a whiff of cruelty."[28] Such endorsement of cruelty in Tertullian, Aquinas, and Kant expressed, on Nietzsche's penetrating pre-Freudian understanding of the unconscious, not reasonable argument, but the return of the repressed (repressed violence—indeed, Christian nonviolence—now expressing itself in wantonly cruel violence). For Nietzsche, the whole theory of strong retributivism rests on the repressive guilt morality that Christianity had put in place after the long dominant shame morality of the pagan world, in particular, the ancient Greek world of *The Iliad* and *The Oresteia* he adored. Nietzsche's critique was never directed against Jews whose cosmopolitanism he admired (he rejected German anti-Semitism precisely because it was a form of ethnic nationalism), but against what he analyzed as the slave guilt morality that Christianity had imposed on the Western ethical mind.[29] Nietzsche may very well have been a repressed homosexual,[30] and Lou Salomé, who knew him as well as anyone (Nietzsche once fell in love with her and proposed marriage, which she rejected), offers an insightful analysis of this deeply neurotic and brilliant man: at the end of life, before his madness, Nietzsche was deeply alone, abandoned by his family and friends (including Richard Wagner as well as Salomé) and obsessed by the traumatic loss of his Christian minister father as a boy (the father, like his son, went mad); that loss was psychologically filled by Nietzsche's incarnating himself (thus, the eternal return) in his father's image of Jesus but as himself the new savior (Zarathustra), sacrificing all (any happiness or love in his own

27. Nietzsche, *On the Genealogy of Morals.*

28. See Nietzsche, *On the Genealogy of Morals*, 46–47.

29. See for a compelling analysis of Nietzsche's views along these lines, Young, *Friedrich Nietzsche.*

30. For a compelling argument to this effect, see Kohler, *Zarathustra's Secret.* For a contrary view, see Young, *Friedrich Nietzsche.*

life) for humankind,[31] high priest of an anti-Christianity because it had repudiated the sexual and emotional repression of his homosexuality. This explains his repudiation of the sexual and emotional asceticism he thought Christianity had imposed on Western culture, both religious and philosophical (for example, in Kant's strong retributivism).[32] Nietzsche argued that Kant's death of God has led to moral nihilism because Kant and others did not credibly offer an empirically based alternative, but rather a perpetuation of a guilt morality that rested on unjust sexual and emotional repression of our human bodies and our animal instincts (Nietzsche was immensely influenced by Darwin's compelling scientific case for our animality[33]). I, like many others (including many contemporary Christians) agree with this aspect of his critique, but view it as consistent with a humane understanding of the ethical imperative, treating persons as equals.

I mention Nietzsche here because he gave perhaps the most influential expression of late-nineteenth-century moral nihilism, and proposed an alternative to the guilt morality of Kant in terms of a return to the shame morality of ancient Greece. So far from questioning patriarchy, Nietzsche rejected the guilt morality of treating others as equals for a modern reintroduction of the shame morality of the ancient Greeks, rejecting both democratic liberalism and feminism because inconsistent with the linchpins of patriarchy, the gender binary and its hierarchy. Nietzsche, as we have seen, despised German anti-Semitism, but his views were interpreted by Hitler to give expression to a genocidal political anti-Semitism and aggressive violence against all forms of democratic liberalism and, of course, feminism.

I do not agree either with Nietzsche's repudiation of all forms of guilt morality (later forms of such morality have, for example, embraced the harm principle as well as feminism) or with his proposed alternative, a return to a shame-based morality. But, his influential views show how important moral nihilism has been in European politics, and I offered elsewhere an analysis of moral nihilism that clarifies the continuing appeal of what I call political religions, all of which express a shame-based

31. See Salomé, *Nietzsche*. Salomé does not bring up Nietzsche's repressed homosexuality, but she did take that view of one of Nietzsche's closest friends, Paul Ree. See, on this point, Young, *Friedrich Nietzsche*, 212–13.

32. See, for his critique of asceticism, Nietzsche, *On the Genealogy of Morals*, 77–136.

33. See, on this point, Young, *Friedrich Nietzsche*.

morality resting on patriarchal psychology deeply hostile to a guilt morality that treats persons as equals, the foundation of both political liberalism and feminism.[34] What characterizes all these views is a sense of the collapse of a long-held patriarchal morality accepted as axiomatic and in the nature of things, an experience of moral nihilism that is shamed by the critique of patriarchy implicit in democratic liberalism (in particular, its liberalism), which expresses itself in the illimitable forms of violence that have characterized the twentieth century and, I fear, may characterize the twenty-first.

RAWLS'S RECONSTRUCTION OF KANT

The importance of the moral and political philosophy of John Rawls is that it has shown how a defensible form of Kantianism that is free of the difficulties in the view so far discussed. I try here to interpret Rawls's argument in a way that makes the basis of our human nature in attachment love, as in Winnicott and others, central to his understanding of human rights.

In an essay by John Rawls that interpreted Kant's argument about the foundations of ethics (the Categorical Imperative), Rawls reformulated the Categorical Imperative in terms of moral constructivism or contractualism, a four-part procedure in which each person without knowing their specific identity and particular ends tests maxims of action in terms of their appeal to practical reason, the fact of reason that enables us, as human, to decide on our actions, and accord a like respect to all other humans who, as human, have practical reason, all coming to an agreement on basic ethical principles.[35] To make sense of this conception, Rawls argues that the goods that are the ends of human action must come in but, following Kant, such goods cannot be the preferences (pleasures over pains) that utilitarians regard as fundamental (which may themselves be unethical—racism and sexism, for example), but must be something more fundamental to being or becoming human, namely, "the fulfillment of true moral needs."[36] Kant for this reason rejects even a preference-based utilitarian conception of happiness as a basis for ethics,

34. See, on this point, Richards, *Love and Violence*, 188–99.

35. See Rawls, *Themes in Kant's Moral Philosophy*. See also Rawls, *Lectures on the History of Moral Philosophy*, 143–328. I develop a similar view, inspired by Rawls (my teacher as an undergraduate at Harvard College) in Richards, *Theory of Reasons*.

36. Rawls, *Themes in Kant's Moral Philosophy*, 507.

because it is an "ideal, not of reason but the imagination."[37] As I argued at some length in chapter 1, there is such a human need, namely, love, our need from infancy to adulthood for loving relationships to one another. As Charles Horton Cooley put it, "it is true of adults as of children, that the mind lives in perpetual conversation,"[38] without which human reason cannot exist, let alone flourish. Is this perhaps the kind of ideal of reason to which Kant referred in *The Critique of Pure Reason*, his way of making sense in the terms of his critical philosophy of "a creative power like the *Platonic* idea"?[39] In effect, the man of good will in Kant is Plato's man through love experiencing the good. Plato certainly saw that love has both cognitive and emotional aspects, as his formulation of love's mirror shows, enabling lovers better to see themselves through the eyes of the beloved. And love's creative power for each and every person would certainly explain why Plato in *The Protagoras*[40] has Socrates raise questions about the utilitarianism of aggregative preferences that he ascribes to the city-planner Protagoras, a man, unlike many of his other interlocutors, whom Socrates clearly respects and even admires. John Stuart Mill argues that "when the young Socrates listened to the old Protagoras, . . . [he] asserted (if Plato's dialogue be grounded in real conversation) the theory of utilitarianism against the popular morality of the so-called sophist."[41] Plato has Socrates articulate utilitarianism as the best normative model for Protagoras's role in city planning in a majoritarian democracy, and Socrates regards this as a not implausible normative basis for such an undertaking, but later appears to question it as a deep theory of ethics itself. In his famous argument about the divided line in *The Republic* Plato distinguishes several forms of knowledge of the divided line and may have had Protagoras in mind who, as an engineer or city planner, may have used and understood as a useful truth the divided line in his work, but, like the other forms of knowledge, did not understand the mathematical proofs that would explain the ratios as universal mathematical truths.[42] Plato has a deeper objection: utilitarianism, as a justification of the Athenian democracy, looks to preferences as normatively fundamental, but preferences as such may be for an evil end like hatred of critical thought

37. Rawls, *Themes in Kant's Moral Philosophy*, 507.

38. Cooley, *Human Nature*, 90.

39. See Kant, *Critique of Pure Reason*, 552.

40. See Plato, *Protagoras*.

41. Mill, *Utilitarianism*, 233.

42. See Plato, *Republic*, 1130–32.

(philosophy) or racism; and utilitarianism looks to majoritarian aggregative preferences for guidance, but such preferences may require the sacrifice of certain goods that are normatively fundamental and should never be sacrificed, like the death of Socrates for teaching philosophy. The mirror of love plays for this reason a pivotal role in Platonic ethics, because such devoted love reveals through love's mirror the goods that cannot be reduced to the pleasures or pains of erotic love that are certainly part of such love, but are not, as utilitarianism supposes, all there is to its attraction and the devotion it elicits. The study of such goods in the individual leads in turn to the understanding of the more abstract ethical goods they instantiate. Plato's thought at this point is very like Kant's reasons for rejecting utilitarian pleasure and pains for the value of dignity, albeit arrived at in a different way (which is why, I suspect, that there is such a surprising reference to Plato in *The Critique of Pure Reason*), and Plato correctly saw its close connection to a reasonable ethics, not utilitarianism certainly, but certainly not, so I believe, the anti-democratic, hierarchical polity endorsed in the *Republic* (which Kant rejected for a democratic liberalism based on respect for human rights).

Love is a human need. We are not born alone nor can we survive alone, having, unlike other animals, extraordinary frailty, dependence, and lack of inborn skills and requiring, as Tomasello observed, a long period of living in relationship to teachers to acquire and develop the interpersonal competences (including language) that distinguish the distinctive role of culture in human life. And injuries to our capacity to love, arising from abandonment or negligence or traumatic abuse, injure not only our capacity to live with others but our capacity to live itself, as Jim Gilligan's work with violent men shows. It is for this reason that Heinz Kohut came to regard love as empathy as "primary needs that had not been responded to in childhood, that had gone into hiding, and whose transference reactivation [in psychoanalysis] is to be welcomed."[43]

Plato's picture of love in *Phaedrus* is, of course homoerotic, and assumes a significant age difference between an older lover and a younger beloved boy, perhaps arising from uncritical patriarchal assumptions dominant in ancient Athens. But, neither homosexuality nor inequality is a necessary feature of love, in particular, the love of equals, which embraces all love relationships, straight and gay; indeed, as I have argued

43. Kohut, *How Does Analysis*, 84.

elsewhere,[44] it is love that has empowered connections across the patriarchal boundaries of race, ethnicity, and religion and thus made possible resistance to the injustices of racism, religious intolerance, sexism, and homophobia. When James Baldwin, then a self-hating black gay man, moved from New York City to Paris and fell in love with and was loved by a white Swiss man, Lucien Happersberger, Lucien's love for him gave Baldwin the loving mirror he had never had, seeing himself, as Lucien did, as the brilliant, tender, beautiful person he was, as all the stereotypes that had afflicted Baldwin fell away because he saw, through his lover's eyes, the person he was and found the ethical voice that would indict the injustices of American racism and homophobia in a way few have ever done before or since.[45] Love's mirror expresses our human capacity to enter into and give weight to the perspectives of those we love, giving expression to self-knowledge as the love of another opens one's heart and mind to the web of relationships that have formed one's psyche, including those that have sometimes nurtured and sometimes deformed a secure and confident sense of living a competent, productive, and good life. It is such love of equals that gives rise to resistance to the patriarchal demands that war on such love, and, in resisting the unreal binaries and hierarchies that patriarchy enforces, such love of equals embraces as well the equality of all persons central to an ethics of universal human rights that patriarchy violently repudiates (see political religions, earlier discussed). The harm patriarchy inflicts on personal life is of a piece with the damage it inflicts on ethical and political life, crippling our distinctively human powers to see ourselves and others as persons, not divided and balkanized and objectified as racism, religious intolerance, sexism, classism, and homophobia require.

Our sense of what ethics is has been, I believe, deformed by the uncritical role that patriarchy has long played in our understanding of it, a point John Stuart Mill powerfully made in *The Subjection of Women*: "The moral training of mankind will never be adapted to the conditions of the life for which all other human progress is a preparation, until they practice in the family the same moral rule which is adapted to the normal condition of human society."[46] Patriarchy has thus damaged moral sensibility in culture generally because it has deformed the love of equals

44. See Richards, *Why Love Leads to Justice*.

45. See Richards, *Why Love Leads to Justice*, 55–57, 215.

46. Mill, *Subjection of Women*, 175.

in personal life, and the road to recovery begins with the love of equals in personal life, which is what Shakespeare saw both in his comedies and his greatest tragedy. Few wrote more perceptively of this journey than the novelist George Eliot, reflecting her own struggles against the religiously patriarchal demands on women she came to see and explore in her novels through her loving egalitarian relationship, breaking the patriarchal Love Laws (condemning adultery), to George Henry Lewes.[47] As she put it in terms that echo Plato: "The first condition of human goodness is something to love," underscoring its ethical implications: "the only true knowledge of our fellow-man is that which enables us to feel with him—which gives us a fine ear for the heart-pulses that are beating under the mere clothes of circumstance and opinion."[48] The framing of personal love in terms of equality (suspending the gender binary and hierarchy), in releasing love from repressive patriarchal demands, releases ethical feeling generally from the binaries and hierarchies that have made treating people as equals so psychologically difficult and even fraught for many. It is the move Jean Piaget observed in the moral development of children from "the ties of authority and unilateral respect" to relationships "defined by equal and mutual respect, the relations of cooperation."[49]

It is precisely because Mill was, unlike almost all other philosophers of his period and earlier,[50] so sensitive to the role patriarchy played in the deformation of conventional understandings of ethics that he argued in *On Liberty* for a principle of free speech and personal autonomy that, while questionable on the utilitarian grounds Mill believed to justify them, anticipate the more philosophically cogent, Kantian basis for such principles made by John Rawls, who regarded Mill's principles of liberty as "quite similar to those of the well-ordered society of justice as fairness"[51] (Rawls's political philosophy). The principles are similar in that both Mill and Rawls give fundamental weight, in their understanding of the liberal imperative to treat persons as equals, to what Rawls calls the basic goods of conscience, speech, association, and opportunity—owed equally to all,

47. See Richards, *Why Love Leads to Justice*, 22, 23–24, 189, 209.

48. Eliot, *Scenes of Clerical Life*, 252, 253.

49. Piaget, *Moral Judgment*, 395.

50. Except perhaps Plato himself who in the *Republic* argues that women may be Guardians, which is to say the philosopher-leaders of the republic Socrates is imaging as a moral ideal. The thought is remarkable for a philosopher of Plato's period or indeed much later periods, both ancient and modern.

51. Rawls, *Lectures on the History of Political Philosophy*, 297.

and, in both cases, these goods play a crucial role in enabling us critically to understand and resist the conventional views, like patriarchy, that have in fact deformed ethical thinking both in personal and political life. These goods play the role they do in Mill's arguments both in *On Liberty* and *The Subjection of Women* not on the utilitarian grounds he supposes, but on the basis of the Kantián values of dignity to which he also appeals. Mill could not ultimately endorse Kant's arguments because Kant's views of ethics were so metaphysically non-empirical (rooted in the noumenal world), and he did not see how such a formal theory could apply to the real world. It is the importance of Rawls's views that he bridges this gap in a reconstruction of Kantian ethics that appeals empirically to human needs, as Kant did, in contractualist thinking about what ethics requires.

In my discussion of needs in my first book, *A Theory of Reasons for Action*, I offered both a conception of needs along the lines Rawls appealed to, and argued love was one among these needs:

> the notion of a need is relative to some idea of what is required for the survival and/or minimal functioning of some other things. In the case of organisms, not all things which are part of the functioning of the organism are thought to be needed, but only those which are typically related to sustaining life, whether the life of the organism or that of other organisms. Thus, in reference to human beings, we speak and think of oxygen, food, water, the exercise of bodily functions of elimination, sexual intercourse, etc., as human needs, because they are viewed as things without which we could not survive, because they are directly necessary to sustain life (oxygen) or because they are part of the minimal organic function by which the life of the organism is sustained (elimination), or the life of the species is sustained (sex). By analogy to this view of bodily needs, what is meant by talking or psychological or spiritual needs like the need for love is that such love is required if a person is to attain some minimum level of satisfactory psychological functioning; and no doubt, part of the appropriateness of such a phenomenon is that one has an underlying idea that, if persons lack such love, the capacity to sustain life may be undermined, with accompanying notions of spiritual death (as, for example, in Strindberg, later Ibsen, and Bergman) and, perhaps, even actual suicide.[52]

It is now, in light of the arguments of Tomasello and others earlier discussed (chapter 1), even clearer to me how and why love is one of these

52. Richards, *Theory of Reasons*, 37–38.

human needs. Its importance to the sense of value in living is nowhere better stated than by King Lear when he confronts his daughter Regan with the life-destroying threat—the lovelessness and humiliation of dignity—that her suggested deprivation of his promised retinue means to him and any human life:

> O, reason not the need! Our basest beggars
> Are in the poorest thing superfluous;
> Allow not nature more than nature needs,
> Man's life is cheap as beast's. (*King Lear*, 2.2.453–456)[53]

We can make sense of Rawls's basic goods naturistically as fundamental ethical demands, since all these goods are nurtured and required reasonably to become and be fully human nurtured by loving relationships and living in relationships to others, based on freedom and equality.[54] We become human in and through loving relationships, starting long before language acquisition in the infant's experience of a self through the mirror of seeing herself or himself through the eyes of a loving mother or father.[55] Rawls himself endorses a view of moral development along these lines:

> the following psychological principle: the child comes to love their parents only if they manifestly first love him . . . Although the child has the potentiality for love, his love of the parents is a new desire brought about by his recognizing their evident love of him and his benefiting from the actions in which their love is expressed . . .
>
> The parents' love of the child is expressed in their evident intention to care for him, to do for him as his rational self-love would incline, and in the fulfillment of these intentions. Their love is displayed by their taking pleasure in his presence and supporting his sense of competence and self-esteem. They encourage his efforts to master the tasks of growing up and they welcome his assuming his own place. In general, to love another means not only to be concerned with his wants and needs, but to affirm his sense of the worth of his own person. Eventually, the love of the parents gives rise to his love in return.[56]

53. Shakespeare, *King Lear*, 255.
54. See Rawls, *Theory of Justice*, 54–257.
55. See Stern, *Interpersonal World*.
56. Rawls, *Theory of Justice*, 463–64.

And this process (a developmental psychology quite like that mapped by the Love Commandments) continues throughout our long experience of being taught by and playing with others as friends and lovers and citizens and persons in an increasingly interdependent world, as they mirror us and we mirror them, including all that expression and communication mean both before and after the acquisition of language, including self-reflection and the role that arts and sciences play in such reflection, and, as Shakespeare's art shows, the union of art and science in revealing truth. Cooley's brilliant observation about the psychosocial roots of the human mind bears, once again, repetition: "it is true of adults as of children, that the mind lives in perpetual conversation."[57] The human rights of conscience, speech, association, and opportunity, although rights protective of moral individualism (the basis of ethics), must be understood in this interpersonal perspective of the mind arising in conversation, imposing ethical duties and obligations of mutual responsibility on ourselves and others to respect the development and exercise of the human mind and heart, which arises interpersonally through the mirror of love and is sustained and developed through such interpersonal relationships. What political liberalism calls for is both respect for the basic goods that make possible real relationships (not the false relationships which patriarchy enforces), and that the distribution of these goods must treat persons as equals. Thus, rights to conscience, speech, association, and opportunity are equal rights, and Rawls's difference principle allows inequality only if it has a tendency to equality.

It was Aristotle, in his discussion of friendship and love in *The Eudemian Ethics*, who, after distinguishing three forms of such love ("one due to excellence, another usefulness, and third to pleasantness"[58]), argues that the first is the primary or focal meaning of love, on which the sense of the others depends derivatively (Aristotle uses the idea of focal meaning elsewhere in his discussions of substance[59]). The primary meaning is, for Aristotle, the love of equals, "that, of good men, . . . a mutual returning of love and choice."[60] Aristotle acknowledges other forms of love, including that of parent/child and husband/wife and even of master/slave, but excludes them from the primary meaning because equality is lacking.

57. Cooley, *Human Nature*, 90.

58. Aristotle, *Eudemian Ethics*, 1958.

59. See Aristotle, *Categories*, 4–5; Aristotle, *Metaphysics*, 1584–85.

60. Aristotle, *Eudemian Ethics*, 1958.

I earlier argued (ch. 5) that the relationship of Jesus to God, on which agape love is modeled, is not asymmetrical, but, as Martin Buber puts it, an I-Thou relationship, through which "we are drawn to and full of love for the intimate person,"[61] "that which in the heart of God is looked for in men."[62] It is such an I-Thou relationship that distinguishes the role of God's love in the life and teaching of the antipatriarchal Jesus and Judaism generally:

> "Thou shalt love the Lord thy God . . . ";—is completely missing in Greece. Aristotle said: "For it would be strange for one to say that he loved Zeus," and held that *philia* (love, friendship) was impossible between man and God.[63]

It is for this reason that Aristotle denies that, in contrast to the antipatriarchal Jesus and the Jewish tradition, we can love God, who is, for Aristotle, very much our superior. Aristotle is, I believe, quite right in making the love of equals the primary meaning of human love, and connecting it to ethical relationships. The conception of the love of equals I am developing, both as an empirical and normative matter, rejects the patriarchal conceptions, which Aristotle naturalizes both in human relationships and our relationship to God, that limit love to certain relationships between adult men and accepts both the subjection of women and slavery as ethical, and that do not give weight to the parent-child relationships that Jean Piaget observed in the moral development of children from "the ties of authority and unilateral respect" to relationships "defined by equal and mutual respect, the relations of cooperation."[64] Indeed, the conception of the love of equals I am using arose from the observation, in my life and others, that resistance to patriarchy arises from the love of equals and gives expression to it, as we see both in the lives and works of George Eliot and John Stuart Mill, as loves, resisting patriarchy, gave voice to ethical progress in the understanding of human rights. In contrast, Aristotle's conception of the love of equals, which he also defends in *The Nicomachean Ethics*, thinks of such love as a form of self-love ("his friend is another self"[65]) and an aid better "to contemplate

61. Buber, *I and Thou*, 108.

62. Buber, *Two Types of Faith*, 79.

63. Bellah, *Religion in Human Evolution*, 326. See Dodds, *Greeks*, 35, 54, citing Aristotle's *Magna Moralia* 1208B.30 and *Nicomachean Ethics* 1159A.5.

64. Piaget, *Moral Judgment of the Child*, 395.

65. Aristotle, *Nicomachean Ethics*, 1843, 1850.

worthy actions and actions that are his own,"[66] the mirroring that Eliot experienced in her relationship to Lewes or Mill in his relationship to Harriet Taylor, releasing each from patriarchal demands and thus giving voice to their human rights and the rights of others.[67]

Rawls's contractualism is, I believe, best understood, as Alexandre Lefebvre has recently persuasively argued,[68] as a general view of ethics as such, not limited, as Rawls later argued,[69] to political argument in a constitutional democracy. Rawls put this view of ethics quite powerfully at the end of *The Theory of Justice*:

> Without conflating all persons into one but recognizing them as distinct and separate, it enables us to be impartial, even between persons who are not contemporaries but who belong to many generations. Thus to see our place in society from the perspective of this position is to see it *sub specie aeternitatis:* it is to regard the human situation not only from all social but also from all temporal points of view. The perspective of eternity is not a perspective from a certain place beyond the world, nor the point of view of a transcendent being, rather it is a certain form of thought and feeling that rational persons can adopt within the world. And having done so, they can, whatever their generation, bring together into one scheme all individual perspectives and arrive together at regulative principles that can be affirmed by everyone as he lives by them, each from his own standpoint. Purity of heart, if one could attain it, would be to see clearly and to act with grace and self-command from this point of view.[70]

When Rawls earlier reconstructed Kant's Categorical Imperative as a four-part contractualism or constructivism, he was thinking of ethics generally in such terms, applied in *A Theory of Justice* to what he calls the circumstances of justice and his just quoted defense of the general view is clearly contractualist applied to such circumstances. Others, including myself[71] and T. M. Scanlon[72] have offered more general views of ethics as contractualist. On a contractualist view applied to the circumstances

66. Aristotle, *Nicomachean Ethics*, 1843, 1850.

67. I am indebted for this discussion of Aristotle to conversations with Donald Levy.

68. See Lefebvre, *Liberalism*.

69. See Rawls, *Political Liberalism*.

70. Rawls, *Theory of Justice*, 587.

71. Richards, *Theory of Reasons*.

72. Scanlon, *What We Owe*.

of justice, each person, not knowing their specific identity (the veil of ignorance), asks what principles they would be prepared to offer to others and accept for themselves, consistent with their status as free and equal, as the ultimate principles to which they and others may appeal in the distribution of the resources made available by a mutually advantageous cooperative life. From this perspective, five principles follow that must be prior to all others: the right of conscience, the right of free speech, the right of associational liberty (including intimate life), equal opportunity, and what Rawls calls the difference principle.

Conscience is a fundamental human right, because protection of independence in forming, expressing, and revising basic convictions about meaning in personal and interpersonal life frees one critically to examine and resist conventions, like patriarchy, that deform conscience. It was Socrates, Plato's teacher, who discovered moral philosophy in his conversations with others in which he held himself and them to demands of consistency and non-contradiction in basic normative beliefs, an argument Kant would later develop as the test for a Categorical Imperative. Moral philosophy thus began in conversation often with young men in love with Socrates and Socrates, sometimes in love with them, and philosophy, as invented by Socrates, was a mirror through which some (like Plato) came to see the incoherence of their conventionally acquired normative beliefs and sometimes came to question and change them. For some, such questioning was humiliating, indeed infuriating (Callicles in *Gorgias*, and Thrasymachus in *Republic*), a shaming of Athenian patriarchal manhood that would condemn Socrates unjustly to death. But, it was through such love that philosophy emerged as a method of developing and cultivating critical conscience. It so challenged conventional Athenian beliefs that Socrates was convicted of heresy and executed; yet, Socrates refused, as friends urged, to flee the Athens whose agonistic democracy had made philosophy feasible but could not accept the role free conscience must play in a democracy that, as we would put it, respects human rights. The Athenian democracy was a great advance in human politics, but it was, as Socrates saw, deeply flawed, shown not only by its murder of Socrates, but by its colonialist imperialistic wars, which destroyed it, and much else (including slavery and the subjection of women). Philosophy like theater is required by democracy precisely because it demands critical thought and reflection as the price citizens must pay to be worthy of the remarkable freedom democracy accords them over themselves and others, perhaps for the first time in human history. It was a point Madison made in No. 55 of *The Federalist*, in favor of representative democracy over Athenian mass assemblies, namely, that it would respect this inalienable human right:

> In all very numerous assemblies, of whatever characters composed, passion never fails to wrest the sceptre from reason. Had every Athenian citizen been a Socrates; every Athenian assembly would still have been a mob.[73]

Freedom of speech is the correlative right that protects the crucial role of expression (linguistic and nonlinguistic) in the interpersonal relationships that make us human and in questioning and resisting unjust patriarchal and other demands. The judicial murder of Socrates was not only a crime against conscience, but against free speech, which must extend in a constitutional democracy to the full range of convictions critical not only of politics, but, in contrast to Athens, constitutional democracy itself.[74] As Madison observed, calling for a Senate in which free speech would be respected in No. 63, *The Federalist*:

> What bitter anguish would not the people of Athens have often escaped, if their government had contained so provident a safeguard against the tyranny of their own passions? Popular liberty might then have escaped the indelible reproach of decreeing to the same citizens the hemlock on one day, and statues on the next.[75]

It was John Stuart Mill's signal contribution to the discourse of free speech to connect the kind of muscular conception of free speech he advocated to exposing and questioning explicitly the role patriarchy had, in his view, historically played in the deformation of ethical thinking, as it may well have played in the death of Socrates (the fury of the patriarchal men shamed by his challenges to their authority).

Associational liberty protects the crucial role of freedom to form interpersonal relationships which are at the heart of the loving relationships through which we are and become human. It may be at the very heart of what motivated Mill to write *On Liberty* and *The Subjection of Women* that he had himself experienced such love in his adulterous relationship to Harriet Taylor (married with children), a relationship condemned by conventional Victorian sexual morality, a love across the patriarchal

73. Hamilton et al., *Federalist*, 270.

74. See, on this point, Richards, *Toleration*, 165–230.

75. Hamilton et al., *Federalist*, 307.

boundaries that led him fundamentally to question such boundaries.[76] In light of the destructive demands that patriarchy imposes on love, this right extends to the relational freedom to intimate love free from the conventional moralisms that unjustly repress it, in particular, loves across the patriarchal boundaries of class and caste, race and ethnicity, religion and gender.

And opportunity is the basic good it is because we are the species, as Tomasello observed, for whom education is indispensable to finding our way in the cultures that distinguish our species and to find meaning not only in our loves but in our vocations, including our contributions to the culture that will outlive us. Teaching and learning and working cooperatively are indispensable to creative and productive cultures scientifically and artistically, a distinctive achievement of our species, and the legacy of a human life well lived under the aspect of our inevitable deaths. Access to such opportunities of education and vocation condemn, in particular, caste systems that confine people rigidly to occupations and ways of life that they are accorded no choice to challenge, indeed that are held in place, as Isabel Wilkerson has argued, by violence.[77] And they condemn as well unregulated access to equal opportunity,[78] what Lefebvre calls "liberaldom,"[79] a supposed meritocracy that betrays a fair equality of opportunity that would take seriously and ameliorate disadvantages relating to class and family background.

The difference principle addresses what inequalities of wealth or status would be acceptable, and finds acceptable only those inequalities that act as necessary incentives to encourage performance for the public good, but such incentives are only justified if the resulting distribution focuses on making the resulting worst-off classes better off. Equality in these resources is not required if, because of disincentive effects on ambition and performance, equality would make the worst off even worse off than they would be with some measure of inequality in wealth and status. On the other hand, because dignity plays such a central role in the view, inequalities would not be allowed which worst off classes would reasonably experience as degrading, even though justified on incentive grounds.

76. See, on this point, Richards, *Why Love Leads*, 24–28.

77. See, on this point, Wilkerson, *Caste*.

78. See, on this point, Lefebvre, *Liberalism*, 103–108.

79. Lefebvre, *Liberalism*, 117.

The argument clarifies as well the foundational role of dignity in the thought of both Kant and Rawls: dignity is the value ascribed to what Kant called "the fact of reason,"[80] namely, respect for the practical reason of each and every person in deciding how to live in relationship to other persons, arising from our distinctively human capacity to understand, enter into, and give weight to the perspectives of others and the cultural forms they nourish and support. Practical reason, in the way both Kant and Rawls understand it, is a fact of reason, the competence that enables us to reflect critically both on our personal and interpersonal end and lives and to act accordingly.[81] What Kant may not have appreciated (in his view of ethics as mysteriously noumenal, not part of the empirical world) is that love and ethics (which he separates) cannot empirically be so sharply separated, a fact Rawls clearly sees (linking love and self-respect, as he put it: "Their [parental] love is displayed by their taking pleasure in his presence and supporting his sense of competence and self-esteem"[82]), and that Plato may have seen something that Freud and later relational psychologists like Kohut and Winnicott have found to be an empirical fact, namely, that interpersonal relationships are what make reason possible for us as humans, and is required to understand reason both in our personal and ethical lives. Ethics for both Kant and Rawls is an expression of our constructive moral powers of our rationality and reasonableness, each of which require, I believe, both a heart and mind nurtured in loving relationship and protected by the human rights grounded in the basic goods that foster the integrity of such relationships. It is a misunderstanding of Rawls's argument to interpret it as egoistic. To the contrary, it offers an interpretation, indeed an expansive interpretation, of the radical empathy of a universalistic ethics of human rights based on the goods each and every person *must* be guaranteed irrespective of utilitarian aggregates to the contrary. Thus, the normative priority of universal human rights, which has, since World War II, become the ethical ideal to which diverse nations and peoples aspire (thus, the Universal Declaration of Human Rights of 1948).

It is a feature of the account I offer of the place of the love of equals as central to ethics that it is joined to an account of how the uncritical cultural acceptance of patriarchy has distorted understanding of the love

80. Kant, *Critique of Practical Reason*, 164.

81. For Rawls on the development of this point in Kant, see Rawls, *Themes in Kant's Moral Philosophy*, 517–23.

82. Rawls, *Theory of Justice*, 463.

of equals and thus ethics itself. The idea of an ethics of care, introduced by Carol Gilligan, arose from her studies of the moral development of girls and young women,[83] revealing, as Sandra Laugier recently put it, "an essential portion of reality [that] has escaped ethics and philosophy."[84] That portion of reality is the importance of care at every stage of human development and the important role that caretakers, often women, play in such care. As Laugier put the point,

> It is quite ironic that Gilligan's approach has been called essentialist. Gilligan has shown how general her approach is: she treats justice and care as two rivaling tones or voices, existing within us all, the voice of care being less quickly stifled in girls than boys. But Gilligan's point of view is radical: it shows that mainstream ethics imposed an extraordinary continuity with "ordinary" experiences—those of women, but not exclusively, she focuses on the voices of all those, including the most disadvantaged, who, *because* they serve others, have no voice in the definition of justice or the common good.[85]

What is radical about this approach is that recent work by Gilligan's students, Judy Chu[86] and Niobe Way,[87] shows how much the moral development of boys into men reveals other realities that have escaped notice, as patriarchy deforms the development of men as well as women. It is because patriarchy attacks the loves across the boundaries it establishes and enforces, requiring disruption and loss of loving relationships, that its psychology regards as normative and highly gendered the two pathological responses to loss—denial, and disassociation for men and compulsive caretaking for women—subverting the voice of repairing relationships that would challenge the injustices thus inflicted on men and women.[88] Even Freud saw the point, albeit mistaking it as a biological not a cultural issue, observing in his late 1938 essay "Analysis Terminable and Interminable" that the "bedrock"[89] of psychological illness is "the 'repudiation of

83. See Gilligan, *In a Different Voice*; Brown and Gilligan, *Meeting at the Crossroads.* See also Richards, *Resisting Injustice and the Feminist Ethics of Care.*

84. See Laugier, "How an Essential Portion of Reality," 23.

85. Laugier, "How an Essential Portion of Reality," 26.

86. Chu, *When Boys Become "Boys."*

87. Way, *Deep Secrets*; Way, *Rebels With a Cause.*

88. See, for fuller exploration of this psychology, Gilligan and Snider, *Why Does Patriarchy.*

89. Freud, "Analysis Terminable and Interminable," 252.

femininity.'"[90] The analysis and critique of patriarchal structures in moral development is thus an imperative—both psychological and ethical—if we are to understand and give emancipatory effect to the love of equals.

Rawls's constructivism in ethics moves beyond Kant in accepting that the basic structure of society shapes the personalities of those who live in that society (which Kant's conception of noumenal freedom denies). Implicitly, his constructivism in which love is central to the human psyche requires, as other liberal theories often do not, that attention be especially paid to those worst off persons and classes, exactly what Sandra Laugier criticizes liberal theories for ignoring. Thus, Rawls's deeply egalitarian argument endorses the social liberalism of his difference principle, requiring that inequalities of wealth and status are only justified if they work out for the benefit of worst-off persons and classes.[91] Inequality in the domain of wealth and status is thus allowed but only if it pays attention to the perspectives of those disadvantaged by the inequality by justifying the inequality to them in terms that advantage them in contrast to equality in this domain. In this respect, Rawls's constructivism demands precisely that ethical attention, as we shall see, be paid to the criminals that Jim Gilligan and others have argued are among the most unjustly despised people in our society (as Simone Weil put the point, "[m]en think they are despising crime when they are really despising the weakness of affliction"[92]).

It was Hegel who tried to connect Kant's metaphysical view of ethics to the history and psychology of persons and cultures he called stages in the phenomenology of spirit, framed by agonistic opposites, later synthesized, as the motor of such development.[93] For Marx, in contrast,

> [m]oral judgments are beside the point. The transformation of the world by capitalism is a necessary stage on the way to the full flowering of human capacities in socialism: "When a great social revolution shall have mastered the results of the bourgeois epoch the market of the world and the modern powers of production . . . then only will human progress cease to resemble that hideous pagan idol, who would not drink the nectar but from the skulls of the slain." [McCarthy quoting Marx].[94]

90. Freud, "Analysis Terminable and Interminable," 250.
91. Rawls, *Theory of Justice*, 75–82.
92. Quoted in Richards, *Love and Violence*, 217.
93. See Hegel, *Phenomenology*.
94. McCarthy, *Race, Empire*, 178.

Thomas McCarthy is surely right: "Today Marx's historical confidence in that 'great social revolution,' like Kant's rational faith in God's or Nature's plan of history, has largely lost whatever powers of reconciliation it might once have possessed."[95] Nothing so rigid or deterministic or necessarily progressive, as both Hegel and Marx supposed, can be true, as both the history of human cultures and contemporary cultures show so clearly; history reveals progress and reaction, learning from many cultures and then forgetting; and there is a mystery about the agonistic motor. But, there is a culture and psychology with all its advances and regressions to be taken seriously. What might it be?

We are the species who must live in and through culture that is made psychologically possible for us through love's mirror which also makes possible, so I have argued, theater, Shakespeare, psychoanalysis, democratic politics, religion, and an ethics of universal human rights. Hamlet may be right when, in response to Rosencrantz's incredulity at Hamlet's remark that Denmark is a prison, he responds (almost quoting Montaigne): "Why then 'tis none for you, for there is nothing either good or bad, but thinking makes it so. To me it is a prison."[96] In a constructivist view of ethics, Hamlet is right that ethics is an expression ultimately of a distinctive form of interpersonal human thought and experience, nothing else, but it also expresses something quite absent from Hamlet's lonely, loveless, traumatized life (without mother, father, lover, former university friends, now, like Polonius, courtiers to the king's homicidal will), namely, love, which makes Hamlet's bitter, ironic observation to his former friends at least humanly understandable (only Horatio stands by him). Love is at the center of what moves us and what we value and what, if we choose to act on it, we can contribute to the lives of others. And injuries to the capacity for love, as by patriarchy, lead to moral nihilism (the root of Hamlet's paralysis), acting out mindless violence to self and others. There is nothing mysterious about any of this, nor deterministic. It is among the choices that make us human.

My approach to ethics is naturalistic and humanistic, and draws support from the importance of a social-psychological science, like that of Jim Gilligan, grounded in a view of the human sciences anticipated by Thucydides, and then shows how Jim's medical approach empirically supports the case for transcending guilt and shame through love based

95. McCarthy, *Race, Empire*, 178.

96. Shakespeare, *Hamlet*, 1203 (II.ii.249–250).

on his work with violent criminals. The study of violence is important in understanding the central significance of love in a human life, because violence psychologically is linked to shame-driven patriarchally rationalized injuries to love and self-esteem.

In looking at violence through the lens provided by Jim Gilligan's medical model, as a problem in public health and preventive medicine (including social psychiatry), it might be helpful to remember that this approach is not untried, nor has its application in the past been doomed to being unsophisticated or oversimplified. Violence was first viewed from a medical perspective in ancient Greece in a masterpiece of historical, political and—not least—psychological analysis by a thinker who has never been surpassed in subtlety and sophistication. Thucydides showed how the empirically based way of thinking that underlies medicine (even in its earliest scientific beginnings) can be applied to the subject of violence with the sensitivity and flexibility that the complexity of the subject requires.[97]

Two millennia later the father of modern epistemology, Immanuel Kant, in the course of describing the "way of thinking" (*Denkungsart*) that is necessary in order to acquire knowledge about human behavior, defended the rationality and appropriateness of these assumptions in the writing of history (and, by implication, all later social science); and he specifically endorsed Hume's praise of Thucydides as the model historian: "The first page of Thucydides, as Hume puts it, is the only beginning of all true history."[98]

Kant's emphasis on the necessity of assuming free will in order to engage in moral legislation and value judgments is so well known that it is often forgotten or overlooked that he was equally emphatic about the indispensability of assuming determinism in order to engage in historical and psychological understanding and explanation, or in other words, to acquire knowledge about people and their relationships. Kant's metaphysical theory of moral freedom is one of the great defects in his critical philosophy, leading Hegel, Marx, and others to create problematic causal theories that would bridge the gap between theory and reality. I argue for an empirically grounded alternative, filling this gap, based on modern science, and have earlier explained my views. What is striking is that, in contradiction to his questionable theory of moral freedom, Kant showed

97. Thucydides, *History of the Peloponnesian War*.

98. Kant, *Idea for a Universal History*, 52, footnote.

himself to be a quite brilliant political scientist when he abandoned his metaphysical theory of freedom for empirical work. Nothing in such empirical work requires, as Kant supposed, denying the role of dignity as a central ethical and political value, let alone exploring how this value is better advanced and realized empirically (for example, by the abolition of prisons).

In an essay on history in which he pays tribute to Thucydides as the creator of the paradigm of "all true history," Kant details the preconditions for what we could call the analysis of human behavior over time (which is, I might add, how both the historical and the psychoanalytic "way of thinking" can be described). In addition to being empirical, he says, it is both deterministic and probabilistic:

> Whatever conception of the freedom of the will one may form in terms of metaphysics, the will's manifestation in the world of phenomena, i.e., human actions, are determined in accordance with natural laws, as is every other natural event. History is concerned with giving an account of these phenomena, no matter how deeply concealed their causes may be, and it allows us to hope that, if it examines the free exercise of the human will *on a larger scale,* it will be able to discover a regular progression among freely willed action. In the same way, we may hope that what strikes us in the actions of individuals as confused and fortuitous may be recognized, in the history of the entire species, as a steadily advancing but slow development of man's original capacities. Thus marriages, births, and deaths do not seem to be subject to any rule by which their numbers could be calculated in advance, since the free human will has such a great influence upon them; and yet the annual statistics for them in large countries prove that they are just as subject to constant natural laws as are the changes in the weather, which in themselves are so inconsistent with their individual occurrence cannot be determined in advance, but which nevertheless do not fail as a whole to sustain the growth of plants, the flow of rivers, and other natural functions in a uniform and uninterrupted course.[99]

Kant applies his empirical method brilliantly later to argue that perpetual peace (the ending of war among states) will be ended at least among those states that are republican democracies,[100] a claim that

99. Kant, *Idea for a Universal History,* 41.

100. See Kant, "Perpetual Peace."

contemporary history apparently confirms.[101] Kant's argument here and elsewhere does not support, indeed contradicts, his metaphysical theory of moral freedom, showing quite plausibly how human conduct can be explained empirically, including why the ethical value, dignity, to which Kant gave such prominence, can be advanced or frustrated by different constitutional arrangements. In this respect, Kant joins Hume as one of the empirical political scientists who best understood and evaluated the forms of constitutionalism, including American constitutionalism, emerging at the end of the eighteenth century. His view, for example, of "the *unsocial sociability* man"[102] and "such warped wood as that which man is made of,"[103] is quite consistent with Hume's theory of the political psychology of faction that was so crucial in Madison's design of the federal system of the U.S. Constitution.[104] At this point, Kant's metaphysical theory of freedom appears more a remnant of patriarchal religious views that still uncritically had a hold on Kant (like his strong retributivism and Puritanical moralism) rather than a consistent working out of his critical philosophy both in epistemology and in ethics. His empirical views, however, lead us to explore the connections of the historical Jesus, who inspired Kant, to democracy.

So, the naturalistic interpretation of Kant that, inspired by Rawls, I have proposed, makes possible the kind of normatively and empirically defensible reconciliation of ethics and history that Hegel and Marx sought, one that reinterprets Kant's Christian theodicy as a reasonable secular conception of universal human rights and democratic constitutionalism that, in the wake of the ethical regression of World War II and the Universal Declaration of Human Rights of 1948 that followed it, inspires diverse peoples now, however imperfectly, to embrace and aspire to realize, as an ethical and political responsibility. Perhaps the

101. See Doyle, "Kant, Liberal Legacies, and Foreign Affairs"; Doyle, *Ways of War and Peace.*

102. Kant, *Idea for a Universal History,* 44.

103. Kant, *Idea for a Universal History,* 46.

104. On Hume's theory of faction and its pivotal influence on the constitutional thought of James Madison, see Richards, *Foundations,* 32–39. The thought underlying Madison's theory of faction (that constitutionalism must take seriously that a majority faction may be hostile to basic human rights) is the same thought Kant articulates when he argues that constitutions must take seriously that sometimes the rulers may be "a nation of devils." See Kant, "Perpetual Peace," 112. Both Madison and Kant appear to have drawn the same conclusions for constitutional constructivism from Hume's theory of faction. I am indebted for this point to conversations with Jeremy Waldron.

most difficult responsibility faced by the cultures of the Christian West is what Thomas McCarthy has proposed, namely, how the injustices inflicted by the racist colonialisms of the West (including slavery) on their colonies and colonized peoples can be acknowledged and faced as a matter "not only of distributive justice but of reparative or restorative justice as well."[105] The argument of this book, which questions the role that hegemonic Christianities historically played in enforcing patriarchal institutions that rationalized violence against outsiders, is a contribution to such discourse. If I am right, the antipatriarchal Jesus inspires and should inspire such resistance.

105. McCarthy, *Race, Empire*, 226–27.

7

Christian Dissent and Democracy

For much of its history, Christianities have been, as I have now argued, more Roman than Christian, a fact institutionalized when Christianity was made the established church of the Roman Empire. I hope I have now shown that this corruption of the life and teaching of the historical Jesus arose from the failure of Christian leaders, starting with Paul, to understand, let alone take seriously the antipatriarchal Jesus. The historical Jesus was not a political or legal thinker, but a visionary prophet of an antipatriarchal kingdom of God that he believed was coming into existence through his life and teaching. Even his disciples failed to understand him, as he often complained, and ultimately, except for Mary Magdalene and a few other women, abandoned him. Paul, who never knew the historical Jesus, understood him even less, and yet was the dominant figure in the development of most of the Christianities we have so far studied in this book. It is a sad, indeed an appalling story—the Inquisition, violent anti-Semitism, the Crusades, the wars of religion, the support Christianities gave autocracies on the model of the Roman Empire (the divine right of kings), the support of the violence of sexism and homophobia, and the like.

The Protestant Reformation, however, unleashed an appeal to democratic conscience that had been theretofore crushed by the enforcement at large by the state of the Augustinian endorsement of violent persecution of dissenting heretics within the Christian tradition. The authority of the Bible, both Hebrew and Christian, was in the hands solely of a literate clerical priestly elite who would communicate their views of its meaning to people generally in sermons and arts (including architecture). Moreover, in Western Christendom the Bible was in Latin (though the Christian Bible had been written in Greek, still used in Eastern Christendom; Jesus, of course, was an oral teacher speaking Aramaic). Most believers were literate neither in Latin nor Greek, so the elite priesthood was the only access of believers to the New Testament. As a Roman Catholic in my childhood, I depended completely on the priests at the weekly masses my family attended for access to the New Testament.

It was the Protestant Reformation that initiated, for the first time in the long history of Christianities, the democratization of access to the New Testament, as translations in the vernacular (for example, Luther's translation of the Bible into German) were not only available but, with the printing press, now very broadly available. What followed was not only the democratization of Christianity, but, in time, democracy itself, and Christian dissent played an increasingly important role, as we shall now see. I will explore this development in the following stages: the development by radical Christians of the argument for toleration and the resulting development of rights-based democratic constitutionalism; the role of radical Christians in the criticism of slavery and its attendant evils of sexism and racism both before, during, and after the Civil War (including Lincoln himself); the discovery and development—on the basis of the teaching of the historical Jesus—of nonviolence leading to resistance and cultural, political, and constitutional change in Britain, India, and the United States; and arguments today coming from within Christianity for new forms of nonviolence and finding common ground with other religious traditions in resisting patriarchy.

THE ARGUMENT FOR TOLERATION

The argument for toleration arose within Christianity—John Locke and Pierre Bayle, both deeply religious Protestants, arguing against the theory of intolerance of Augustine that had informed the view of most Christianities until Locke and Bayle.[1]

Augustine developed his argument to make sense of the schismatic Christian Donatists in light of his deep commitment to a theory of history.

1. See, for further elaboration, Richards, *Toleration*, 85–102.

That theory required Augustine to give a reasonable sense to both biblical prophecy and recent catastrophic events (the sack of Rome by pagans in 410 CE). For Augustine, who associated Roman order with civilization, a redemptive meaning, compatible with the Bible, could be given to Rome's fall only if the spiritual ideals of civilization were transferred from the fallen corrupt world of politics to the institutions of the Catholic Church. If the church alone civilizes, a concern to maintain the authority of the church has a kind of world historical significance, especially for a working bishop like Augustine. Accordingly, resistance to the authority of the church by schismatic Christians, such as the Donatists, appeared to Augustine, who also believed in an original sin that flawed human nature and was only redeemed by Jesus's sacrifice, came to see the resistance of the Donatists as the product not of reasonable disagreement, but of the culpable ignorance of persons who know the truth but willfully deny it through a corruption of the will. Such people so lack freedom and rationality that others may justly intervene, paternalistically, to protect them from themselves for the same reason that we protect the insane from their own self-destructive irrationalities. The analogy is, for Augustine, exact. Heresy reflects a corrupt will lacking rational capacities; and the self-destructiveness is of the worst kind—eternal damnation. Indeed, the ground for coercive intervention by the state on behalf of the church is even stronger, since the destructiveness of the heretical madman inflicts damage on those he corrupts as well, from which society may justly be protected. While Augustine himself urged leniency in the treatment of heretics, the Augustinian argument for intolerance was later elaborated by Thomas Aquinas, among others, to justify capital punishment of heretics.[2]

The argument of John Locke's four *Letters Concerning Toleration* is as classically authoritative for the Anglo-American tradition as Pierre Bayle's contemporary defense in his *Philosophique Commentaire* is for the French and European democratic tradition. No other statements of the argument for toleration are more profound or more influential. Both thinkers worked within a Calvinist heritage, wrote in a common cultural environment of the Netherlands, knew one another, and shared many common philosophical premises. Locke, however, writes his argument in the context of the more general rights-based democratic theory of *The Second Treatise of Government*: the state's violation of basic human rights

2. See Richards, *Toleration*, 87–88, for supporting citations.

(in particular, the right to conscience) may justify disobedience and, in extremis, rebellion.

Augustine's arguments center on the idea of the culpable and vincible ignorance of persons who know the truth but willfully deny it through a corruption of the will, to which we owe nothing but the contempt and opposition due a diabolic fault in the soul. Thus, the heretic is owed no respect, because her freedom is enslaved by her will and her rationality is at war with itself.

Neither Locke nor Bayle denies the existence of the erring conscience, that is, people may believe false religious propositions on inadequate grounds. They deny, however, the moral and political interpretation given to the erring conscience by Augustine and those using Augustinian arguments in England and France to justify persecution of dissenters from the established Anglican or Catholic churches, respectively (both Locke and Bayle were such dissenters). They deny, in particular, that the nature of religious questions and the ways in which people believe them allow grounds for repression that does not itself rest on contempt for the freedom and rationality of the person. Any such theory of persecution itself expresses, Locke emphasizes, contempt for the equal rationality of persons in using reasoning in diverse ways consistent with experience equally available to all and with free conscience. At bottom, one theological system, among others equally reasonable, is made the measure of rationality. This, of course, fails to accord the respect due free and rational persons.

This conception—that ethical independence and the right to conscience are mutually supportive—leads to the most radical departure of this argument from other political traditions, namely, Locke's principle that religious ends are not a legitimate state concern, but only secular goods like life, liberty, and what Jefferson would later call the pursuit of happiness. This argument was naturally opposed as undermining public morality and political stability, especially when it was later elaborated to encompass disestablishment (in Virginia, and under the First Amendment of the United States Constitution). Past political experience was, for Locke and Bayle, a poor guide once the diversity of religious thought was unleashed by the Reformation. For them, such political experience was itself based on an unsound theory of intolerance and on a corrupt conception of public morality. The argument from past experience proved, of course, wrong. The argument for the right to conscience did not undermine public morality; it led to a new conception of what ethics is, made possible by the ethical independence that respect for conscience fosters. That was, I believe, exactly Locke's and Bayle's prophetic point.[3]

Neither Locke nor Bayle gave the argument for toleration the expansive scope it was later to enjoy (denying such toleration to Catholics or atheists, neither of whom they believed, erroneously, could or would themselves be tolerant).[4] And while Locke himself did not regard the argument for toleration as inconsistent with a tolerant and latitudinarian established church, it was in the United States that Thomas Jefferson and James Madison argued, as Jefferson put it in drafting the bill disestablishing the Anglican Church in Virginia, "where he [Locke] stopped, we may go on."[5] The anti-establishment clause of the First Amendment of the U.S. Bill of Rights rests on their common view that no state tax money should go to the support of sectarian religious teaching. Based on their view of how Christianity had betrayed its emancipatory humanistic promise once it became the established church of the Roman Empire and states modeled on that precedent, they argued that disestablishment was not so much designed to protect politics from religion, but religion from politics, a fact demonstrated in their view by how Christianities, as established churches, had betrayed the life and teaching of the historical Jesus.[6]

RADICAL CHRISTIAN RESISTANCE TO SLAVERY, SEXISM, AND RACISM: THE GRIMKE SISTERS

It is again from within Christianity that radical Christians (most notably, the Quakers) oppose slavery, and play an important role in the antislavery abolitionist movements in both Britain and the United States. But, in antebellum American, when many Christian churches in both the South and North condemned abolitionism, it was two women and sisters, Angelina and Sarah Grimke, who had observed slavery at first hand in their native South Carolina and then converted to Quakerism and moved North to support not only the abolition of slavery but to criticize as well what they regarded as its attendant evils—racism and sexism.

Quakerism is remarkable among Christianties not only for taking the salient role of nonviolence in both the historical Jesus's life and

3. See, for supporting argument and citations, Richards, *Toleration*, 89–95.

4. See, on this point, Richards, *Toleration*, 95–98.

5. Quoted at Richards, *Toleration*, 112.

6. See, for further argument and defense, Richards, *Toleration*, 104–16.

teaching so seriously (refusing, as pacifists, to fight in wars), but for their repudiation of the patriarchal shame culture, based on honor, that Jesus had also challenged. As the brilliant social historian Bertram Wyatt-Brown put it:

> In almost every feature, the Quaker credo directly challenged the tenets of honor. Though condemned as subversive for shattering custom, the Friends made themselves walking testaments of pious shamelessness. They adopted the Beatitudes and tried to live by them. In fact, the most zealous among them elevated shame, translated into humility, to the penultimate in virtue, second only to godliness. In public, plain clothes, plain speech, and the use of the intimate form of address and greeting were all designed to set Friends apart, but also serve as implicit criticism of a world of ranks, brute strength, and self-aggrandizement. Like the early Christians, Quakers appealed largely to the honorless—the servant and tenants classes, the cottagers of Wales, the small artisans of England.
>
> . . . First and foremost, the Friends repudiated the intimate connections between community approval or rejection and the individual. Instead, one's duty was the solitary business of seeking God, for all men were equipped with a divinity permitting the search for the Light Within . . . Hospitality or honorable largess was to be offered only to those in need, without any expectation of return . . . In sexuality, continence before marriage was to be observed regardless of one's gender. Women were accorded the right to speak in meetings. In dealings with outsiders and menials, one was to recognize that all human beings were children of God. In short, there was scarcely any aspect of primal honor, including military virtue . . . , that the Quakers did not dramatically transform, modify, or reject outright. Opposition to slavery, a much later development, eventually became part of the Friends' challenge to worldliness.[7]

What I find so remarkable about the Grimke sisters is that, as Quakers, they not only spoke at meetings, but exercised powers of public speech and writing about the true meaning of Christianity and the proper interpretation of the Bible that most Christianities had theretofore reserved solely to a hierarchical priesthood of men, anticipating by well over a century the emergence of a serious search for the historical antipatriarchal Jesus earlier discussed in the work of Elizabeth Schüssler Fiorenza, among others. Writing and speaking as women, from their

7. Wyatt-Brown, *Southern Honor*, 75–76.

experience as women and their intimate understanding of the indignities of American slavery, they indict not only slavery, but what they argued was its supporting evils—racism and sexism.

Angelina and Sarah Grimke eloquently testified to the injuries that American slavery and racism had inflicted on the very minds and hearts of its perpetrators and its victims; their searing portraits of the tyrannies of Southern women bespoke the former, and their memorialization of the degradation of the slaves to illiterate permanent heathens the latter. Their confrontation with American sexism prodded them to think more deeply than any American of their generation or indeed long after about the roots of the opposition they had always faced, first as Southern women and later as expatriate women in the North, from other women as well as men. If slavery and racism were, as Sarah Grimke had described them, "this heart-breaking, this soul-destroying system,"[8] so too, on examination was sexism, in view of its blatant contempt for women's inalienable right to conscience. The failure to respect what Angelina Grimke called "the fundamental principle of moral being"[9] discredited the conventional morality that expressed such contempt, "the unchristian doctrine of masculine and feminine virtues."[10]

Both Angelina and Sarah Grimke were, by the American measure of the time, quite religiously heterodox, but their moral independence as Christians centered, like most Americans of the time, on Bible interpretation. They therefore naturally thought that the institutional failure of American religions to embody the principle of equality in their practice (including, of course, a central role for women as scholars, preachers, and teachers) was the consequence of the failure of American religion adequately to understand the central place of equality in reasonable Bible interpretation. This was the main argument of the Grimkes' central contribution to abolitionist feminism, Sarah Grimke's *Letters on the Equality of the Sexes and the Condition of Women.*[11]

Sarah Grimke's arguments centers, first, on making her case that the dominant biblical interpretations of normatively influential texts of the Hebrew Bible and the New Testament wrongly ascribed to them the moral ideology of separate spheres and the inferiority of women, and, second, on showing how this had happened. Both aspects of her position

8. Quoted in Richards, *Women, Gays,* 93.

9. Quoted in Richards, *Women, Gays,* 93.

10. Quoted in Richards, *Women, Gays,* 93.

11. See, for further discussion and citations, Richards, *Women, Gays,* 94–102.

brilliantly elaborated the argument for toleration to the ends of feminist liberation. The dominant misogyny of Bible interpretation assumed, on examination, a wholly corrupted and illegitimate political epistemology that unreasonably entrenched a masculine hierarchy of power and privilege over women (including masculine monopoly of Bible interpretation); this corrupt epistemology narrowed the terms of debate to the cramped measure of masculine self-protection, and for this illegitimate reason excluded women from reasonable participation in its dialogue.

Grimke's substantive exercises in Bible interpretation applied a normative conviction that she took to be to the entire narrative and, thus understood, to be reasonably supported by the narrative, namely, that all persons, made in the image of God, have the creative powers of "a moral and responsible being."[12] As such, each person was ultimately ethically responsible for one's self and accountable as such directly to God and no other person (as Jesus had argued against the Pharisees in the Gospel of John). In the light of this normative perspective, Grimke's substantive exercise in Bible interpretation had two strategies: first, to show that the texts most commonly urged as supporting women's moral inferiority did not reasonably require that reading; and second, to point to the often ignored texts that support women's equality as moral agents. As regards, the former, two texts were central: the Adam and Eve narrative and the epistles of St. Paul.

Grimke's reading of the Adam and Eve narratives argued that it cannot be interpreted to justify women's inferiority as God's punishment for the Fall. In fact, both Adam and Eve shared equal moral fault in the Fall: certainly, "Adam's ready acquiescence with his wife's proposal, does not savor much of that superiority in *strength of mind,* which is arrogated by man."[13] Properly understood, God's statement, "Thou will be subject unto thy husband, and he will rule over thee,"[14] was a prophecy of man's corrupt subjection of women, not a normative command for such subjection. The contrary view reflected the failure of male Bible interpreters to note the ambiguity of the pertinent Hebrew word for "will" (between the normative "shall" and the predictive "will"), a failure Grimke explained in terms of "translators . . . accustomed to exercise lordship over their wives and seeing only through the medium of perverted judgment."[15]

12. Quoted at Richards, *Women, Gays,* 94.
13. Quoted at Richards, *Women, Gays,* 95.
14. Quoted at Richards, *Women, Gays,* 95.
15. Quoted at Richards, *Women, Gays,* 95.

Grimke's hermeneutic principle was that, among two readings of an ambiguous texts, the one should be preferred that better coheres with the basic normative purposes of the text as a whole—in this case, the primary ethical principle that all persons are equal moral agents. The prophetic interpretation of the text better accorded with this principle since all persons retains this status, albeit some of them exercised it wrongly to the disadvantage of others.

Grimke appealed to this hermeneutic principle in repudiating the misogynist interpretation traditionally assigned to various passages in Paul's epistles, for example, "Wives submit yourselves unto your own husbands as unto the Lord."[16] For Grimke, the traditional reading cannot be believed because it conflicted with the primary ethical principle of the Bible, the equality of all persons. "Now I must understand the sacred Scriptures as harmonizing with themselves, or I cannot receive them as the word of God."[17] Other reasonable readings were available that interpreted such passages without compromising this principle. Such passage might, for example, be contextualized to a specific historical circumstance (converted Christian woman married to unconverted men) urging women in those circumstances patiently to bear evil. This interpretation granted that husbands had no right to oppress women, but insisted that the response to such evil not appeal to what Grimke took to be un-Christian principles of violent resistance.

Grimke's affirmative interpretive case, as had her sister's, relied heavily on the role of powerfully active female prophets in the Hebrew Bible and the comparably important role by women as preachers in early Christianity.[18] Grimke's argument was very much in the radical Protestant spirit of the argument for toleration as it had been interpreted by Bayle and Locke. As we have seen, Locke and Bayle had there argued that the Augustinian tradition (dominant in their period in both Catholic and Protestant thought and practice) illegitimately enforced on society at large a corrupt political epistemology that narrowed both the scope of discussion and participants therein to the measure of the entrenched interests of a dominant political and religious hierarchy. Both Locke and Bayle argued as religious Protestants who claimed that this enforced political epistemology included a corrupt tradition of Bible interpretation that betrayed the humane tolerance central to pre-Augustinian Christianity.

16. Quoted at Richards, *Women, Gays*, 95.

17. Quoted at Richards, *Women, Gays*, 95.

18. See, for further discussion and citations, Richards, *Women, Gays*, 96.

Sarah Grimke's central claim was that the dominant Christian tradition endorsing the subjection of women was similarly illegitimate, giving rise to an unreasonable genre of Bible interpretation that betrayed early Christianity's and the historical Jesus's treatment of women as the moral and spiritual equals of men.

Grimke indicted the unreasonable exclusion of women from Christian ministry and all the consequences this exclusion inevitably had for the development of the corrupt tradition of misogynist Bible interpretation:

> it is manifest, that if women were permitted to be ministers of the gospels, as they unquestionably were in the primitive ages of the Christian church, it would interfere materially with the present organized system of spiritual power and ecclesiastical authority, which is now vested solely in the hands of men.[19]

She based her argument on the political illegitimacy of this exclusion of women not only on the usual grounds urged by Locke and Bayle (the failure of respect the rights of persons to conscience, speech, and the like), but on further grounds associated with the traditional political and religious treatment of women.

For Sarah Grimke, consistent with Angelina's similar arguments, the essential issue of political illegitimacy was posed in terms of a morally precise analogy between the rights-based subjection of women and people of color held in slavery. Her argument included both diachronic and synchronic claims.

Diachronically, Grimke argued very much along the lines of Gerda Lerner's exploration of similar themes that women's subjugation was the historically generative pattern for slavery.[20] Dating this subjugation from the fall of Adam and Eve, Grimke claimed that "[t]he lust of dominion was probably the first effect of the fall; and as there was no other intelligent being over whom to exercise it woman was the first victim of this unhallowed passion . . . Here we see the origin of that Upas of slavery, which sprang up immediately after the fall, and has spread its pestilential branches over the whole face of the known world."[21] The nerve of the issue of enslavement was "to regard women as property, and hence we

19. Quoted in Richards, *Women, Gays*, 96.

20. See Lerner, *Creation of Patriarchy*, 76, 99. See also Lerner, *Creation of Feminist Consciousness*.

21. Quoted in Richards, *Women, Gays*, 96.

find them sold to those, who wished to marry them, as far as it appears, without any regard to those sacred rights which belong to woman, as well as to man in the choice of a companion."[22] Women, objectified as property, are thus not only exchanged as slaves, but were the model for the institution of slavery (later generalized to include men as well).

Synchronically, Grimke argued that the illegitimacy of the contemporary deprivations of rights of women was based on the same grounds as slavery as an institution. She pointed to the systematic unity among the deprivations of rights to which women, like slaves, were subject: voting rights, rights to bring legal actions against her master-husband, freedom from chastisement, liberty of religious and moral conscience, and work and property rights. Such laws "approximate too nearly to the laws enacted by slaveholders for the government of their slaves,"[23] and were illegitimate for the same reason: the failure to take seriously women as persons with inalienable moral rights of moral agency and self-government. Such unjust denials of central rights of moral agency led to a cultural construction of woman's roles that "have a tendency to lessen them in their own estimation of moral and responsible beings . . . teaching them practically the fatal lesson to look upon man for protection and indulgence."[24] This debasing insult to "self-respect"[25] was, in turn, extended to the devaluation of women's work, including care. Grimke, like her sister, was a probing critic of American racism as the root of American slavery, and generalized that argument to criticize sexism as the unjustifiable basis of the subjection of women.

The brilliance of Grimke's analysis of these matters was to anatomize the common indignity to women and the slave on what she, like her sister, called "the same platform of human rights."[26] Under Grimke's analysis, both the enslavement of blacks (and its associated racism) and the subjection of women (and its associated sexism) instantiated a common radical moral evil: the politically illegitimate failure to regard a whole class of persons as bearers of human rights and their debasement to a servile status on that basis; both exemplified the evil of what I call moral slavery. Such moral slavery turned on three related kinds of radical evil: the denial of rights of conscience and free speech; the denial of

22. Quoted in Richards, *Women, Gays*, 97.

23. Quoted at Richards, *Women, Gays*, 97–98.

24. Quoted at Richards, *Women, Gays*, 98.

25. Quoted at Richards, *Women, Gays*, 98.

26. Quoted at Richards, *Women, Gays*, 98.

associational liberty, including intimate life on terms of equal respect; and the denial of the right to work. Moral slavery, thus understood, deadened moral sensibility and responsibility, and Grimke, anticipating later critics of both racism and sexism, observed how it distorted consciousness, making the same point about the injuries of sexism that W. E. B. Dubois would later make of those of racism:

> a world which yields him [a black person] no true self-consciousness, but only lets him see himself through the revelation of the other world. It is a peculiar sensation, this double-consciousness, this sense of always looking at one's self through the eyes of others, of measuring one's soul by the tape of a world that looks on in amused contempt and pity.[27]

RADICAL CHRISTIAN RESISTANCE TO SLAVERY AND RACISM: THEODORE PARKER, FREDERICK DOUGLASS, AND ABRAHAM LINCOLN

We can see the importance of such a fundamental challenge to the conventional Bible pro-slavery interpretation of the dominant Christianities in the antebellum period in both North and South, culminating in the Civil War, in Matthew Stewart's recent compelling study of the role quite radical challenges to conventional modes of Bible interpretation played in some of the leading abolitionist figures before, during, and after the Civil War, including Theodore Parker, Frederick Douglass, and Abraham Lincoln himself.[28] The most radical challenge came from Ludwig Feuerbach, a German philosopher whose view that religion was a projection of human sentiments, including love, we have had occasion to mention earlier,[29] as Winnicott had a psychological view similar but not the same as his, a matter we will discuss in a later chapter. Feuerbach was a central figure ending the dominance in German thought, called by Stewart,

> the Hegelian slumber, . . . with the publication of [his] . . . 1841 best-seller, *The Essence of Christianity.* "The spell was broken: the 'system' was exploded and cast aside," Karl Marx recalls, "One must himself have experienced the liberating effect of this book to get an idea of it. Enthusiasm was general, we all became at

27. Quoted in Richards, *Women, Gays,* 99.
28. See Stewart, *Emancipation of the Mind.*
29. See Feuerbach, *Essence of Christianity.*

> once Feuerbachians." And, most memorably, "There is no other road for you to truth and freedom except that leading through the book of fire [Feuerbach]." Feuerbach's accomplishment, says Marx, is to "abstract from Hegel's abstraction . . . and talk . . . instead . . . of man."
>
> In Feuerbach's words, God is the "species-essence of Man." What humans in the past have called "God"—and what the Hegelians obtusely called "Spirit"—is just a word that stands for our common humanity. It is an artifact of human consciousness, not the creator of it. Feurbach thus reduces theology to anthropology and declares that the aim of the philosophy of the future must be to liberate humanity from its enslavement to the fictional deities of its own making. "God himself is a materialist," he adds for good measure, and "Spinoza is the Moses of modern free-thinkers and materialists."[30]

Marx had acutely observed,

> at the outset of the war [the Civil War], the goal of the Confederacy, "is supplanting the hitherto existing democracy by the unrestricted oligarchy of 300,000 slaveholders . . ." In an 1864 letter to Abraham Lincoln, Marx asserts without fear of contradiction that the war began when an "oligarchy of 300,000 slaveholders dared to inscribe for the first time in the annals of the world, 'slavery' on the banner of Armed Revolt."[31]

Theodore Parker, the American transcendentalist and abolitionist reforming minister of the Unitarian Church, had made the same argument about the American Slave Power long before Marx, noting the entrenched power under the Constitution of the Southern states that led them to dominate the Senate, House, Presidency, and the Supreme Court—an argument Lincoln appealed to in his Second Inaugural Address pointing a finger at the Southern oligarchy.[32] While Marx, however, saw the role of religion in proslavery thought as yet another example of "enslavement to fictional deities of its own making," Parker argued within Christianity for a radical theological position in an 1841 sermon titled *A Discourse on the Transient and Permanent in Christianity* that the traditions of historic Christianities did not reflect the truth. Rather, he stressed the immediacy of God and saw the church as an expression of

30. Stewart, *Emancipation of the Mind*, 204–5.
31. Stewart, *Emancipation of the Mind*, 59.
32. See, on this point, Stewart, *Emancipation of the Mind*, 59–60.

communion, looking on a personal relationship to the historical Jesus as the supreme expression of God. Rejecting all miracles and revelation, he regarded the Bible as full of contradictions. Retaining his belief in God, he suggested people should experience God intuitively and personally, and that they should center their religious beliefs on individual experience.[33] Parker came to think of himself as an ethical prophet on the model of Jesus, questioning Christianities just as Jesus had questioned conventional views within Judaism, and became a central figure in political abolitionism, urging resistance to the stricter Fugitive Slave Act, protested (as had Lincoln) the Mexican war, worked for and with many fugitive slaves, and was a member of the Secret Six, supporting financially the abolitionist John Brown, arguing for the right of slaves to kill their masters and defending Brown's action.[34] He died in Europe in 1860. He had predicted the inevitable success of the abolitionist movement in words later to be quoted by Martin Luther King:

> I do not pretend to understand the moral universe; the arc is a long one, my eye reaches but little ways; I cannot calculate the curve and complete the figure by the experience of sight; I can divine it by conscience. And from what I see I am sure it bends towards justice.[35]

Parker came to identify Nature's God with the laws of nature "in the manner of [Thomas] Paine and his German admirers," but goes on to write, "The law of nature . . . represents the modes of action of God himself, his thought made visible."[36] Parker's engagement with Feuerbach

> illustrates the gravitational pull of German radicalism on this thought . . . We learn from Parker that Feuerbach is a "speculative atheist," and this is something very different from a "practical atheist." Feuerbach is a good man who means only to save religion from its abusers . . . "The 'atheism' of . . . Feuerbach," Parker argues, is "higher and better than the theological idea of God, as represented by Jonathan Edwards, the great champion of New England divinity." As a matter of fact, Feuerbach and people like him aren't really atheists at all: "When a philosopher

33. See, on this point, Wikipedia, "Theodore Parker," 3–4, and the sources cited in Stewart, *Emancipation of the Mind*, 323–24.

34. See, on these points Wikipedia, "Theodore Parker," 3–6.

35. Quoted at Wikipedia, "Theodore Parker," 7, including citations there to King's paraphrase of these words.

36. Stewart, *Emancipation of the Mind*, 210.

says there is no God, I do not believe he thinks so, only that he thinks that he thinks so."[37]

It was through a German émigré, Ottilie Assing, fleeing from the abortive German revolution of 1848, that Frederick Douglass came to read and take quite seriously indeed the works of Ludwig Feuerbach:

> Feuerbach's ideas struck Douglass "like a ray of light, and accomplished a complete revolution of his opinions," Ottiline Assing writes to Ludwig Feuerbach himself. This was a reverse conversion experience of world-historical significance, or so she maintains. "I add with great satisfaction that it was German radicalism that works that revolution, and that to our great, venerated Feuerbach above all others our thanks are due for having pointed out the path to intellectual liberty to that distinguished man, after he had freed himself from the fetters of slavery."
>
> At some point later in life, Douglass acquired a marble bust of Feuerbach. He also picked up a matching sculpture of David Friedrich Strauss [the German historian of Jesus]. In his home on Cedar Hill in Washington, D.C., he placed the two busts on the mantelpiece overlooking his writing desk, where they might gaze upon him as he composed many of his speeches and books. On the shelves over the desk, one can still find several German grammar books, a few guides for travelers to Germany, and a copy of Feuerbach's *Essence of Christianity*. Douglass's interest in the freethinkers of Germany was no summer fling.[38]

It is against this background that we can understand Sojourner Truth's question to Douglass in the midst of an abolitionist speech he gave after his first meeting with John Brown: "Frederick, Is God dead?"[39]

> "No," Frederick replies, "and because God is not dead slavery can only end in blood."
>
> What Douglass did not explain to his "good and old friend" was that "God," if yet alive, now stood for something that she and her fellow believers would not have recognized as divine. It referred instead to a certain idea of nature—the same idea of "God or nature" that presided over the intellectual world of the first American Revolution.[40]

37. Stewart, *Emancipation of the Mind*, 212–13.
38. Stewart, *Emancipation of the Mind*, 284.
39. Quoted at Stewart, *Emancipation of the Mind*, 197.
40. Stewart, *Emancipation of the Mind*, 197–98.

William Herndon had been Lincoln's junior law partner since 1843, and shared with Lincoln a

> common interest in reading. . . . Herndon writes to Parker with Lincoln in mind. "You know probably what I recommended and whose books." The bookshelf in Lincoln's office, curated by Herndon, ultimately included such spine-stiffening authors as John Stuart Mill, the Hegelian popularizer Victor Cousins, Ludwig Feuerbach, David Friedrich Strauss, and, of course, Theodore Parker.[41]

Lincoln's religious views appear to have been at least as heterodox as Parker's:

> Lincoln's close, lifelong friend Jesse Fell (1808–1887), elaborating on the subject in a long letter written after Lincoln's death, concludes, on central Christian doctrines such as the divinity of Jesus, the infallibility of written revelation, the innate depravity of men, the performance of miracles, future rewards and punishments, and "many other subjects," Lincoln "held views utterly at variance with what are usually taught in the Church . . . "[42]

On the other hand, Charles Strozier's illuminating psychoanalytic exploration of Lincoln's remarkably loving egalitarian relationship to Joshua Speed[43] reveals how and why Lincoln may have come to an understanding of and been moved by the antipatriarchal Jesus discussed in this book. Both Lincoln and Speed shared a common history of good-enough mothering (in Lincoln's case to both his mother and stepmother) and strained relationship to their fathers,[44] and common struggles in both their vocations (in Lincoln, politics; in Speed, business) and relationships to women. Their intimate love for one another, which Strozier regards as mirroring in both love and psychoanalysis,[45] enabled each of them to find their vocations and loves (both marry). For Lincoln, such love enabled him to come through the two clinical depressions and suicidal thoughts he suffered, one in connection with the death of the woman he first loved, and the second his jilting of the woman, Mary Todd, he eventually married

41. Stewart, *Emancipation of the Mind*, 20.

42. Stewart, *Emancipation of the Mind*, 35–36.

43. Strozier, *Your Friend Forever.*

44. On Lincoln's relationship to his natural mother and stepmother, see Strozier, *Your Friend Forever*, 63–65; and to his father, 66–69. On Speed's relationship to this mother, see 15; on his relationship to his father, see 14–19.

45. See, on this point, Strozier, *Your Friend Forever*, 114–15, 167.

as well as Speed's departure to his home in Kentucky and marrying. Strozier's discussion of the intimate letters Lincoln wrote to Speed,[46] as well as Speed's to him, reveal the kind of care Jesus brought to the despairing. And Lincoln himself, solaced by Speed's mother and her feeling for Jesus, apparently underwent a change in his view of religion.[47] Strozier suggests "evidence that Lincoln changed spiritually in 1841, perhaps under the tender ministrations of Lucy Speed [Joshua's Speed's mother]."[48] If so, Lincoln's sense of the antipatriarchal Jesus would explain psychologically why Theodore Parker's unorthodox view of Christianity appealed to him in the way it apparently did.

There is compelling evidence that Lincoln's thought, as he tried to reenter American politics as senator from Illinois and later as the Republican candidate for president, was centrally influenced by Parker. In 1858, Herndon brought to Lincoln's attention a lecture by Parker, "The Effect of Slavery on the American People," which,

> Lincoln read with interest and returned it. In another lecture that caught Lincoln's attention, Parker describes his vision of a future society without an aristocracy and a church without a priesthood. This one went over well, too. Then Lincoln seems to have had a look at an 1854 sermon on "The Dangers Which Face the Rights of Man in America." . . .
>
> America, Parker explains in his 1854 talk on the rights of man, is divided between two utterly contradictory ideas. On the one hand, there is "the idea of Freedom." It is the idea that humans are natural equals, that they recognize one another and realize themselves through collaboration in the world, and that legitimate government derives from the consent of the governed . . . On the other hand, there is a second idea: the "Idea of Slavery." . . .
>
> "It is plain America cannot long hold these two contradictions in the national consciousness," Parker concludes. Then he condenses the case in a memorable phrase: "Unless there is national unity of idea in fundamentals, a nation is a 'house divided against itself'; of course it cannot stand" (The quotation marks . . . [are to], specifically Matthew 12:25 and Mark 3:25).[49]

46. Strozier, *Your Friend Forever,* 171–74.

47. Strozier, *Your Friend Forever,* 143.

48. Strozier, *Your Friend Forever,* 143.

49. Stewart, *Emancipation of the Mind,* 265–67.

Lincoln insisted, despite Herndon's doubts, on using Parker's idea and language in his 1858 House Divided speech to the Republican State Convention to the delight of Parker, but to the despair of Herndon when he lost the election.[50]

Lincoln, as we earlier saw, had a look as well at Parker's 1854 sermon, speaking to the normative contradiction in American political culture. That speech had concluded that,

> the thing we must learn if our government "of all, by all, and for all" is not to perish from the earth, Parker argues, is that slavery must end. According to Herndon, with this collection of works, Lincoln liked especially the following expression, which he marked with pencil, and which he in substance afterwards used in his Gettysburg Address: "Democracy is direct self-government, over all the people, for all the people, by the people."[51]

There is, finally, the impact of Parker on Lincoln's Second Inaugural Address:

> in the sentence that impressed Frederick Douglass more than anything any other the president had said, . . . where Lincoln conjectures that "all the wealth piled by the bond-man's two hundred and fifty years of unrequited toil shall be sunk." . . .

William Herndon certainly thought he knew where Lincoln got this idea:

> I remember once, after having one of Theodore Parker's sermons on slavery, saying to Mr. Lincoln substantially this: "I have always noticed that ill-gotten wealth does no man any good. This is as true of nations as individuals. I believe that all the ill-gotten gain wrenched by us from the negro through his enslavement will eventually be taken from us, and we will be set back where we began."[52]

Lincoln's Second Inaugural Address, delivered March 4, 1865 (he was to be assassinated a month later on April 14, 1865), expressly addresses the competing Bible interpretations that led to the conflict, and there is no doubt where, following Theodore Parker, he stood ethically:

> Neither party expected for the war that magnitude or the duration which it has already attained. Neither anticipated that

50. See, on this point, Stewart, *Emancipation of the Mind*, 267–71.

51. Stewart, *Emancipation of the Mind*, 266.

52. Stewart, *Emancipation of the Mind*, 93.

the cause of the conflict might cease with, or even before, the conflict itself should cease. Each looked for an easier triumph, and a result less fundamental and astounding. Both read the same Bible, and pray to the same God; and each invokes his aid against the other. It may seem strange that any men should dare to ask a just God's assistance in wringing their bread from the sweat of other men's faces; but let us judge not, that we be not judged [Matt 7:1]. The prayers of both could not be answered—that of neither has been answered fully.

The Almighty has his own purposes: "Woe unto the world because of offenses! For it must needs be that offenses come; but woe to that man by whom the offense cometh." [Matt 18:7] If we shall suppose that American slavery is one of those offenses which, in the providence of God, must needs come, but which, having continued through his appointed time, he now wills to remove, and that he gives to both North and South this terrible war, as the woe due to those by the offense came, shall we discern therein any departure from those divine attributes which the believers in a living God always ascribe to him? Fondly do we hope—fervently do we pray—that this mighty scourge of war may speedily pass away. Yet, if God wills that it continue until all the wealth piled by the bondman's two hundred and fifty years of unrequited toil shall be sunk, and until every drop of blood drawn with the lash shall be paid by another drawn with the sword, as was said three thousand years ago, so still it must be said, "The judgments of the Lord are true and righteous altogether." [Psalms 19:9]

With malice toward none; with charity for all; with firmness in the right, as God gives us to see the right, let us strive on to finish the work we are in; to bind up the nation's wounds; to care for him who shall have borne the battle, and for his widow, and his orphan—to do all which may achieve and cherish a just and lasting peace among ourselves, and with all nations.[53]

CHRISTIAN NONVIOLENCE IN SOCIAL MOVEMENTS

My book, *Disarming Manhood: Roots of Ethical Resistance*,[54] published in 2005, discusses the movement of nonviolent resistance to injustice as a remarkably cosmopolitan movement, each form of the movement

53. Lincoln, "Second Inaugural Address."

54. Richards, *Disarming Manhood.*

self-consciously building on earlier movements: starting with William Lloyd Garrison's antebellum radical movement in the United States, then Leo Tolstoy on nonviolence against theocratic czarist Russia, Gandhi's satyagraha in India against British imperialism, and Martin Luther King Jr.'s civil rights movement in the United States. The movement in these four stages is remarkable for what they share: their common appeal to the historical Jesus on nonviolence, and the crucial role played in each case by relationships to mothers or female caretakers and their caretakers' form of highly personal forms of religion, often Christianity, well outside the traditional forms of patriarchal Christianities of their period in which women's moral agency played little or no role in the interpretation of Jesus and the tradition that appealed to him.

All of these figures knew of and were inspired by one another, but the relationship of King's nonviolent movement to Gandhi's satyagraha was particularly close. As we saw in an earlier chapter, if the forces of conscience (whether based on Christian agape or Renaissance humanism) can have this force through nonviolence effectively resisting and ending British colonialism in India, Reinhold Niebuhr argues—in a passage that inspired King[55]—the same might be true if nonviolence was used by the forces of humanist Christian or secular conscience in the United States exposing the contradictions of racist violence and subjugation of people of color withing both American Christianity and democratic constitutionalism.[56] Gandhi had been assassinated in 1948 long before King became active in the United States, but King went to India to study satyagraha, which informed how such a movement could and should be developed in the United States.

Nothing, as we have seen, was more central to the life and teaching of the historical antipatriarchal Jesus than nonviolence, but it was a teaching that, with the exception of Christians like the Quakers, Hutterites, and others,[57] was largely ignored by dominant Christianities (consider the wars of religion among Christians, violent pogroms against the Jews, and the Crusades, to mention only a few examples). It is thus a real historical questions why this teaching should have been the basis of the remarkable and often successful resistance movements of Gandhi and King, and others.[58]

55. See, on this point, Richards, *Disarming Manhood*, 146–49.

56. Niebuhr, *Moral Man*, 238–56.

57. See ch. 1 on guilt versus shame cultures.

58. See Chenoweth, *Why Civil Resistance Works.*

It is a historical question that requires us further to explore shame and guilt cultures, a topic I introduced in chapter 1 and have made reference to throughout the argument of this book. The shame culture of patriarchy has, I believe, been dominant in human cultures at least since the rise of high civilizations, and was contested by Socratic moral philosophy in ancient Athens and the antipatriarchal Jesus studied in the book, both of whom developed inward forms of independent moral conscience based on culpable injustices and harms to others, the mark of guilt cultures. The hegemonic power of still dominant patriarchal cultures in both cases (including the Athenian democracy) explains why, in both cases, their criticisms of patriarchal conventions of group insularity were experienced as insults to patriarchal authority, eliciting the violence of their respective states, condemning them to death.

The life and teaching of the antipatriarchal historical Jesus—in particular, nonviolence—could, I believe, only have any broader resonance in cultures in which the transition from shame to guilt cultures has advanced to the point in which still existing patriarchal shame cultures can now be contested not just by individuals, but by groups that, appealing to democratic values of free speech and accountable representative democracies now more widely accepted, can use free speech to protest their exclusion from democratic values now enjoyed at large, but not yet fully by them. This was the case in varying degrees in Garrison's antebellum America and in Gandhi's Britain and in King's America. In each such case, of course, the measure of increasing democratic values was still limited and patriarchal values of Southern and Northern racism both in antebellum America and King's America and British racism against its colonial subjects were still sufficiently powerful that violence can and was unleashed against any resistance (for example, the lynchings in the American South, a form of violent terror that continued to exist until the civil rights movement in the 1950s).

But, it was not the appeal to the contradictions in the ostensible democratic values of Britain or America that would have been enough to explain the emergence, development, and ultimate success of nonviolent resistance in both cases. It was, at this point, crucially important that the life and teaching of the historical antipatriarchal Jesus on nonviolence was appealed to by social movements that themselves brilliantly used nonviolence, often greeted, as it was, by the irrational violence of racism under threat, that exposed to the democratic conscience of their communities that racism had no rational basis, only irrational violence.

Nonviolence against violence was the key to the moral dramaturgy that exposed the public mind to ugly truths it had long ignored.

But, we can only understand how this could have occurred and gotten as far as it did if we take seriously the underlying psychology of the remarkable men and women who led these movements and the crucial role that the antipatriarchal religion of mothers or women caretakers, including Jesus on nonviolence, played in the life and thought of these leaders. King decided, contrary to his father's advice, that he had to disobey a state court order not to demonstrate, leading to his imprisonment in Birmingham City Jail. His father comments: "Well, you didn't get this nonviolence from me. You must have got it from your Mama."[59] King has gotten these convictions from his mother and grandmother, black women who had developed their own personal relationships to the Jesus who called for nonviolence, not from the patriarchal leaders like King's father (himself a minister). Black women of the South had developed their own mini-reformation resisting Christian patriarchy, and imparted it to their sons as the authentic historical Jesus. Of course, their resistance extended only so far (not, for example, to questioning gender roles in marriage—both Gandhi and King were, as husbands, quite patriarchal[60]), but it is historically remarkable that their resistance extended as far as it did and had the impact on a successful nonviolent social movement that it had.

It is even more remarkable historically that there could have been an appreciative audience in the North and even in the South that broke the political stasis, long maintained by Southern politicians in Congress, against any significant federal civil rights legislation. Patriarchy may still have been culturally powerful in both the North and South, but there were other subterranean forces at work—not yet seen nor acknowledged by the dominant psychology of the time, including, as we shall see in the next chapter, Freud's. There is what Winnicott called a human nature whose development required good-enough mothering, and American women were themselves at this time forming or about to form their own feminist social movement, on the model of the civil rights movement, based on their own convictions of their democratic moral equality resisting patriarchal gender roles. The sons and daughters of such women and even their husbands, like my own father, who shared their views,

59. See, on this point, Richards, *Disarming Manhood*, 137.

60. See, on this point, Richards, *Disarming Manhood*, 120–30, 172–80.

developed a capacity for guilt politically responsive to the claims of the civil rights movement. As a consequence, the Congress of the United States, with the pivotal support of then President Lyndon B. Johnson (a man of the South), approved the most important civil rights legislation in American history, the Civil Rights Act of 1964 and the Voting Rights Act of 1965.

THE PSYCHOLOGY OF PEACEMAKING: THE END OF THE TROUBLES IN NORTHERN IRELAND

Today is a time of despair over seemingly intractable levels of violence between peoples with long histories of unjust humiliation on religious and ethnic grounds inflicted on one another and often by one another, turning to violence as a response to such humiliation, exemplified by the current Hamas-Israel war, but many other all too contemporary endless wars. In his *The End of the Troubles in Northern Ireland: On the Psychology of Peacemaking,*[61] Charles B. Strozier, a leading psychologist of such violence, offers a message of hope showing how a psychoanalytically informed conception of peacemaking is possible between the most intractable enmities, religious and ethnic enmities rooted in histories of unjust humiliation and seemingly endless retributive violence between the Protestants and Catholics of Northern Ireland.

Strozier takes us not only into the background history of the conflict, including British colonial history (Ireland as Britain's first colony), but into the histories of each of the leading figures on both sides of the conflict, including John Hume, David Trimble, Ian Paisley, Gerry Adams, Martin McGuiness, and, above all, the remarkable John Alderdice, a psychoanalyst, Presbyterian, and political leader who was to play a pivotal role in the institutions that were to bring the warring parties together into a democratic peace. There is also the crucial role played by Irish-American leaders, like Tip O'Neil and Teddy Kennedy and President Clinton (reflecting the shift of Irish-Americans from their sometime support of the IRA), whose appointment of George Mitchell was pivotal in successfully negotiating the Good Friday Accords. And there is as well the role played by leaders in Ireland and Britain, and even the invitation of the conflicting parties to South Africa by President Nelson Mandela to an "indaba," a Zulu word for the meeting of minds, using the South African

61. Strozier, *End of the Troubles.*

experience of reconciliation as a model for the Irish leaders on both sides. Groups of women and the European Union also played a role.

What makes the violent conflict in Northern Ireland of such interest, from the perspective of the argument of this book, is that both the fundamentalist Protestantism of the fanatic Ian Paisley and the form of Catholicism appealed to by Jerry Adams leading the IRA, both grounded ostensibly in Christianities, were political religions, in the terms of chapter 5, criticized by Protestants like John Alderdice and Catholic Church leaders for turning to violence, betraying the nonviolence of Jesus of Nazareth, but in service of an essentially nationalist reading of Christianity as serving either the nationalism of the Protestants wedded to Great Britain or the nationalism of the IRA wedded to the Irish state. The political use or abuse of Christianity is most salient, as Strozier makes clear, in the 1981 hunger strike of Bobby Sands and others against

> the refusal of British authorities to treat the IRA inmates as political prisoners, rather than common criminals, which meant wearing their civilian clothes and being granted other privileges. They were not protesting their sentences or other aspects of the criminal justice system, nor their objection to the British control of Northern Ireland. They just wanted to be treated with respect as imprisoned soldiers.[62]

Sands and the others conceived themselves as nonviolent martyrs on the model of the unjust crucifixion of Jesus of Nazareth, though both Protestants like John Alderdice and leaders of the Catholic Church rejected the analogy, and indeed some regarded their acts as suicide, and, as such, forbidden.[63] Support for Sands before his death was shown by his election to parliament, and, after his and the death of the others, the deaths of these young men and the intransigence of the British led to the end of the hunger strike, but played a pivotal role in moving Catholic opinion in the North to support for Jerry Adams and the IRA and led to Protestant opinion to support John Alderdice's nonviolent leadership of the small Alliance Party as an alternative to Ian Paisley and the parties that supported his views.[64]

Strozier has woven a complex tapestry, a rich and unforgettable psychologically astute history of how people for whom violence has become

62. Strozier, *End of the Troubles*, 249. See also 59, 92, 95–98.

63. For fuller discussion, see O'Malley, *Biting at the Grave.*

64. Strozier, *End of the Troubles*, 45–50.

their only mode of communication can be brought finally to participate in common democratic institutions, finding a democratic voice and road to a democratic peace, and how such institutions are, in fact, in the interest of everyone. What is of interest, from the psychoanalytic perspective on Christianities taken in this book, is the role played in the peacemaking by a psychoanalyst and Christian, John Alderdice, showing not only how compatible psychoanalysis is with Christianity, but how, as Winnicott believed, it could play a role in understanding the role of political religions among warring Christianities, including the long history of British and Protestant violence against Catholics, and, when nonviolence by Catholics did not work as a strategy, the turn to terrorism of the IRA. What would have surprised Winnicott was that precisely the transference love analysts had for analysands could be brought to bear by someone like Alderdice in developing relationships not only to his fellow Christians in Northern Ireland, but to the Irish-American leaders in the United States, to a new generation of British leaders, to the European Union, and even to South African leaders like Nelson Mandela. It is central to such peacemaking that constitutional democracies in the United States, Britain, the European Union, and South Africa—all of whom had themselves experienced the violence of war and civil war and developed constitutional democracies as an alternative—could have and did play the role they did in bringing the warring parties into a sense of the peace of democratic institutions, based on voice and listening. In defense of the role he played, as a Christian and psychoanalyst in these events, Alderdice appealed to other religious leaders to take seriously the prophetic tradition in Judaeo-Christianity which often opposed politics and any role as a political religion:

> I said that I believed that the role of the church was to be prophetic. They agreed but I went on to challenge them and to say that the prophets did not act as apologists for the people of Israel; they challenged them with the charge that they were not living as God wanted them to be. I said that they seemed to me to be chaplains for their people, not prophets, but I warned them that the prophets were often stoned and killed by their own people.[65]

There is an illuminating analogy in the role the psychoanalyst John Alderdice played in Northern Ireland peacemaking and the role James

65. Quoted by Strozier, *End of the Troubles*, 53.

Gilligan played as a psychotherapist to the violent men he studied in American prisons. In both cases, Alderdice and Gilligan discovered that for violent men (including the role such men played in violent political religions) the humiliation of patriarchal manhood elicited their violence, and violence was indeed their only voice. It is for this reason that the listening of transference love even for such seemingly intractable violence in men can elicit in favorable circumstances a responsive democratic voice, the key to democratic institutions.

AN ECUMENICAL TWENTY-FIRST-CENTURY CHRISTIANITY EMBRACING SCIENCE, PHILOSOPHY, AND OTHER RELIGIONS

The contemporary search for the historical Jesus, which we have now discussed at some length, has had different consequences in the life and thought of its advocates. But, I am particularly struck with where this search has led Marcus J. Borg, a member of the Jesus Seminar, coming to the view that through this search he has come, as he put it in the title of one of his books, to *The God We Never Knew*,[66] and in another, to *Meeting Jesus Again for the First Time*.[67] Borg has come to see that it is the uncritical acceptance of patriarchy that has deformed historical Christianities, reading the gospel through a patriarchal lens and thus abandoning what is most distinctive in the remarkable moral personality of the historical Jesus as an ethical prophet, namely, the antipatriarchal basis of both his life and thought.[68] He notes, for example, Jesus's questioning of the purity codes,[69] his rejection of the patriarchal family,[70] and his questioning of the honor codes central to patriarchy,[71] which leads Borg to reject both the sexism[72] and homophobia[73] of traditional Christianities. He rejects

66. Borg, *God We Never Knew*.

67. Borg, *God We Never Knew*.

68. See, on this point, Borg, *God We Never Knew*, 69–71.

69. Borg, *Meeting Jesus Again*, 50–53.

70. Borg, *Meeting Jesus Again*, 81–82.

71. Borg, *Meeting Jesus Again*, 82.

72. Borg, *Meeting Jesus Again*, 57.

73. Borg, *Meeting Jesus Again*, 59.

as well the need for an after life,[74] and a last judgment.[75] What is central to his Christianity is a personal relationship to Jesus, as our beloved, and "our healing, here on earth."[76] Politically, such ethically based Christianity opposes systems of unjust domination, as Walter Wink has argued.[77]

Should this contemporary understanding of Christianity be limited to Christianity? In his important philosophical study of comparative religion, the philosopher John Hick argues reasonably it cannot.[78] Hick offers powerful criticisms of Augustine's views of both original sin and predestination,[79] offering Irenean theodicy as a reasonable alternative,[80] and questions as well the resurrection narratives.[81] Kant was, he argues, correct that morality is part of our human nature, and independent of religion.[82] And he argues that Christianities, like other religions, have mythological elements which have unjustifiably led them on inadequate grounds to denigrate all other religions;

> the dogma of the deity of Christ—in conjunction with the aggressive and predatory aspects of human nature—has contributed to the evils of colonialism, the destruction of indigenous peoples, anti-Semitism, destructive wars of religion and the burnings of heretics and witches. But on the other hand it is also possible to understand the idea of divine incarnation mythologically, as indicating an extraordinary openness to the divine presence in virtue of which Jesus' life and teachings have mediated the reality and love of God to millions of people in successive centuries. Thus, whereas understood literally the doctrine of a unique divine incarnation in Christ has divided humanity and has shrunk the image of God to that of the tribal deity of the West, understood mythologically it can continue to draw people to God through Christ without thereby sundering them from the rest of the human family.[83]

74. Borg, *God We Never Knew*, 163.
75. Borg, *Meeting Jesus Again*, 85, 103.
76. Borg, *God We Never Knew*, 167.
77. Borg, *God We Never Knew*, 69. See also Wink, *Engaging the Powers*.
78. Hick, *Interpretation of Religion*.
79. Hick, *Interpretation of Religion*, 207–8.
80. Hick, *Interpretation of Religion*, 118–22, 359–60.
81. Hick, *Interpretation of Religion*, 101–2.
82. See, on these points, Hick, *Interpretation of Religion*, 39, 96–99, 150, 200, 240–46.
83. Hick, *Interpretation of Religion*, 372.

What absorbs us in Jesus are not these mythologies, including unhistorical birth narratives or the Trinity: rather, "Jesus' moral teaching shines in its own light as true and as claiming our response."[84]

What distinguishes the historical Jesus from Muhammed was, Hick argues, that

> Jesus was born into the artisan class of a subject people ruled by the Romans. He was thus entirely without political power or influence and was accordingly free of any need to think of ordering or reforming the society of which he was a part.[85]

Muhammed, in contrast to Jesus, "was born into the dominant tribe of Arabia . . . , and was thus close to the center of power."[86] His message, however, challenged the existing power structure in Mecca, and he had to flee for his life.

> Islam would have been suppressed or wiped out if it had not resorted to the same methods as the neighboring tribes . . . Islam was thus brought . . . to the stage of morally compromised participation in the harsh dynamics of history to which Christianity arrived only with its integration into the Roman Empire. . . . Thus the integration with society that took nearly three centuries in the case of Christianity, and in which the founder himself accordingly had no part, occurred in the case of Islam within the lifetime of its founder, and was perforce one of his major preoccupations.[87]

It was the very distance of the historical Jesus from these preoccupations that made the search for his historicity so revelatory in the development, as we have seen, of both ethics and democracy by figures (among them, Locke, Bayle, Kant) often appealing to Jesus in criticism of the Christianities that, in their view, misunderstood and disfigured his ethical teaching.

Hick focuses on this teaching as the core of what is of lasting value in Christianity, but argues:

> Since morality is thus generated by the inter-personal nature of personality, its basic principle is mutuality, or acceptance of the other as another person, someone else of the same nature as oneself. The fundamental moral claim is accordingly to treat

84. Hick, *Interpretation of Religion*, xxxv.
85. Hick, *Interpretation of Religion*, 32.
86. Hick, *Interpretation of Religion*, 332.
87. Hick, *Interpretation of Religion*, 334.

> others as having the same value as myself. This is in effect a transcription of the Golden Rule found in the Hindu, Buddhist, Confucian, Taoist, Zoroastrian, Jain and Christian scriptures and in the Jewish *Talmud* and the Muslim *Hadith* and is likewise a translation of Kant's concepts of a rational person as an end and of right action as action which our rationality, acknowledging a universal impartiality transcending individual desires and aversions, can see to be required.[88]

And, while "Christianity is the first religious tradition to have been influenced by the scientific enterprise and to be largely transformed by its new outlook and knowledge,"[89] Hick surmises "that the Hindu and Buddhist traditions will be able to assimilate the scientific outlook as relatively easily as post-Confucian China, whereas Islam may perhaps find the process as traumatic as Christianity has done."[90]

Hick argues, on the basis of quite detailed investigations of a range of non-Christian religious traditions, that they share not only ethical essentials but a common spirituality in which the model for God's love is mother love.[91] As one of the Buddhist scriptures puts it:

> As a mother cares for her son,
> Her only son, all her days,
> So towards all living things living
> A man's mind should be all embracing.[92]

Hick concludes that, in view of all that other religious traditions share with Christianity (as Christians have now come to understand a Christianity based on the historical Jesus), contemporary twentieth- and twenty-first-century Christianity is and should be pluralistic in embracing how much they share with other religious traditions, and how much they have to learn from one another about their searches for meaning in human life and perhaps even in the universe.[93]

What they may have to learn is that the orthodox Christian insistence on an afterlife may be questionable, as Nietzsche argued, for its

88. Hick, *Interpretation of Religion*, 149.
89. Hick, *Interpretation of Religion*, 329.
90. Hick, *Interpretation of Religion*, 329.
91. See, on this point, Hick, *Interpretation of Religion*, 316–31.
92. Quoted at Hick, *Interpretation of Religion*, 320.
93. See, on this point, Hick, *Interpretation of Religion*, 342–80.

sanguinary cruelties, including damnation of unbelievers. John Stuart Mill took a similar view, but went on, pointing to the Buddhist view that:

> they [Buddhists] could find nothing more transcendent to hold out as the capital prize to be won by the mightiest efforts of labour and self-denial, that what we are so often told is the terrible idea of annihilation. Surely this is a proof that the idea is not really or naturally terrible; that not philosophers only, but the common order of mankind, can easily reconcile themselves to it, and even consider it as a good; and that it is no unnatural part of the idea of a happy life, that life itself be laid down, after the best that it can give has been fully enjoyed through a long lapse of time; when all its pleasures, even those of benevolence, are familiar, and nothing untasted and unknown is left to stimulate curiosity and keep up the desire of prolonged existence.[94]

It is this kind of consulting and learning from other religions that Karl Jaspers argued as a contemporary possibility on the basis that something like it had earlier occurred in the axial religions of 500 BCE.[95] Certainly, Robert Bellah's important study of these religions shows a remarkable convergence on "some idea of 'transcendence'"[96] in them, making possible an analogous independent ethical assessment of conventional values and rulers in these cultures.[97] If Hick is right, we are closer to Jasper's hope than Jaspers, despairing after Germany's turn to fascist nationalism, believed likely or probable. Albert Schweitzer argued lines similar to Hick, in his study of Indian thought, that the most important exponents of modern Indian thought, including Gandhi, crucially integrated into their arguments syncretically non-Indian thought, including Christianity.[98]

Hick does not himself regard as successful attempts by philosophers like Richard Swinburne to infer the existence of a just God and the problem of evil on the basis of probability arguments.[99] What philosophers try to explain in these and other ways can also be explained in naturalistic terms. But today even philosophers committed to naturalism have come to the view that purpose must be introduced in some way to explain what

94. Mill, *Three Essays on Religion*, 121–22.
95. Jaspers, *Origin and Goal of History*.
96. Bellah, *Religion in Human Evolution*, 475.
97. See, for fuller discussion, Bellah, *Religion in Human Evolution*, 264–566.
98. Schweitzer, *Indian Thoughts*, 209–49.
99. See, Hick, *Interpretation of Religion*, 104–6.

we now know about the universe and our place in it, as creatures who can understand and reflect on it.[100]

In his *Towards a World Theology*,[101] Wilfred Cantwell Smith makes a different but complementary argument to that made by John Hick. Smith argues as a historian of comparative religion, and thus does not try to excavate, as Hick does, common Kantian normative themes in the religions he studies. Smith's approach is interpretive, suggesting, in the mode of a concluding question, whether all the religions (Christianity, Islam, Hinduism, Buddhism, Sikhs, Jews) he discusses and even secular perspectives share "a truth-reality that explicitly transcends conception but in so far as conceivable is that to which man's religious history has at its best been a response, human and in some sense inadequate?"[102] What Smith means by transcendence is what he takes to be the historically universal search, a search he calls one of faith, responding to our human need to be:

> saved from nihilism, from alienation, anomie, despair; from the bleak despondency of meaninglessness. Saved from unfreedom; from being the victim of one's own whims within, or of pressures without; saved from being merely an organism reacting to its environment.[103]

Smith's interpretive argument is historically predictive: when we examine with care not the origins of religion (which he dismisses as "the 'big-bang' theory"[104]), but their development over time, including the role they play in the lives of humans today, we find indications, because of levels of communication made possible by the contemporary world, of a possible or even probable convergence on a common life of belief and action that is broadly shared, indeed universal, arising from a "corporate critical self-consciousness."[105]

There is no doubt Smith assumes such a convergence will be on common humane beliefs and ways of life, but, in contrast to John Hick, he refuses to engage in the normative criticism of at least some of the belief systems he discusses (notably, the caste system in Hinduism, and the

100. See, for example, Goff, *Why?* Goff does not, however, believe his arguments support theism.

101. See Smith, *Towards a World Theology*.

102. Smith, *Towards a World Theology*, 185.

103. Smith, *Towards a World Theology*, 168.

104. Smith, *Towards a World Theology*, 154.

105. Smith, *Towards a World Theology*, 59.

patriarchal priesthoods of some Christianities). Nonetheless, he clearly is critical and for very good reason, of the historical treatment "of blacks in the United States by white scholars; of the role of women by male scholars; of homosexuality by heterosexual investigators,"[106] and acknowledges as well the impact on Christian Bible interpretation of the "Protestant and Jewish encounter,"[107] by which I take it he means the perspectives of Jewish scholars on the role of anti-Semitism in the framing of the Gospels (a topic discussed at length earlier in this book). As an alternative route to the universalism of Hick's version of Christianity, Smith commands respect and even the hope he might historically be right.

There is another notable feature of Smith's argument that, if anything, clarifies his own version of Christianity, which very much complements the argument of this book. Smith claims to dismiss "the 'big-theory theory,'" which he concedes was very much the inspiration of the search for the historical Jesus characteristic of Luther and the Protestant Reformation, the tradition of Smith's own Presbyterian convictions. But, while on the one hand denying anything like "the 'big-theory theory,'" his own version of Christianity rests on his own highly personal relationship to Jesus of Nazareth, suggesting exactly a search for the historical Jesus like that of Winnicott and the other historians of the historical Jesus we have now studied at some length. Indeed, he puts the point in exactly the way Winnicott put it in repudiating original sin and predestination, arising not from the life and teaching of Jesus, but Paul and others:

> If St. Paul or anybody else thought or thinks that only Christians can be saved, St. Paul was wrong. It is Christ, and the God who has given me faith through Christ, that save me from believing so blasphemous a doctrine.[108]

Indeed, as I argue in the last chapter, Winnicott's psychological understanding of religion illuminates what may be true in Smith's historically based argument for a universalist understanding of religion.

There is one more notable proposal about how contemporary Christianity, in light of our better understanding of the historical Jesus, can today reasonably be regarded as sharing convictions of other belief systems (including other religions), a proposal very much illuminated by the psychoanalytic approach to Jesus and Christianities taken in this

106. Smith, *Towards a World Theology*, 69.

107. Smith, *Towards a World Theology*, 192.

108. Smith, *Towards a World Theology*, 171.

book. The proposal I have in mind is one dealing with the relationship of Christianity to Judaism, from which Christianity emerged. It arises from the pathbreaking historical study of Rosemary Ruether, herself an important feminist Christian, exploring the central role played among many Christianities, both in the formation of the Gospels and major Christian theologians (including, among others, Augustine), by an irrationalist anti-Semitism certainly not justified by the life and teaching of the antipatriarchal Jesus (himself a Jew and conceiving himself as a prophet in the Jewish tradition), but fabricated to rationalize Paul's proselytizing mission to the gentiles and corresponding denial that the Jews were any longer God's chosen people (as Jesus certainly assumed).[109] Ruether's scholarship is compelling, exposing to critical ethical examination, at some length, the quite *central* role anti-Semitism played in the construction of many Christianities and the role this construction played, in association with Hitler's pseudo-science of race,[110] in the genocidal evils it rationalized, not least the murder of six million innocent Jews in the Holocaust. What is of interest, from the psychoanalytic perspective taken in this book, is how, at the conclusion of her argument, Ruether characterizes both the psychological roots of such anti-Semitism and what is required for Christians ethically to rethink their understanding of Christianity and its relation to Judaism.

On the first issue, Ruether regards the political psychology of Christian anti-Semitism as an irrationalism, "the psychopathology representing Christian anti-Judaism,"[111] a psychopathology essentially resting on the denial and repudiation of the life and teaching of the historical Jesus. As she puts the point:

> I believe that the paradigmatic and proleptic view of the messianic work of Jesus is the only theologically and historically valid way of interpreting it consistent with biblical faith and historical realism. It is the only way we can reconnect Christianity with the context of this event in its original Jewish setting and so rediscover the historical Jesus, who must ever elude an anti-Judaic Christianity. It represents the way we should have read the New Testament . . . It is the way we needed to appropriate this apocalyptic expectation once its imminence had faded from

109. Ruether, *Faith and Fratricide.*

110. See, for a brilliant study of the role pseudo-science played in Hitler's genocidal anti-Semitism, Lifton, *Nazi Doctors.*

111. Ruether, *Faith and Fratricide*, 245.

> sight, rather than transposing it into that messianic absolutism which generated Christian totalitarianism and imperialism.[112]

To say Christian anti-Semitism is a psychopathology is to say that, psychoanalytically, it arises from the repression by Christianities of an irrational hatred so terrible that it could not be acknowledged but held in the unconscious in the same way Augustine repressed his hatred for his mother and Luther his hatred for his father—rage arising from traumatic loss covered by idealization and expressing itself as the irrational violence of Christianities against Jews for refusing to convert and thus questioning and threatening the falsifying idealizations on which Christianities had come to rest. Because the irrationalism is a psychopathology, "[t]he Christian anti-Judaic myth can never be held in check, much less overcome, until Christianity submits itself to the therapy of Jewish consciousness that allows 'the return of the repressed,'"[113] namely, confronting that a religion consciously idealized as one of love rests on unconscious irrational hatred and a history of irrational violence, arising from the "very suppression of Jewish history and experience from Christian consciousness," which "is tacitly genocidal."[114] Only in this way can Christianities recover their connection to the historical Jesus, so clearly a Jew and rooted in the Jewish prophetic tradition, *a Christianity worthy of Jesus.*

On the second issue, Ruether proposes nothing less than a new covenantal Christian theology that no longer regards the Christian covenant as superseding the Jewish covenant. Because Ruether's argument is at this point psychoanalytic, Christians of conscience like Ruether can only acknowledge and then confront the psychopathology on which Christianities have rested if they enter into what would essentially be a relationship of transference love to Jews as an analyst seeing themselves as Christians through the eyes of Jews—in effect, a dialogue with and mutual respect for the life and experience of Jews, secular and religious, "establishing a new education for a new consciousness, the sort of new consciousness that would make us grapple with the need for a new way of formulating Christian identity that allows space for the Jewish brother to live—live not on our terms, but on his."[115] In this way, the very image of a loving God, central to the Love Commandments that both Judaism and

112. Ruether, *Faith and Fratricide*, 250.

113. Ruether, *Faith and Fratricide*, 259.

114. Ruether, *Faith and Fratricide*, 258.

115. Ruether, *Faith and Fratricide*, 259.

Christianity share, will no longer exclude but embrace the Jews. Ruether concludes:

> What this will mean for Christian identity, we do not yet know. It means at least a certain relativization of Christian absolutism which can accept the independent salvific validity of the Jewish tradition, the authenticity of this alternative way of appropriating the biblical heritage.[116]

116. Ruether, *Faith and Fratricide*, 260.

8

Psychoanalysis on Religion and Ethics

Freud and Winnicott

IT WAS A LETTER of Winnicott to his sister that inspired the inquiry of this book. It is worth now repeating the relevant part of the letter in full:

> I shall probably be accused if I say that Christ was a leading psychotherapist, (I don't know why, but Violet is fond of saying that what I say is blasphemy, when there is no connection whatever between what I have said and the term.) It is not less true that extreme acts and religious rituals and obsessions are an exact counterpart of these mind disorders, and by psychotherapy, many fanatics or extremists in religion can be brought (if treated early) to a real understanding of religion and its use in setting a high ethical standard.[1]

What struck me is Winnicott's view that psychotherapy enabled "a real understanding of religion and its use in setting a high ethical standard."

But there is another letter of Winnicott to his fellow analyst Bion showing that whatever he meant by Jesus as "a leading psychotherapist" was not the interpretation of Jesus of the dominant Christianities of Augustine and Luther. Again, the relevant letter was as follows:

> I, like you, was brought up in the Christian tradition (Wesleyan) and I have no desire to throw away all that I listened to over and over again and tried to digest and sort out.

1. Winnicott, "Letter to His Sister."

> It is not possible for me to throw away religion just because the people who organize the religions of the world insist on belief in miracles. What I wanted to know is, have you met with the amazing book by Robert Graves and his friend Joshua Podro, called the Nazarene Gospel Restored? It is not possible to buy this book but it is in most of the libraries. Naturally it is frowned upon by all the Christian churches because it deals with the reconstruction of the Jesus which was current but not much recorded before an attempt was made to get accepted records somewhere in the first and second centuries. In other words, by a tremendous amount of erudition and research these authors have been able to make a reconstruction of the original story, and I find a study of this book absolutely fascinating and very important for the understanding of the Bible story that we came to know so well. I wish I could buy a copy of this book, and send it to you but unfortunately it is out of print.[2]

What was it in *The Nazarene Gospel Restored* that so excited Winnicott and he wanted to share with another analyst, Bion, something that meant there might be something of enduring value even to them as analysts, so that they need not "throw away religion just because the people who organize the religions of the world insist on belief in miracles"? What captivated Winnicott was that the historical Jesus, according to *The Nazarene Gospel Restored*, Jesus was not only independent of Paul, but that Paul had indeed been "[c]harged with heresy"[3] by Jesus's brother, James the Just, having transferred "the title deeds of the Heavenly Kingdom from the Children of the House [the Jews] to unclean and lawless hands [the Romans]."[4] We know what Winnicott objected to:

> Religions have made much of original sin, but have not all come round to the idea of original goodness. That which by being gathered together in the idea of God is at the same time separated off from the individuals who collectively create and re-create this God concept. The saying that man made God in his own image is usually treated as an amusing example of the perverse, but the truth in this saying could be made more evident by a restatement, such as: man continues to create and re-create God as a place to put that which is good in himself, and which he

2. Winnicott, "Letter to Bion."
3. Graves and Podro, *Nazarene Gospel*, 821.
4. Graves and Podro, *Nazarene Gospel*, 827.

> might spoil if he kept it to himself along with all the hate and destructiveness which is also to be found there.[5]

Both original sin[6] and predestination[7] were central features of Paul's interpretation of Christian doctrine in *Romans,* elaborated, as we saw earlier, by Augustine and Luther, and both were associated either with Augustine's view that human sexuality as such separated us from God's love and could only be redeemed by celibacy, or Luther's view that human nature as such was depraved and could only redeemed by the experience of Jesus's agape love. It was this psychological conception of an intrinsically corrupt human will that not only rationalized the repression of sexuality, but contempt as well for human competences to be sovereign in their own lives and sovereigns as democratic equals. It is thus the doctrine of original sin that rationalized Augustine's support for the Roman imperial autocracy, who enforced brutally the repression of any Christianity with whom Augustine doctrinally disagreed, as well as Luther's endorsement of state violence against peasants and Jews. Augustine works very much within the framework of imperial Roman patriarchy, which he used to entrench his views. It is psychologically astonishing that this man offered probably the earliest extant description of the essential difference between a shame culture and a guilt culture in contrasting the "earthly city" (Roman shame culture) with the "heavenly city" (Roman shame culture):

> Glory, the object of the Romans' burning ambition, is the judgment of men when they think well of others. That is why virtue is superior to glory, since it is not content with the testimony of men, without the witness of a man's own conscience. Hence the Apostle says, "This is our glory: the testimony of our own conscience."[8]

But it is the very contradictions in Augustine's psyche (his unconscious hatred of his beloved mother) that could explain how so much unconscious hatred could be projected onto others, and through a theory that consciously prominently appealed to love!

It was psychoanalysis, as understood and practiced by Winnicott and others, that would enable us to free Christianities from such

5. Winnicott, "Morals and Education," 378.

6. See Rom 5:12–15.

7. See Rom 8:28–31.

8. Augustine, *City of God*, V.12 (Bettenson, 199).

psychological contradictions, and thus to achieve "a real understanding of religion and its use in setting a high ethical standard." To understand what Winnicott meant by such "a real understanding," we must consider Freud's very different psychology of religion, and how and why Winnicott's view is so different.

FREUD ON ETHICS AND RELIGION

It was Freud, so otherwise hostile to conventional religion in *Future of an Illusion*,[9] who urged thinking more psychologically about religion as "a therapeutic attempt"[10] to give a foundation to ethics. Freud saw that "equal love was expressly enunciated by Christ: 'Inasmuch as ye have done it have done unto one of the least of my brethren, ye have done it under me,'" and saw as well his "democratic strain."[11] But he questioned Jesus's ethics of love as a prescription because it failed to take seriously the biological drive to aggression he called Thanatos (harming both others and the self),[12] shown, so he argued, by the way in which what he called "the narcissism of small differences" had unleashed, despite the Christian claim of "universal love between men," "the extreme intolerance on the part of Christendom towards those who remained outside it,"[13] namely, Christian anti-Semitism. The consequence was Freud's pessimistic, indeed despairing, views on the problem of violence. Thus, in his response to Einstein's query of "Why war?", he pointed to "the innate and ineradicable inequality of men" and their "need of an authority which will offer an unqualified submission,"[14] in effect, endorsing a quasi-Hobbesian absolutism. However, his view of aggression did not have a psychological basis, as Ian Suttie, Jim Gilligan, and others have shown,[15] indeed was a pseudo-science (Thanatos), not based on psychological observation. In effect, because aggression could not be explained within his framework, he made aggression an instinct, like biologically rooted appetites of hunger and thirst, and failed to engage the cultural roots of

9. See Freud, *Future of an Illusion*.

10. See Freud, *Civilization and Its Discontents*, 142.

11. Freud, *Group Psychology*, 94.

12. See Freud, *Civilization and Its Discontents*, 109–10.

13. Freud, *Civilization and Its Discontents*, 114.

14. Freud, *Why War?*, 212.

15. See Suttie, *Origins of Love and Hate*; Sagan, *Freud, Women*; Carveth, *Still Small Voice.*

Christian anti-Semitism in its denigration of sexuality as such, "carnal Israel," as Augustine put it in his rationalization of Christian anti-Semitism (see chapter 4). The validity of Freud's psychologically acute observation of how the irrationality of anti-Semitism can be seen in how Christian narcissism ignores how little they differ from those they persecute is thus lost in a conception of aggression that Freud normalizes, as if that makes the irrationality more rooted in human nature rather than an unjustly stigmatizing cultural tradition.

Philip Rieff in his book *Freud: The Mind of the Moralist*,[16] reads Freud's views quite accurately. Freud was, on Rieff's reading, no sexual liberationist. Sexual repression had, in his view, been carried too far: thus his sympathy for homosexuals,[17] and even for how the constraints placed on women's sexuality stunted their talents.[18] What was needed "is to free men from their sick communities."

> Yet he also treated the neurotic as a social dilemma, as one unable to relate himself effectively to the established community. The prevailing image of psychoanalysis as reintegrating the neurotic, making him again a constructive member of society, must be studied closely, for this does not signify that the patient gives his assent to the demands society makes upon his instinctual life . . . [19]

But Freud's limited belief "in freedom makes itself felt most strongly in Freud's denial that psychoanalysis does criticize society or that it has any 'concern with judgments of value.'"[20] We are left, Rieff argues, only with psychological man,[21] or, as he later put it, "the triumph of the therapeutic,"[22] in which some form of faith (Jung, Reich, D. H. Lawrence) replaces reason.

If Freud is a moralist, he is a rather conservative one, uncritically assuming, as Carol Gilligan and I have argued elsewhere, a patriarchal framework,[23] the lens through which he came to interpret ethics in terms of a punitive patriarchal father and guilt as the legacy of the parricidal

16. Rief, *Freud.*
17. See Freud, "Letter to the Mother of a Homosexual."
18. See Freud, "'Civilized' Sexual Morality."
19. Rief, *Freud,* 330.
20. Rief, *Freud,* 331.
21. See Rief, *Freud,* 329–57.
22. See Rief, *Triumph of the Therapeutic.*
23. See Gilligan and Richards, *Deepening Darkness,* 160–90.

murder of the father and guilt as the punishment inflicted by the superego for any deviation from patriarchal norms, a theory based on the now discredited Lamarckian view that such parricide at the beginning of culture would be inherited biologically through the generations (an argument he makes both in an early work *Totem and Taboo* [1913], and his last book, *Moses and Monotheism* [1939]). In effect, his erroneous biological theory of violence, Thanatos, is hard wired into a erroneous biological view of human development. It is quite extraordinary that an observer as sensitive as Freud should have paid no attention to his own experience of mothering or mothering generally,[24] a blindness undoubtedly enforced by the rigid patriarchal lens through which Freud came to understand his work.

The appeal of biological explanations for Freud apparently reflects his

> earlier training and career as a neurologist [that] led him to resist the acceptance of psychological explanations as ultimate; and he was engaged [in 1895] in devising a complicated structure of hypotheses intended to make it possible to describe mental events in purely neurological terms. This project culminated in the 'Project' ['The Project for a Scientific Psychology'] and was not long afterwards abandoned. To the end of his life, however, Freud continued to adhere to the chemical aetiology of the 'actual' neuroses and to believe that a physical basis for all mental phenomena might be found.[25]

In this, Freud's thinking reflects the dominant physical sciences of his time, from which his discovery of psychoanalysis (except for his biological theory of Thanatos) clearly departs, though he apparently hoped for some reconnection in the future. It is, of course, striking that, as Robert Jay Lifton's pathbreaking *The Nazi Doctors* makes clear, it was precisely such pseudo-scientific biological views that would rationalize Nazi genocide as "applied biology."[26]

Freud was, of course, also working within a highly patriarchal Austrian culture, one of the most politically anti-Semitic in Europe (Hitler was Austrian), and the patriarchal lens he adopted in his work reflects what must have been continuing patterns of unjust traumatic humiliation of a justifiably proud man who thought of himself as a Roman conqueror.

24. See, on this point, Whitebook, *Freud*.

25. Freud, "Editor's Introduction," xxiv.

26. Lifton, *Nazi Doctors*, 129, 438.

Freud was, to his cost, sufficiently patriarchal as a man to experience such unjust humiliation as infuriating and, as a patriarchal man, eliciting violence certainly in his unconscious, which explains, I believe, the role violence played in his theory of ethics, the superego as the punishing father. That it was largely unconscious is confirmed by Freud's astonishing difficulties in even seeing let alone dealing realistically with the anti-Semitic violence that, had he not left Vienna quite late, would have cost him his and his daughter's (Anna Freud) life, as it did his sisters. Freud had been blinded by patriarchy in the same way his hero, Oedipus, had been blinded by his own pride. It is a sad and terrifying story, showing what psychoanalysis has shown us and should have shown Freud, the limits of our vaunted ostensibly but often narcissistic scientific rationality when disassociated from loving egalitarian relationships.

Even those, like Herbert Marcuse, who argued that Freud's mythology of Thanatos could be the basis of a more optimistic, progressive critique of the role of violent hierarchies in contemporary cultures, argued within the framework of Freud's mythology.[27] The consequence was Marcuse's failure, like other members of the Frankfurt School,[28] to understand, let alone take seriously, the role of shame-driven patriarchal culture in rationalizing violence targeting scapegoats (on the basis of religion, ethnicity, gender, sexual orientation, and the like), unleashing, as in Nazi Germany, the genocidal evils of racism and anti-Semitism of which they, like others, had been the damaged victims.[29] No doubt, Marcuse made central to his argument the evil of "patriarchal despotism"[30] and endorsed, appealing to Plato on love,[31] ending the "surplus repression"[32] of "pregenital polymorphous eroticism,"[33] supporting the role sexual liberation played, and was increasingly to play, in the feminist, gay rights, and other resistance movements. But, in contrast to Fromm and others,

27. For Marcuse's critique of Freud, see Marcuse, *Psychoanalysis, Politics*, 62–82. For his alternative, arguing that an unleashing of the repressions on erotic sexual life would diminish propensities to hierarchy and violence, see Marcuse, *Eros and Civilization*; Marcuse, *One-Dimensional Man*. See also Brown, *Life Against Death*; Brown, *Love's Body*.

28. See, for fuller discussion, Jay, *Dialectical Imagination*.

29. See, for acknowledgment of this point, Adorno, *Minima Moralia*.

30. Marcuse, *Eros and Civilization*, 61.

31. Marcuse, *Eros and Civilization*, 210–11.

32. Marcuse, *Eros and Civilization*, 88, 131, 224.

33. Marcuse, *Eros and Civilization*, 215.

whom he criticizes,[34] Marcuse fails to understand what Arendt (yet another German Jew, like Marcuse, who escaped Hitler) saw, namely, the war of totalitarianism (fascism and Stalinism) on human rights and liberal constitutional democracy and the crucial role of defending and deepening democratic liberalism,[35] treating people as equals (love as empathy), as the key to resistance to populist authoritarianism and totalitarianism. In consequence, his critique of modern industrial society,[36] failing to identify its threat to democratic liberalism, is much less powerful than it would otherwise be.

WINNICOTT ON ETHICS AND RELIGION

Winnicott never accepted Freud's biological theory of Thanatos ("I simply cannot find value in his [Freud's] idea of a Death Instinct"[37]), and argued this turn in Freud's thought disabled him from taking the role of culture seriously:

> Freud did not have a place in his topography of the mind for the experience of things cultural. He gave new value to inner psychic reality, and from this came a new value for things that are actual and truly external. Freud used the word 'sublimation' to point the way to a place where cultural experience is meaningful, but perhaps he did not get so far as to tell us where in the mind cultural experience is.[38]

Winnicott's discussion of Freud's *Moses and Monotheism* illustrates their very different understandings of human evolution. Whereas for Freud, it is the unconscious repression of the parricidal rage of sons against their fathers that is crucial to moral development, Winnicott attributes the empirical inadequacy in Freud's account to what Winnicott and others had subsequently discovered, namely, "that a great deal happens associated with need, and apart from wish, and apart from (pregenital)

34. Marcuse, *Eros and Civilization*, 238.

35. See, for example, Arendt, *Origins of Totalitarianism*; Arendt, *On Revolution*; Arendt, *Lectures on Kant's Political Philosophy*; Arendt, *Life of the Mind*; Arendt, *Responsibility and Judgment*; Arendt, *Thinking Without a Banister*.

36. See Marcuse, *One-Dimensional Man*. For more despairing forms of a similar argument, see Horkheimer and Adorno, *Dialectic of Enlightenment*; Horkheimer, *Eclipse of Reason*.

37. Winnicott, "Personal View of the Kleinian Contribution," 330.

38. Winnicott, "Location of Cultural Experience," 429.

id-representative clamouring for satisfaction,"[39] namely, the relationship to the mother, and its later development including the loving relationship to the father:

> As the baby moves from ego strengthening due to its being reinforced by the mother's ego to having an identity of his or her own—that, as the inherited tendency to integration carries the baby forward in the good-enough or average expectable environment—the third-person [the father] plays or seemed to play a big part. The father may or may not have been a mother-substitute, but at some time he begins to be felt to be there in a different role, and it is here I suggest that the baby is likely to make use of the father as a blue-print for his or her own integration when just becoming at times a unit. If the father is not there the baby must take the same development but more arduously, or using some other fairly stable relationship to a whole person.[40]

Where Freud sees moral development in terms of parricidal wishes and repression, Winnicott finds the development of loving relationships to the mother and third persons, including what he calls "use" by which he means a child coming into a real relationship to a person by experiencing that the person stays in relationship and the child sees the person as an independent person because they survive the child's destructive impulses directed at the person's independence.[41]

Winnicott's own theory of culture developed from his discovery and "formulation of the transitional phenomena"[42] in the play of child and mother:

> I have claimed that when we witness an infant's employment of a transitional object, the first non-me possession, we are witnessing both the child's first use of a symbol and the first experience of play . . . An essential part of my formulation of transitional phenomena is that we agree never to make the challenge to the baby: did you create this object, or did you find it conveniently lying around? That is to say, an essential feature of transitional phenomena and objects is a quality of our attitude when we observe them.
>
> The object is a symbol of the baby and the mother (or a part of the mother). This symbol can be located. It is at the place in

39. Winnicott, "Use of an Object in the Context of Moses and Monotheism," 34.
40. Winnicott, "Use of an Object in the Context of Moses and Monotheism," 35.
41. See Winnicott, "Use of an Object and Relating Through Identifications."
42. Winnicott, "Location of Cultural Experience," 430.

> space and time where and when the mother is in transition from being (in the baby's mind) merged in with the infant and alternatively being experienced as an object to be perceived rather than conceived of. The use of an object symbolizes the two now separate beings, baby and mother, *at the point in time and space of the initiation of their state of separateness . . . This is the place that I have set out to examine,* the separation that is not a separation but a form of union.[43]

Winnicott has discovered the development of intersubjective imagination in the play of child and mother and human beings with other human beings generally, "the 'electricity' that seems to generate meaningful or intimate contact, that is a feature, for instance, when two people are in love."[44] He argues "that the time has come for psychoanalytic theory to pay tribute to . . . cultural experience which is a derivative of play,"[45] arising in the trust of child in mother, "the building up of confidence based on experience, at the time of maximal dependence, before the enjoyment and employment of separation and independence."[46]

Winnicott claims with characteristic humility that his reframing of psychoanalysis does not "clash with Freud's structural theory of the mind in terms of ego, id, and superego," but his reframing is in fact quite radical in its aims:

> What I say does affect our view of the question: what is life about? You may cure your patient and not know what it is that makes him or her go on living. It is of first importance for us to acknowledge openly that absence of psychoneurotic illness may be health, but it is not life. Psychotic patients who are all the time hovering between living and not living force us to look at the problem, one that really belongs *not to psychoneurotics but to all human beings.* I am claiming these same phenomena that are life and death to our schizoid or borderline patients appear in our cultural experiences. It is these cultural experiences that provide the continuity in the human race that transcends personal existence. I am assuming that cultural experiences are in direct continuity with play, the play of those who have not heard of games.[47]

43. Winnicott, "Location of Cultural Experience," 430–31.
44. Winnicott, "Location of Cultural Experience," 432.
45. Winnicott, "Location of Cutural Experience," 435.
46. Winnicott, "Location of Cutural Exerience," 435.
47. Winnicott, "Location of Cultural Experience," 433.

Another signal difference with Freud is that culture for Winnicott is transmitted not biologically, but through interpersonal cultural relationships transmitted through care and teaching (so central and distinctive a part of our development as humans):

> The accent indeed is on experience. In using the word culture I am thinking of the inherited tradition. I am thinking of something that is in the common pool of humanity, into which individuals and groups of people contribute, and from which we may all draw *if we have somewhere to put what we find.*

There is a dependence here on some kind of recording method. No doubt a very great deal was lost of the early civilizations, but in the myths that were a product of oral tradition there could be said to be a cultural pool giving the history of human culture spanning six thousand years. This history through myth persists to the present time in spite of the efforts of historians to be objective, which they never can be, though they must try

> Perhaps I have said enough to show both what I know and what I do not know about the meaning of culture. It interests me, however, as a side issue, that in any cultural field *it is not possible to be original except on the basis of a tradition.*[48]

Winnicott's view of the centrality of culture in human development offers a psychoanalysis no longer content, as Freud's was, to lead to a health consistent with adaptation to conventional life, but to both an essentially normative perspective on what he called the true vs. false self and the role that perspective might play whether in psychoanalysis or in culture more generally in the criticism of the traditions in which one has been brought up. In particular, psychoanalysis, as least as developed by Winnicott and other analysts, might ground movements in both ethics and politics to challenge and change conventional views politically and constitutionally, including patriarchal views and institutions. As I observed earlier, in "Some thoughts on the Meaning of the Word Democracy,"[49] Winnicott connected his views of the importance of good-enough mothers to the defense of democracy, but also pointed to the dark side of such long dependence. As he put it,

48. Winnicott, "Location of Cultural Experience," 432. On the role of play in human and non-human animals, see Burghardt, *Genesis of Animal Play.*

49. Winnicott, "Some Thoughts on the Meaning of the Word Democracy."

> In psycho-analytical and allied work, it is found that all individuals have in reserve a certain fear of *woman*. Some individuals have this fear to a greater extent than others, but it can be said to be universal. This is quite different from saying that an individual fears a particular woman. This fear of *woman* is a powerful agent in social structure, and it is responsible for the fact that in very few societies does a woman hold the political reins. It is also responsible for the immense cruelty to women, which can be found in customs that are accepted by almost all civilizations.[50]

Winnicott remarkably thus uses his view of good-enough mothering better to understand an unconscious misogyny rooted, so he argues, in the experience infants have of such one-sided dependence on women, "when the infant is doubly dependent because totally unaware of dependence."[51] It is striking that Winnicott should thus have anticipated the insights of comparable psychoanalytically informed feminists, like Dorothy Dinnerstein,[52] Nancy Chodorow,[53] and Jessica Benjamin.[54]

Nothing was more central to Freud's critique of religion than that religion was, as he concluded in *The Future of an Illusion*, "in their psychological nature, an illusion."[55] Freud appears to confuse perceptual illusions like refraction (a stick in water that appears bent, though we know it is straight) with delusions, which, as J. L. Austin pointed out, "*does* suggest something totally unreal, not really there at all."[56] Freud is thinking of religious belief as delusions, as if believers know there is no reality to which their belief refers, which is, of course, false, as there have been and still are reasonable arguments allegedly proving God's existence (for example, Thomas Aquinas on the five ways, proofs for God's existence,[57] and Swinburne on the empirical probability of God's existence[58]), which people believe and not unreasonably believe. He nowhere offers arguments that they are always false, let alone that they are always believed to

50. Winnicott, "Some Thoughts on the Meaning of the Word Democracy," 416.

51. Winnicott, "Some Thoughts on the Meaning of the Word Democracy," 416.

52. Dinnerstein, *Mermaid and the Minotaur*.

53. Chodorow, *Reproduction*.

54. Benjamin, *Bonds of Love*.

55. Freud, *Future of an Illusion*, 33.

56. Austin, *Sense and Sensibilia*, 23.

57. See, for extended discussion of this point, Bamforth and Richards, *Patriarchal Religion*, 152–66.

58. See Swinburne, *Existence of God*.

be false, like paranoid delusions of persecution. What interests me, at this point in my argument, is the very different view Winnicott takes of what he discovered in the role of transitional objects in distinctively human development in relationships within and framed by culture and what that discovery meant for understanding the role of play in human culture and the importance of culture generally in understanding human development (Winnicott argued, as we have seen, that Freud never understood the role of culture in human psychology). What Winnicott observed in human development could not be understood in Freud's terms:

> It is usual to refer to "reality-testing", and to make a clear distinction between apperception and perception. I am here staking a claim for an intermediate state between a baby's inability and growing ability to recognize and accept reality. I am therefore studying the substance of an *illusion,* that which is allowed to the infant and which in adult life is inherent in art and religion.[59]

Winnicott points, in particular, to the cultural forms "art and religion," about which he insists that, like transitional objects, they may be "an illusion," but one "which is allowed to the infant and which in adult life is inherent in art and religion." Winnicott does not mean by "illusion" what Freud means, namely, that religious believers suffer from delusions that there is no reality to which their belief corresponds, which is, as I observed, false. For Winnicott, what made transitional objects so striking is that the belief in them certainly does not affirm a reality but neither does it deny such a reality, but is a form of imagination that leaves that question open, and that is its point in human life and development, indeed in human creativity generally. Why, for Winnicott, is such illusion "allowed . . . in adult life . . . inherent in art and religion"? And indeed, not just allowed, but, for Winnicott, *indispensable* to the role of imagination in our creativity in the sciences and arts and ethics in the discovery of truths not otherwise accessible to us, truths that make life worth living. The difference from Freud could not be more striking in either art or religion, but let us start with art, and then turn to religion.

Freud clearly saw the connection between the narratives of analysands and literary narratives, and indeed drew psychological insight from tragic theater, both ancient Greek and Shakespearean. Freud's understanding of this process takes the form of what he took to render tragedy consistent with his pleasure principle:

59. Winnicott, "Transitional Objects and Transitional Phenomena," 407.

> If, as has been assumed since the time of Aristotle, the purpose of drama is to arouse "terror and pity" and so "to purge" the emotions, we can describe the purpose in rather more detail by saying that it is a question of opening up sources of pleasure or enjoyment in our emotional life . . . The spectator is a person who experiences too little, who feels that he is a "poor wretch to whom nothing of importance can happen," who has long been obliged to damp down, or rather displace his ambitions to stand in his own person at the hub of world affairs; he longs to feel and to act and to arrange things according to his desires—in short, to be a hero. And the playwright and actor enable him to do this by allowing him *to identity himself with* a hero. They spare him something, too. For the spectator knows quite well that actual heroic conduct such as this would be impossible for him without pains and sufferings and acute fears, which would almost cancel out the enjoyment. He knows, moreover, that he has only *one* life and that he might perhaps perish even in a *single* such adversity. Accordingly, his enjoyment is based on an illusion; that is to say, his suffering is mitigated by the certainty that, firstly, it is someone other than himself who is acting and suffering on the stage and, secondly, that after all it is only a game, which can threaten no damage to his personal security. In these circumstances he can allow himself to be a "great man," to give way without a qualm to such suppressed impulses as a craving for freedom in religious, political, social and sexual matters and to "blow off steam" in every direction.[60]

Freud clearly sees the role in the psychology of theater of what he had discovered in transference love, namely, that the mirror of the analyst enables analysands to discover and explore their own background and history, including the identifications that have shaped their sense of themselves, including their ideals. But the account could be of any genre of theater, for example, melodrama, in which idealized heroes vie with denigrated villains, and there is nothing of what so moved Aristotle in those tragedies that gave rise to terror and fear, namely, "complex tragedy, depending on reversal and recognition."[61] It was Freud that based his discovery of the Oedipus Complex on such a play, the *Oedipus Rex* of Sophocles, and recognition (by Oedipus that he has killed his father and married his mother) and reversal (disowning the kingship and blinding himself in a life of exile). And we see the same patterns, recognition and

60. Freud, "Psychopathic Characters on the Stage," 305–6.

61. Aristotle, *Poetics*, 29.

reversal, in many of the tragedies by Shakespeare. But Freud's account of the psychology of theater gives no account of the role these features played in the tragedies that so influenced the development of his psychological views. Why?

Freud's discovery of the importance of the Oedipus Complex arose as the consequence of his own self-analysis in *The Interpretation of Dreams*, and it was Erich Fromm who observed that his account "is at the same time the *acknowledgement and the denial* of the crucial phenomenon: man's longing for mother's love . . . ; by explaining it as sexual the *emotional*—and true—meaning of the tie is denied."[62] Freud's "strictly patriarchal attitude"[63] had blinded him to the continuing emotional bond to the mother in the lives of men, as well as to her earlier role in their development, including their moral development. Evidence for this is that the Oedipus narrative is a narrative of a patriarchally enforced traumatic child abuse: a boy, on the basis of fears arising from prophecies, is not only abandoned by his parents, but crippled by them, a choice patriarchy allows and indeed enforces. Why is this not seen? Why did Freud not see it?

Freud's interpretation arose from his own self-analysis, and his analysis would lead to his sense of himself as a hero like Aeneas concerned never to be defeated, as he supposed his father had been, by an anti-Semite. But self-analysis is not transference love, but rather transference self-love. Freud paid a price in his insight into himself and others for this pivotal failure, as we can see in the story he told of how the Oedipus Complex had historically developed, namely, the parricidal murder in the primal horde of the father by brothers.[64] Freud may have stopped too early in his self-analysis at the point of discovering his shame of his father, but not experiencing his love for his father as well, his ambivalence. Patriarchy blinded him to his own full experience of his mother, his father, and himself. His mother does not exist, his father is demonized (thus parricide).[65]

We can see the consequence of this in the defects in Freud's understanding of the psychology of theater in which tragic recognition and turning is replaced by heroic melodrama. He thus misses, I believe, the distinctive historical place of tragic theater, a place that can only be understood if we take seriously the role of patriarchy and resistance to

62. Fromm, *Sane Society*, 42.

63. Fromm, *Sane Society*, 43.

64. See, on this point, Freud, *Group Psychology*, 122–28.

65. See, on this point, Whitebook, *Freud*.

that role in the transition from shame to guilt cultures and the place of tragic theater as a mirror for the psychological forces unleashed by this transition. Freud's own analysis was not an experience of transference love, and his view of theater reflects, I have come to believe, a similarly motivated patriarchal astigmatism, seeing the love of fathers as always patriarchal and problematic for this reason (love cannot be commanded or willed).

Love exists even under patriarchy, which is shown by the forms of art that express a love that gives a mirror to patriarchally inflicted tragedies. (Shakespeare writes, as I have argued elsewhere,[66] out of such love.) Freud thought of sublimation evidently as a defense to the repression of Eros, but I have come to believe with Hans Loewald that sublimation is not a defense mechanism at all,[67] but the fuller expression of what Erich Fromm called "productive love"[68] and Thomas Merton called love as "personal revolution,"[69] a love that offers a mirror that persons may better see how "his love and reason are crippled" by patriarchy, because "he does not experience himself nor his fellow man in their—and his own—human reality." Tragedy is not, as Freud believed, a pleasurable illusion of our heroism, but an expression of love communicating both knowledge and emotion about the threat patriarchy inflicts on love and the aim of love, which is justice, freed "from the ties to blood and soil."[70]

Zevedei Barbu, in his illuminating book on the historical psychology of the transition in Britain in the seventeenth century, regards the plays of Shakespeare, in particular, as important not only as the great literature they are but as documentary insights into the underlying psychology of the underlying psychological crisis.[71] The psychological focus of Barbu's analysis is the questioning of the previous medieval religious consensus in light of the impact on British cultural and political development of the Renaissance and Reformation. Barbu's focus is on the removal of the constraints on and repressions of thought and feeling in Britain during this period, and he interprets Shakespeare's plays as expressing and exploring the consequences of the new forms of thought

66. See Richards, *Love and Violence*, 48–72.

67. Loewald, *Essential Loewald*, 439–530.

68. Fromm, *Sane Society*, 33.

69. Merton, *Love and Living*, 28.

70. Fromm, *Sane Society*, 58.

71. See, for Barbu's argument along these lines, Barbu, *Problems of Historical Psychology*, 166–72.

and feeling—including not only doubt, but erotic and aggressive energies now released and thus now depicted and explored with a depth and psychological complexity not seen since the great period of the ancient Greek theater of Athens.

Jan Kott, in his pathbreaking study of Shakespeare's plays, *Shakespeare Our Contemporary*,[72] analyzed the tragic structure of these plays as reflecting the destructiveness of "the Grand Mechanism,"[73] a "mechanism whose cogs are both great lords and hired assassins, a mechanism which forces people to violence, cruelty, and treason; which constantly claims new victims."[74] Commenting on *Richard III*, Kott observes of this and other plays:

> There is no tragedy of history without awareness. Tragedy begins at the point when the king becomes aware of the working of the Grand Mechanism. This can happen when he falls victim to it, or when he acts as executioner. These are the points at which Shakespeare carries out his great confrontations, contrasting the moral order with the order of history. . . . Richard III is the mastermind of the Grand Mechanism, its will and awareness. Here for the first time Shakespeare has shown the human face of the Grand Mechanism. A terrifying face, in its ugliness and the cruel grimace of its lips. But also a fascinating face.[75]

Kott had come to see this "terrifying face" in the totalitarian politics of Stalinism in his native Poland, and found in Shakespeare "our contemporary" because the tragedies and histories reveal what he came to see as the destructiveness of political patriarchy both in private and public life. In Britain, the questions raised by these plays prepared the way for the first fundamental questioning of absolute monarchy since democratic Athens, questions which were to culminate in the emergence of arguments for toleration, free speech, and constitutional democracy in the English Civil War and, after the Glorious Revolution, in the development of British democratic constitutionalism, all of which crucially framed both the American Revolution and the Constitution of 1787 and Bill of Rights of 1791.[76]

72. Kott, *Shakespeare.*

73. Kott, *Shakespeare,* 11.

74. Kott, *Shakespeare,* 38.

75. Kott, *Shakespeare,* 41.

76. See, on these points, Walzer, *Revolution of the Saints*; Woodhouse, *Puritanism and Liberty*; Bailyn, *Ideological Origins of the American Revolution*; Wood, *Creation of*

When Winnicott thus offers his view of culture as play, based on his discovery of transitional objects, he sees the role of illusion there as the same role illusion plays in the arts, as, in experiencing an art like Shakespeare's tragic theater, we are shown through an imaginative art deeper truths of human psychology than those available from psychology, as Jim Gilligan discovered in trying to understand the violent criminals with whom he worked as a therapist.[77] Imagination, through its illusions, plays a role in discovering the truths the arts communicate in a way Gilligan found that the supposedly scientific psychiatry of his time did not. Imagination has played a pivotal role even in creative breakthroughs in the hard physical sciences, not only the crucial role of mathematics in these sciences (which Plato anticipated), but the role of imaginative thought experiments (Einstein). What Gilligan's work shows is that in the *human* sciences psychological truth *requires* artistic imagination (Shakespeare on violence).

If that is true about the arts, one can see why Winnicott thought the same was true of religion, in particular, his conception of the psychological connection of religion to ethics in the historical Jesus. Freud certainly thought of the Christianities deriving from Paul that they were not only illusions, but dangerous illusions, as "the narcissism of small differences" had paradoxically unleashed, despite the Christian claim of "universal love between men," "the extreme intolerance on the part of Christendom towards those who remained outside it."[78] There was, as we have seen in the argument of this book, an extraordinary gap between the life and teaching of the historical Jesus and what later Christianities made of him, which is one way of making sense of Freud's Voltairean horror of Christianities, and even of religion in general. But Freud's ethical despair about the roots of violence in Thanatos was itself a mythology, one he uncritically accepted as the basis of his conception of the punishing superego, guilt arising from his own mythology of the parricide of the patriarchal father. So, Freud has replaced one dangerous illusion with yet another.

Winnicott's opposing view arises not from mythology, but from his empirical studies of the role of the good-enough mother (including transitional objects) in her relationship to her child and the similar role in later relationships in the development of a human life. This is the

---

the American Republic; Adair, *Fame*; Richards, *Toleration*; Richards, *Foundations*; Richards, *Conscience, Revolution and Constitutionalism*.

77. See Gilligan and Richards, *Holding a Mirror*, 1–17.

78. Freud, *Civilization and Its Discontents*, 114.

empirical basis of his observation that the psychology of religion in general and Christianity in particular is based in loving relationships and is projected on to an imagined ethical God, a transitional object, which Winnicott understands in terms of the life and teaching of the historical Jesus. Jesus was undoubtedly radically imaginative transforming the Jewish prophetic tradition on which he depended and creatively transformed but in terms of a kingdom of God that was antipatriarchal and existed at the time nowhere, and indeed threatened the existing Roman patriarchy that had subjugated Israel. But it was, for Winnicott, the very fact that religio-ethical culture allowed such imaginative construction of something that did not yet exist that made its illusions (whether true or not of the world as it then existed) so *ethically* imperative in the advance of human culture. Ethics, on the view I have (following Rawls) taken of it, is constructed by humans as an expression of a moral nature that treats persons as equals, which requires us to exercise our imaginative capacities of empathy and mind-reading to enter into the experience of other persons who are equally persons in what Jesus called the kingdom of God and Kant the kingdom of ends, and to construct an ethics treating persons as equals consistent with this moral equality.

Winnicott's theory of culture as play correctly highlights the importance of imagination in the development of a culture, starting from tradition but tradition transformed and advanced by the imaginative play of creativity in human experience, as we can see not only in the sciences and the arts, but in the psychological connection, as Winnicott saw it, of religion to ethics, as well as to politics. Such creativity is a crucial feature of the role human linguistic capacity has played in the cultural advances distinctive of the human species in all these domains,[79] not least in religion, ethics, and politics. Jesus was creative in this way, as was Socrates, the Grimke sisters, Theodore Parker, Frederick Douglass, Abraham Lincoln, as well as Gandhi and King. Rawls's use of the veil of ignorance in his ethical and political philosophy is an act of creative imagination of this sort, as we see and understand Kant in a deeper, more empirically and normatively truthful, and yet more critical way.

Important Christian theologians, Christopher and Richard Hays (father and son),[80] within the Methodist tradition of Winnicott and the Lutheran tradition of Tillich and Niebuhr, have recently powerfully

79. See, on this point, Taylor, *Language Animals*; Taylor, *Cosmic Connections*.

80. On the recent death of Richard Hays, see Gabriel, "Richard B. Hayes, 76, Dies."

argued that, notwithstanding the biblical texts condemning gay sex,[81] a better understanding of the prophetic tradition within Judaism and the teachings of Jesus that clearly appeal to that tradition (notably, Isaiah and Jeremiah[82]), as well as Jesus's open table embrace of outcasts and sinners, as well as of Samaritans, earlier discussed in this book, compel a rethinking of the view that the Bible condemns gay people and their relationships, a view these theologians once endorsed and now, much to their credit, repudiate. Some of their textual appeals, notably to Peter and Paul, are not, in my view, supported by the historical Jesus, and would be more convincing without these appeals. What is compelling in their overall account is the role of the creative imaginations of prophets, challenging dominant views in both the Jewish and Christian traditions, working within and yet questioning those traditions, and Jesus's clear role as a prophet in these traditions. Their argument is a model of how the prophetic tradition within Judeo-Christianity should be understood and elaborated.

What I find even more compelling in their views is their overall account of the implicit role of the Love Commandments both in Judaism and the teaching of Jesus. As we earlier observed (chapter 5), the love of God plays a role in Christianity and Judaism that it did not play in Greek thought:

> "Thou shalt love the Lord thy God . . . ";—is completely missing in Greece. Aristotle said: "For it would be strange for one to say that he loved Zeus," and held that *philia* (love, friendship) was impossible between man and God.[83]

The role love plays in Judeo-Christianity converged with Winnicott's view of the origin of religion and ethics in good-enough mothering (consider, for example, the feminine images of God in the Bible[84]), and his view of the antipatriarchal Jesus as arising from such an intimate I-Thou relationship of equality, not hierarchy, with a loving God (in contrast to Paul's view of agape love), and thus calling ethically for treating persons

81. Gen 19:1–9; Lev 18:22, 20:13; 1 Cor 6:9–11, 1 Tim 1:10; and Rom 1:18–32.

82. On Jesus's appeal to Isaiah to justify his calling, Hayes and Hayes, *Widening of God's Mercy*, 197, 114–15; Isaiah on opening the door to eunuchs, 97–101, and to foreigners, 101–6; Jeremiah, on God changing his mind, 87–88; Isaiah and Jeremiah, on critiques of temple authorities.

83. Bellah, *Religion in Human Evolution*, 326. See Dodds, *Greeks*, 35, 54, citing Aristotle's *Magna Moralia* 208B.30 and *Nicomachean Ethics* 1159A.5.

84. See, on this point, Hayes and Hayes, *Widening of God's Mercy*, 20–36.

as equals, connecting religion to ethics. Christopher and Richard Hays think of God's love in terms of mercy, but mercy assumes "forebearance and compassion by one person to another who is in his power and has no claim to receive kindness."[85] But, their over-all argument, based on both the Hebrew and Christian Bibles, is much closer to the love of what Winnicott called a good-enough mother or nurturant parent, whose love for a child strives to find and support what is best in the child, correcting what is bad, supporting what is good, ultimately realized in a conversation of equals (certainly not assuming the child "has no claim to receive kindness"). Such a conversation is not one-sided, as nurturant parents may come through love of their child as the person he or she is to realize their own view of the child was flawed and harmful (I draw here on experience, the experience of the love of my parents and sister, see Introduction). Through love, such nurturant parents, like the Judeo-Christian God, come to change their minds through love, as the theologians make so clear in their revelatory over-all argument. Such love is not mercy, which assumes a one-sided and nonreciprocal hierarchy, but the love Plato called mirroring, the center of our being and becoming human. The two Love commandments thus have, for Winnicott, a psychological foundation: it is through our love for the good-enough mother or other nurturant parent who has loved us, that we come empathetically to love others as we have some to love ourselves.

At this point, Christopher and Richard Hays, like Winnicott and Jesus, listened closely and respectfully to actual outcasts to the dominant tradition, namely, gay men and women, and have come to understand that love plays the same role in their lives that it does for others, and thus accord them the respect for their human rights that the central teaching of the antipatriarchal Jesus requires, treating all persons as equals. Jesus refused to use the language of moral judgment of the Pharisees about these outcasts and was condemned for his refusal, responding that he regarded himself as a physician, engaging in open table fellowship with them, listening and engaging with them about their unjust suffering, entering into their worlds, expressing an understanding and concern that was evidently therapeutic (thus, Jesus as "a leading psychotherapist"). If anything, Jesus regards such outcasts (Mary Magdalene, among others) as, if anything, more loving than those who heaped condemnatory moral judgment on them, and Mary very likely for this reason alone does not

85. *Oxford Edition of the Oxford English Dictionary*, "Mercy," 1:851.

abandon Jesus and alone experiences the resurrection, and was, I have come to think, the leading disciple. What Winnicott offers, which the theologians do not, is an understanding of the distinctive imaginative human psychology centered in love that explains how such love is connected to ethics, indeed to progress in ethical thought and practice.

We can see the same dynamic in the transition of the evangelical pastor, Bill White, who, starting from the homophobic premise that "I hate homosexuality. I hate it more than anything else in the world,"[86] experienced a leap of faith in accepting his gay son, Timothy White, as he and his wife, Katy, come to thank God for the "full, true, vibrant life in Christ, Father, Thank you that you created our son gay. Forgive me for how poorly I received that gift."[87] Once again, as with Christopher and Richard Hays, Bill White listened closely not only to his son but other gays in his church, as Jesus had embraced outcasts in open table fellowship, and, though he suffered loss of church members because of his rejection of evangelical homophobia, he found in his loving relationship to the antipatriarchal Jesus the love of Jesus for his son and his and his wife's love for their son, as the person he was.

It is remarkable to me that Winnicott's psychological argument at this point converges with, yet deepens, the comparable arguments John Stuart Mill made in his *Three Essays on Religion*[88] that offer skeptical arguments, both empirical and normative, about the ways in which religion in general and Christianity in particular had been understood. The skepticism that is quite close to that of Winnicott is the ways in which what Mill had come to regard "the life and sayings of Jesus" as bearing:

> a stamp of personal originality combined with profundity of insight, which if we abandon the idle expectation of finding scientific precision where something very different was aimed at, must place the Prophet of Nazareth, even in the estimation of those who have no belief in his inspiration, in the very first rank of the men of sublime genius of whom our species can boast. When this pre-eminent genius is combined with the qualities of probably the greatest moral reformer, and martyr to that mission, who ever existed upon earth, religion cannot be said to have made a bad choice in pitching on this man as the ideal representative and guide of humanity; not, even now, would it

86. White, "How My Dad Reconciled His God and His Gay Son," 8.
87. White, "How My Dad Reconciled His God and His Gay Son," 11.
88. Mill, *Three Essays on Religion.*

> be easy, even for an unbeliever, to find a better translation of the rule of virtue from the abstract into the concrete, than to endeavour so to live that Christ would approve our life.[89]

Yet Mill, like Winnicott, sharply distinguishes this understanding of Jesus from "the Paulism which is the foundation of ordinary Christianity,"[90] which had corrupted, in his view, the ethical teaching of Jesus. Mill and Winnicott agree on this point. However, Winnicott appeals, unlike Mill, explicitly to an understanding of the historical antipatriarchal Jesus that I have defended at length in this book, and it is not surprising that Mill, with his extraordinary indictment of the injustice of sexism in *The Subjection of Women,* should implicitly have come to regard Jesus in very much the terms of the antipatriarchal Jesus. The convergence with Winnicott's view of Jesus is confirmed as well by the similar ways Mill argues that justice cannot be done to either the life or teaching of Jesus until we take seriously that "the exercise of imagination" advances ethical understanding "without running counter to the evidence of fact,"[91] an emphasis on the imaginative freedom of the moral reformers, like Socrates and Jesus, both murdered for their resistance to conventional Athenian and Roman patriarchal morality, that was central to Mill's justification for an expansive understanding of free speech.[92] It should strike us that early Christians, like Justin Martyr, as they moved from Pagan Platonic philosophy to Christianity, were so moved by Socrates prefiguring Jesus.[93] What Winnicott distinctively brings to Mill's argument is an empirically grounded psychology of the role of creative imagination that offers empirical support for the crucial role both Mill and Winnicott argued was fundamental to prophetic ethical progress. Winnicott thus deepens our understanding of the psychology of ethical progress beyond even Mill, including, as we earlier saw, the role resistance to the patriarchal Love Laws had played in Mill's defense of his adulterous love for Harriet Mill, the ethical emancipation that made possible both *On Liberty* and *The Subjection of Women.*[94] And love across the patriarchal boundaries was the heart of the matter, as it was for Jesus, Winnicott, and Mill.

89. Mill, *Three Essays on Religion,* 254–255.
90. Mill, *Three Essays on Religion,* 97.
91. Mill, *Three Essays on Religion,* 245.
92. See Mill, *On Liberty,* chs. 2–3, 17–76.
93. Justin Martyr, *Complete Works,* 271–72.
94. On this point, see Richards, *Why Love Leads to Justice,* 22–30.

Winnicott's developmental views offer a psychological basis for understanding as well Mill's suggestion that Manicheanism, which Augustine had accepted before his conversion to Christianity,

> allows it be believed that all the mass of evil which exists was undesigned by, and exists not by the appointment of, but in spite of the Being whom we are called upon to worship. A virtuous human being assumes in this theory that exalted character of a fellow-labourer with the Highest, a fellow-combatant in the great strife; contributing his little, which by the aggregation of many like himself becomes much, towards that progressive ascendancy, and ultimately complete triumph of good over evil, which history points to, and which this doctrine teaches us to regard as planned by the Being to whom we owe all the benevolent contrivance we behold in Nature.[95]

The good-enough mother, for Winnicott, as I earlier suggested, both teaches and learns from her child as the child develops, clarifying how in a religion arising from such relationships, we can come to see ourselves as playing a prophetic role in understanding God's changes of mind, teaching as well as learning from persons made in the image of the loving relationship of equals. Love in Christianity, properly understood, is of a God, love, whom we *need*, as much as God *needs* us, as we work together to moral maturity, growth, and progress against what is, I have come to believe, the main impediment to such growth, patriarchy and the dehumanizing structures patriarchy endorses and, through violence, defends, an evil still invisible to many of us (men, in particular). Winnicott took, I believe, this view, and came to regard psychoanalytic therapy as a way, among others, to reveal and address the traumatic and dehumanizing subordination of outcasts patriarchy requires.

It is the psychological connection of violence to a humiliated patriarchal manhood, the subject of the life and work of Jim Gilligan, that enables us to see as well why nonviolence was so central to the life and teaching of the antipatriarchal Jesus and why the most patriarchal of peoples, the Romans, killed him for living, advocating, and teaching it. Our culture, including most Christianities, have found this, among all his teachings, the most difficult to understand or to live, offering, rather, theories of just wars that, even when plausible and well-intentioned,[96] do not address the underlying connection between patriarchy and violence

95. Mill, *Three Essays on Religion*, 116–17.

96. See, for example, Fisher, *Morality and War*.

central to the life and teaching Jesus. We can, however, see in the heterodox Christianities studied in this book (chapter 7) the ethical and psychological truth that Jesus revealed to us and contemporary experience confirms, namely, that "[p]sychological violence lies at the core of the traditional socialization of boys in our culture,"[97] and how transformative it was and it can be in future to take this truth seriously and help men and women act on it; it confirms, I believe, my view of the antipatriarchal Jesus that contemporary psychoanalysts who take such therapy seriously paraphrase the aims of such therapy in terms familiar from the life and teaching of Jesus: "we want the weak to rise and the mighty to melt."[98] Such rethinking will require as well what Gilligan has argued in his critique of retributivism in criminal justice, which perpetuates the violence it claims to end, a rethinking of why even liberals like Kant and Mill linked justice to the legitimacy of coercion[99] when nonviolent alternatives demonstrably often (not always) better achieve justice, as heterodox Christianities and others (Jim Gilligan) clearly show. Loving your enemies, for many among Jesus's most impossible demands, is among his most realistic if we understand how the violence patriarchy requires and endorses rests on a fear of the vulnerability to loving connection that makes us human and moves us to struggle for a more humane life and politics. The life and teaching of Jesus on nonviolence call for us both to see and act on this connection, among the most "impossible" demands in a patriarchal culture, excoriating and violently repressing, as it does, the place of antipatriarchal love in our human natures, and those, like Jesus, whose life and teaching, including his role as a physician, address our patriarchally endorsed fear of love. It is through such love and the trust and confidence and faith such love inspires and sustains that we resist patriarchal demands, which no longer have the hold, based in fear of love, on us they once had.

Patriarchy, on the view I have taken of it in this book, calls for violence whenever patriarchal demands are challenged, and it is this political psychology that explains why the life and teaching of the antipatriarchal Jesus, which challenged these demands, were met by repressive violence, indeed, the worst punishment Rome could inflict, crucifixion. The argument of this book has shown as well, I believe, that it was the persistence

97. Real, *I Don't Want to Talk About It*, 198. See also 229.

98. Real, *Us*, 132.

99. For Mill on this point, see Mill, *Utilitarianism*, 277–301; for Kant, *Metaphysics of Morals*, 388.

of patriarchy among the Christianities, which were ostensibly inspired by Jesus but became more Roman than Christian, that explains how and why any challenge to their view of Jesus as supporting patriarchy led them to endorse violence against such heretics and dissenters, including not only Jews but the heterodox Christianities that appeal to the antipatriarchal Jesus, as well as many others.

The problem persists. For example, its analysis (the violence of patriarchy against Christians and non-Christians who resist patriarchy) clarifies as well, I have come to think, the role of what Kristin Kobes Du Mez calls the "militant masculinity"[100] developed and supported by American white evangelicals who wrongly read the life and teaching of Jesus as requiring a rigid patriarchal code in personal and public life today, now in their view at threat by feminists and gays and lesbians, and thus requiring violent repression both at home and rationalizing wars to defend threats to Christian nationalism from abroad (the unjust wars in Vietnam and Iraq[101]). Defense of this patriarchal code thus calls for parents to "dare to discipline"[102] their children, including use of corporal punishment, rather than imitating Jesus, so tenderly nurturant of babies and children in the Gospels; and the Gospel passage, Matthew 11–12, in which Jesus observes that the "[k]ingdom of heaven suffers violence, and violent men take it by force"[103] is taken not to observe the unjust violence against the nonviolence of John the Baptist and his follower Jesus, but to endorse violence. What makes the overall historical argument of Du Mez about this development so powerful is that it clarifies at its end why so many of these evangelicals have politically supported and brought to power a man, Donald Trump, whose appeal to them is not his theology and certainly not his ethics (as it may have been in their support of Billy Graham)[104] but only and solely his manly violence in attacking anyone critical of him and what they take to be his support of a Christian nationalism, a tribal shame culture in fact quite foreign to and repudiated by the sense of ethical responsibility to others (treating persons as equals) and

100. Du Mez, *Jesus and John Wayne*, 3.

101. See Du Mez, *Jesus and John Wayne*, 48–57, 137–38, 184–85, 197, 208, 209, 216, 227, 231–32, 235.

102. Du Mez, *Jesus and John Wayne*, 80.

103. Quoted in Du Mez, *Jesus and John Wayne*, 174.

104. See, on this point, Du Mez, *Jesus and John Wayne*, 22–39, 44–57.

personal guilt in failure of such responsibility in the life and teaching of the historical antipatriarchal Jesus.[105]

Winnicott's sense of such personal responsibility, central to his distinction of the true vs. false self, has been for me the most resonant feature of his view of psychoanalysis, as it was, I believe, implicitly as well for Mill. It centers in what you would expect to be central to a view of the human psyche arising in and flourishing in loving relationships of care and concern, but it is for me the most truthful feature of his view of psychoanalysis that even good mothers sometimes uncritically enforce on their children views that denigrate and defame the only loving egalitarian relationships in which they flourish, as was the case with my family and my own homosexuality. Winnicott has an extraordinary sensitivity, undoubtedly arising from his own loving relationships to a withdrawn depressive mother and rather patriarchal father, as to how a sensitive child in such a situation must withdraw into an incommunicable secret self, the only way to preserve his true self from a domination that cripples the sense of value in living. Winnicott often writes about child development in terms of the emergence of the child's sense of "I am,"[106] the individual one uniquely is, but an individual that a patriarchal culture like America not only condemned but rendered unspeakable, accepting consensual homosexual sex as something the British common law authority in colonial America, William Blackstone, hesitated even to discuss, "the very mention of which is a disgrace to human nature . . . a crime not fit to be named: '*peccatum illud horrible, inter christianos non nominandum*,'" noting ancient law called for burning at the stake, but now capital punishment by hanging.[107] In such a culture, gay loving relationships—the basis of a life worth living—are not a cultural possibility.

Winnicott has an extraordinary understanding of children, like myself and so many others (perhaps most others, I am inclined to think), who have thus been culturally directed into lives of wealth and status and even accomplishment, but lives not worth living.[108] I have come to understand my self and my life as a secret self, and Winnicott has given a quite precise name to my struggle to loving relationship, namely, the creative play with one's ethical and political culture (in my case,

105. See, in particular, Du Mez, *Jesus and John Wayne*, 250–94.

106. See, for example, Winnicott, "Therapeutic Consultations in Child Psychiatry," 78.

107. Blackstone, *Commentaries*, 215–16.

108. See, for a similar view, Riker, *Kohut's Self Psychology*.

Italian-American Catholic) finding a voice, perhaps a prophetic voice within that culture that, in transforming oneself, transforms others as well. The is what Winnicott meant by a life worth living, grounded in the cultural creativity expressive of the secret self and advancing as well an ethical and political/constitutional culture more just, because more loving to others as well. What compelled him about Jesus of Nazareth, as it compels me, is that Jesus was also such a creative ethical prophet of an ethics of treating persons as equals and even of a democracy, demanded in his name by later heterodox Christians, based on liberal equality.

In "Morals and Education,"[109] Winnicott explains as clearly as he ever did the critical implications of his view for both religion and ethics, in particular, his criticism of the role original sin had played in the Christianities that were the dominant Christian tradition, Catholic and Protestant. In sharp contrast to Freud, religious experience arises in and from the care and concern of good-enough mothering, and guilt arises from the experience of acts and failures of love to those we love, an experience that develops over time in other relationships, including to lovers, friends, fellow citizens, and the like. It is the experience of good arising from such relationships that is, for Winnicott, the basis of God as loving, and, correspondingly the experience of traumatic harm of God as evil or tolerating evil. The argument I earlier developed about Augustine and Luther was, I believe, along the psychoanalytic lines Winnicott would have offered for understanding how the conception of a loving God, to whom they always appealed consciously, could have become, because of unconscious hatred of parents, so unloving, indeed endorsing evil.

Winnicott's religious views originated in his family's Wesleyan Methodism, and I am struck by William James's objection to his psychology of religious experience by a Methodist: "I do not see why Methodists need object to such a view. Pray go back and recollect one of the conclusions to which I sought to lead you . . . You may remember how I there argued against the notion that the worth of a thing can be decided by its origin."[110] I earlier (chapter 4) framed my discussion of the psychology of religion in line with the psychological perspective of William James in his pathbreaking *The Varieties of Religious Experience*. James was not a conventional religious believer,[111] but, himself crippled by a depression connected to the demands of a domineering father, closely examines

109. See Winnicott, "Morals and Education."

110. James, *Varieties*, 237.

111. See James, *Varieties*, xxiv.

the testimony of those who have experienced what he called the two kinds of religious experience, that of the healthy minded and the sick minded. It is the psychological role that religious experience plays in the sick minded that particularly interests James. James, a central figure in American pragmatism, takes no interest in the tradition of philosophical arguments for the existence of God,[112] but, as a pragmatist, explores its "cash values,"[113] for example, bringing a relief to neurotic suffering. Accordingly, in *Varieties,* his interest, as a psychologist, is in the psychology of religion, not its origin or truth, and he thus insists that nothing he documents, for example, in the psychological role of crisis and conversion in Methodism (Winnicott's religion of origin) should reasonably be interpreted as questioning its truth, but only pointing to its psychological value empirically.[114]

Winnicott's interest as a psychoanalyst in religion is, I believe, consistent with this program, including James's considered view in *Varieties* that religious experience was an aspect of the unconscious, what he called the "subconscious self"[115] or the "[o]ver belief."[116] James had critiqued the idea of the unconscious in his earlier work, *The Principles of Psychology*, but Donald Levy has shown that parts of his argument do not work and other parts accept a form of unconscious.[117] In *Varieties*, James quite clearly accepts the unconscious, citing Freud among others,[118] and sees that it plays a role in religious experience. He also saw something that Winnicott certainly saw in the historical Jesus: that it is through religion that "in communion with the Ideal new force comes into the world,"[119] namely, an antipatriarchal conception of ethics.

Winnicott's psychoanalysis of religious experience enables him to go further than James or Mill were able to go in understanding religious experience in general and of Christianities in particular. This is, I believe, quite appropriate since our argument shows that the life and teaching of the historical Jesus uses a form of psychoanalysis, and I believe it remained central in the life and work of two of the main figures shaping

112. See, for example, James, *Varieties,* 63, 73–74.

113. James, *Varieties,* 443.

114. See, on this point, James, *Varieties*, 237.

115. James, *Varieties,* 511.

116. James, *Varieties,* 518.

117. See, on this point, Levy, *Freud Among the Philosophers*, 64–82.

118. James, *Varieties,*233–36, 478–84.

119. James, *Varieties,* 521.

the direction of Christianities, Augustine and Luther. For Winnicott, the psychoanalysis of religious experience begins with the experience of love, either a strict parent morality or a nurturant morality, or some mixture of them. It is aspects of such early experience, including acts and omissions of what he called generically the good mother, that explain how love, which is the center of Christianity, is understood or misunderstood.

As I earlier observed, the role love plays in Judaeo-Christianity converged with Winnicott's view of the origin of religion and ethics in good-enough mothering, and his view of the antipatriarchal Jesus as arising from such an intimate I-Thou relationship of equality, not hierarchy, with a loving God (in contrast to Paul's view of agape love), and thus calling ethically for treating persons as equals, connecting religion to ethics. The two Love commandments thus have, for Winnicott, a psychological foundation: it is through our love for the good-enough mother and her love for us, that we come empathetically to love others as we love ourselves. Alison Gopnik shows that recent research on babies confirms such a development from quite early on: "[l]iterally from the time they are born children are empathic . . . and three-year-olds understand rules and try to follow them."[120] Indeed,

> The new research shows that children have some of the foundations of morality from the time they're very young, even from the time they are born. But these foundations aren't just innate, unchanging 'moral grammar' or a hardwired set of emotional reactions. Instead, children's moral thinking, and so our own, changes as we learn more about the world and ourselves. Just as children are born with theories about the world, but also with powerful capacities for changing those theories, they seem to be born with certain fundamental moral ideas, but also with powerful capacities to change their moral judgments and actions.[121]

Winnicott adopts a form of Feuerbach's projection view of religious experience, but does not draw the same conclusions as Feuerbach (who regarded Christianity itself as a delusion[122]). The projection account may be psychologically true, but this is a feature of how the human psyche comes to religious convictions. It says nothing about the truth and value of such convictions if they are integrally connected, as Winnicott

120. Gopnik, *Philosophical Baby*, 204.

121. Gopnik, *Philosophical Baby*, 203–4.

122. See Wikipedia, "Ludwig Feuerbach"; *Stanford Encyclopedia of Philosophy*, Ludwig Andreas Feuerbach.

believed, to defensible ethical and democratic values, as we have seen in the role of heterodox Christianities in the development of constitutional democracy, the abolition of slavery and emancipation of women, the successful anti-racist and anti-colonial nonviolence of Gandhi and King, peacemaking in Northern Ireland, and much else (chapter 7). Indeed, it is the very heterodox character of such prophetic Christianities that may sometimes make them more appealing both ethically and politically than more conventional secular arguments; it has been observed, for example, about the distinctive appeal of James Baldwin's art and essays, in contrast to other arguments during the period he lived, that: "Baldwin kept Christianity and took away the dogmatisms. We can go back as far as Baldwin and still relate to what we're hearing as a living truth, not a historical one."[123]

For Winnicott, such convictions and their consequences for ethics and democracy are rooted in the role love plays in the growth and flourishing of the human psyche, as it did in Baldwin's loving mother and his love for her[124]—a fact as permanent a feature of our humanity as our capacity for reason itself. Indeed, good-enough mothering, an indispensable feature of our survival as a species, gives rise not only to a child's need for and faith in such secure relationships, but our continuing need as humans for such relationships: what Jesus called "the kingdom of God" and Kant "the kingdom of ends." It suggests an empirical foundation for the role faith plays in all the religions, including the secular forms Mill called "the Religion of Humanity."[125] If so, the psychological connection of religion to ethics may be an ineliminable feature of our human natures, or, as Wilfred Smith put it, "religion, and each of what used to be called 'the religions', is inherently human; and integrally so."[126] And I believe Winnicott came to the view that there was both ethical truth and value in such convictions, which explains why he wanted to establish an empirical/psychoanalytical basis for them against the Christianities that had debased and transmogrified them and to defend religion in general and Christianity in particular against Freud's psychology of religion that repudiated any connection to a defensible ethics that included democratic voice, nonviolence, and treating persons as equals as central tenets of its teaching.

123. Pinckney, *Baldwin's Spell*, 25

124. See, for illuminating discussion of this point, Phillips, "House Is Not a Home."

125. Mill, *Three Essays on Religion*, 118, 119.

126. Smith, *Towards a World Theology*, 53.

There is, finally, my own personal response to the terrifying isolation and death of Jesus—crucified unjustly essentially for being a nonviolent ethical prophet whose views upset Roman authorities, abandoned by his male disciples (except Mary Magdalene and a few other women), the despair on the cross ("'Eli, Eli, lama sabachthani?,' that is, 'My God, my God, why have you forsaken me'"[127]), the sense of homelessness ("Foxes had holes, and birds of the air have nests, but the Son of Man has nowhere to lay his head"[128]). The belief in the resurrection of such a remarkable loving man and his ethically revolutionary teaching makes sense psychologically as a response to such evident despair, indeed redeems it. Accordingly, the resurrection has long been a distinctive feature of Christian belief, and there are liberal Christians today who hold to the view and offer arguments in support of it.[129] Others, like Elaine Pagels, point to the views of Gnostic Christianity that are quite like the psychoanalytic understanding of the antipatriarchal Jesus defended by Winnicott as a reasonable alternative to patriarchal orthodox Christianity.[130]

Beliefs in the resurrection can, however, be explained naturalistically, as John Hick points out,[131] and he ultimately sees a legitimate role for these beliefs if believers accept as well the beliefs, including the ethical and other spiritual beliefs, they share with other traditions. Religious pluralism is, for Hick, a reasonable requirement of religious belief in the twenty-first century and beyond.

The resurrection story has always moved me; if anything has continued to appeal to me about Christianity in contrast to other religions and belief systems throughout my life, from boyhood to now, it is the resurrection. My doubts about it are not only that belief in it can be explained naturalistically as the traumatic response to a terrifying, indeed catastrophic loss of the most loving man Mary Magdalene and others had ever experienced as the very human and humane person Jesus clearly was. My lack of belief is not, unlike the resurrection, doubts that it occurred, but of something I do not doubt, that Jesus was crucified, in particular, the role that the *idea* of crucifixion has played in the rationalization of Christian ascetism and self-inflicted masochism (including the

127. Coogan, *New Oxford Bible*, 1825, Matt 27:46–47.

128. Coogan, *New Oxford Bible*, 1794, Matt 9:20–21.

129. See the works of N. T. Wright on this point. Wright, *Simply Jesus*; Wright, *Simply Christian*; Wright, *Resurrection of the Son of God*.

130. Pagels, *Gnostic Gospels*, 119–41.

131. Hick, *Interpretation of Religion*, 101–4.

extraordinary role of "the ideology of martyrdom [as] . . . an essential component of Christian identity"[132] (foreign to the historical Jesus's view of open table fellowship and of himself as a "bridegroom" and his disciples as "wedding guests,"[133] who should not fast but celebrate). In contrast, Augustine argues that we can only love God when we abandon our sexuality and sensuality as embodied beings entirely. Christianities have, in my view, played a deplorably negative role in the history of Western views of sexuality and gender because, essentially, they warred on human nature, in particular, a human nature in which loving relationships play a central role in a creative life worth living.[134] Christianities, based in love, have warred on love, something a secular critic of Christianity like Freud, to his credit, saw clearly, and some Christians, like Dostoyevsky, to their credit, saw as well—the unforgettable image of the Grand Inquisitor in *The Brothers Karamazov* (a metaphor for established religion) condemning Jesus.[135] My doubts about the ways in which Christianities have handled love are illustrated by the way a believer like René Girard focuses on *belief* in a redemptive resurrection after the sanguinary crucifixion of the innocent Jesus as what alone releases us from competitive hierarchy (based on punishing guilty scapegoats) into Christian religious belief.[136] In contrast, I have argued in this book *that the care and teaching* of the antipatriarchal Jesus speak to *all* of us in a way that *belief* in the resurrection may not.

There is a further point that explains and perhaps justifies my skepticism, namely, what I find to be the wholly convincing argument of Ernst Troeltsch that the ethical problem in Christianities can be traced to the model of the "Patriarchalism of love"[137] they have uncritically accepted both in their conceptions of religious and personal love, which are inextricably connected. The radical hierarchy that agape love assumes for Augustine and Luther illustrates the problem, and the corresponding endorsement of gender hierarchy in matters of personal love and beyond. John Stuart Mill correctly diagnosed the psychological depth of

132. See Fredriksen, *Ancient Christianities*, 61.

133. Coogan, *New Oxford Bible*, 1877, Luke 5:24.

134. For a powerful recent statement along these lines by a theologian of this critique of historical and contemporary Christianities, foreign to the life and teaching of the antipatriarchal Jesus, see MacCulloch, *Lower than the Angels*.

135. Dostoyevsky, *Brothers Karamazov*, 322–44.

136. See Girard, *All Desire If a Desire For Being*.

137. Troeltsch, *Social Teaching*, 1:285.

the problem of patriarchy when he pointed to its intractable roots in our conceptions of gender hierarchy in intimate life, which was Troeltsch's point as well. For me, the greatest challenge for Christianity is taking seriously what it means and should mean for lovers to treat one another as equals, the central theme in Jesus's loves for his disciples and others is that, after washing the feet of the disciples, he says "servants are not greater than their master, nor are messengers greater than the one who sent them"[138] and accordingly:

> I give you a new commandment, that you love one another, just as I have loved you, you also should love one another. By this everyone will know that you are my disciples, if you have love for one another.[139]

My own earlier account is framed by my view of the antipatriarchal Jesus, and I have come to believe that what Winnicott meant by Jesus as "a leading psychotherapist" is very much along the lines I have defended now at some length, and explains the form of Christianity Winnicott would have defended and the life he led as a remarkably hard-working analyst and advocate of more humane treatment of juvenile delinquents, prisoners, homosexuals, and the like, an imitation of a loving Jesus whose love knew no boundaries very much like the life and work of my friend, the psychiatrist and prison reformer James Gilligan, the most Christian man I have ever known.[140] It also explains why psychoanalysis or something like psychoanalysis has always and remarkably been a feature of Christianity, as it was in Jesus himself, and always in those moved by his life and teaching, albeit often through patriarchy seeing him through a glass, darkly. Jesus, for Christians, is the beloved, indeed for some the only lover worth having, the lover who best mirrors us, "the divine mirror."[141]

Love, as I understand it, is constitutive of the human psyche because it is through the mirroring in loving attachments (from infancy on forward) that we become human, seeing ourselves through the eyes of others as others see themselves through ours. I have experienced the grace of such love in relationships in which we, the lovers, have found ourselves though what Plato called the mirror of those who loved us, entering deeply into our psyches as we enter theirs. We find ourselves as

138. Coogan, *New Oxford Bible,*1942, John 13:16–17.

139. Coogan, *New Oxford Bible,* 1943, John 13: 34–36.

140. See Rodman, *Winnicott.*

141. See Rohr, *Universal Christ,* 226–29.

persons in loving relationship to other persons, and such free and equal love crosses all the boundaries that conventionally divide and balkanize our communities. It may be one way of understanding or making contemporary sense of what Jesus of Nazareth meant when he called us "to love your neighbor as you love yourself,"[142] transcending the polarities of both guilt and shame ethics. I am not conventionally religious, but Jesus's appeal to interpersonal love ministering to those Simone Weil called the afflicted, among whom she included criminals,[143] as well as his call for a nonviolence of listening and dialogue and an egalitarian ethics, deeply move me, as it has moved many, religious and non-religious, to find their liberalism of human rights within the ongoing project Tom Holland has called "the Christian Revolution."[144] The very idea of God becoming human (the incarnation) and sharing our vulnerabilities and sufferings bespeaks an antipatriarchal love of equals in the intimate space or our most intimate and creative personal loving relationships, an image of the divine defined by empathy, whose humility in becoming our equals reveals what the love of equals is and calls for, as Shakespeare shows us in Lear's struggle, as an absolute monarch and warrior, to repudiate hierarchy and through the experience of love becoming human. The emphasis on humility is surely one of the most striking features of Jesus's teaching: "learn from me; for I am gentle and humble in heart,"[145] "All who exalt themselves will be humbled, and all who humble themselves shall be exalted."[146] Isabel Wilkerson correctly distinguishes pity ("looking down from above") from the role of humility in "radical empathy . . . [which] means putting in the work to educate oneself and to listen with a humble heart to understand another's experience from their perspective not as we imagine we would feel."[147]

Kant may have had this in mind when he argues that Jesus's "union with us may therefore be regarded as a state of *abasement* of the Son of God if we represent to ourselves this God-like human being, our

142. Coogan, *New Oxford Bible*, 1854, Mark 12:31.

143. "Men think they are despising crime when they are really despising the weakness of affliction. A being in whom the two are combined affords them an opportunity of giving free play to their contempt for afflictions on the pretext that they are scorning crime. He is thus the object of the greatest contempt. Contempt is the contrary of attention" (Weil, *Waiting for God*, 95).

144. See Holland, *Dominion*. See also Siedentop, *Inventing the Individual.*

145. Coogan, *New Oxford Bible*, 1799, Matt 11:29.

146. Coogan, *New Oxford Bible*, 1817, Matt 23:12.

147. Wilkerson, *Caste*, 386.

prototype [for an ethics of equal respect], in such a way that, though himself holy and hence not bound to submit to sufferings, he nonetheless takes these upon himself"[148] (in effect, questioning the role hierarchy had played in earlier conceptions of ethics, including utilitarianism[149]). What moved so many in Christianity was precisely its development of a guilt ethics that questioned patriarchy's endorsement of the abject status of slaves and the subjection of women ("It is highly likely that women were a clear majority in the churches of the third century"[150]), and it has moved me as well, both as a child and as an adult. But I have been critical of the role a form of unjust sacrifice of the self has played in the guilt ethics developed by Christian thinkers like Augustine and Luther and ostensibly post-Christian thinkers like Kant, as well as in the masochistic personality of Simone Weil herself.[151] The experience of the love of equals has shown me an alternative way to transcend the objectionable polarities of guilt and shame cultures that tempt many to political religions that are deeply unjust and inhuman.

It strikes me that these views, both inspired by and yet critical of Christian and post-Christian thinkers, may themselves be better understood and even illuminated by seeing them as reflecting longstanding concerns strikingly similar in some respects to a radical critic of religion, politics, and science like the poet and artist William Blake.[152] Blake indicted the moralism of his late eighteenth- and early-nineteenth-century British culture, as I do our twenty-first-century American culture, precisely because it enforced repressive patriarchal codes that used a misogynist denigration of sexual love to rationalize retributive violence in personal and public life.[153] Blake thought of great artists like Shakespeare and

148. Kant, *Religion Within the Boundaries of Mere Reason*, 104.

149. Even utilitarianism, for Kant, because it subordinated the interests of the few to the aggregate interests of the many, violated his understanding of equal respect, requiring human rights that could not be abridged on utilitarian grounds. Rawls has this idea in mind, I believe, when he criticizes utilitarianism because "it does not take seriously the distinction between persons," Rawls, *Theory of Justice*, 27.

150. Fox, *Pagans and Christians*, 310.

151. See, on this point, Toril Moi, "I Came With a Sword."

152. See, for illuminating interpreters of Blake's art along these lines, Frye, *Fearful Symmetry*; Bloom, *Blake's Apocalypse*; Bloom, *William Blake*; Eaves, *Cambridge Companion to William Blake*. For an excellent biography, see Ackroyd, *Blake*.

153. For Blake's critique of the mysterious Christian God as "Nobodaddy," Blake, *Complete Poetry and Prose*, 471–47. On "cruel Patriarchal pride," see 173, and the role of "strong & mighty Shame" in enforcing its demands, 153, including the destruction of love through repressive codes of "cold chastity," 161, and the connection of such

Milton as prophetic because their art shows how the exercise of our imaginative powers in love of others in art enlarges our moral imaginations about how to understand and resist a culture based on unjust violence, as Shakespeare's art clearly does.[154] Blake argued, as I do, that this requires not the denial of ethics, but a shift in the understanding of what ethics is, a shift that centers in the love of equals in relationship across the patriarchal boundaries that divide us.

Unlike Blake, however, my argument is not hostile to science, but based on the forms of the empirical human sciences that were seminally developed by Darwin, Marx, and Freud, but my interest in patriarchy was not shared by any of these inspiring human scientists, and I am critical of them for this reason, not seeing the persistence of patriarchy as the central problem in human culture, an impediment to human progress and indeed hostile to such progress. But, perhaps the most interesting difference between my views and these thinkers is my disagreement with Freud, whose discovery of transference love is the basis of my over-all argument. It was Freud, so otherwise hostile to conventional religion, who urged thinking more psychologically about religion as "a therapeutic attempt"[155] to give a foundation to ethics. Freud saw that "equal love was expressly enunciated by Christ: 'Inasmuch as ye have done it have done unto one of the least of my brethren, ye have done it under me,'" and saw as well his "democratic strain."[156] But, he questioned Jesus's ethics of love as a prescription because it failed to take seriously the biological drive to aggression (harming both others and the self).[157]

In contrast, Jim Gilligan has offered an alternative, more plausible cultural-psychological view, of violence arising from the shaming of patriarchal manhood and the cultural practices that so damage our needs for love and self-esteem, and thus rationalize violence as, like Freud, in

repression to violence, "I am drunk with unsatiated love/I must rush again to War: for the Virgin has frownd & refusd," 222. And, on retributive moralism, "And he who takes vengeance alone if the criminal of Providence;/'If I should dare to lay my finger on a grain of sand/In way of vengeance; I punish the already punishd: O whom/Should I pity if I pity not the sinner who has gone astray," 194, and its Manichean binaries, failing to see "Every Harlot was once a Virgin: every Criminal an Infant Love!," 212, and the wanton cruelties of criminal justice to which a loving god demands alternatives, "Tho thou art taken to prison & judgment, starved in the streets/I will command the cloud to give thee food & the hard rock/To flow with milk & wine," 213.

154. For a powerful similar argument, see Shelley, "Defence of Poetry."

155. See Freud, *Civilization and Its Discontents*, 142.

156. Freud, *Group Psychology*, 94.

157. See Freud, *Civilization and Its Discontents*, 109–10.

the nature of things. This view of love is thus based on factual experience, including what Gilligan found in his therapeutic work with violent criminals. It is a view that leads not to Freud's naturalization of violence and appeal to autocracy, but to empirically based views, like those of Thucydides critical of the Athenian majoritarian democracy and Kant on a liberal democracy of human rights and Gilligan on prisons and the unjust inequalities and corruptions of democracy they perpetuate,[158] all of which can, in light of the argument of this book, be understood as addressing how patriarchal culture must be seen and criticized and constitutional democracy fostered.

It is on the basis of experience that I offer the love of equals as a psychological alternative to the polarities of guilt ethics in Kant and shame ethics in Nietzsche, and question the role patriarchy has played in retarding, indeed killing, love and empathy as the psychological basis of ethics. I am thus doing what Freud urged, interpreting religion psychologically as "a therapeutic attempt," offering love, in the sense developed in this book, as such an empirically grounded therapy. As I argued in my discussions of Augustine, love as empathy (treating persons as equals) was, in my view, the heart of Christianity's appeal for Augustine and others, as one can see in the role the Platonic role of love's mirror plays in Augustine's thought. But, if I am right, patriarchy has corrupted and distorted Christianity's mirror of love (explaining why, in Paul's words, "now we see in a mirror, dimly, but then we see will see face to face"[159]). Paul has in mind, as do Augustine and Thomas Aquinas, that we will only see God "face to face" (the *visio dei*) in an afterlife no longer burdened by our corrupting bodies and sexuality. If Paul is quite disastrously wrong about our sexuality and its corruption of an ethically defensible human love, as I believe, we can experience such love here and now face to face, the face of those we love as equals.[160] But, to do so, we must come to understand how patriarchy has distorted not only religion, but much else in our traditions, and we cannot understand or give effect to our most defensible values, including the mirror of love and its place in ethics and

158. See, on this point Gilligan, *Why Some Politicians are More Dangerous than Others*.

159. Coogan, *New Oxford Bible*, 2054, 1 Cor 13:12.

160. It is a love connected to ethics and courage, of which a Holocaust survivor wrote in a letter to her children about those who did not survive: "Their voices did not bleat like sheep. Their voices told of victory overcoming evil by dying like men without somebody's blood on their hands," cited in Hedges, *Greatest Evil Is War*, 158.

religion and liberal democracy, until we take seriously the dimensions of the problem we face, in particular, the problem of patriarchally endorsed violence in our public and private lives, a violence that kills love and through the resulting death of self (as the self is brought to life and lives through love) mindlessly perpetuates itself in an unending cycle of Roman violence and idealization of war at home and abroad.[161]

Many—both religious and, like myself, nonreligious—find Jesus one of the most compelling figures in human history. That is certainly my experience and I believe the experience of many others, religious and nonreligious. I came to my view of Jesus in this book from an outsider's perspective, as a gay and nonreligious man, because, as I show at the beginning of my argument, Winnicott's understanding of psychoanalysis so illuminated my own life and struggles to equal love. Many in our increasingly secular society share either this or related perspectives, religious or not. Yet, like me, they may find in this book how and why Jesus so moves them, as he moves me, and even how and why—given the hegemonic power of patriarchy in human history and in the life and times of Jesus and the subsequent history of Christianities and even today—he has been so difficult to see face to face, and yet moves something deep in our human natures, the love of equals that he believed was coming into existence through his life and teaching. From this perspective, the life and teaching of the antipatriarchal Jesus rest on a deep psychological truth of our human nature—our need for love that exists and moves us despite the cultural forms that would disfigure and repress it. And it rests as well on an ethical truth, rooted in the role of love in human nature, that we are most human when we treat other persons as equals.

In living and teaching as he did, Jesus, in my view, nonviolently resisted one of the ancient world's most successful and violent hegemonic patriarchies, and was killed for it, as, in the ancient world, Socrates was killed (nonviolently resisting an ostensibly democratic patriarchy), and, in the modern world, Martin Luther King Jr. and Mohandas Gandhi were murdered (nonviolently resisting other democratically flawed, violent patriarchies). The tragic paradox of the historical Christianities of Augustine and Luther is that, in accommodating themselves to the Roman patriarchy that killed Jesus, they have buried the antipatriarchal Jesus. Constitutional democracy (inspired, as we have seen, by heterodox Christianities that resist patriarchy) calls for nonviolent deliberative

161. On the idealization of war, see Hedges, *Greatest Evil Is War.*

democratic voice to resolve conflict, a voice, like that of Jesus, that fundamentally threatens patriarchy, resting, as it does, on violence. It is for this reason that liberal democracy, more than ever, rests on deliberative voice, the foundation of universal human rights, a voice that exposes the injustices that rest on the violent repression of voice, and thus resists injustice, as both Jesus and Socrates did.

Bibliography

Ackroyd, Peter. *Blake: a Biography*. New York: Ballantine, 1995.

Adair, Douglass. *Fame and the Founding Fathers*. New York: Norton, 1974.

Adorno, Theodore. *Minima Moralia: Reflections from Damaged* Life. Translated by E. F. N. Jephcott. London: Verso, 1974.

Adorno, T. W., et al. *The Authoritarian Personality*. New York: Harper & Row, 1950.

Ainsworth, Mary S., and John Bowlby. "An Ethnological Approach to Personality Development." *American Psychologist* 46 (1991) 333–41.

Aisenstein, Marila, and Elsa Rappoport de Aisenberg. *Psychosomatics Today: A Psychoanalytic Perspective*. London: Routledge, 2022.

à Kempis, Thomas. *The Imitation of Christ*. Translated by John C. Graham. John C. Graham, 2023.

Altemeyer, Bob. *Authoritarian Specter*. Cambridge, MA: Harvard University Press, 1996.

———. *Right-Wing Authoritarianism*. Manitoba, Canada: The University of Manitoba Press, 1981.

Appignanesi, Lisa, and John Forrester. *Freud's Women*. New York: Other Press, 2001.

Arendt, Hannah. *Lectures on Kant's Political Philosophy*. Edited by Ronald Beiner. Chicago: University of Chicago Press, 1992.

———. *Life of the Mind*. San Diego, CA: A Harvest/HBJ Book, 1971.

———. *On Revolution*. New York: Penguin, 1963.

———. *Origins of Totalitarianism*. Repr. Orlando: A Harvest Book, 1976.

———. *Responsibility and Judgment*. Edited by Jerome Cohn. New York: Schocken, 2003.

———. *Thinking Without a Banister: Essays in Understanding 1953–2003*. New York: Schocken, 2018.

Aristotle. *Categories*. In *The Complete Works of Aristotle*, edited by Jonathan Barnes, 1:3–24. Princeton: Princeton University Press, 1984.

———. *Eudemian Ethics*. In *The Complete Works of Aristotle*, edited by Jonathan Barnes, 2:1922–81. Princeton: Princeton University Press, 1984.

———. *Metaphysics*. In *The Complete Works of Aristotle*, edited by Jonathan Barnes, 2:1552–728. Princeton: Princeton University Press, 1984.

———. *Nicomachean Ethics*. In *The Complete Works of Aristotle*, edited by Jonathan Barnes, 2:1729–867. Princeton: Princeton University Press, 1984.

———. *Poetics*. Translated by Malcolm Heath. London: Penguin, 1996.

———. *Politics.* In *The Complete Works of Aristotle*, Translated and edited by Jonathan Barnes, 2:1968–2129. Princeton: Princeton University Press, 1984.

Astin, A. E., et al. *The Cambridge Ancient History Second Edition Volume VIII Rome and the Mediterranean to 133 B.C.E.* Cambridge: Cambridge University Press, 1989.

Atack, Carol. *Plato: A Civic Life.* London: Reaktion, 2025.

Augustine. *City of God.* Translated by Henry Bettenson Harmondsworth. Middlesex: Penguin, 1972.

———. *Confessions.* Translated by Henry Chadwick. Oxford: Oxford University Press, 2008.

———. *Homilies on the Gospel of John. Homilies on the First Epistle of John. Soliloquies I.* Edited by Philip Schaff and Henry Wace. A Select Library of Nicene and Post-Nicene Fathers of the Christian Church, Second Series 7. Grand Rapids, MI: Eerdmans, 1978–1979.

———. "Homily 7 on the First Epistle of John." Edited by Philip Schaff and translated by H. Browne. Nicene and Post-Nicene Fathers, First Series 7. Buffalo, NY: Christian Literature Publishing Co., 1888. Revised and edited for New Advent by Kevin Knight. http://www.newadvent.org/fathers/170207.htm.

———. *Literal Meaning of Genesis, Volume 2.* Translated by John Hammond Taylor. New York: Newman, 1958.

———. *On the Trinity, Books IX–XV.* Edited by Philip Schaff and translated by Arthur West Haddan. Nicene and Post-Nicene Fathers, First Series 3. Tyler, TX: Veritatis Splendor, 2021.

Austin, J. L. *Sense and Sensibilia.* London: Oxford University Press, 1962.

Bach, J. S. *Matthaus Passion.* Peter Schreier, with Theo Adam et al. Full opera vocal score and libretto. Recorded 1984. Philips 4757761, compact disc.

Bailyn, Bernard. *The Ideological Origins of the American Revolution.* Cambridge, MA: Harvard University Press, 1967.

Bakan, David. *Sigmund Freud and the Jewish Mystical Tradition.* Princeton, NJ: Van Nostrand, 1958.

Bamforth, Nicholas C., and David A. J. Richards. *Patriarchal Religion, Sexuality, and Gender: A Critique of New Natural Law.* Cambridge: Cambridge University Press, 2008.

Barbu, Zevedei. *Problems of Historical Psychology.* New York: Grove, 1960.

Barrett, Anthony A. *Agrippina: Sex, Power and Politics in the Early Empire.* New Haven, CT: Yale University Press,1996.

———. *Livia: First Lady of Imperial Rome.* New Haven, CT: Yale University Press, 2002.

Baudry, Francis. "Winnicott's 1968 Visit to the New York Psychoanalytic Society and Institute: A Contextual View." *The Psychoanalytic Quarterly* 77 (2009) 1059–90.

Bauman, Richard A. *Women and Politics in Ancient Rome.* London: Routledge, 1992.

Beard, Mary. "Priesthood in the Roman Republic." In *Pagan Priests: Religion and Power in the Ancient World*, edited by Mary Beard and John North, 17–48. Ithaca, NY: Cornell University Press, 1990.

Beele, Beatrice, et al. *Infant Research and Psychoanalysis.* Leece, Italy: Frenis Zero, 2018.

Bellah, Robert N. *Religion in Human Evolution: From the Paleolithic to the Axial Age.* Cambridge, MA: Harvard University Press, 2011.

Bellah, Robert N., and Hans Joas. *The Axial Age and Its Consequences.* Cambridge, MA: Harvard University Press, 2012.

Benedict, Ruth. *Chrysanthemum and the Sword: Patterns of Japanese Culture*. Repr. Boston: A Mariner Book, 2005.

———. *Patterns of Culture*. Repr. Boston: Houghton Mifflin Company, 2005.

Benjamin, Jessica. *Bonds of Love: Psychoanalysis, Feminism, and the Problem of Domination*. New York: Pantheon, 1988.

———. *Shadow of the Other: Intersubjectivity and Gender in Psychoanalysis*. New York: Routledge, 1998.

Blackstone, William. *Commentaries on the Laws of England*. Repr. Chicago: University of Chicago Press, 1979.

Blake, William. *The Complete Poetry and Prose of William Blake*. Edited by David V. Erdman. Berkeley: University of California Press, 2008.

Bloom, Harold. *Blake's Apocalypse: a Study in Poetic Argument*. Ithaca: Cornell University Press, 1963.

———. *William Blake*. New York: Chelsea House, 1985.

Boas, Franz. *Kwakiutl Ethography*. Chicago: University of Chicago Ethnography, 1966.

———. *Mind of Primitive Man*. Repr. London: Forgotten Books, 2012.

Borg, Marcus J. *The God We Never Knew*. New York: HarperOne, 1998.

———. *Meeting Jesus Again for the First Time: The Historical Jesus and the Heart of Contemporary Faith*. New York: HarperCollins, 1994.

Boyarin, Daniel. *Carnal Israel: Reading Sex in Talmudic Culture*. Berkeley: University of California Press, 1993.

Bowlby, John. *Attachment and Loss*. New York: Basic, 1980.

Bowman, Alan K., et al. *The Cambridge Ancient History Second Edition, Volume X, The Augustan Empire, 43 B.C.E.-A.D. 69*. Cambridge: Cambridge University Press, 1996.

Bowman, Alan K., et al. *The Cambridge Ancient History, Volume XI: The High Empire, A.D. 70–192*. Cambridge: Cambridge University Press, 2000.

Bowman, Ian K., et al. *The Cambridge Ancient History, Volume XII: The Crisis of Empire, A.D. 193–337*. 2nd ed. Cambridge: Cambridge University Press, 2005.

Brajelton, T. Berry. *The Neonatal Behavioural Assessment Scale*. 3rd ed. London: MacKeither, 1995.

Brooten, Bernadette J. *Love Between Women: Early Christian Responses to Female Homoeroticism*. Chicago: University of Chicago Press, 1996.

Brown, Lyn Mikel, and Carol Gilligan. *Meeting at the Crossroads: Women's Psychology and Girls' Development*. Cambridge, MA: Harvard University Press, 1992.

Brown, Norman O. *Life Against Death: The Psychoanalytical Meaning of History*. 2nd ed. Middletown, CT: Wesleyan University Press, 1985.

———. *Love's Body*. Berkeley: University of California Press, 1966.

Brown, Peter. *Augustine of Hippo: A Biography*. Repr. Berkeley: University of California Press, 2000.

———. *The Body and Society: Men, Women, and Sexual Renunciation in Early Christianity*. New York: Columbia University Press, 1988.

Bruner, Jerome. *Actual Minds, Possible Worlds*. Cambridge, MA: Harvard University Press, 1986.

Buber, Martin. *I and Thou*. Victoria, BC: Must Have, 2021.

———. *Two Types of Faith*. Translated by Norman P. Goldhawk. Syracuse: University of Syracuse Press, 2003.

Bultmann, Rudolf. *Gospel of John: A Commentary*. Translated by G. R. Beasley-Murray. Oxford: Basil Blackwell, 1972.

———. *History of the Synoptic Tradition*. Translated by John Marsh. Oxford: Basil Blackwell, 1968.

———. *Jesus Christ and Mythology*. New York: Charles Scribner's Sons, 1958.

———. *Theology of the New Testament*. Translated by Kendrick Grobel. Waco, TX: Baylor University Press, 2007.

Burghardt, Gordon M. *The Genesis of Animal Play: Testing the Limits*. Cambridge, MA: MIT Press, 2005.

Buruma, Ian. *The Wages of Guilt: Memories of War in Germany and Japan*. Repr. New York: New York Review Book, 2015.

Buttrick, David. *Speaking Jesus: Homiletic Theology and the Sermon on the Mount*. Louisville, KY: Westminster John Knox, 2002.

Cameron, Averil, and Peter Garnsey. *The Cambridge Ancient History Volume XIII The Late Empire, A.D. 337–425*. Cambridge: Cambridge University Press, 1998.

Cantarella, Eva. *Pandora's Daughters: The Role and Status of Women in Greek and Roman Antiquity*. Translated by Maureen B. Fant. Baltimore: The Johns Hopkins University Press, 1987.

Capps, Donald. *Erik Erikson's Verbal Portraits: Luther, Gandhi, Einstein, Jesus*. Landham, MD: Rowman & Littlefield, 2014.

Carveth, Donald L. *The Still Small Voice: Psychoanalytic Reflections on Guilt and Conscience*. Repr. London: Routledge, 2018.

Cassidy, Jude, and Philip R. Shaver, eds. *Handbook of Attachment Theory: Theory, Research, and Clinical Application*. 2nd ed. New York: Guilford, 2008.

Champlin, Edward. *Nero*. Cambridge, MA: Belknap Press of Harvard University Press, 2003.

Chenoweth, Erica. *Why Civil Resistance Works: The Strategic Logic of Nonviolent Conflict*. New York: Columbia University Press, 2011.

Chodorow, Nancy J. *The Reproduction of Mothering*. Berkeley: University of California Press, 1999.

Chu, Judy. *When Boys Become "Boys."* New York: New York University Press, 2013.

Cohen, Josh. *All the Rage: Why Anger Drives the World*. London: Granta, 2024.

Congdon, David W. *Rudolph Bultmann: A Companion to His Theology*. Eugene, OR: Cascade, 2015.

Coogan, Michael D., ed. *New Oxford Annotated Bible*. 5th ed. Oxford: Oxford University Press, 2010.

Cooley, Charles Horton. *Human Nature and the Social Order*. Repr. New Brunswick: Transaction, 2009.

Critchley, Simon. *Mysticism*. New York: New York Review Books, 2024.

Crook, J. A., et al. *The Cambridge Ancient History Second Edition, Volume IX, The Last Age of the Roman Republic, 146–43 B.C.E.* Cambridge: Cambridge University Press, 1994.

Crossan, John Dominic. *God and Empire: Jesus Against Rome Then and Now*. New York: HarperCollins, 2008.

———. *The Historical Jesus: The Life of a Mediterranean Jewish Peasant*. New York: HarperCollins, 1992.

———. *Jesus: A Revolutionary Biography*. New York: HarperCollins, 1994.

Daly, Mary. *Beyond God the Father: Toward a Philosophy of Women's Liberation*. Boston: Beacon, 1973.

———. *The Church and the Second Sex*. Repr. Boston: Beacon, 1985.

Darwall, Stephen. *The Second-Person Standpoint: Morality, Respect, and Accountability.* Cambridge, MA: Harvard University Press, 2006.

Dinnerstein, Dorothy. *The Mermaid and the Minotaur.* New York: Other Press, 1999.

Dixon, Suzanne. *The Roman Family.* Baltimore: The Johns Hopkins University Press, 1992.

———. *The Roman Mother. Norman, Oklahoma; Oklahoma University Press, 1988.*

———. *Reading Roman Women.* London: Duckworth, 2001.

Dodd, C. H. *The Parables of the Kingdom.* London: Collins, 1961.

Dodds, E. R. *The Greeks and the Irrational.* Berkeley: University of California Press, 1959.

Donald, Merlin. *A Mind So Rare: The Evolution of Human Consciousness.* New York: W.W. Norton, 2001.

———. *Origins of the Modern Mind: Three Stages in the Evolution of Culture and Cognition.* Cambridge, MA: Harvard University Press, 1991.

Dostoyevsky, Fyodor. *The Brothers Karamazov* Translated by David McDuff. London: Penguin, 2003.

Doyle, Michael M. "Kant, Liberal Legacies, and Foreign Affairs." *Philosophy and Public Affairs* 12 (1983) 205–235.

———. *Ways of War and Peace: Realism, Liberalism, and Socialism.* New York: Norton, 1997.

Du Mez, Kristin Kobes. *Jesus and John Wayne: How White Evangelicals Corrupted a Faith and Fractured a Nation.* New York: Liveright, 2021.

Eaton, Joseph W., and Robert J. Weil. *Culture and Mental Disorders: A Comparative Study of the Hutterites and Other Populations.* New York: The Free Press, 1955.

Eaves, Morris. *The Cambridge Companion to William Blake.* Cambridge: Cambridge University Press, 2003.

Ehrman, Bart D. *Jesus: Apocalyptic Prophet of the New Millennium.* New York: Oxford University Press, 1999.

Eliot, George. *Scenes of Clerical Life.* Edited by Thomas A. Noble. Oxford: Oxford University Press, 2015.

Erikson, Erik H. *Childhood and Society.* New York: W.W. Norton, 1993.

———. "The Galilean Sayings and the Sense of 'I.'" *Psychoanalysis and Contemporary Thought* 19 (1996) 291–337.

———. *Young Man Luther: A Study in Psychoanalysis and History.* New York: W.W. Norton, 1993.

Evans, John K. *War, Women and Children in Ancient Rome.* London: Routledge, 1991.

Everitt, Anthony. *Augustus: The Life of Rome's First Emperor.* New York: Random House, 2006.

———. *Cicero: The Life and Times of Rome's Greatest Politician.* New York: Random House, 2003.

Eyben, Emiel. "Fathers and Sons." In *Marriage, Divorce, and Children in Ancient Rome,* edited by Beryl Rawson, 14–143. Oxford: Clarendon, 2004.

Ferenczi, Sandor. "Confusion of Tongues Between Adult and Child." *International Journal of Psychoanalysis* (1949), 30, 225.

Ferenczi, Sandor, et al. *Psycho-Analysis and the War Neuroses.* Repr. London: Forgotten Books, 2012.

Feuerbach, Ludwig. *Essence of Christianity.* Translated by George Eliot. Repr. Amherst, NY: Prometheus, 1989.

Fisher, David. *Morality and War: Can War be Just in the Twenty-First Century.* Oxford: Oxford University Press, 2011.

Ford, Clellan S., and Frank A. Beach. *Patterns of Sexual Behavior.* New York: Harper & Row, 1959.

Ford, Richard Q. *Jesus' Parables Speak to Power and Greed: Confronting Climate Change Denial.* Eugene, OR: Cascade, 2022.

———. *The Parables of Jesus: Recovering the Art of Listening.* Minneapolis: Fortress, 1997.

Fox, Robin Lane. *Pagans and Christians.* New York: Alfred A. Knopf, 1987.

Fredriksen, Paula. *Ancient Christianities: The First Hundred Years.* Princeton: Princeton University Press, 2024.

———. *From Jesus to Christ.* 2nd ed. New Haven, CT: Yale University Press,1988.

———. *When Christians Were Jews: The First Generation.* New Haven, CT: Yale University Press, 2018.

Freud, Sigmund. "Analysis Terminable and Interminable." In *The Standard Edition of the Complete Psychological Works of Sigmund Freud,* translated by James Strachey, 23:216–53. London: The Hogarth Press,1964.

———. *Beyond the Pleasure Principle.* In *The Standard Edition of the Complete Psychological Works of Sigmund Freud,* translated and edited by James Strachey, 17:7–64. London: The Hogarth, 1955.

———. *Civilization and Its Discontents.* In *The Standard Edition of the Complete Works Psychological Works of Sigmund Freud,* translated and edited by James Strachey, 21:64–145. London: the Hogarth Press, 1961.

———. "'Civilized' Sexual Morality and Modern Nervous Illness." In *The Standard Edition of the Complete Psychological Works of Sigmund Freud,* translated and edited by James Strachey, 9:181–204. London: The Hogarth, 1959.

———. "The Dynamics of Transference." In *Standard Edition of the Complete Psychological Works of Sigmund Freud,* translated and edited by James Strachey, 12:99–108. London: The Hogarth, 1958.

———. "Editor's Introduction." In *The Standard Edition of the Complete Psychological Works of Sigmund Freud,* translated and edited by James Strachey, 2:ix–xxviii. London: The Hogarth, 1959.

———. *Future of an Illusion.* In *The Standard Edition of the Complete Psychological Works of Sigmund Freud,* translated by James Strachey, 21:5–56. London: The Hogarth, 1961.

———. *Group Psychology and the Analysis of the Ego.* In *The Standard Edition of the Complete Psychological Works of Sigmund Freud,* translated and edited by James Strachey, 18:69–143. London: The Hogarth, 1955.

———. "A Letter from Freud (to the Mother of a Homosexual)." Wikisource. https://en.wikisource.org/wiki/A_Letter_from_Freud_(to_a_mother_of_a_homosexual).

———. "Observations on Transference-Love." In *Standard Edition of the Complete Psychological Works of Sigmund Freud,* translated and edited by James Strachey 12:157–171. London: The Hogarth, 1958.

———. "Psychopathic Characters on the Stage." In *Standard Edition of the Complete Psychological Works of Sigmund Freud,* translated and edited by James Strachey, 7:305–310. London: The Hogarth, 1958.

———. "Recommendations to Physicians Practising Psycho-Analysis." In *Standard Edition of the Complete Psychological Works of Sigmund Freud*, translated and edited by James Strachey, 7:1011–120. London: The Hogarth, 1958.

———. "Remembering, Repeating and Working-through." In *Standard Edition of the Complete Psychological Works of Sigmund Freud*, translated and edited by James Strachey, 7:147–56. London: The Hogarth, 1959.

———. *Studies on Hysteria*. In *The Standard Edition of the Psychological Works of Sigmund Freud*, translated and edited by James Strachey, 2:1–306. London: The Hogarth, 1973.

———. *Why War?* In Sigmund Freud, *The Standard Edition of the Complete Psychological Works of Sigmund Freud*, translated and edited by James Strachey, 22:197–218. London: The Hogarth, 1964.

Fromm, Erich H. *The Art of Loving*. Repr. New York: Harperperennial, 2006.

———. *Escape from Freedom*. Repr. New York: Henry Holt and Company, 1965.

———. *Man for Himself: An Inquiry into the Psychology of Ethics*. Repr. New York: Henry Holt and Company, 1990.

———. *Sane Society*. Repr. New York: Henry Holt and Company, 1990.

Frst, Joachim. *Hitler*. New York: Vintage, 1975.

Frye, Northrop. *Fearful Symmetry: A Study of William Blake*. Princeton: Princeton University Press, 1969.

Funk, Robert W., and the Jesus Seminar. *The Acts of Jesus: What Did Really Do?* New York: HarperCollins, 1998.

Funk, Robert W., et al. *The Gospel of Jesus According to the Jesus Seminar*. 2nd ed. Salem, OR: Polebridge, 2015.

Funk, Robert W., et al. *The Parables of Jesus Red Letter Edition The Jesus Seminar*. Salem, OR: Polebridge, 1988.

Funk, Robert W., et al. *The Five Gospels: What Did Jesus Really Say?* New York: HarperCollins, 1997.

Gabriel, Trip. "Richard B. Hayes, 76, Dies; Theologian Had a Stunning Change of Heart." *New York Times* (January 26, 2025) B10.

Gardner, Jane F. *Women in Roman Law and Society*. Bloomington: Indiana University Press, 1995.

Garff, Joakim. *Soren Kierkegaard: A Biography*. Translated by Bruce H. Kirmmse. Princeton: Princeton University Press, 2005.

Gibbon, Edward. *Decline and Fall of the Roman Empire*. 3 vols. New York: The Modern Library, 1977.

Gifford, Carolyn De Swarte. "Politicizing the Sacred Texts: Elizabeth Cady Stanton's *The Woman's Bible*." In *Searching the Scriptures: A Feminist Introduction Volume One*, edited by Elisabeth Schüssler Fiorenza, 52–63. New York Crossroad, 1993.

Gilligan, Carol. *Birth of Pleasure*. New York: Alfred A. Knopf, 2002.

———. *In a Different Voice: Psychological Theory and Women's Development*. Cambridge, MA: Harvard University Press, 1982.

———. *In a Human Voice*. Cambridge: Polity, 2023.

———. "Moral Injury and the Ethic of Care: Reframing the Conversation about Differences." *Journal of Social Philosophy* 45 (2014) 89–106.

Gilligan, Carol, and Naomi Snider. *Why Does Patriarchy Persist?* Cambridge: Polity, 2018.

Gilligan, Carol, and David A. J. Richards. *Darkness Now Visible: Patriarchy's Resurgence and Feminist Resistance.* Cambridge: Cambridge University Press, 2018.

———.*Deepening Darkness: Patriarchy, Resistance, and Democracy's Future.* Cambridge: Cambridge University Press, 2009.

Gilligan, James. *Preventing Violence.* New York: Thames & Hudson, 2001.

———.*Terrorism, Fundamentalism and Nihilism: Analyzing the Dilemmas of Modernity."* In *The Future of Prejudice: Applications of Psychoanalytic Understanding toward Its Prevention,* edited by Henri Parens and Stuart Twemlow, 37–62. New York: Rowman & Littlefield, 2006.

———. *Violence: Reflections on a National Epidemic.* New York: Vintage, 1997.

———. *Why Some Politicians Are More Dangerous Than Others.* Cambridge: Polity, 2011.

Gilligan, James, and David A. J. Richards. *Holding a Mirror up to Nature.* Cambridge: Cambridge University Press, 2022.

Gilmore, David D. *Manhood in the Making: Cultural Concepts of Masculinity.* New Haven, CT: Yale University Press, 1990.

Girard, Rene. *All Desire If a Desire For Being.* Essential Writings Selected by Cynthia L. Haven. London: Penguiin, 2023.

Goff, Philip. *Why?: The Purpose of the University.* Oxford: Oxford University Press, 2023.

Goldberg, Susan, et al., eds. *Attachment Theory: Social, Developmental, and Clinical Perspectives.* Hills, NJ: The Analytic, 2000.

Goldsworthy, Adrian. *Caesar: Life of a Colossus.* New Haven, CT: Yale University Press, 2006.

Gopnik, Alison. *Philosophical Baby: What Children's Minds Tell Us About Truth, Love, and the Meaning of Life.* New York: Farrar, Straus and Giroux, 2009.

Graves, Robert. *King Jesus: A Novel.* New York: Farrar Straus Giroux 1946.

———. *White Goddess: A Historical Grammar of Poetic Myth.* Repr. New York: Farrar, Straus and Giroux, 1997.

Graves, Robert, and Joshua Podro. *Jesus in Rome.* London: Cassell & Company, 1957.

———.*Nazarene Gospel Restored.* London: Cassell and Company, 1953.

Guntrip, Harry. "My Experience of Analysis with Fairbairn and Winnicott." *Int. J. Psycho-Anal* (1996) 77, 739–754.

Hallett, Judith P. *Fathers and Daughters in Roman Society: Women and the Elite Family* Princeton: Princeton University Press, 1984.

Hamilton, Alexander, et al. *The Federalist.* Edited by Terence Ball. Cambridge: Cambridge University Press, 2007.

Hannay, Alastair. *Kierkegaard: A Biography.* Cambridge: Cambridge University Press, 2001.

Harris, William V. *War and Imperialism in Republic Rome* 327–70 *B.*Vermes, .*A.* Oxford: Clarendon, 1965.

Hart, H. L. A. *Punishment and Responsibility: Essays in the Philosophy of Law.* 2nd ed. Oxford: Oxford University Press, 2008.

Hayes, Christopher B., and Richard B. Hays. *The Widening of God's Mercy: Sexuality Within the Biblical Story.* New Haven, CT: Yale University Press, 2024.

Heather, Peter. *Christendom: The Triumph of Religion, AD* 300–1300. New York: Alfred A. Knopf, 2023.

Hedges, Chris. *Greatest Evil Is War.* New York: Seven Stories, 2022.

Hegel, G. W. F. *Phenomenology of Spirit.* Translated by A. V. Miller. Oxford: Oxford University Press, 1977.

Hengel, Martin. *The Charismatic Leader and His Followers.* Translated by James Greig Eugene, OR: Wipf & Stock, 2005.

Herman, Judith L. *Trauma and Recovery—from Domestic Abuse to Political Terror.* NewYork: Basic, 1992.

———. *Truth and Repair: How Trauma Survivors Envision Justice.* New York: Basic, 2023.

Hick, John. *An Interpretation of Religion: Human Responses to the Transcendent* 2nd ed. New Haven, CT: Yale University Press, 2004.

———. "An Irenaean Theodicy." In *Philosophy of Religion: The Big Questions,* edited by Eleanor Stump and Michael J. Murray, 222–27. Oxford: Blackwell, 1999.

Hitler, Adolf. *Mein Kampf.* Boston: Houghton Mifflin, 1962.

Holland, Tom. *Dominion: How the Christian Revolution Remade the World.* New York: Basic, 2019.

Holmes, Jeremy. *John Bowlby and Attachment Theory.* 2nd ed. New York: Routledge, 2014.

Horkheimer, Max. *Eclipse of Reason.* New York: Oxford University Press, 1949.

Horkheimer, Max, and Theodor W. Adorno. *Dialectic of Enlightenment: Philosophical Fragments.* Translated by Gunzelin Schmid Noerr. Stanford: Stanford University Press, 2002.

Hrdy, Sarah Blaffer. *Father Time: A Natural History of Men and Babies.* Princeton: Princeton University Press, 2024.

———. *Mothers and Others: The Evolutionary Origins of Mutual Understanding.* Cambridge, MA: Harvard University Press, 2009.

Huizinga, Johan. *Homo Ludens: A Study of the Play-Element in Culture.* Eastford, CT: Martin Fine, 2014.

Hunsberger, Bruce E., and Bob Altemeyer. *Atheists: A Groundbreaking Study of America's Nonbelievers.* Amherst, NY: Prometheus, 2006.

Immerwahr, Daniel. *How To Hide an Empire: A History of the Greater United States.* New York: Farrar, Straus and Giroux, 2019.

Jackowski, Karol. *Silence We Keep: A Nun's View of the Catholic Priest Scandal.* New York: Harmony, 2004.

James, William. "On a Certain Blindness in Human Beings." In *Writings 1878 1899,* 841–60. New York: The Library of America, 1992.

———. *Varieties of Religious Experience.* New York: Penguin, 1982.

———. "Will to Believe." In *The Will to Believe,* 1–31. New York: Dover, 1956.

Jaspers, Karl. *Origin and Goal of History.* Translated by Michael Bullock. Repr, London: Routledge, 2021.

Jay, Martin. *The Dialectical Imagination: A History of the Frankfurt School and the Institute of Social Research, 1923–1950.* Berkeley: University of California Press, 1996.

Jeremias, Joachim. *The Parables of Jesus.* 3rd rev. ed. Translated by S. H. Hooke. London: SCM, 2003.

———. *Rediscovering the Parables.* Translated by S. H. Hooke. London: SCM, 1966.

Jefferson, Thomas. *Jefferson Bible.* Repr. Washington, DC: Smithsonian, 2011.

Johnson, Luke Timothy. *The Real Jesus: The Misguided Quest for the Historical Jesus and the Truth of the Traditional Gospels.* New York: HarperCollins, 1996.

Josephus. *The Jewish War Books I-II.* Translated by H. St. J. Thackeray. Cambridge, MA: Harvard University Press, 1997.

———. *The Jewish Wars Books III-IV.* Translated by H. St. J. Thackeray. Cambridge, MA: Harvard University Press, 1997.

Justin Martyr. *Complete Works: Dialogue with Trypho First and Second Apology.* Edited by Philip Schaff. Ante-Nicene Fathers. 1885.

Kant, Immanuel. *Critique of Practical Reason* in Immanuel Kant, *Practical Philosophy.* Translated by Mary J. Gregor, 153–271. Cambridge: Cambridge University Press, 1999.

———. *Critique of Pure Reason.* Translated by edited by Paul Guyer. Cambridge: Cambridge University Press, 1998.

———. *Groundwork of the Metaphysics of Morals.* In *Practical Philosophy,* translated by Mary Gregor and Jens Timmermann, 37–108. Cambridge: Cambridge University Press, 2012.

———. *Idea for a Universal History with a Cosmopolitan Purpose, Kant's Political Writings.* Edited by Hans Reiss. Cambridge: Cambridge University Press, 1977.

———. *Lectures on Ethics.* Edited by Peter Heath and J. B. Schneewind and translated by Peter Heath. Cambridge: Cambridge University Press, 2001.

———. *Metaphysics of Morals.* In *Practical Philosophy*, translated by Mary J. Gregor, 365–603. Cambridge: Cambridge University Press, 1999.

———. "Perpetual Peace: A Philosophical Sketch." In *Kant's Political Writings*, Edited by Hans Reiss, 93–130. Cambridge: Cambridge University Press, 1999.

———. *Religion Within the Boundaries of Mere Reason.* In *Religion and Rational Theology*, edited by Allen W. Wood, 39–216. Cambridge: Cambridge University Press, 2005.

Kaplan, Bert, and Thomas F. A. Plaut. *Personality in a Communal Society: An Analysis of the Mental Health of the* Hutterites. Lawrence: University Press of Kansas, 1956.

Kierkegaard, Søren. *Concluding Unscientific Postscript to Philosophical Fragment.* Translated and edited by Howard V. Hong and Edna H. Hong. Princeton: Princeton University Press, 1992.

———. *Concept of Anxiety: A Simple Psychologically Oriented Deliberation in View of the Dogmatic Problem of Hereditary Sin.* Translated by Alastair Hannay. New York: Liveright Publishing, 2014.

———. *Concept of Irony.* Translated by Lee M. Capel. Bloomington: Indiana University Press, 1965.

———. *Either/Or: A Fragment of Life.* Abridged and translated by Alastair Hannay. New York: Penguin 1992.

———. *Fear and Trembling.* Translated by Alastair Hannay. London: Penguin, 2003.

———. *Moment and Late Writings.* Translated by Howard V. Hong and Edna H. Hong. Princeton: Princeton University Press, 1998.

———. *Practice in Christianity.* Edited and translated by Howard V. Hong and Edna H. Hong. Princeton: Princeton University Press, 1991.

———. *Sickness unto Death* Translated by Alastair Hannay. London: Penguin, 2004.

———. *Stages on Life's Way.* Edited and translated by Howard V. Hong and Edna H. Hong. Princeton: Princeton University Press, 1988.

———. *Works of Love.* Translated by Howard and Edna Hong. New York: HarperPerennial, 1962.

Klausner, Joseph. *Jesus of Nazareth: His Life, Times, and Teaching*. Translated by Herbert Danby. Eugene, OR: Wipf & Stock, 2020.

Kohler, Joachim. *Zarathustra's Secret: The Interior Life of Friedrich Nietzsche*. New Haven, CT: Yale University Press, 2002.

Kohut, Heinz. *Analysis of the Self: A Systematic Study of the Psychoanalytic Treatment of Narcissistic Personality Disorders*. Chicago: University of Chicago Press, 2000.

———. *How Does Analysis Cure?* Chicago: University of Chicago Press, 1984.

———. *Restoration of the Self*. New York: International Universities Press, 1977.

Korsgaard, ChSanders, istine M. *Fellow Creatures: Our Obligations to Other Animals*. New York: Oxford University Press, 2018.

Kott, Jan. *Shakespeare Our Contemporary*. Translated by Boleslaw Taborski. New York: W.W. Norton, 1974.

Lakoff, George. *Moral Politics: How Liberals and Conservative Think*. Chicago: University of Chicago Press, 2016.

Langlands, Rebecca. *Sexual Morality in Ancient Rome*. Cambridge: Cambridge University Press, 2006.

Laplanche, J., and J.-B. Pontalis. *Language of Psycho-Analysis*. Translated by Donald Nicholson-Smith. New York: W.W. Norton, 1973.

Laugier, Sandra. "How an Essential Portion of Reality has Escaped Ethics and Philosophy." In *What Gender does to the Humanities and Social Sciences*, edited by Armelle Andro et al., 23–26. Paris: Pantheon Sorbonne, 2021.

Lear, Jonathan. *Freud*. 2nd ed. London: Routledge, 2005.

———. *Happiness, Death, and the Remainder of Life*. Cambridge, MA: Harvard University Press. 2000.

———. *Love and Its Place in Nature: A Philosophical Interpretation of Freudian Psychoanalysis*. New Haven, CT: Yale University Press, 1990, 1998.

———. *Open Minded: Working Out the Logic of the Soul*. Cambridge, MA: Harvard University Press, 1998.

———. *Radical Hope: Ethics in the Face of Cultural Devastation*. Cambridge, MA: Harvard University Press, 2006.

Lefebvre, Alexandre. *Liberalism as a Way of Life*. Princeton: Princeton University Press, 2024.

Lerner, Gerda. *Creation of Feminist Consciousness: From the Middle Ages to 1870*. New York: Oxford University Press, 1993.

———. *Creation of Patriarchy*. New York: Oxford University Press, 1986.

Levy, Donald. "Definition of Love in Plato's Symposium." *Journal of the History of Ideas* 40 (1979) 285–91.

———. *Freud Among the Philosophers*. New Haven, CT: Yale University Press, 1996.

Lifton, Robert Jay. *Nazi Doctors: Medical Killing and the Psychology of Genocide*. New York: Basic, 2017.

Lincoln, Abraham. "Second Inaugural Address." March 4, 1865. https://www.owleyes.org/text/second-inaugural-address/read/text-of-lincolns-speech.

Lintott, Andrew. *Constitution of the Roman Republic*. Oxford: Oxford University Press, 2004.

———. *Violence in Republican Rome*. Oxford: Oxford University Press, 1999.

Little, Margaret I. *Psychotic Anxieties and Containment: A Personal Record of an Analysis with Winnicott*. Northvale, NJ: Jason Aronson, 1990.

Livy. *The Early History of Rome.* Translated by Aubrey De Selincourt. London: Penguin, 2002.

Loewald, Hans W. *The Essential Loewald: Collected Papers and Monographs.* Hagerstown, MD: University Publishing Group, 2000.

Luther, Martin. *Commentary on Galatians.* Translated by Theodore Graebner. N.d.: Digireads.com, 2019.

———. *Commentary on Genesis, Volume 1.* Translated by J. N. Lenker. Eisleben, Germany: J.N. Lenker, 1904.

———. *Commentary on Romans.* Translated by J. Theodore Mueller. Grand Rapids, MI: Kregel, 1976.

———. *First Lectures on the Psalms I.* In *Luther's Works*, edited by Hilton C. Oswald, 10: 11–519. Saint Louis: Concordia, 1974.

———. *First Lectures on the Psalms II.* In *Luther's Works*, edited by Hilton C. Oswald, 11:1–533 Saint Louis: Concordia, 1976.

———. *Lectures on Romans.* In *Luther's Works*, edited by Hilton C. Oswald, 25:1–524. Saint Louis: Concordia, 1972.

———. *Saint Paul's Epistle to the Galatians.* Translated by Haroldo Comacho Irvine. Minneapolis: Fortress, 2018.

MacCulloch, Diarmaid. *Lower Than the Angels: A History of Sex and Christianity.* London: Allen Lane, 2024.

Machiavelli, Niccolo. *The Prince and Discourses.* New York: The Modern Library, 1950.

MacMullen, Ramsay. *Christianizing the Roman Empire A.D.* 100–400. New Haven, CT: Yale University Press, 1984.

Mahler, Margaret S., et al. *The Psychological Birth of the Human Infant: Symbiosis and Individuation.* New York: Basic, 2000.

Marcuse, Herbert. *Eros and Civilization: A Philosophical Inquiry into Freud.* Boston: Beacon, 1966.

———. *One-Dimensional Man.* Boston: Beacon, 1964.

———. *Psychoanalysis, Politics, and Utopia* London: Repeater, 2022.

McCarthy, Thomas. *Race, Empire, and the Idea of Human Development.* Cambridge: Cambridge University Press, 2009.

McDonnell, Miles. *Roman Manliness: Virtues and the Roman Republic.* Cambridge: Cambridge University Press, 2006.

McLynn, Neil B. *Ambrose of Milan: Church and Court in a Christian Capital.* Berkeley: University of California Press, 1994.

Mead, George Herbert. *Mind, Self, and Society.* Repr. Chicago: University of Chicago Press, 2015.

Meeks, Wayne A. *The Moral World of the First Christians.* Philadelphia: Westminster, 1986.

Meier, Christian. *Caesar: A Biography.* Translated by David McLintock. New York: Basic, 1982.

Meier, John P. *A Marginal Jew: Companions and Competitor.* New York: Doubleday, 2001.

———. *Marginal Jew: Law and Love.* New Haven, CT: Yale University Press, 2009.

———. *A Marginal Jew: Mentor, Message, Miracles.* New York: Doubleday, 1994.

———. *A Marginal Jew: Probing the Authenticity of the Parables.* New Haven, CT: Yale University Press, 2016.

———. *A Marginal Jew: The Roots of the Problem and the Person.* New York: Doubleday, 1991.

Melville, Herman. *Moby-Dick.* New York: Penguin, 1992.

Merton, Thomas. *Love and Living.* Orlando: A Harvest Book, 1967.

Meyer, Marvin. *Gospel of Thomas: The Hidden Sayings of Jesus.* New York: HarperCollins, 1992.

Mill, John Stuart. *On Liberty.* In *The Basic Writings of John Stuart Mill*, edited by Dale E. Miller, 3–119. New York: Modern Liberty, 2002.

———. *Subjection of Women.* In *Essays on Sex Equality*, edited by Alice S. Rossi, 125–242. Chicago: University of Chicago Press, 1970.

———. *Three Essays on Religion.* Delhi: Skilled Books, n.d.

———. *Utilitarianism, The Basic Writings of John Stuart Mill.* Edited by Dale E. Miller. New York: The Modern Library, 2002.

Miller, Robert J. *Jesus Seminar and Its Critics.* Farmington, MN: Polebridge, 1999.

Mitchell, Stephen A. *Hope and Dread in Psychoanalysis.* New York: BasicBooks, 1993.

———. *Relational Concepts in Psychoanalysis: An Interpretation.* Cambridge, MA: Harvard University Press, 1988.

Modell, Arnold H. *Object Love and Reality: An Introduction to a Psychoanalytic Theory of Object Relations.* New York: International Universities Press, 1968.

———. *Other Times, Other Realities: Toward a Theory of Psychoanalytic Treatment.* Cambridge, MA: Harvard University Press, 1990.

———. *The Private Self.* Cambridge, MA: Harvard University Press, 1993.

———. *Psychoanalysis in a New Context.* New York: International Universities Press, 1984.

Moi, Toril. "I Came With a Sword." *London Review of Books* 43 (2021) 7–10.

Murray, Lynne. *Social Baby: Understanding Babies' Communication from Birth.* Guildford: The Children's Project, 2014.

Myers, David G., and Letha Dawson Scanzoni. *What God Has Joined Together: The Christian Case for Gay Marriage.* New York: HarperCollins, 2005.

Nagel, Thomas. *Moral Feelings, Moral Reality, and Moral Progress.* New York: Oxford University Press, 2023.

Niebuhr, Reinhold. *Moral Man and Immoral Society: A Study in Ethics and Politics* Repr. Louisville, KY: Westminster John Knox, 2021.

———. *Nature and Destiny of Man.* 2 vols. Louisville, KY: Westminster John Knox Press, 2021.

Nietzsche, Friedrich. *On the Genealogy of Morals.* Translated by Douglas Smith. Oxford: Oxford University Press, 1996.

Nygren, Anders. *Agape and Eros.* Translated by Philip S. Watson. Philadelphia: Westminster, 1953.

Ogilvie, R. M. *A Commentary on Livy Books 1–5.* Oxford: Clarendon, 1965.

Okin, Susan Moller. *Women in Western Political Thought.* Princeton: Princeton University Press, 1979.

O'Malley, Padraig. *Biting at the Grave: The Irish Hunger Strikes and the Politics of Despair* Boston: Beacon, 1990.

Oxford Edition of the Oxford English Dictionary. "Mercy." Oxford: Oxford University Press, 1971.

Outka, Gene. *Agape: an Ethical Analysis.* New Haven, CT: Yale University Press, 1972.

Pagels, Elaine. *Adam, Eve, and the Serpent.* New York: Random House, 1988.

———. *Gnostic Gospels.* New York: Vintage, 1979.

Palmer, R. E. A. *Archaic Community of the Romans.* Cambridge: Cambridge University Press, 1970.

Parker, Stephen E. *Winnicott and Religion.* Lanham, MD: Jason Aronson, 2011.

Paxton, Robert O. *Anatomy of Fascism.* New York: Vintage, 2004.

Perrin, Norman. *Rediscovering the Teaching of Jesus.* New York: Harper & Row, 1967.

Phillips, Adam. *Winnicott.* Cambridge, MA: Harvard University Press, 1988.

Phillips, Caryl. "A House Is Not a Home: The Importance of Place to James Baldwin." *Times Literary Supplement* no. 6349 (December 6, 2024) 3–5.

Piaget, Jean. *Moral Judgment of the Child.* New York: The Free Press, 1997.

Pinckney, Darryl. *Baldwin's Spell, in The New York Review of Books* 77 (2025) 23–25.

Plato. *Crito.* In *Plato: Complete Works,* edited by John M. Cooper and translated by G. M. A. Grube, 37–48. Indianapolis: Hackett, 1997.

———. *Gorgias.* In *Plato: Complete Works,* edited by John M. Cooper and translated by Donald J. Zeyl, 791–869. Indianapolis: Hackett, 1997.

———. *Phaedrus.* In *Plato: Complete Works,* edited by John M. Cooper and translated by Alexander Nehamas and Paul Woodruff, 506–56. Indianapolis: Hackett, 1997.

———. *Protagoras.* In *Plato: Complete Works,* edited by John M. Cooper and translated by Stanley Lombardo and Karen Bell, 746–90. Indianapolis: Hackett, 1997.

———. *Republic.* In *Plato: Complete Works,* edited by John M. Cooper and translated by G. M. A. Grube, revised by C. D. C. Reeve, 971–1223. Indianapolis: Hackett, 1997.

Polybius. *The Rise of the Roman Empire.* Translated by Ian Scott-Kilvert. London: Penguin, 1979.

Pomeroy, Sarah B. *Goddesses, Whores, Wives, and Slaves: Women in Classical Antiquity.* New York: Schocken, 1995.

Rawls, John. *A Brief Inquiry into the Meaning of Sin and Faith.* Edited by Thomas Nagel. Cambridge, MA: Harvard University Press, 2009.

———. *Lectures on the History of Moral Philosophy.* Edited by Barbara Herman. Cambridge, MA: Harvard University Press, 2000.

———. *Political Liberalism.* New York: Columbia University Press, 2005.

———. *Themes in Kant's Moral Philosophy.* In *Collected Papers,* edited by Samuel Freeman, 497–528. Cambridge, MA: Harvard University Press, 1999.

———. *Theory of Justice.* Cambridge, MA: Harvard University Press, 1971.

Rawson, Beryl, ed. *Marriage, Divorce, and Children in Ancient Rome.* Oxford: Clarendon, 2004.

Real, Terrence. *I Don't Want to Talk About It: Overcoming the Secret Legacy of Male Depression* New York: Scribner, 1997.

———. *Us.* New York: Rodale, 2024.

Regan, Richard, SJ. *Conflict and Consensus: Religious Freedom and the Second Vatican Council.* New York: Macmillan, 1967.

Reich, Wilhelm. *Character Analysis* 3rd ed. New York: Orgone Institute Press, 1949.

Renan, Ernest. *The Life of Jesus.* Translated by Anonymous. Amherst, NY: Prometheus, 1991.

Richards, David A. J. *Conscience and the Constitution: History, Theory, and Law of the Reconstruction Amendments.* Princeton: Princeton University Press, 1993.

———. *Disarming Manhood: Roots of Ethical Resistance.* Athens, OH: Ohio University Press, 2005.

———. *Foundations of American Constitutionalism*. New York: Oxford University Press, 1989.

———. *Free Speech and the Politics of Identity*. Oxford: Oxford University Press, 1999.

———. *Fundamentalism in American Religion and Law: Obama's Challenge to Patriarchy's Threat to Democracy*. Cambridge: Cambridge University Press, 2010.

———. *Identity and the Case for Gay Rights: Race, Gender, Religion as Analogies*. Chicago: University of Chicago Press, 1999.

———. *Love and Violence: Insights from Shakespeare on Ethics, Psychology, Theater, and Law*. Cambridge: Ethics International Press, 2023.

———. "Patriarchal Religion in U.S. Constitutional Law." *Contemporary Psychoanalysis* 59 (2023) 23–42.

———. *Resisting Injustice and the Feminist Ethics of Care in the Age of Obama: "Suddenly. . .All the Truth Was Coming Out."* New York: Routledge, 2013.

———. *Revolution and Constitutionalism in Britain and the U.S.: Burke and Madison and Their Contemporary Legacies*. New York: Routledge, 2024.

———. *Rise of Gay Rights and the Fall of the British Empire*. Cambridge: Cambridge University Press, 2013.

———. *Sex, Drugs, Death and the Law: An Essay on Human Rights and Decriminalization*. Totowa, NJ: Rowman & Littlefield, 1977.

———. *A Theory of Reasons for Action*. Oxford: Oxford University Press, 1971.

———. *Toleration and the Constitution*. New York: Oxford University Press, 1986.

———. *Why Love Leads to Justice: Love Across the Boundaries*. Cambridge: Cambridge University Press, 2015.

———. *Women, Gays, and the Constitution: The Grounds for Feminism and Gay Rights in Culture and Law*. Chicago: University of Chicago Press, 1998.

Rief, Philip. *Freud: The Mind of the Moralist*. Chicago: University of Chicago Press, 1979.

———. *Triumph of the Therapeutic: Uses of Faith after Freud*. Chicago: University of Chicago Press, 1987.

Riker, John Hanwell. *Kohut's Self Psychology for a Fractured World: New Ways of Understanding the Self and Human Community*. London: Routledge, 2024.

Rodman, F. Robert. *Winnicott: Life and Work*. Cambridge, MA: Da Capo, 2003.

Rogers, Leoandra Onnie, and Niobe Way. "Child Development in an Ideological Context: Through the Lends of Resistance and Accommodation." *Child Development Perspectives* (2021) 242–48.

Rohr, Richard. *Universal Christ: How a Forgotten Reality Can Change Everything We See, How For, and Believe*. New York: Convergent, 2021.

Rosaldo, Michelle Z. *Knowledge and Passion: Ilongot Notions of Self and Social Life*. Cambridge: Cambridge University Press, 1980.

———. "Shame of Headhunters and the Autonomy of Self." *Ethos* 11 (1983) 135–51.

Ruether, Rosemary. *Faith and Fratricide: The Theological Roots of Anti-Semitism*. Eugene, OR: Wipf & Stock, 1997.

———. *Sexism and God-Talk: Toward a Feminist Theology*. Boston: Beacon, 1993.

Sagan, Eli. *Freud, Women, and Morality: The Psychology of Good and Evil*. New York: Basic, 1988.

Saller, Richard P. *Patriarchy, Property and Death in the Roman Family*. Cambridge: Cambridge University Press, 1994.

Salome, Lou. *Nietzsche.* Translated by Siegfried Mandel. Redding Ridge, CT: Black Swan, 1988.

Sanders, E. P. *The Historical Figure of Jesus.* London: Penguin, 1993.

———. *Jesus and Judaism.* Minneapolis: Fortress, 1985.

Saturri, Edmund N., and William Werpehowski. *The Love Commandments: Essays in Christian Ethics and Moral* Philosophy. Washington, DC: Georgetown University Press, 1992.

Sauer, Hanno. *Invention of Good and Evil: A World History of Morality.* Translated by Jo Heinrich. New York: Oxford University Press, 2024.

Scanlon, T. M. *What We Owe to Each Other.* Cambridge, MA: Harvard University Press, 1998.

Scanzoni, Letha Dawson, and Virginia Ramey Mollenkott. *Is the Homosexual My Neighbor: A Positive Christian Response.* New York: HarperCollins, 1994.

Schillebeeckx, Edward. *Jesus: An Experiment in Christology.* Translated by Hubert Hoskins. New York: A Crossroad Book, 1979.

Schofield, Malcolm. *How Plato Writes: Perspectives and Problems.* Cambridge: Cambridge University Press, 2023.

Schüssler Fiorenza, Elisabeth. *Congress of Women: Religion, Gender, and Kyriarchal Power.* Eugene, OR: Wipf & Stock, 2016.

———. *Discipleship of Equals: A Critical Feminist Ekklesia-logy of Liberation.* New York: Crossroad, 1993.

———. *In Memory of Her: A Feminist Theological Reconstruction of Christian Origins.* New York: Crossroad, 2002.

———. *Searching the Scriptures: A Feminist Commentary.* New York: Crossroad, 1994.

———. *Searching the Scriptures: A Feminist Introduction, Volume One.* New York: Crossroad, 1993.

Schweitzer, Albert. *Indian Thoughts and Its Development.* Translated by Mrs. Charles E. B. Russell. Boston: Beacon, 1936.

———. *J.S. Bach* 2 vols. Translated by Ernest Newman. New York: Dover, 1966.

———. *Mysticism of Paul the Apostle.* Translated by William Montgomery. Baltimore: The Johns Hopkins University Press, 1998.

———. *Out of My Life and Thought, An Autobiography.* New York: a Mentor Book, 1961.

———. *Philosophy of Civilization.* Amherst, NY: Prometheus, 1987.

———. *Psychiatric Study of Jesus: Exposition and Criticism.* Translated by Charles R. Joy. Boston: Beacon, 2011.

———. *Quest for the Historical Jesus.* Garden City, NY: Dover, 2023.

Seymour, Miranda. *Robert Graves: Life on the Edge.* New York: Henry Holt, 1995.

Shakespeare, William. *Hamlet.* 2nd ed. Boston: Houghton Mifflin Company, 1997.

———. *King Lear.* Edited by R. A. Foakes. London: Bloomsbury, 2017.

Shay, Jonathan. *Achilles in Vietnam: Combat Trauma and the Undoing of Character.* New York: Scribner, 1994.

Shelley, Percy. "A Defence of Poetry." In *Percy Shelley Classics,* 51–85. Middletown, DE: Percy Shelley Classics, 2020.

Siedentop, Larry. *Inventing the Individual: The Origins of Western Liberalism.* London: Allen Lane, 2014.

Smith, Wilfred Cantwell. *Towards a World Theology: Faith and the Comparative History of Religion.* Maryknoll, New York: Orbis, 1981.

Stanford Encyclopedia of Philosophy. "Ludwig Andreas Feuerbach." *https://plato.stanford.edu/entries/ludwig-feuerbach/*.

Stanton, Elizabeth Cady. *Woman's Bible*. Bexar County, TX: Bibliotech, 2019.

Stark, Rodney. *Rise of Christianity: A Sociologist Reconsiders History*. Princeton: Princeton University Press, 1996.

Stenner, Karen. *Authoritarian Dynamic*. Cambridge: Cambridge University Press, 2005.

Stern, Daniel N. *Interpersonal World of the Infant: A View from Psychoanalysis and Developmental Psychology*. New York: Basic, 1985.

Stern, Donnel B. *Relational Freedom: Emergent Properties of the Interpersonal Field*. London: Routledge, 2015.

———. *Unformulated Experience: From Disassociation to Imagination in Psychoanaysis*. Hillsdale, NJ: The Analytic, 2003.

Stewart, Matthew. *Emancipation of the Mind: Radical Philosophy, the War over Slavery, and the Refounding of America*. New York: W.W. Norton, 2024.

Strauss, David Friedrich. *Life of Jesus, Critically Examined*. Translated by George Eliot. New York: CosimoClassics, 2009.

Strozier, Charles B. *End of the Troubles in Northern Ireland: On the Psychology of Peacemaking*. London: Ethics International, 2025.

———. *Your Friend Forever, A. Lincoln: The Enduring Friendship of Abraham Lincoln and Joshua Speed*. New York: Columbia University Press, 2016.

Strozier, Charles B., et al. *New World of Self: Heinz Kohut's Transformation of Psychoanalysis and Psychotherapy*. New York: Oxford University Press, 2022.

Suetonius. *The Twelve Caesars*. Translated by Robert Graves. London: Penguin, 1979.

Sullivan, Harry Stack. *Interpersonal Theory of Psychiatry*. New York: W.W. Norton, 1997.

Suttie, Ian D. *Origins of Love and Hate*. London: Free Association, 1999.

Swinburne, Richard. *Existence of God*. Oxford: Clarendon, 1979.

Tacitus, *Annals of Imperial Rome*. Translated by Michael Grant. London: Penguin, 1996.

———. *A Dialogue on Oratory*. In *Agricola, Germania, Dialogus*, translated by W. Peterson, 231–47. Cambridge, MA: Harvard University Press, 1970.

Taylor, Charles. *Cosmic Connections: Poetry in the Age of Disenchantment*. Cambridge, MA: Harvard University Press, 2024.

———. *Language Animals: The Full Shape of the Human Linguistic Capacity*. Cambridge, MA: Harvard University Press, 2016.

Taylor, Graeme J. "Psychoanalysis and Psychosomatics: A New Synthesis." *Journal of the American Academy of Psychoanalysis* 20 (1992) 251–75.

Thucydides. *History of the Peloponnesian War*. Translated by Rex Warner. London: Penguin, 1972.

Tillich, Paul. *Love, Power and Justice*. London: Oxford University Press, 1954.

———. *Morality and Beyond*. Louisville, KY: Westminster John Knox, 1963.

———. *Systematic Theology*. 3 vols. Chicago: University of Chicago Press, 1967.

Toibin, Colm. *Testament of Mary*. New York: Scribner, 2012.

Tomasello, Michael. *Becoming Human: A Theory of Ontogeny*. Cambridge, MA: Harvard University Press, 2019.

———. *A Natural History of Human Thinking*. Cambridge, MA: Harvard University Press, 2014.

———. *A Natural History of Morality*. Cambridge, MA: Harvard University Press, 2016.

Treggiari, Susan. *Roman Marriage*. Oxford: Clarendon, 1991.

Troeltsch, Ernst. *Social Teaching of the Christian Churches.* 2 vols. Translated by Olive Wyon. New York: Harper & Brothers, 1960.

Tronick, Edward. *The Power of Discord: Why the Ups and Downs of Relationship Are the Secret to Building Intimacy, Resilience, and Trust.* New York: Little, Brown Spark, 2020.

van der Kolk, Bessel, et al. *Traumatic Stress: The Effects of Overwhelming Experience on Mind, Body, and Society.* New York: Guilford, 1996.

Vermes, Geza. *Authentic Gospel of* Jesus. London: Penguin, 2003.

———. *Changing Faces of Jesus.* New York: Penguin, 2000.

———. *Jesus and the World of Judaism.* London: SCM, 1983.

———. *Jesus the Jew: A Historian's Reading of the Gospels.* Philadelphia: Fortress, 1981.

———. *Religion of Jesus the Jew.* Minneapolis: Fortress, 1993.

Vlastos, Gregory. *Socrates: Ironist and Moral Philosopher.* Ithaca: Cornell University Press, 1991.

Walbank, F. W., et al. *Cambridge Ancient History: The Rise of Rome to 220 B.C.E.* 2nd ed. Cambridge: Cambridge University Press, 1989.

Walzer, Michael. *Revolution of the Saints.* Cambridge, MA: Harvard University Press, 1965.

Warner, Marina. *Alone of All Her Sex: The Myth and the Cult of the Virgin Mary.* New York: Vintage, 1983.

Way, Niobe. *Deep Secrets: Boys' Friendships and the Crisis of Connection.* Cambridge, MA: Harvard University Press, 2011.

———. *Rebels With a Cause: Reimagining Boys, Ourselves, and Our Culture.* New York: Dutton, 2024.

Weil, Simone. *Waiting for God.* Translated by Emma Crauford. New York: HarperPerennial 2009.

White, Robert. *Ego and Reality in Psychoanalytic Theory in Psychological Issues, Volume* 3. New York: International Universities Press, 1963.

White, Timothy. "How My Dad Reconciled His God and His Gay Son." *New York Times,* February 16, 2025. https://www.nytimes.com/interactive/2025/02/05/opinion/coming-out-evangelical-pastor.html.

Whitebook, Joel. *Freud: An Intellectual Biography.* Cambridge: Cambridge University Press, 2017.

Whitman, James Q. *Hitler's American Model: The United States and the Making of Nazi Race Law.* Princeton: Princeton University Press, 2017.

Wikipedia. "Glastonbury." https://en.wikipedia.org/wiki/Glastonbury.

———. "Hasmonean Dynasty." https://en.wikipedia.org/wiki/Hasmonean_dynasty.

———. "Ludwig Feuerbach." https://wnwikipedia.org/wiki/Ludwig-feuerbach/.

———. "List of Hymns by Martin Luther." https://en.wikipedia.org/wiki/List_of_hymns_by_Martin_Luther.

———. "Richard Whiting." https://en.wikipedia.org/wiki/Richard_Whiting_(abbot).

———. "Theodore Parker." https://en.wikipedia.org/wiki/Theodore_Parker.

Wilkerson, Isabel. *Caste: The Origins of Our Discontents.* New York: Random House, 2020.

Wink, Walter. *Engaging the Powers: Discernment and Resistance in a World of Domination.* Minneapolis: Fortress, 1992.

Winnicott, D. W. "Aggression in Relation to Emotional Development." In *The Collected Works of D.W. Winnicott*, edited by Lesley Caldwell and Helen Taylor Robinson, 3:313–347. New York: Oxford University Press, 2017.

———. "Capacity to Be Alone." In *The Collected Works of D.W. Winnicott*, edited by Lesley Caldwell and Helen Taylor Robinson, 6:241–48. New York: Oxford University Press, 2017.

———. "Children Learning." In *The Collected Works of D.W. Winnicott*, edited by Lesley Caldwell and Helen Taylor Robinson, 8:313–18. New York: Oxford University Press, 2017.

———. "Communicating and Not Communicating Leading to a Study of Certain Opposites." In *The Collected Works of D.W. Winnicott*, edited by Lesley Caldwell and Helen Taylor Robinson, 6:433–445. New York: Oxford University Press, 2017.

———. "Communication Between Infant and Mother, and Mother and Infant, Compared and Contrasted." In *The Collected Works of D.W. Winnicott*, edited by Lesley Caldwell and Helen Taylor Robinson, 8:227–37. New York: Oxford University Press, 2017.

———. "Creativity and Its Origins." In *The Collected Works of D.W. Winnicott*, edited by Lesley Caldwell and Helen Taylor Robinson, 9:299–317. New York: Oxford University Press, 2017.

———. "Ego Distortion in Terms of True and False Self." In *The Collected Works of D.W. Winnicott*, edited by Lesley Caldwell and Helen Taylor Robinson, 6:159–71. New York: Oxford University Press, 2017.

———. "Fate of the Transitional Object." In *The Collected Works of D.W. Winnicott*, edited by Lesley Caldwell and Helen Taylor Robinson, 5:523–28. New York: Oxford University Press, 2017.

———. "Further Clinical Material on the Theme of a Male Patient's Exploitation of His Female Self." In *The Collected Works of D.W. Winnicott*, edited by Lesley Caldwell and Helen Taylor Robinson, 5:519–22. New York: Oxford University Press, 2017.

———. "Holding and Interpretation: Fragment of an Analysis." In *The Collected Works of D.W. Winnicott*, edited by Lesley Caldwell and Helen Taylor Robinson, 4:303–474. New York: Oxford University Press, 2017.

———. "Ideas and Definition." In *The Collected Works of D.W. Winnicott*, edited by Lesley Caldwell and Helen Taylor Robinson, 9:359–60. New York: Oxford University Press, 2017.

———. "Letter to His Sister, Violet." In *The Collected Works of D.W. Winnicott*, edited by Lesley Caldwell and Helen Taylor Robinson, 1:53–55. New York: Oxford University Press, 2017.

———. "Letter to Melanie Klein." In *The Collected Works of D.W. Winnicott*, edited by Lesley Caldwell and Helen Taylor Robinson, 4:59–62. New York: Oxford University Press, 2017.

———. "Letter to Wilfred R. Bion." In *The Collected Works of D.W. Winnicott*, edited by Lesley Caldwell and Helen Taylor Robinson, 8:157–58. New York: Oxford University Press, 2017.

———. "Location of Cultural Experience." In *The Collected Works of D.A. Winnicott*, edited by Lesley Caldwell and Helen Taylor Robinson, 7:429–36. New York: Oxford University Press, 2017.

———. "Memorandum from Paddington Green Children's Hospital Psychology Department on Homosexuality and the Law." In *The Collected Works of D.W.*

Winnicott, edited by Lesley Caldwell and Helen Taylor Robinson, 6:27–30. New York: Oxford University Press, 2017.

———. "Mind and Its Relation to the Psyche-Soma." In *The Collected Works of D.W. Winnicott*, edited by Lesley Caldwell and Helen Taylor Robinson, 3:245–57. New York: Oxford University Press, 2017,

———. "Mirror–Role of Mother and Family in Child Development." In *The Collected Works of D.W. Winnicott*, edited by Lesley Caldwell and Helen Taylor Robinson, 8:211–18. New York: Oxford University Press, 2017.

———. "Morals and Education." In *The Collected Works of D.W. Winnicott*, edited by Lesley Caldwell and Helen Taylor Robinson, 6:377–88. New York: Oxford University Press, 2017.

———. "Mother's Contribution to Society." In *The Collected Works of D.W. Winnicott*, edited by Lesley Caldwell and Helen Taylor Robinson, 5:293–96. New York: Oxford University Press, 2017.

———. "Personal View of the Kleinian Contribution." In *The Collected Works of D.W. Winnicott*, edited by Lesley Caldwell and Helen Taylor Robinson, 6:325–32. New York: Oxford University Press, 2017.

———. *Piggle: An Account of the Pschoanalytic Treatment of a Little Girl*. In *The Collected Works of D.W. Winnicott*, edited by Lesley Caldwell and Helen Taylor Robinson, 11:197–318. New York: Oxford University Press, 2017.

———. "Playing: Creativity and the Search for the Self." In *The Collected Works of D.W. Winnicott*, edited by Lesley Caldwell and Helen Taylor Robinson, 8:169–79. New York: Oxford University Press, 2017.

———. "Primary State of Being: Pre-Primitive Stages." In *The Collected Works of D.W. Winnicott*, edited by Lesley Caldwell and Helen Taylor Robinson, 11:149–51. New York: Oxford University Press, 2017.

———. "Some Thoughts on the Meaning of the Word Democracy." In *The Collected Works of D.W. Winnicott*, edited by Lesley Caldwell and Helen Taylor Robinson, 3:407–21. New York: Oxford University Press, 2017.

———. "Therapeutic Consultations in Child Psychiatry." In *The Collected Works of D.W. Winnicott*, edited Lesley Caldwell and Helen Taylor Robinson, 5:519–22. New York: Oxford University Press, 2017.

———. *Through Paediatrics to Psycho-Analysis: Collected Papers*. New York: Brunner-Routledge, 1992.

———. "Transitional Objects and Transitional Phenomena." In *The Collected Works of D.W. Winnicott*, edited by Lesley Caldwell and Helen Taylor Robinson, 5:405–20. New York: Oxford University Press, 2017.

———. "Tree." In *The Collected Works of D.W. Winnicott*, edited by Lesley Caldwell and Helen Taylor Robinson, 6:499–500. New York: Oxford University Press, 2017.

———. "Use of an Object and Relating Through Identifications." In *The Collected Works of D.W. Winnicott*, edited by Lesley Caldwell and Helen Taylor Robinson, 8:355–64. New York: Oxford University Press, 2017.

———. "Use of an Object in the Context of *Moses and Monotheism*." In *The Collected Works of D.W. Winnicott*, edited by Lesley Caldwell and Helen Taylor Robinson, 9:33–38. New York: Oxford University Press, 2017.

Witherington, Ben, III. *The Jesus Quest: The Third Search for the Jew of Nazareth*. 2nd ed. Downers Grove, IL: InterVarsity, 1997.

Wood, Gordon S. *The Creation of the American Republic, 1776–1787*. New York: Norton, 1969.

Wood, Susan E. *Imperial Women: A Study in Public Images 40 B.C.E.-AD 69*. Leiden: Brill, 1999,

Woodhouse, A. S. P., ed. *Puritanism and Liberty*. London: Dent, 1938.

Woolf, Virginia. *Three Guineas*. Jane Marcus edition. Orlando, FL: Harvest, 2006.

Wordsworth, William. *Selected Poems*. London: Penguin, 2004.

Wright, Jacob L. *Why the Bible Began: An Alternative History of Scripture and Its Origins*. Cambridge: Cambridge University Press, 2023.

Wright, N. T. *Resurrection of the Son of God*. Minneapolis: Fortress, 2003.

———. *Simply Christian: Why Christianity Makes Sense*. New York: HarperOne, 2006.

———. *Simply Jesus: A New Vision of Who He Was, What He Did, and Why He Matters*. New York: HarperOne, 2012.

Wyatt-Brown, Bertram. *Southern Honor: Ethics and Behavior in the Old South*. Oxford: Oxford University Press, 2007.

Yerushalmi, Yosef Hayim. *Freud's Moses: Judaism Terminable and Interminable*. New Haven, CT: Yale University Press, 1991.

Young, Julian. *Friedrich Nietzsche: A Philosophical Biography*. New York: Cambridge University Press, 2010.

Young-Bruehl, Elisabeth. *Why Arendt Matters*. New Haven, CT: Yale University Press, 2006.

General Index

Scripture Index

www.ingramcontent.com/pod-product-compliance
Lightning Source LLC
LaVergne TN
LVHW100512110826
845146LV00002B/611

* 9 7 9 8 3 8 5 2 4 2 5 8 0 *